THINKING ABOUT POLITICAL PSYCHOLOGY

In this volume, political psychologists take a hard look at political psychology. They pose, and then address, the kinds of tough questions that those outside the field would be inclined to ask and those inside should be able to answer satisfactorily. Not everyone will agree with the answers the authors provide, and in some cases, the best an author can do is offer well-grounded speculations. Nonetheless, the chapters raise questions that will lead to an improved political psychology and will generate further discussion and research in the field.

The individual chapters are organized around four themes. Part I tries to define political psychology and provides an overview of the field. Part II raises questions about theory and empirical methods in political psychology. Part III contains arguments ranging from the position that the field is too heavily psychological to the view that it is not psychological enough. Part IV considers how political psychologists might best connect individual-level mental processes to aggregate outcomes.

James H. Kuklinski is a professor in the Department of Political Science and the Institute of Government and Public Affairs at the University of Illinois at Urbana-Champaign. He has served on the boards of the *American Political Science Review*, the *American Journal of Political Science*, the *Journal of Politics*, *Legislative Studies Quarterly*, and *Political Behavior*, and he has published articles in these and other journals.

This series has been established in recognition of the growing sophistication in the resurgence of interest in political psychology and the study of public opinion. Its focus will range from the kinds of mental processes that people employ when they think about democratic processes and make political choices to the nature and consequences of macrolevel public opinion.

We expect that some of the works will draw on developments in cognitive and social psychology and relevant areas of philosophy. Appropriate subjects would include the use of heuristics, the roles of core values and moral principles in political reasoning, the effects of expertise and sophistication, the roles of affect and emotion, and the nature of cognition and information processing. The emphasis will be on systematic and rigorous empirical analysis, and a wide range of methodologies will be appropriate: traditional surveys, experimental surveys, laboratory experiments, focus groups, in-depth interviews, and others. We intend that these empirically oriented studies will also consider normative implications for democratic politics generally.

Politics, not psychology, will be the primary focus, and it is expected that most works will deal with mass publics and democratic politics, although work on nondemocratic publics will not be excluded. Other works will examine traditional topics in public opinion research, as well as contribute to the growing literature on aggregate opinion and its role in democratic societies.

List of books in series appears on page following index

THINKING ABOUT POLITICAL PSYCHOLOGY

EDITED BY

JAMES H. KUKLINSKI

University of Illinois at Urbana-Champaign

CAMBRIDGE
UNIVERSITY PRESS

PUBLISHED BY THE PRESS SYNDICATE OF THE UNIVERSITY OF CAMBRIDGE
The Pitt Building, Trumpington Street, Cambridge, United Kingdom

CAMBRIDGE UNIVERSITY PRESS
The Edinburgh Building, Cambridge CB2 2RU, UK
40 West 20th Street, New York, NY 10011-4211, USA
477 Williamstown Road, Port Melbourne, VIC 3207, Australia
Ruiz de Alarcón 13, 28014 Madrid, Spain
Dock House, The Waterfront, Cape Town 8001, South Africa

http://www.cambridge.org

First published 2002
Reprinted 2003

Printed in the United Kingdom at the University Press, Cambridge

Typeface Sabon 10/12 pt.   *System* QuarkXPress [BTS]

A catalog record for this book is available from the British Library.

Library of Congress Cataloging in Publication Data
Thinking about political psychology / edited by James H. Kuklinski.
    p.   cm. – (Cambridge studies in political psychology and public opinion)
    Includes bibliographical references and index.
    ISBN 0-521-59377-8
    1. Political psychology.   I. Kuklinski, James H.   II. Series.
JA74.5 .T43   2001
320′.01′9–dc21   2001035589

ISBN   0 521 59377 8   hardback

Contents

vii

Contents

List of Contributors

Pamela Johnston Conover, *Professor of Political Science, University of North Carolina, Chapel Hill, North Carolina*

Jon A. Krosnick, *Professor of Psychology and Political Science, Ohio State University, Columbus, Ohio*

James H. Kuklinski, *Professor of Political Science, University of Illinois, Urbana-Champaign, Illinois*

Arthur Lupia, *Professor of Political Science, University of California at San Diego, San Diego, California*

Robert C. Luskin, *Associate Professor of Political Science, University of Texas, Austin, Texas*

Michael MacKuen, *Burton Craige Professor of Political Science, University of North Carolina, Chapel Hill, North Carolina*

Wendy M. Rahn, *Associate Professor of Political Science, University of Minnesota, Minneapolis, Minnesota*

Thomas J. Rudolph, *Assistant Professor of Political Science, University of Illinois, Urbana-Champaign, Illinois*

Donald D. Searing, *Burton Craige Professor of Political Science, University of North Carolina, Chapel Hill, North Carolina*

James A. Stimson, *Raymond Dawson Professor of Political Science, University of North Carolina, Chapel Hill, North Carolina*

John L. Sullivan, *Regents Professor of Political Science, University of Minnesota, Minneapolis, Minnesota*

Introduction: Political Psychology and the Study of Politics

JAMES H. KUKLINSKI

Fields of scientific inquiry follow a common pattern. At the outset, excitement and enthusiasm prevail as a small group of founders offers a new conceptual framework and, usually, a new, related methodology. Sometimes the specific topics of inquiry are also new, at other times only the ways to think about them. Other, often young, scholars adopt the new perspective, and before long it becomes an active, visible part of the discipline. Typically, this very growth in prominence portends the beginning of a leveling off, if not decline, in research activity. Continuing scholarship takes the form of adding small increments of knowledge to the key central questions that the founders had posed much earlier.

Often missing from this sequence is a self-evaluation by the practitioners themselves. Concerned, as they should be, with substantive questions, the researchers don't stop to scrutinize what they do and how it fits into the larger discipline of which they are part. The criticisms usually come from elsewhere and consequently tend to undercut rather than strengthen the field.

In this volume, political psychologists take a hard look at political psychology. They pose, and then address, the kinds of tough questions that those outside of the field would be inclined to ask and those inside should satisfactorily be able to answer. Not everyone will agree with the answers the authors provide, and, in some cases, the best an author can do is offer well-grounded speculations. Nonetheless, the chapters raise questions that, if taken seriously, will lead to an improved political psychology.

But, one might protest, the idea of political psychologists evaluating political psychology is equivalent to the idea of police officers monitoring their own department. In both cases, the conclusions are foreordained, such that the scientific field in one case and the department in the other will be evaluated more positively than it should be. It is indeed true that most of the chapters that follow find an important role for political psychology in the larger discipline. It is also true that these same chapters set forth hard-hitting criticisms and formidable challenges for future research. Moreover, the expectation is that this volume will generate further commentary, not stifle it.

The individual chapters are organized around four themes. The remainder of this introduction delineates these themes and briefly summarizes the individual contributions.

DEFINING POLITICAL PSYCHOLOGY

Fields of scientific inquiry should be definable. Sullivan, Rahn, and Rudolph offer a tour de force of political psychology, and in the process show how diverse and ill-defined the field is. Political psychologists, unlike, say, students of rational choice, do not share a single set of assumptions or even a general perspective. As Sullivan, Rahn, and Rudolph state in their opening paragraph, the field "includes – has always included – a wide diversity of theories, approaches, quantitative and qualitative research methods, and verdicts." They identify three distinct eras – the first dominated by studies of personality, the second by attitude theory and change, and the third by human cognition and information processing – and note that today all three perspectives are a part of what is normally called political psychology.

The diversity in fact is even wider and deeper. Even within the currently dominant information-processing perspective, which is the focus of this volume, scholars examine a variety of cognitive processes ranging from attribution to cognitive heuristics to on-line processing. Researchers have also begun to ascertain how affect and emotions interact with cognition to shape political judgments.

So what, exactly, is political psychology? A simple answer is also a pretty good one: the study of mental processes that underlie political judgments and decision making. Because there are many mental processes, and to date no general framework that integrates them, a political psychologist can – must? – focus on those that seem most applicable to the political task people are facing. This freedom to pick and choose is both a plus and a minus. On the one hand, the wide range of perspectives on political decision making can be compared and contrasted within the academic marketplace. In time, presumably, the strongest and most beneficial will prevail. On the other hand, the accumulation of agreed-upon evidence is slow and, at worst, could not occur at all.

Sullivan, Rahn, and Rudolph also note that political psychologists have overwhelmingly used psychoanalysis to study elites and information processing to study citizens. In principle, this dichotomy need not and should not exist. That it does reflects the extreme difficulty of gaining access to public officials for the purpose of conducting the kinds of surveys and experiments that are at the core of the information processing perspective. Unfortunately, the dichotomy precludes systematic comparisons of the two groups. One outstanding question, for example, is whether elected officials and other political activists make the same kinds of errors – anchoring, overconfidence, and so on – that ordinary citizens make. Or do the institutional settings in which they function reduce such errors? Lacking equivalent experiments across the two groups, we really cannot say. To assume that the latter make better political judgments is understandable, but it might not be right.

Similarly, political psychologists have not been inclined toward cross-national analysis. This is an opportunity lost. Differences in political structures – presidential versus parliamentary systems, two-party versus multiparty systems, and so on – are natural manipulations that facilitate examining how structures affect and interact with individual decision making.

THEORY AND CONTEXT

A typical psychological study entails formulating a hypothesis and then testing it experimentally (political psychologists often substitute experimental surveys for the laboratory). Both Lupia and Conover and Searing find problems with this venerable approach to research, although for very different reasons.

Lupia argues for a closer relationship between formal theory and political psychology. In his words, "interactions between political psychologists and rational choice theorists can generate substantial *gains from trade*" (italics in the original). Political psychologists tend to use experiments to test hypotheses and make inferences. By design, experiments simplify the world by holding constant everything except those factors that interest the researcher. This very strength, the isolation of a cause-and-effect relationship, is also the experiment's primary vulnerability. It is a big inferential leap from an experiment to a much more complex political environment. Whether the experimental results hold in the real world is always open to question.

How, then, can researchers maintain the strength of experiments while at the same time increase confidence that the experimental results are externally valid? One answer might be to uncover similar relationships in the real world. As Lupia argues, however, the complexity of politics renders this a difficult if not impossible task; indeed, it is this complexity that motivates experimental work in the first place. Lupia proposes, instead, that experimentally oriented political psychologists look to formal models. Based on a deductive logic, these models begin with a set of assumptions from which the researcher then can derive precise and testable implications. However, models also simplify – they must be analytically tractable – and thus they are not especially good analogues of actual human behavior, either.

What Lupia recommends, therefore, is the joint use of axiomatic theory and experiments. On the one hand, rigorous theory leads to precise predictions about human behavior that not only shape the design of the experiment but also serve as the test criteria. On the other, experimental research directs theorists to a realistic set of assumptions about political decision makers and also provides the vehicle by which to test their models empirically. In Lupia's words, "an explanation that combines political psychology and rational choice theory trumps explanations that ignore either or both approaches." As he cautions, however, a formal model is no panacea for a badly designed experiment, nor is a poorly formulated model a panacea for experimental research. Lupia (also see Lupia and McCubbins 1998) then presents an illustrative study, of political persuasion, that includes a formal model of the relationship between speakers (public officials) and listeners (citizens) and an experiment embedded in a national survey designed to test its implications.

Lupia's study builds on the idea that the typically uninformed citizen must use available cues that more informed others provide. Reviewing the major psychological studies of persuasion of the past fifty years, Lupia argues that past work has not satisfactorily explained what differentiates a persuasive from a nonpersuasive cue. Specifically, none of the extant models identifies the necessary or sufficient conditions for cue persuasion.

The formal theoretical framework that Lupia offers begins with the theorem that "perceived common interests and perceived speaker knowledge are each necessary for persuasion." Satisfaction of both necessary conditions, plus the condition that the listener be sufficiently uncertain about two (or more) alternatives so as to be open to influence, comprise the sufficient condition. But listeners often cannot directly observe a speaker's knowledge and common interest, and thus they will look to speaker attributes that help them decide whether or not the speaker is knowledgeable and shares their interests. As a matter of empirical research, the task for the researcher is to identify such attributes, for only they can have a nonspurious correlation with cue persuasiveness. Speaker attributes that people ignore might be statistically related to persuasiveness, but they cannot be a cause of it.

Elaboration of the basic model entails introducing a third actor, an observer. This leads to the revised theorem that if the observer believes

4

his interests conflict with both the speaker's and the listener's, and if the speaker has an incentive to be truthful, then the speaker can persuade the observer. An Illinois liberal who hears Jesse Helms criticize a pending bill before his most devoted North Carolina constituents should be persuaded to favor it.

The call for increased formalization in political psychology warrants serious consideration. Rational choice theorists have demonstrated its value, and there is no obvious reason why political psychologists should not benefit from it. This said, two comments are in order.

First, it would be wrong to leave the impression that deduction belongs solely to the realm of rational choice and experimental testing of hypotheses to political psychology. Zaller's *The Nature and Origins of Mass Opinion* (1992) is a notable example of deductive reasoning in political psychology. Borrowing from extant psychological research on persuasion, Zaller systematically deduces a set of predictions that he then tests. Although most other research programs in political psychology admittedly are less axiomatic, they too build on assumptions about individual thought processes. The on-line processing model (Lodge, McGraw, and Stroh 1989), for example, takes as its point of departure the importance of affect and the limitations of long-term memory. Given these features of human thinking, it follows that people will forget the specific events that occur during a political campaign but will incorporate their reactions toward the events via a "running tally" of affect toward the candidates.

The second observation is the more crucial. It is one thing to propose that political psychologists use formal theory, quite another to propose that they use rational choice theory. Lupia understandably recommends bringing political psychology into a rational choice framework. To be sure, he rejects the traditional assumption of omniscience found in rational choice models and adopts the psychology-sounding idea "that people do the best they can with the knowledge and skills they have." Nonetheless, he employs a signaling model that has its roots fully in economics and that assumes the ordinary citizen to be a rational, strategic actor. Whether political psychologists will readily adopt a rational choice framework that they themselves might modify further remains to be seen. Some of the most influential psychological research on which political scientists draw portrays people as incapable of even approximating the canons of rationality in their decision making. For example, they consistently and unknowingly use rules of thumb that lead to biased errors in judgment (Kahneman, Slovic, and Tversky 1982; Kahneman and Tversky 1979). Emotions are not an element of rational choice models, and yet they apparently precede and are a necessary condition for rational thinking (Damasio 1994; LeDoux 1996). More generally, the diversity of political psychology, noted earlier, would seem to preclude an easy incorporation of the one field into the other.

Conover and Searing use their study of citizenship in the United States and Great Britain to offer a fundamentally different set of recommendations for the field of political psychology. Not only do these recommendations eschew formalization, they also challenge the very foundations of the kinds of empirical research that political psychologists conduct. The authors' recommendations draw heavily on interpretivist ideas.

The authors explicitly state their central presumption as follows: "there are no context-free thinking processes . . . and . . . political thinking . . . is therefore best studied in the cultural and political contexts of meaning in which it occurs." By implication, this means, first, that people cannot be studied in laboratories or via traditional surveys and, second, that the pursuit of universal laws is ill-directed ("there are . . . only particular citizens thinking and behaving in particular times and places, thinking particular thoughts and applying particular decision rules"). Conover and Searing readily acknowledge the radical nature of their premise, which departs markedly from the assumptions underlying their own past work.

The second implication, that social scientists should not strive for universal generalizations, is perhaps the more profound, for it runs counter to a widely accepted principle that motivates nearly all empirical research in political psychology and the study of public opinion more generally.

What is it that Conover and Searing believe political psychologists should do? The single word that best captures their answer is "discover." Typically, researchers set forth hypotheses that they then verify (or not, although the latter occurs infrequently unless it is someone else's hypothesis that is being rejected). More importantly, in Conover and Searing's eyes, the researchers also select the concepts and language that motivate the hypotheses. Very much in the interpretivist tradition, the authors urge researchers to discover the categories that people use in their everyday lives rather than impose them. This entails, in turn, identifying the political culture within which people function and that shapes how they interpret and give meaning to the world around them. In short, political thinking is contextual, and the most directly relevant context is the political culture.

As an empirical matter, focus groups and in-depth interviews replace experiments and surveys. Conover and Searing discuss how they themselves are employing focus groups to identify the descriptive categories that people use when thinking about citizenship and their roles as citizens. Some of their focus groups consist of students and parents, others of eight adults plus a moderator who asks the participants a set of questions that are accompanied by specific probes. Other than that, the subjects simply talk with one another, using their own concepts, themes, and language. All of the sessions are recorded, and the researchers then use the transcripts to create a coding scheme. Thus the final coding scheme emerges from the participants' own words and the meanings they share.

Interestingly, the focus groups lend themselves to experimental manipulation that could define more precisely what the boundaries of a culture are. Suppose, for example, that one were to undertake some of the focus groups with uneducated rural residents and others with educated urban residents. Suppose, furthermore, that the two demographic groups use distinctly different concepts and language. To ascertain whether the different cultures are due to education or place of residence (or both), one would then conduct parallel focus groups in which one or the other demographic is held constant.

The authors are aware of the possibilities for experimental manipulation, and in fact undertake one that is fundamentally important: they compare citizens' concepts and language across countries. If national cultures exist, their focus groups presumably will reveal them. In one of their early discoveries, Conover and Searing find that the citizens of the United States and Great Britain define their roles differently.

In prescribing comparative political psychology, the authors are not content to remain at the micro level of analysis. Rather, "once the study of political psychology moves into this comparative world, the case for adding qualitative and historical analysis to its strategies of inquiry becomes compelling, since qualitative case-oriented studies are, for good reason, the dominant tradition in comparative politics." In other words, comparative political psychology lends itself to connecting the psychology of individual thought to the institutions – family, school, media, voluntary associations – of a particular culture.

Adopting the prescription for this case-oriented approach requires accepting the twin ideas that universal laws are not attainable and (thus) that social scientists should be engaged in discovery. Many political psychologists will reject this idea out of hand, pointing to its single case orientation as the very thing that is wrong with comparative politics. Why transport this weakness into one's own field? Nonetheless, the Conover and Searing prescriptions warrant a second thought. One of the principal criticisms of political psychology is that in reducing everything to mental processes it loses sight of politics and political institutions. The authors offer one way to help ensure that this does not happen. Moreover, theirs is simultaneously a call for comparative political psychology, which currently is notable for its absence.

One can be sure that many political psychologists will resist the argument that research findings are necessarily limited to a particular time and place. Nonetheless, Conover and Searing's chapter is intended to provoke debate about a goal of social science – generalization – that most social scientists have long taken for granted. Such a discussion is particularly important to political psychology, where laboratory-based research has already raised questions about ecological validity. If laboratory findings cannot be generalized anyway – this is a point of debate, not a conclusion – then the call for a case-oriented political psychology at least warrants a hearing.

Krosnick raises some fundamental issues even for those who conduct more traditional modes of research, such as experiments and analysis of survey data. To make his case, Krosnick focuses on attitude perception research, to which he has made substantial contributions. What he has to say, however, applies equally well to all topical areas within political psychology.

The first lesson to be learned, he argues, is that political psychologists rely far too heavily on cross-sectional data, even when those data are not appropriate for the task at hand. As he pointedly states, "nearly every causal hypothesis of significance in political psychology is tested initially using cross-sectional data." It is easy to understand why: cross-sectional data, either survey or experimental, are the most readily available.

Using the projection hypothesis as his example, Krosnick thoroughly documents how researchers tried but failed to use cross-sectional data as a legitimate test of the hypothesis. Some, for example, employed models that extracted correlated measurement error. Others used instrumental variables to account for possible mutual causation between variables. Despite the creative and highly sophisticated statistical maneuvers, however, no one fully succeeded in either eliminating alternative hypotheses or ascertaining causal direction. Krosnick's point is that no one could, since cross-sectional data simply are not appropriate for the kinds of tests the projection hypothesis calls for.

The second lesson goes hand in hand with the first: not only do political psychologists typically begin with cross-sectional data, they also unthinkingly use linear measures of association. This characterization, of course, applies to just about all areas of political science. Krosnick demonstrates, in a highly detailed and careful manner, precisely why linear measures do not always work in tests of the projection hypothesis. Specifically, he convincingly argues that "although measures of linear association are well suited to estimating the magnitude of positive projection onto liked candidates, assessing negative projection with a measure of linear association is wholly inappropriate."

More generally, Krosnick shows how not using the right data or not using the right statistical analysis leads to contradictory and often wrong conclusions. His most important message is that researchers can avoid the problems of wasted time and wasted effort by carefully considering what it will take to test their hypothesis correctly. Linear statistical analysis of cross-sectional data might be the easiest route, but more often than not it is also the wrong one. Although Krosnick's discussion applies specifically to a single hypothesis, his discussion is required reading for everyone who conducts survey or experimental research. It sets a new standard for thinking through the relationship between theory and data analysis *before* the research begins.

THE PSYCHOLOGY–POLITICS NEXUS

The single most consistent criticism of political psychology (and political behavior more generally) is its neglect of politics or, at best, its reduction of politics to a psychological phenomenon. For the most part, political psychologists have dismissed the criticism out of hand and pursued their research unabated. The three chapters in Part III address the issue directly, albeit very differently.

Rahn, Sullivan, and Rudolph begin by documenting the dramatic growth in published research on political psychology during the last decade or so. Although publications on rational choice grew more rapidly, the increased influence of psychologically oriented research is undeniable, which renders questions about its value to the study of politics even more crucial.

Rahn, Sullivan, and Rudolph begin at the beginning: when critics deem political psychology to be insufficiently political, what do they mean by "insufficiently political?" They offer three plausible constructions of what the "naysayers" (their term) might have in mind and refute all three. The first possibility is that political psychologists do not pay enough attention to the role of elites in mass political behavior. This criticism, they argue, fails on the evidence. Numerous works have considered the connection between mass decision making, on the one hand, and elite discourse and behavior, on the other. To be sure, the authors continue, these studies typically incorporate elites as informational sources, not strictly as political actors, but the provision of political cues and messages is an integral part of the political process.

Second, perhaps the critics deem political psychology to be insufficiently political because it concentrates too heavily on the individual as the unit of analysis. After all, it is aggregate opinion, not individual choices and judgments, that elected officials see, hear, and pay attention to. True, admit Rahn, Sullivan, and Rudolph, but even students of macro politics draw on psychological models developed at the individual level, and "the question is not whether we will rely on psychological models to explain both individual and aggregate phenomena, but whether we will rely explicitly or implicitly, naively or with expertise, on such models." An even stronger assertion, which Rahn, Sullivan, and Rudolph do not make, is that the nature of collective opinion will never be fully understood without understanding the psychological processes underlying the individual decisions that get aggregated in democratic societies.

Finally, Rahn, Sullivan, and Rudolph speculate that what critics really have in mind is a specific approach, best exemplified by the Stony Brook School. This approach relies heavily on experimentation, some of it involving students, and delves deeply into psychic processes. Best known is the on-line processing model, which is described with nonpolitical-sounding terms like "updating" and "judgment operators" (Lodge et al. 1989). Reductionism, Rahn, Sullivan, and Rudolph state, is an inherent feature of political psychology for which researchers need not apologize. Moreover, the study of the most extremely micro psychological processes might well have big payoffs for the more traditional concerns in political science. It just takes time and hard work to get there.

Moving from the defensive to the offensive, Rahn, Sullivan, and Rudolph posit that just about everyone would identify the three most basic elements of politics as power, conflict, and governing. If political psychology is to be sufficiently political, therefore, it should have something to say about each. The authors then review literatures that, in toto, speak to all three elements of politics. In fact, they conclude, it is impossible to imagine how political scientists would study power, conflict, and governing without psychological concepts.

Rahn, Sullivan, and Rudolph conclude with a typology of extant research. The first category consists of research that directly applies psychological concepts and theories to political phenomena. As they note, most of the burgeoning literature on mass political cognition falls into this category, which begs the question "How worthwhile to political science are these straightforward applications?" The authors offer a strong argument that these direct applications have enriched our understanding of politics.

The second category of research also applies psychological concepts and theories, but less directly than the first. In this case, the researchers reformulate the psychological ideas so that they are specific to politics. Although Brady and Sniderman (1985) borrow the idea of a decision-making heuristic from psychology, for example, they do not merely apply an already identified heuristic to political decision making. Instead, they develop the idea of a "likability heuristic," which citizens can use effectively to predict political groups' policy positions. Finally, Rahn, Sullivan, and Rudolph observe that some political psychologists have actually helped to reformulate psychological theory by demonstrating that psychological processes deemed to be universal in fact are domain-specific. These processes either do not operate in political decision making at all or they operate in a way that is far removed from the original theory.

Krosnick begins where Rahn, Sullivan, and Rudolph leave off, turning the question of whether political psychology is sufficiently political on its head. The truly crucial question, he argues, is whether political psychology is sufficiently psychological. He answers in the negative and proposes that what political psychologists currently do is best captured by the term "psychological political science." They implicitly or explicitly import ideas developed in psychology to study decision making in the political domain. What political psychologists do not but should do – Krosnick views this as imperative – is help to generate valid generalizations about the mind. "One could say that the name we have settled on for our enterprise places the priority on the goals of *psychology* and suggests that political psychology is a subtype of the larger discipline of psychology generally. In this sense, it could be viewed as comparable to social psychology or cognitive psychology or consumer psychology or health psychology."

Krosnick's provocative (to psychologists and political scientists alike) prescription immediately raises two questions: (1) If the goal of psychology is to derive generalized statements about mental processes, why focus on a single context? (2) Why should political scientists aspire to contribute to psychology when the current one-way borrowing appears to serve them well? With respect to the first question, Krosnick offers three reasons why domain-specific research can contribute to psychology more generally. First, even though psychologists might pretend otherwise, there is no context-free psychological research. When people enter the experimental laboratory, they bring with them experiences they have had in the outside world. Researchers who are intimately familiar with politics will better be able to identify the effects of these experiences on laboratory-derived outcomes and to design more effective experiments that take these potential contaminations into account. Second, many psychologists study what are already manifestly political phenomena, such as aggression, altruism, stereotyping, intergroup relations, and the like. Especially at the level of international relations, Krosnick argues, many of these processes are the vehicle by which nations interact with each other. Finally, by focusing specifically on the political domain, political psychologists true to their name can begin to develop new constructs and think more precisely about how variables might interact – something, it should be noted, that political scientists have not done particularly well.

Political psychologists not true to their name can endorse Krosnick's preceding argument but still wonder why they should concern themselves with establishing psychological generalizations. After all, most political psychologists are political scientists who care much more about gaining insight into political phenomena than contributing to another discipline. To heed Krosnick's call to become more sensitive to the accumulation of psychological knowledge, therefore, political psychologists will need to see potential payoffs. Krosnick hints at rather than directly enumerates what those payoffs might be.

Most fundamentally, by contributing to psychology generally, political psychologists can become more equal partners with the psychologists from whom they borrow. Krosnick identifies what currently is an undeniable and unfortunate imbalance. Political psychologists pay a lot of attention to psychological research, while psychologists ignore political science. Political science departments hire psychologists, but almost never does a psychology department hire a political scientist. The Ohio State University Summer Program in Political Psychology attracts many more political scientists who want to learn psychology than psychologists who want to learn political science. Only by contributing to the field from which they now only borrow will political psychologists change this imbalance and thus avoid what could become an inferiority complex.

Even more compelling, political psychology that contributes to psychological theory is also good political science. Krosnick underlines this point, even though it is not his purpose, in reviewing some of his own work. To take one example, Krosnick and Berent (1993) used experiments to ascertain whether verbally labeling some widely used questionnaire items – ideology and partisan identification in the National Election Studies (NES), for example – and not others – the traditional NES 7-point policy scales, for example – might contribute to the relatively greater stability of responses to the former. They derived their hypothesis from psychological research on decomposition, which had found that splitting a single question into several questions leads to more accurate answers. Not only did Krosnick and Berent find support for their hypothesis, which should serve as a cautionary flag to users of the NES, but they also helped to establish the validity of the decomposition thesis by documenting its existence in a new domain.

To Krosnick, then, those who criticize political psychology as insufficiently political miss the more crucial point that political psychologists have not been faithful to their name. Because they have practiced psychological political science, they have contributed little to psychological theory and have not maximized the leverage that can be gained from employing psychological concepts and theories to understand politics.

Rahn, Sullivan, and Rudolph argue that political psychologists indeed address political questions and therefore have no reason to apologize for what they do. Krosnick advocates an even more psychologically oriented endeavor that will contribute to basic psychological theory. Luskin, in the third chapter in Part III, comes down on the side of taste, which is to say he recommends that the discipline be yielding in what it deems to be political. This is not to say that Luskin refrains from voicing his own tastes. On the contrary, he states his views with considerable emphasis.

Luskin accepts Krosnick's portrayal of political psychology as psychological political science, and then proceeds to ponder how far into the human psyche a researcher can delve and still find political relevance. To find political relevance is not only to find that elites influence mass thinking, which most work has done, but also to find an influence of citizen attitudes and behavior on politics. Luskin believes that this latter influence has been found at the aggregate level: "At least in the aggregate, what ordinary citizens think, feel, and do about politics clearly makes some difference to elites, institutions, the policies they produce, and the political system."

Where political psychologists and their critics part is on the need to study citizen decision making at lower levels of analysis, what Luskin calls the "native individual levels of analysis," which can vary from partisan identification to on-line processing to neural networking. In the eyes of the critics, if the effects of these individual-level processes and characteristics are manifested in the aggregate, there is no reason to conduct research at the individual level. Why, these skeptics ask, "pursue the sequence of causal relations back beyond the aggregate opinions and participation that directly affect politics"? In their minds, it is precisely when political scientists delve into lower-level mental processes that their research becomes insufficiently political.

Not so, Luskin counters. For one thing, people hold self-defined interests, which appear as values. Knowing how well they link their values to their policy and candidate preferences is fundamental to evaluating their effectiveness in politics. Moreover, people vary in their ability to make this association. Those who are politically sophisticated do better than those who are not. Researchers who eschew individual-level measures in favor of aggregated ones miss this variation and thus a crucial part of the story about citizens and politics. Finally, Luskin demonstrates that estimating aggregate-level relationships hinges on the assumption that all individual-level processes and relationships are linear and additive. Because this assumption is not tenable, aggregate-level parameters almost certainly will be biased and inconsistent.

One of the most established traditions in the study of public opinion is what Luskin calls "aggregated measurement of cognitive structure." Dating back at least to Converse, this approach entails correlating variables across individuals. In this case, individual-level variables are used, but they are measured in an aggregate fashion, which, Luskin notes, is distinct from aggregating individual-level measures. Although trained in this tradition, Luskin finds fault with it. Most significantly, the correlations hide wide individual variation in both cognitive structure and structuredness (i.e., sophistication). Division of the sample into relevant groups helps but does not overcome the problem. Putting this aside, other problems remain. First, with decent filters, something approaching half of the sample can drop out, simply because large numbers of people can't answer the survey questions. Second, even when researchers correct for measurement error in their statistical models, the parameters they report grossly underestimate the true level of respondent ignorance. Third, correlational analysis of aggregated individual-level data cannot capture the complexities of political thinking that political scientists should want to identify.[1]

What, then, should be the nature of the research that political psychologists conduct? By no means does Luskin endorse everything that researchers have done. Just as aggregation creates problems, so does "psychological disaggregation" to the level of cognitive mapping, as exemplified by research on schemas. This level, Luskin asserts, is simply too remote from politics. Similarly, political psychology experiments that look at reactions to stimuli at the moment miss the accumulation of responses that occur over the duration of a campaign or a political debate and thus don't tell us what we need to know.

For Luskin, sufficiently political political psychology might look to Kahneman and Tversky's corpora on prospect theory and heuristics and come to grips with how (and with what biases) people value and judge the probabilities of outcomes. He also finds potential in the psychological research on emotions and social categories. In his view, these are psychological concepts and processes that are not too causally distant from politics, and thus they can help us understand the relationship between citizens and politics.

POLITICAL PSYCHOLOGY AND AGGREGATE OPINION

Discussions of what it takes for political psychology to be sufficiently political inevitably must come to grips with one of the most formidable problems in nearly all of the sciences: level of analysis. The level of analysis problem poses two distinct if related challenges for political scientists: identifying the proper level, given a research question, and discovering

---

1 It should be emphasized that Luskin is *not* arguing against aggregation. As he aptly puts it, the question is *when* to aggregate. In his view, when individual-level data are available, the researcher should first model and estimate at the individual level and *then* aggregate.

the connections between individuals and the larger collective of which they are a part. These challenges take on special importance for political psychology. Most social scientists agree that aggregate public opinion is what influences politics, yet political psychology's natural level of analysis is the individual mind. It is this seeming disjuncture that has led critics to question the very relevance of political psychology to the study of politics. If it is to be relevant, its practitioners must demonstrate the value of their research to understanding collective opinion.

Stimson's contribution, an extension of his earlier work on policy mood (1991), serves to lay a foundation for the task that political psychologists face. It begins with these two sentences: "Public opinion matters in a democracy because it is presumed to influence government. The level at which that is realized is the macro, the polity." Accordingly, the research that Stimson reports in *Public Opinion in America* (1991) begins with fully aggregated NES data – aggregated across issues and individuals – and examines changes in the survey marginals over time. His more recent work (Erikson, MacKuen, and Stimson, in press) (forthcoming) tracks the relationship between these aggregated trends in public opinion and congressional policy making. This research omits the individual entirely and could not be further removed from the mental processes that political psychologists routinely study.

Stimson proposes to close the so-called micro–macro gap by taking individual-level data from the General Social Survey (GSS) series and aggregating them by relevant characteristics such as education and ideology. His purpose is to determine what underlies the global patterns – the shifts in marginals – he identified in *Public Opinion in America*. Do they reflect a general movement among all citizens, shifts among only an opinion elite, or, conversely, shifts among peripheral citizens who know little about politics? This is not a trivial question. In his earlier work, Stimson assumes the first, which, if wrong, is the classical ecological fallacy. The GSS data show that changes in aggregate opinion on a series of spending priorities questions arise from relatively uniform shifts across all segments of the citizenry. "The systematic patterns in the aggregate *do not arise from systematic movements by only a relative handful of citizens* (italics in the original).

Using some sophisticated statistical analysis, Stimson also shows that the over-time movement of mood is not a compositional effect resulting from changes in the types of people who comprise the population and thus the sample surveys. It is not the case, for example, that changes in the proportion of well-educated or high-income people explain the shifts in policy mood. Finally, since Stimson construes policy mood as left–right ideology, he examines whether mood tracks longitudinally with ideological self-identification, the more commonly used measure of left–right ideology. It does. Specifically, after Stimson accounts for unreliability in the self-identification measure, he finds that people's policy preferences drive their self-identifications.

Note that Stimson's approach to closing the micro–macro gap does not depend at all on political psychology. All it requires are appropriate individual-level demographics by which the researcher can aggregate. It is an approach, in other words, that renders political psychology unnecessary. However, both Luskin and MacKuen believe that political psychology can – and must – play a more central role in the study of mass politics. Luskin argues that political psychology is indispensable to understanding the nature of collective opinion. MacKuen places emphasis on revealing the mechanisms that link individual citizens to the polity and on how people's shared collective life defines what is political for them as individual citizens. Because he focuses on the dynamics of these mechanisms, emergent properties take on special importance in his discussion.

Luskin's second contribution to this volume builds on the first. Motivated by his enduring interest in political knowledge (or sophistication), Luskin asks whether psychological disaggregation and physical aggregation can lead to erroneous conclusions about citizen competence. He believes not only that they can but that they inevitably will. Both can obscure political ignorance and thus portray the citizenry in a more positive light than is warranted.

Consider, for example, Lane's research (1962, 1969, 1973; also see Hochschild 1981) that uses intensive, probing interviews to identify the nature of political cognition. This sort of psychological *disaggregation*, Luskin argues, is too microscopic a focus that "makes gossamer cognition, barely visible in everyday conversation, look impressive." In other words, research at this level of analysis loses perspective. To find that individual persons "reason," as Lane did, does not help social scientists understand how, if at all, ordinary citizens deal with politics. By contrast, Converse's study of ideological thinking and issue constraint (1964) does, since liberal–conservative ideology drives elected officials' behavior. In other words, it is reasonable to ask whether citizens think in the some terms as their representatives.

On the other side, studies that *aggregate* can also inflate citizen competence. To support his claim, Luskin points to two streams of research. First, some scholars (Lupia 1994; Popkin 1991; Sniderman, Brody, and Tetlock 1991) have argued, with considerable success, that even uninformed citizens make reasonably good political judgments by using heuristics, such as watching what the better informed do. The implication, therefore, is that the citizenry as a whole adequately performs its function of assessing policies and candidates. Not necessarily so, Lusin cautions. To reach their conclusions, these scholars have aggregated, and the aggregated data might not be conveying an accurate portrayal. For example, those who believe political heuristics to be an effective decision-making tool often report statistical means to make their case. These means obscure the large proportions of respondents who make wrong judgments. Moreover, researchers need to correct the means for guessing, which they rarely do. Finally, and as Luskin also argues in his first contribution, the means inflate accuracy because missing data are simply ignored.

A related but distinct line of research contends that collective public opinion is rational and provides elected officials with meaningful information because even though individual citizens are uninformed and make errors in judgment, these errors are random and thus cancel out in the aggregation process (Page and Shapiro 1992). Luskin challenges this thesis (also see Kuklinski and Quirk 2000) on the grounds that individual-level studies raise serious questions about how meaningful the aggregate opinion is. Several studies, for example, indicate that increased information among the least informed would markedly change the distributions of preferences for candidates and for public policies (Althaus 1998). As Luskin notes, currently available empirical evidence on whether increased information moves opinion to the left or the right does not speak as one voice. All the more reason, in his view, for a political psychology that can begin to sort out the answers and thus enlighten studies of aggregate opinion.

MacKuen begins exactly where Luskin begins: showing why Converse's analysis of and conclusions about citizens' political beliefs are superior to Lane's. And, again, the verdict is that "the highly idiosyncratic views Lane heard [are] hardly connected to the politics of government. For politicians to deal with their constituents they need . . . a systematic organization of political views." Converse recognized this, and thus established criteria that could be used to evaluate individual political reasoning as it applies to real-world politics. In other words, although both Lane and Converse borrowed from psychology, only the latter showed "how individual psyches connect to the broader political system."

More generally, MacKuen construes the micro–macro gap as falling along two (not orthogonal) dimensions: time and population. The latter is the more familiar and consists of what Luskin calls "physical aggregation." It ranges from Stimson's (1991) and Page and Shapiro's (1992) work on mood and collective opinion, respectively, to reductionist research on political schemas (Conover and Feldman 1984) and on-line information processing (Lodge et al. 1989). The micro-oriented research also adopts a short time frame, ranging from the millisecond of response-time measures to the time it takes to complete a laboratory experiment. By contrast, macro studies of politics typically examine historical change that occurs over decades, if not centuries. Moving from the micro to the macro level entails much more than mindless additive summing over individuals and milliseconds. Social scientists must identify the mechanisms that translate individual behavior into collective outcomes, including interpersonal interactions. They must also ascertain how the collective outcomes influence individual beliefs and behavior. In short, the polity and the individuals who comprise it act on each other over time, and the crucial task is to elucidate this dynamic process.

The standard aggregate model is linear "in the sense that individuals independently form the aggregate by adding up their experiences." To the extent that this model is accurate, current aggregate studies suffice. However, MacKuen proposes, three complications render this simple connection between micro and macro problematic. First, the very process of aggregation produces something different from a simple sum of the individual parts. The "citizenry" incorporates different sorts of people – some are more wealthy and/or educated than others, some pay more attention to politics, and so on – and politicians will pay more attention to some than to others. Moreover, there will be slight changes in the composition of the citizenry over time, and these very small changes can have consequences – for who wins and loses in campaigns and for the kinds of policies that receive majority support. In the same vein, some citizens pay more attention than others, and at certain times everyone pays more attention to politics than at other times. And social relations influence both what people see when they do attend to politics and how they react to what they see. Because of these interpersonal relationships, non-linearities – unpredictable occurrences – characterize mass politics, which the simple addition of individual attitudes and behaviors will not capture.

The second complication for aggregation is that macro phenomena shape what individuals see, do, and believe. Politicians, for example, grossly oversimplify and construct a macro polity, through their language, that will serve their purposes. Once this collective image has been established – business versus labor, blacks versus whites, and so on – individuals use it as a mirror to see how they relate to others. Often, they construct mental schemas and stereotypes to judge their political worlds. Once in place, these mental constructions obstruct proper reactions to new events and situations. These dynamic processes require psychologically based studies that must occur prior to aggregation.

Finally, and most important from the standpoint of a dynamic process, studies that use aggregated data likely will miss the effects of a feedback system: the macro polity shapes individual beliefs and behavior, which in turn influence the larger collective, which in turn conditions individual thinking and behavior, and so on. For example, if the poor do not receive adequate representation, then they must accept the class-biased rhetoric of politicians or drop out. In either case, the result will be to reinforce the rhetoric and thus place them even further on the margins of political life. Or, to cite another of MacKuen's examples, a famous basketball player dies from an overdose of drugs, which leads politicians to start making speeches on the terrible drug problem, which in turn encourages their constituents to communicate their concern about drugs. All of a sudden the nation is facing a heretofore unrivaled drug problem, even though statistics indicate that drug use has been declining. Again, sole reliance on aggregated data will not adequately capture this dynamic process. Nor, it should be said, will political psychology studies that depend on static, micro-level experiments.

One might construe the three preceding complications as spelling the death knell of aggregate-level studies. The presence of feedback and the possibility of nonlinear, emergent relationships, especially, raise serious doubts about their utility. MacKuen is careful to point out, however, that it is not at all clear that the simple macro conceptualization, rooted in the linear model, must be abandoned. On many counts, it appears to work well. Page and Shapiro (1992), for example, demonstrate that the public acts in sensible and expected ways. This said, MacKuen has made a strong case for the relevance of political psychology to the study of politics.

FINAL COMMENT

Political psychology is almost as old as political science itself, and there is every reason to expect that nothing less than the demise of the latter will undo the former. Political psychology is a staple in the study of politics. Nonetheless, its future utility to the discipline as a whole will depend heavily on political psychologists' willingness and ability to demonstrate the relevance of their research to the study of politics. The chapters in this volume raise issues that the next generations of political psychologists will need to address. As these chapters attest, some important steps have been taken already.

References

Althaus, S. L. 1998. "Information Effects in Collective Preferences." *American Political Science Review* 92:545–58.

Brady, H. E., and P. M. Sniderman. 1985. "Attitude Attribution: A Group Basis for Political Reasoning." *American Political Science Review* 79:1061–78.

Conover, P. J., and S. Feldman. 1984. "How People Organize the Political World: A Schematic Model." *American Journal of Political Science* 28:95–126.

Converse, P. E. 1964. "The Nature of Belief Systems in Mass Publics." In D. E. Apter, ed., *Ideology and Discontent*. New York: Free Press. 206–61.

Damasio, A. R. 1994. *Descartes' Error: Emotion, Reason, and the Human Brain*. New York: G. P. Putnam's Sons.

Erikson, R. S., M. B. MacKuen, and J. A. Stimson. Forth-coming. *The Macro Polity*. New York: Cambridge University Press.

Hochschild, J. L. 1981. *What's Fair? American Beliefs about Distributive Justice*. Cambridge, MA: Harvard University Press.

Kahneman, D., P. Slovic, and A. Tversky. 1982. *Judgment Under Uncertainty: Heuristics and Biases*. New York: Cambridge University Press.

Kahneman, D., and A. Tversky. 1979. "Prospect Theory: An Analysis of Decision Under Risk." *Econometrika* 47:263–91.

Krosnick, J. A., and M. K. Berent. 1993. "Comparisons of Party Identification and Policy Preferences: The Impact of Survey Question Format." *American Journal of Political Science* 37:941–64.

Kuklinski, J. H., and P. J. Quirk. 2000. "Reconsidering the Rational Public: Cognition, Heuristics, and Mass Opinion." In A. Lupia, M. D. McCubbins, and S. L. Popkin, eds., *Elements of Reason*. New York: Cambridge University Press.

Lane, R. E. 1962. *Political Ideology: Why the American Common Man Believes What He Does*. New York: Free Press.

———. 1969. *Political Thinking and Consciousness: The Private Life of the Public Mind*. Chicago: Markham.

———. 1973. "Patterns of Political Belief." In J. Knutson, ed., *Handbook of Political Psychology*. San Francisco: Jossey-Bass.

LeDoux, J. 1996. *The Emotional Brain: The Mysterious Underpinnings of Emotional Life*. New York: Simon & Schuster.

Lodge, M., K. M. McGraw, and P. K. Stroh. 1989. "An Impression-Driven Model of Candidate Evaluation." *American Political Science Review* 83:399–419.

Lupia, A. 1994. "Shortcuts versus Encyclopedias: Information and Voting Behavior in California Insurance Reform Elections." *American Political Science Review* 88:63–76.

Lupia, A., and M. D. McCubbins. 1998. *The Democratic Dilemma: Can Citizens Learn What They Need to Know?* New York: Cambridge University Press.

Page, B. I., and R. Y. Shapiro. 1992. *The Rational Public: Fifty Years of Trends in Americans' Policy Preferences*. Chicago: University of Chicago Press.

Popkin, S. L. 1991. *The Reasoning Voter: Communication and Persuasion in Presidential Campaigns*. Chicago: University of Chicago Press.

Sniderman, P. S., R. A. Brody, and P. E. Tetlock. 1991. *Reasoning and Choice: Explorations in Political Psychology*. New York: Cambridge University Press.

Stimson, J. A. 1991. *Public Opinion in America: Moods, Cycles, and Swings*. Boulder, CO: Westview Press.

Zaller, J. R. 1992. *The Nature and Origins of Mass Opinion*. New York: Cambridge University Press.

Part I Defining Political Psychology

I

The Contours of Political Psychology: Situating Research on Political Information Processing

JOHN L. SULLIVAN
WENDY M. RAHN
THOMAS J. RUDOLPH

The field of political psychology has a long history and a broad purview. It includes – has always included – a wide diversity of theories, approaches, quantitative and qualitative research methods, and verdicts. This is as true today as it has been true historically. There are, therefore, diverse issues and problems that have received long-standing attention in this interdisciplinary field. Yet, despite these many concerns, it is possible to identify some ebb and flow in the extent to which particular paradigms have characterized different research eras in political psychology.

The purpose of this chapter is threefold. First, we will attempt to provide the reader with a very broad (and hence somewhat cursory) overview of the breadth of concerns that have characterized the modern era of research in political psychology. Second, we will identify what we believe are some central trends in the evolution of "defining work" in this subfield. And, third and most important in the current context, we will locate the research reported in this volume within the diversity and central tendencies of broader issues in political psychology. The work reported in this volume is limited in scope, and we want to identify these limitations explicitly. At the same time, we hope to make it clear that by accepting a narrow purview and bringing to bear the considerable intellectual and scholarly energies of some of the best scholars in the field, considerable payoff in depth of knowledge is possible. We think that the papers published in this and a companion volume have realized this potential payoff.

Most recently, William McGuire (1993), a psychologist, characterized the history of political psychology as progressing through "three eras." The first era (1940s and 1950s) he characterized as dominated by research on personality and culture. The second era, during the 1960s and 1970s, he identified as focused on political attitudes and voting behavior. And, according to McGuire, the third era, of the 1980s and 1990s, is characterized by an emphasis on political ideology and belief systems.

Although such judgments are necessarily subjective and reflect one's perspective on the field, as well as one's own location among the panoply of research agendas included under the rubric of political psychology, we would modify McGuire's topology slightly. In our view, McGuire's demarcation of eras underestimates the continuity of certain issues and theoretical approaches.

It seems to us that political psychology was most certainly dominated by a focus on personality and politics from the 1940s up to and including much of the research conducted as late as the 1960s. The theoretical perspective adopted by most political psychologists of this era is best characterized as explicitly or implicitly psychoanalytic. Certainly this is true of the modern origins of the field in the work of Harold Lasswell, and it is true as well of the adaptations and applications introduced in the middle to late 1960s by scholars such as Robert Lane, James David Barber, and Fred Greenstein. We will identify these developments more specifically in the sections that follow.

A second era began before the emphasis on personality and politics had quite reached its zenith. During this time, many academic psychologists moved away from psychoanalysis and adopted a more Skinnerian or "behavioristic" approach, while research in social psychology began to focus heavily on attitude theory and change. Many scholars of political behavior began to focus heavily on social psychological models of voting in the 1950s and 1960s and also applied these models to political belief systems, mostly in the 1960s. Most of these scholars seem to have identified themselves as "political behavioralists" rather than "political psychologists," and thus two separate but related streams of research developed at this time. These two foci – on personality and politics and on social psychological models of belief systems and voting behavior – were often explicitly linked by scholars in the field, and neither really dominated the research agenda in political psychology in the 1960s.

Political behavioralists' emphasis on quantification coupled with their understanding of scholarly "rigor," however, led them to reject the psychoanalytic orientation that had dominated research on personality and politics (e.g., McClosky 1967). To the extent that they investigated the role of personality in politics, they did so by administering personality inventories and relying on "trait theories" of personality. With a strong focus on attitudes and voting, many of them abandoned the study of personality and politics altogether,[1] in part because most measures of personality did not predict voting behavior or partisanship, and in part because many of these scholars were more centrally located in behavioral political science departments and did not appear to identify themselves centrally as political psychologists.

During this time, even among those who did identify themselves most centrally as political psychologists, much of the initiative in the field came from social psychologists such as Irving Janis, Robert Abelson, and David Sears rather than from personality and individual-difference psychologists. Thus, by the late 1960s and early 1970s, it was broadly true that the momentum among political psychologists had shifted from the study of personality to the study of belief systems, attitudes, and voting behavior. To be sure, humanistic political psychologists such as Jeanne Knutson (1972), Walter Anderson (1973), and others continued to focus on stages of personality development. Their central concerns, however, shifted from stages of psychosexual development to Piaget's and Kohlberg's work on stages of moral development and Maslow's work on human development and the needs hierarchy.[2] Thus the late 1960s and the first half of the 1970s were characterized by dual paradigms, with the long-term momentum shifting toward the political behavioralists, whose focus and training were perhaps more allied with the concerns of political science than with the subfield of political psychology.

Finally, the third stage of the modern era began to evolve in the 1970s and achieved full flower in the 1980s and early 1990s. It is characterized by a focus on human cognition and information processing, the perspective and agenda represented by much of the work published in this volume and its companion. In part due to the success of the interdisciplinary "cognitive science" revolution, social psychology turned away from an almost exclusive focus on attitude theory to a strong emphasis on social cognition. Social psychologists began to study very precisely how people perceive, store, process, recall, and use information from their social environment. In turn, then, political psychologists began to turn their attention to how people similarly deal with information about their political world. This eventually led to a paradigm shift in political psychology, with the concept of "schema theory" replacing temporarily the concept of "attitude theory," although the debate about new wine in old bottles

1 For example, a 1972 collection of articles on public opinion and political attitudes had no articles on personality and politics. See Nimmo and Bonjean (1972).
2 Wilcox (1974) published a collection of articles on public opinion and political attitudes that had a section devoted to "traits." In that collection only Knutson's (1974) analysis of Maslow focused on personality.

continues (Conover and Feldman 1991; Kuklinski, Luskin, and Bolland 1991; Lodge and McGraw 1991; Miller 1991).

The era when an emphasis on political information processing dominated the agenda evolved slowly during the 1980s, in part because the training of many political scientists studying political behavior continued to be mostly within political science rather than within the more interdisciplinary field of political psychology. Those with interdisciplinary training picked up more rapidly on the new emphasis on social and political cognition.

The pace with which political science began to pay attention to recent developments in political and social cognition was quickened by two factors. The first was the continuing debate about ideological constraint and belief systems. This amplified the appeal of work in political cognition, which focused on how people actually process and store political information and how they make decisions, rather than on identifying how they do not store information and how they do not make decisions. Secondly, at about the same time, political science became enamored of economic models of politics, including political economy and rational choice. During the late 1980s, it became increasingly evident that there were fundamental contradictions between evolving work in political cognition and the increasingly popular rational choice models of politics. This heightened political scientists' interest in the cognitive science revolution and led more mainstream political scientists to pay attention to developments in political psychology. It became apparent by the early 1990s that political psychologists presented one of the major critiques of rational choice theory, as well as alternatives to it. The work of Quattrone and Tversky (1988), Simon (1985), Rosenberg (1995), Monroe and Maher (1995), McDermott (1998), Green and Shapiro (1994; but see Friedman 1996), and others identified fundamental empirical weaknesses underlying the assumptions of most rational choice models of politics. In addition, the careful work of the Stony Brook School and others on political cognition identified how people actually process political information and make political judgments, while David Sears (1993) and his colleagues (Sears, Hensler, and Speer 1979; Sears, Lau, Tyler, and Allen 1980), George Marcus (1988), and Roger Masters and Dennis Sullivan (1993) broadened our understanding of political decision making to include affect and symbolic reactions, neither of which have been properly addressed by rational choice models.

Though it too was slow to incorporate the role of affect into models of political judgment, the political cognition literature in recent years has increasingly elevated the importance of affect. Marcus and Mac-Kuen (1993) argue that citizens' affective judgments enhance the efficiency of information processing during campaigns. Distinguishing between positive and negative emotions, they show that anxiety stimulates political learning, while enthusiasm spurs campaign involvement. Similarly, Nadeau, Niemi, and Amato (1995) find that the interaction of anxiety and an expectation of success increases issue importance, which, in turn, promotes political learning. The influence of affect has also been demonstrated in work on political tolerance (Marcus, Sullivan, Theiss-Morse, and Wood 1995). In particular, individuals' emotions, when coupled with perceptions of threat, lead to greater intolerance. Political psychologists have shown increasing care in distinguishing between cognitive and affective dimensions of political thought. Such distinctions have been critical in recent analyses of political conceptualization (Just, Crigler, and Neuman 1996), candidate evaluations (Lavine, Thomsen, Zana, and Borgida 1998), and social policy opinions (Nelson 1999). With its emphasis on both affect and cognition, political psychology has contributed to a richer understanding of political decision making.

Rather than simply asserting the primacy of one approach over the other, a promising line of inquiry has begun to search for ways in which psychology-based and rational-choice models of decision making might be reconciled. We wish to highlight three such studies. Through the development of his "serial shift" concept, Jones (1994) formulates a model that is potentially consistent with both approaches. By positing fixed preferences, Jones allows individuals to behave rationally within a single decisional domain. Since attentiveness to preferences shifts by decisional context, he argues, individuals may also display the response instabilities so commonly found in studies of framing. In his analysis of impression formation, Bianco (1998) argues that rational choice and political psychology are not necessarily incompatible. By formalizing models in which individuals behave as either rational actors or motivated tacticians, Bianco actually finds that both models yield identical predictions about impression formation in campaigns. The two approaches produce, as the title of his article claims, "different paths to the same result." A final example is Chong's *Rational Lives* (2000). Chong incorporates individuals' psychological dispositions and their rational calculations of expected utility into a single model designed to inform our understanding of political norms and values.

In short, then, we have characterized the modern development of the field of political psychology as one whose emphasis has gradually shifted from personality and politics, to political attitudes and beliefs, and then to political cognition and information processing. In turn, there is evidence of an evolving emphasis on the role of affective factors in politics.

It is clear, however, that although these overall developments may indeed be discerned, no new development has entirely supplanted previous foci of interest. Thus, work on personality and politics continues, evolves, and changes its theoretical focus (e.g., Altemeyer 1996; Doty, Winter, Peterson, and Kemmelmeier 1997; Feldman and Stenner 1997); research on political attitudes and beliefs does not always, even today, emanate from the new perspectives generated by research on human information processing; and many political behavioralists have not been informed and/or persuaded by the newer paradigm.

With this as a backdrop, we will proceed to describe the diversity of recent work in political psychology, and thus to locate properly the work published in this and the accompanying volume. We will discuss the history of the field within a broader framework of presenting and discussing theoretical approaches, including early and contemporary examples.

PSYCHOANALYTICALLY BASED APPROACHES

Psychoanalytic approaches to politics owe a great intellectual debt to Harold Lasswell (1948). Lasswell argued that Freud's theory, applied to politics, meant that scholars should not take stated reasons for political action at face value – not primarily because there are hidden *political* agendas, but because political motivations, like all motivations, are deeply *human*. As such, motives for political action are obscure not only to most observers but also to the actors themselves. Political action is, in Lasswell's view, aimed at self-gratification or aggrandizement but is disguised and rationalized as public-spirited. Comprehending both of these realities requires considerable psychological insight.[3]

Others have built on Lasswell's theoretical approach in two main ways. First, some scholars apply psychoanalytic theory to the analysis of selected political leaders on the assumption that the roles played by these leaders are politically so powerful, and their own actions so consequential, that understanding how individual leaders function psychologically

---

3 Recent research in the psychology of memory and the relationship between memory for information and social judgments and evaluations has heavily "cognitized" but basically left unaltered the profound psychoanalytic insight that people are often unaware of the reasons for their preferences. Individuals' self-reports for these reasons instead "focus on explanations that are salient and plausible. The problem is that what seems like a plausible cause and what actually determines people's reactions are not always the same thing" (Wilson and Schooler 1991:182). People appear to be much better "rationalization actors" than rational actors, a point made nearly a century ago by Graham Wallas (1908; see also Plous 1993). In addition, recent advances in techniques for measuring implicit memory (as opposed to explicit memory, such as memory that is tested in recall and recognition tasks) have brought cognitive psychology closer to Freud's realm than perhaps many political psychologists realize (see von Hippel, Jonides, Hilton, and Narayan 1993).

will provide tremendous analytic leverage. Much of this work is weak and overly psychological, with little acknowledgment of the synergy provided by the political context. Not all psychological predispositions are acted out the same way in different political contexts, and the nature of the times limits not only the psychological predispositions of the actors themselves, but also how these predispositions work their political effects.

In any case, psychobiographies such as Langer's (1972) secret report on Adolf Hitler, done for the Secret Service during World War II, are purely psychoanalytic and almost completely reductionist. They are fascinating to read and they provide considerable nonintuitive insight into the character of the leader under analysis, but they show very little political sophistication.

Alexander and Juliette George's (1964, 1998) analysis of Woodrow Wilson is an example of a psychobiography that is psychoanalytically based but is not merely psychoanalytic.[4] Political and psychological insights coexist. Wilson's characteristic defense mechanisms – reaction formation and projection, to name two – are described within explicit political contexts that explain why they are manifested, as they apparently are, under some political circumstances but not others. The Georges also recognize explicitly a primary valid use of psychobiography – to explain political actions that we have difficulty comprehending if we rely solely on conventional political explanations and theories. The puzzle they address is why Wilson failed to obtain Senate ratification of the League of Nations Treaty when, by conventional political standards, he should have succeeded. More specifically, why did he fail to compromise when he reasonably could have had most of what he wanted by demonstrating a modicum of flexibility? Wilson's rigid approach and his self-righteousness tipped the Georges that something nonobvious and psychological was probably involved.

Finally, relying on the psychology of adaptation, which has psychoanalytic roots but is grounded much more in the language of everyday discourse, James David Barber (1992) takes psychobiography into the commercially successful realm of topologies. Perhaps even more than the Georges, Barber relies on the nature of the times and the political context of individual leaders' experiences to depict the interaction between psychological predispositions, on the one hand, and political, institutional, and historical imperatives, on the other.

Psychoanalytically based theories have been applied to the analysis of ordinary citizens as well as political leaders, exemplified by the in-depth

4 For a psychobiographical analysis of a more recent president, see Renshon's (1995, 1996) studies of Bill Clinton.

clinical research conducted by Robert Lane (1962, 1969). Lane examined the links between consciousness and political thinking, studying how ordinary human needs are translated into political ideologies. Carrying on Lasswell's tradition, he argues that political attitudes and ideologies do not merely express one's economic self-interest or one's sense of civic virtue, but rather are formulated by a complex interaction between our character, as shaped in the family, and the life circumstances (including, of course, economic as well as psychological ones) that we face during adulthood. Much of what constitutes these circumstances is political, and is connected to the interface between (individual) economic and political success and failure.

Finally, psychoanalytic theories and their derivatives have been applied to politics in the study of war, enmification, and peace-making. Much of this work is recent and represents a research arena where the theoretical focus of the first era survived fairly intact and now coexists with the newer approaches and foci of the second and third eras. Vamik Volkan, Sam Keen, and Ervin Staub, for example, have noted the almost universal tendency either to have or to create political enemies. Volkan (1988) provides an explicit psychoanalytic interpretation of the psychogenic process by which this tendency may reflect a universal need. He traces the deepest origins of enmification to stranger anxiety, a rather universal occurrence in children (at about eight months of age) that produces one's sensing another as a bad presence. By about age three, the child, under the influence of the family, begins to select targets to externalize his or her unintegrated black-and-white self, and projects images, good and bad, onto objects in the environment. The particular targets selected to serve as good versus bad objects are often determined by ethnicity and nationality. Later, the child's identification with peers, parents, leaders, and teachers leads to a fuller identification with their religion, ethnicity, nationality, and so on. This unconscious urge to be like similar others contributes to the crystallization of the concepts of "ally" and "enemy." Volkan further argues that if one has multiple identifications, the sense of self suffers and there may be less crystallization of the concepts of ally and enemy. If there are no suitable targets of externalization, both positive and negative, then the child will lack the ability to protect and regulate a sense of self. The need to have enemies – as well as allies – thus develops quite naturally from the normal development of identification. Volkan then applies his theory to ethnic and national political conflict, a timely political issue in the last years of the twentieth century.

Keen (1986) also takes a psychoanalytic approach. Drawing on Jungian psychology, he illustrates how individual psychological processes of enmification can be aggregated to characterize entire societies. Staub (1989) identifies how the psychological dispositions and processes of enmification can predispose societies toward political genocide. He situates these psychological tendencies within broader historical, economic, and political contexts that interact to increase the likelihood that such atrocities will actually occur. He argues that difficult life conditions – particularly economic conditions and political changes that frustrate basic goals and needs – play a catalytic role in political genocide. So also do cultural and social characteristics, particularly a national sense of superiority that is coupled with self-doubt, and an exaggerated sense of respect for and obedience to political authority. Finally, authoritarian political structures play a central role. Within this context, Staub identifies and describes in some detail the psychological characteristics and processes that not only predispose some individuals to acts of extreme political aggression, but also allow the aggression to occur even when psychological predispositions are absent. His analysis is fully contextualized yet general, psychological yet sensitive to social, economic, and political preconditions. He also draws on a much broader range of psychological theory and research, reaching well beyond psychoanalytic approaches.

Emmification and political genocide raise profoundly difficult questions that require interdisciplinary research strategies. To understand the complex issues involved in recent genocides – such as those in Cambodia, Argentina, Turkey, and the former Yugoslavia, not to mention Nazi Germany – we need to practice methodological eclecticism, to draw on multiple theoretical foci, and to synthesize work on individuals and political institutions. A collaboration between psychology and political science is required. During the twentieth century, there may have been an explosion of technical knowledge and rationality, but it also was characterized by more state-supported genocide than in any comparable period. Why and how so many good and ordinary people are able to become bystanders or even perpetrators of torture, terrorism, and genocide is an urgent question of the greatest importance – and psychological as well as political explanations are required for any attempt at a comprehensive answer.

In summary, although psychoanalytic theories characterized the mainstream of the first era in the development of modern political psychology, they have not been abandoned entirely. There has not been much mainstream research on American political behavior that either focuses on psychoanalytic strategies or assesses the role of personality in politics, but, as we have noted, they persist in other areas of research.

Other approaches to political psychology draw on personality and dispositional theories quite different from psychoanalysis. Before her death, for example, Jeanne Knutson (1972, 1974) applied humanistic psychology – particularly Abraham Maslow's theory of the development of human needs – to the analysis of political behavior. Others, including Anderson (1973), followed suit, but among the approaches applying humanistic psychology to politics, perhaps only Ronald Inglehart's (1977, 1990, 1997; Abramson and Inglehart 1995) has had a lasting impact on mainstream political science. His translation of Maslow's theory of human needs into a political theory of the development of post-material values has generated considerable research and controversy. Whether it is better to examine the political impact of postmaterial values using solely political approaches, or to examine psychological explanations as well, is hotly debated. From our perspective, it seems obvious that the additional leverage provided by an analysis that incorporates both approaches can only improve our understanding of these social and political developments. That a psychological approach by itself is insufficient is a claim with which we agree.

Finally, other dispositional approaches have provided insights into the impact of personality on political behavior and attitudes without adopting a fully psychoanalytic perspective.[5] For example, McClosky (1967) has written a number of significant papers relating political attitudes to personality characteristics such as anomie, self-esteem, dogmatism, and so on. Sniderman (1975) found a strong relationship between political tolerance and self-esteem, a finding corroborated by Sullivan, Piereson, and Marcus (1982) and McClosky and Brill (1983). These studies are concerned with issues such as leadership recruitment, political involvement, and support for civil liberties, and they have examined simultaneously the role of social, psychological, and political factors in determining individual levels of tolerance. They have also considered the broader political implications of the individual-level findings.

DEVELOPMENTAL AND SOCIAL LEARNING APPROACHES

Beginning with the earlier work of Richard Merelman (1969) and R. W. Connell (1971), and continuing more recently with the work of Timothy Cook (1985) and Shawn Rosenberg (1988; Rosenberg, Ward, and Chilton 1988), political psychologists have applied theories of cognitive and moral development to the political realm.[6]

For the most part, the best works in the now moribund field of political socialization have been in this genre. They draw on Piaget's research on genetic epistemology and Lawrence Kohlberg's on moral development to understand how the structure and content of political thought

---

5 Work on the authoritarian personality will be mentioned later.
6 The oldest coauthor of this chapter even taught a graduate-level political science seminar in 1973 entitled "Developmental Psychology and Political Behavior."

evolve with maturation and experience. These works have provided new perspectives on political science issues such as how ordinary citizens actually structure their political thinking (Rosenberg 1988) and what role moral development plays in political tolerance judgments (Wagner 1986). An underlying premise of this approach might be that the development of political thought and behavior is an integral part of general human development and that an understanding of the former cannot be divorced entirely from an understanding of the latter. Political behavior and thought are, quite simply, part and parcel of all human behavior and thought.

Political scientists have often adopted the position that unless childhood or adolescent patterns of political thinking and behavior can be directly linked to adult behavior in a sort of one-to-one correspondence, the study of political socialization cannot be justified. If the primacy principle cannot be validated, then the study of political socialization should be abandoned. We think this is an overly narrow viewpoint. Developmental approaches, whether explicitly stage-oriented or not, encourage a process orientation that links the structure and content of thought at one point with the entire web of thought and action that preceded the present. Socialization patterns at the individual level continue throughout the life cycle, and societal patterns change in ways not unrelated to the past. Understanding the present cannot be divorced from a comprehension of the past, both for individuals and for social and political aggregations.

Political psychologists have also relied on social learning theory to examine diverse political issues such as the diffusion of innovations in political campaigns and elections (Hershey 1984), the psychological basis of political authoritarianism (Altemeyer 1996), the emergence of torture among soldiers and citizens working on behalf of authoritarian regimes or terrorists fighting against powerful regimes (Bandura 1990; Haritos-Fatourcos 1988), the social-psychological basis of charismatic leadership (Madsen and Snow 1991), and the socialization experiences that distinguish heroic political rescuers from mere bystanders (Monroe 1996; Oliner and Oliner 1988).

Hershey explicitly takes social learning theory into a deeply political context and relies on it to provide a framework for understanding how successful political tactics and strategies spread from one campaign or campaign organization to another. Tactics that work in one campaign diffuse to others; those that do not go nowhere.

Altemeyer (1996) furnishes a much-needed psychometric updating of work on authoritarianism, which provides a powerful explanation of individual social and political intolerance toward unpopular and nonconformist groups and ideas. Unlike earlier scholars, Altemeyer places

33

authoritarianism in a social context and takes it out of the realm of psychoanalysis, viewing it as an attitude cluster with social roots and political consequences.

Madsen and Snow (1991), drawing on Albert Bandura's theory of human coping behavior, develop a conception of charismatic political authority in which the leader's ability to restore individuals' perceived self-efficacy figures prominently. The "charismatic bond" between leader and follower is established when individuals relinquish their own control of events to another – a proxy – who is deemed more able to cope with environmental stresses. Because such bonding is psychologically reliev-ing, individuals experience strong positive affect, reinforcing their com-mitment to the leader. The restoration of efficacy is thus the basis for charismatic leadership, a hypothesis Madsen and Snow (1991) test with a case study of Juan Peron's rise to power in Argentina.

Finally, the Oliners (1988) analyze social, psychological, and political reasons why some gentiles risked their lives to save Jews during World War II and why some remained bystanders (see also Monroe 1996). What is the role of acquiescence in encouraging perpetrators of extreme political aggression? What allows some individuals to break out of the mold of compliance with unjust authority? Surely, the answers to these important questions require a blend of social, historical, psychological, and political analysis. Putting psychological tendencies into a full context such as the Holocaust provides an opportunity to contextualize psycho-logical approaches to political questions.

Developmental and social learning approaches have been applied to a wide variety of political questions, in a variety of ways, some more explicitly political and contextual than others. These research approaches were introduced during the second era in the development of political psychology. Developmental approaches became central to the study of political socialization, which has since faded as a central concern in political science and political psychology. Social learning approaches were introduced to political psychology after learning theories sup-planted psychoanalysis among academic psychologists. They have con-tinued to play a role during the third era, as evidenced by the recency of research such as Altemeyer's and the Oliners'. In both of these cases, social factors were seen as supplanting the central role of personality in influencing both political authoritarianism and political altruism.

When one reads this variety of research in political psychology, one begins to develop new insights into old questions, to appreciate and understand the importance of some questions that more purely "politi-cal" political scientists might not be asking, and to realize the seamless nature of the connections among political contexts, psychological prin-ciples, and political and psychological theories.

SOCIAL PSYCHOLOGICAL APPROACHES

Although often overlooked in reviews of social psychological approaches to the study of politics, research focusing on conformity in politics is actually quite informative and germane. Beginning with the studies of Sharif and Asch, experimental social psychologists have studied the power of conformity in group settings. Today, the findings generated by the conformity paradigm have been examined within vastly different political contexts, generating new contextual theories of political psychology and sociology.

Noelle-Neumann (1984), for example, studying mass society and politics in Germany, discovered what she called the "spiral of silence" – a phenomenon whereby those on one side of a major political issue perceive that the tide of history and politics is turning against it and in favor of its opponents, who also understand this. The consequence is that the former silence themselves, while the latter are assertive and speak out, thereby exaggerating the size and power of the latter group and reinforcing the impression of their inevitable victory. Noelle-Neumann conducted a series of studies on the German electorate to determine the etiology of the spiral of silence and attributed it to the fear of social isolation, ruling out alternative explanations such as a bandwagon effect (but see Mutz 1998 for an alternative mechanism to explain shifts in opinion).[7] Because the fear of social isolation appears to be widespread, if not universal, the spiral of silence is a general social and psychological phenomenon. It applies to issues of fashion, fame, and even college-age drinking (Prentice and Miller 1993), as well as politics. Noelle-Neumann's explanation for it is largely social-psychological. Yet it is of the utmost political relevance, and the circumstances under which it occurs or is suppressed can only be explained by a combination of political insight and social-psychological awareness.

The effects of majority opinion in shaping individuals' opinions have recently been demonstrated through contextual analysis of political communication at the county and dyadic levels. Huckfeldt, Beck, Daltow,

---

7 Mutz (1998) provides an integrated theoretical framework that explains the multiple mechanisms through which impersonal influence shapes mass opinion. She suggests that only the very well informed have the capacity to engage in rational calculations of expected utility, while the uninformed rely on heuristic processing. The vast majority of individuals, she argues, do not fit at either end of this information spectrum. Consequently, she concludes, a cognitive response model provides the most appealing explanation of the process through which collective opinion shapes individuals' judgments.

Levine, and Morgan (1998) posit that political communication often involves ambiguous political messages. Such ambiguity, they argue, encourages people to employ "contextually-based cognitive shortcuts" when evaluating this information. Though cast in Bayesian terms, their model clearly reflects the influence of research on individuals' cognitive processes. Since the distribution of preferences in macroenvironments (counties) affects the distribution of preferences in microenvironments (discussion networks), members of political majorities are more likely to encounter others with similar political beliefs. Additionally, since perceptions of discussants' preferences are influenced by the perceived composition of microenvironments, members of political majorities are more likely to think that people agree with them even if they do not. The reverse is true for members of the minority. In sum, the authors conclude that the use of inferential devices or judgmental heuristics such as the "personal experience heuristic" creates a political bias that sustains majority opinion.

While Noelle-Neumann, Mutz, and Huckfeldt et al. examine conformity at the societal or local level, Janis (1982) examines it in elite decision-making groups. He discovers how the need to maintain in-group esprit de corps, and the tendency of highly cohesive groups to discourage dissent by means of various social and psychological mechanisms, can lead to disastrous foreign policy decisions. Janis (1982) finds tendencies toward political conformity among the elites that can be very similar to those found among ordinary citizens. Clearly, other purely political explanations are available for the fiascos studied by Janis – particularly the Bay of Pigs, his prototype. But, as in the case of Woodrow Wilson and the Georges, purely political explanations are inadequate to explain the rather massive nature of the miscalculations involved. The extent to which obvious and critical information was known but ignored during the decision making leaves ample space for psychological explanations to emerge preeminent. Similar issues have also been addressed in the literature on obedience to law (Gamson, Fireman, and Rytina 1982; Tyler 1990).

A better-known genre of social psychological theories applied to political analysis is the one dealing with political attitudes. It includes cognitive dissonance, schema theory, attribution theory, self-perception theory, and other aspects of research and theory in social and political cognition and information processing. In the 1960s and 1970s, scholars such as Jervis (1976), Holsti (1967), and De Rivera (1968) applied social-psychological attitude theory to foreign policy decision making, while others, including the authors of the *American Voter*, constructed attitude models to explain public opinion and voting behavior.

Deborah Larson (1985) has outlined the elements of five social psychological theories most pertinent to elite decision making: attitude change theory, cognitive dissonance theory, attribution theory, self-perception theory, and schema theory. She tries to construct alternative historical records based on these five theories, and then compares and contrasts these hypothetical records with the actual history of how the containment policy evolved. She then assesses which theory fits the record best. Larson concludes that self-perception theory provides the best fit. The central question addressed – for example, what explains foreign policy decision making with regard to the U.S. cold war containment policy? – is of immense concern to political scientists, and Larson's analysis is deeply political and historical, as well as social and psychological.

Finally, most of the burgeoning "mass political cognition" literature falls under the rubric of social psychological attitude theory. In the area of mass political behavior and attitudes, there has been a virtual *explosion* of recent work relying on social psychological theory, methods, and findings. While there are numerous examples of this type of work, we focus on four different types of political cognition research: (1) work that makes use of ideas about knowledge structures (e.g., cognitive categories and schemas); (2) the on-line model of political information processing; (3) priming and accessibility; and (4) dual-process models.

Research on schema theory, attitude availability, accessibility, and priming has provided new perspectives on old questions in the political behavior field. The old "attitude constraint" argument and perspective have been largely abandoned, in part because political scientists are weary of the debate and in part because work on schema theory and attitude accessibility has outdated it. We no longer argue about whether ordinary citizens are "ideological" or whether they hold "constrained beliefs." Instead, we ask how political attitudes and values are structured, and how they affect political behavior and elections. Conover and Feldman (1984), for example, use Q-methodology to assess how political attitudes are structured given that they are not generally organized into tight nodes of liberalism or conservatism. Research by Lodge and Hamill (1986), Lau (1989), and Miller, Wattenburg, and Malanchuk (1986) suggests that by examining the structure and content of citizens' political schemas, we can draw on generalized knowledge of schema theory better to understand how political knowledge structures are used by citizens to evaluate issues, candidates, and partisanship. (See our other chapter in this volume for a more detailed discussion.) Others have investigated how information about political candidates is stored and structured in individuals' memories (McGraw and Steenbergen 1995) and whether such cognitive organization might be affected by multicandidate contexts (Rahn 1995).

Milton Lodge and his colleagues (Lodge, McGraw and Stroh 1989; Lodge, Steenbergen, and Brau 1995; McGraw, Lodge and Stroh 1990; McGraw and Pinney 1990), in a series of political cognition experiments, examine the applicability of two different information processing models of judgment formation. The on-line/memory-based distinction, while somewhat oversimplified (see Hastie and Pennington 1989; Lodge 1995), was developed in the social cognition field to integrate a wide range of studies that explore the links between memory for information about a stimulus object and the generation of summary impressions and evaluations about that object. A convincing demonstration of the role of memory in such judgments proved to be elusive; many studies in social cognition had documented a surprisingly weak link between memory and evaluations. The on-line/memory-based distinction was developed in social cognition in order to provide a theoretical understanding of the conditions under which it could be expected that judgments would be based on the specific contents of memory for the stimulus object, or when such judgments had their basis in a "pre-stored" running evaluation, so that generating summary impressions does not require the retrieval of specific information about the stimulus object.

Using political candidates, public policies, or political attitudes on matters such as tax compliance (Scholz and Lubell 1998; Scholz and Pinney 1995) as the target of evaluations, the Stony Brook scholars consider the utility of these two models to characterize political information processing. Their studies suggest that judgments about political objects may have on-line components, at least for the more sophisticated, interested, and experienced members of the public.

Another important area of application of social cognitive ideas is the research that makes use of ideas about priming or the accessibility of cognitive categories. The accessibility literature in political science covers a range of topics. Perhaps best known is the application of the priming hypothesis to the study of the role of the media in citizens' evaluations of presidents (e.g., Iyengar and Kinder 1987; Krosnick and Brannon 1993; Krosnick and Kinder 1990). These notions have also been applied to the study of the role of self-interest and sociotropic judgments (Mutz 1992; Young, Thomsen, Borgida, Sullivan, and Aldrich 1991), the determinants of vote choice (Lau 1989; Mendelsohn 1996), political persuasion (Mutz 1998), and political attitude importance (Krosnick 1990). Research has also shown that the utility of partisan or ideological orientations in judgment situations is conditional on the accessibility of those orientations (Huckfeldt, Levine, Morgan, and Sprague 1999). All of these applications have extended our understanding of long-standing issues in political behavior.

And finally, students of political behavior have been making use of ideas drawn from the dual-process models of information processing. Dual-process ideas have their origins in the social cognition research on schemas and other cognitive structures. As it became increasingly clear that the "cognitive miser" metaphor was inappropriate for some people in some situations, social psychologists attempted to formulate more general models of information processing that allow people more flexibility in their cognitive strategies. Given insufficient motivation or high information processing costs, people may behave as if they were cognitive misers. Given incentives to perform well (either socially or individually induced) or low cost barriers, people may follow more resource-consuming processing strategies. The "motivated tactician" (Fiske and Taylor 1991) metaphor has been formalized into a variety of dual-process models. Several researchers in political science have used these models as inspiration for the study of attitude formation (Mondak 1992), attitude change (Peffley and Hurwitz 1992), the role of party images in candidate evaluations (Rahn 1993), the conditional importance of racial stereotypes (Hurwitz and Peffley 1997; Peffley, Hurwitz, and Sniderman 1997), and the counterfactual reasoning abilities of political elites (Tetlock 1999).

Another advance brought about in part by work in political psychology is the reassessment of the "minimal effects" hypothesis about the mass media. When the oldest coauthor of this chapter was in graduate school, the political effects of the media were summarily dismissed as intuitively important but scientifically untenable. Iyengar and Kinder's (1987) work has shown not only that the media have more than minor effects on the political agenda, and on political evaluations and choices, but more specifically how these effects work through priming and framing (Iyengar 1991). As noted by Bartels (1993), measurement error has often hindered nonexperimental efforts to document media effects. In recent years, however, researchers using nonexperimental data have demonstrated the effects of media exposure on individuals' policy and candidate preferences (Dalton, Beck, and Huckfeldt 1998; Zaller 1996), vote choice (Mendelsohn 1996), and economic evaluations (Hetherington 1996). The attitude accessibility paradigm illustrated by these research projects may even hold some promise for integrating the political science literature on media effects, political campaigns and elections, and voting behavior and public opinion (Jacobs and Shapiro 1994; Lavine, Sullivan, Borgida, and Thomsen 1996; Shaw 1999). Accessibility, however, is by no means the only mechanism that can explain media effects. Media frames can influence public opinion by increasing the salience of certain information rather than merely making it more accessible (Druckman 1999; Nelson, Clawson, and Oxley 1997; Nelson and Kinder 1996).

Finally, social psychological theory and research on affect and cognition, the development of group identifications, and stereotyping and prejudice have been used explicitly in attempts to understand and explain political intolerance (Kuklinski, Riggle, Ottati, Schwarz, and Wyer 1991; Marcus et al. 1995; Theiss-Morse, Marcus, and Sullivan 1993), ethnic and religious political conflict (Bar-Tal, Graumann, Kruglanski, and Stroebe 1989; Granberg and Sarup 1992), and international bargaining and negotiation (White 1986). Much of this literature has been both political and psychological, as well as explicitly directed at political action and change, more so than most straight political science scholarly attempts to analyze related topics.[8]

Social psychology theory and methods have thus characterized the second and third eras discussed earlier. Although mainstream research has evolved from the structure and content of attitudes to the psychological mechanisms by which citizens perceive, store, and process political information, other streams of research have continued to rely on other approaches from social psychology. The research reported in this volume is largely mainstream work that characterizes the latter years of the third era and may presage the development of a fourth, with greater emphasis on affect and a more balanced conception of the role of political cognition in shaping political decision making and behavior.

SUMMARY AND CONCLUSIONS

The point of our selective but broad overview of psychological approaches to political analysis was to illustrate the diversity both of the psychological models employed and of the political questions that these models have addressed; to identify significant trends in the field; and thus to help locate more carefully the work represented in this volume.

Among the diverse themes represented historically and currently in research agendas included under the rubric of political psychology, the chapters represented here fit squarely within the mainstream represented

---

8 The scholars who have adopted psychological approaches to political problems such as ethnic and national relations, and intergroup bargaining and conflict, have often attempted to enact political change to deal with problems of racism, ethnic and national hostility, and education. There are a large number of national and international conferences directed toward such goals, using political psychology as a base for political action.

by the third era and the evolving fourth era, if there is one. Overall, although the work in this volume reflects one of the major research streams in modern political psychology, much is left out. In attempting to achieve our explicit purposes, we also hope we have addressed the political importance and centrality of the questions that political psychologists are addressing, in this volume and elsewhere. We also hope we have made an implicit case for interdisciplinary research, because it often addresses questions and research agenda that strict disciplinarians do not consider central. At its base, human behavior is not parceled out precisely the way American academic social scientists have organized their fields of study. The most fruitful ways to understand what we may call "political" or "economic" or "social" questions are not necessarily limited to "political" or "economic" or "social" theories, concepts, or approaches.

We believe that all types of knowledge – psychological, social, political, and economic – as well as individual, institutional, and aggregate – are important and add to our understanding of politics, just as they add to our understanding of the broader human endeavor. We suspect that some of the most intriguing research being done today is interdisciplinary, and that our institutional structures are beginning to recognize this and even encourage it.

References

Abramson, Paul R., and Ronald Inglehart. 1995. *Value Change in Global Perspective*. Ann Arbor: University of Michigan Press.

Altemeyer, Bob. 1996. *The Authoritarian Specter*. Cambridge, MA: Harvard University Press.

Anderson, Walt. 1973. *Politics and the New Humanism*. Pacific Palisades, CA: Goodyear.

Bandura, Albert. 1990. "Mechanisms of Moral Disagreement." In Walter Reich, ed., *Origins of Terrorism: Psychologies, Ideologies, Theologies, States of Mind*. Princeton, NJ: Wilson Center.

Bar-Tal, Daniel, Carl F. Graumann, Arie W. Kruglanski, and Wolfgang Stroebe. 1989. *Stereotyping and Prejudice: Changing Conceptions*. New York: Springer-Verlag.

Barber, James David. 1992. *The Presidential Character: Predicting Performance in the White House*, 4th ed. Englewood Cliffs, NJ: Prentice-Hall.

Bartels, Larry M. 1993. "Messages Received: The Political Impact of Media Exposure." *American Political Science Review* 87:267–85.

Bianco, William T. 1998. "Different Paths to the Same Result: Rational Choice, Political Psychology, and Impression Formation in Campaigns." *American Journal of Political Science* 42:1061–81.

Chong, Dennis. 2000. *Rational Lives*. Chicago: University of Chicago Press.

Connell, R. W. 1971. *The Child's Construction of Politics*. Melbourne, Australia: Melbourne University Press.

Conover, Pamela J., and Stanley Feldman. 1984. "How People Organize the Political World: A Schematic Model." *American Journal of Political Science* 28:95–126.
    1991. "Where Is the Schema? Critiques." *American Political Science Review* 85:1364–9.
Cook, Timothy. 1985. "The Bear Market in Political Socialization and the Costs of Misunderstood Psychological Theories." *American Political Science Review* 70:1079–93.
Dalton, Russell J., Paul A. Beck, and Robert Huckfeldt. 1998. "Partisan Cues and the Media: Information Flows in the 1992 Presidential Election." *American Political Science Review* 92:111–26.
De Rivera, Joseph H. 1968. *The Psychological Dimension of Foreign Policy.* Columbus, OH: Charles E. Merrill.
Doty, Richard M., David G. Winter, Bill E. Peterson, and Markus Kemmelmeier. 1997. "Authoritarianism and American Students' Attitudes About the Gulf War, 1990–1996." *Personality and Social Psychology Bulletin* 11: 1133–43.
Druckman, James N. 1999. "Do Party Cues Limit Framing Effects?" Paper presented at the annual meeting of the American Political Science Association, Atlanta, September 2–5, 1999.
Feldman, Stanley, and Karen Stenner. 1997. "Perceived Threat and Authoritarianism." *Political Psychology* 18:741–70.
Fiske, Susan T., and Shelley E. Taylor. 1991. *Social Cognition,* 2nd ed. New York: McGraw-Hill.
Friedman, Jeffrey, ed. 1996. *The Rational Choice Controversy.* New Haven, CT: Yale University Press.
Gamson, William A., Bruce Fireman, and Steven Rytina. 1982. *Encounters with Unjust Authority.* Homewood, IL: Dorsey Press.
George, Alexander L., and Juliette L. George. 1964. *Woodrow Wilson and Colonel House: A Personality Study.* New York: Dover Press.
    1998. *Presidential Popularity and Performance.* Boulder, CO: Westview Press.
Granberg, Donald, and Gian Sarup. 1992. *Social Judgment and Intergroup Relations.* New York: Springer-Verlag.
Green, Donald P., and Ian Shapiro. 1994. *Pathologies of Rational Choice Theory: A Critique of Applications in Political Science.* New Haven, CT: Yale University Press.
Haritos-Fatourcos, Mika. 1988. "The Official Torturer: A Learning Model for Obedience to the Authority of Violence." *Journal of Applied Social Psychology* 18:1107–20.
Hastie, Reid, and Nancy Pennington. 1989. "Notes on the Distinction between Memory-Based Versus On-line Judgments." In John N. Bassili, ed., *On-line Processes in Person Perception.* Hillsdale, NJ: Erlbaum.
Hershey, Marjorie Randon. 1984. *Running for Office: The Political Education of Campaigners.* Chatham, NJ: Chatham House.
Hetherington, Marc J. 1996. "The Media's Role in Forming Voters' National Economic Evaluations." *American Journal of Political Science* 40:372–95.
Holsti, Ole. 1967. "Cognitive Dynamics and Images of the Enemy." In David Finlay, Ole Holsti, and Richard Fagen, eds., *Enemies in Politics.* Chicago: Rand McNally.
Huckfeldt, Robert, Paul Allen Beck, Russell J. Dalton, Jeffrey Levine, and William Morgan. 1998. "Ambiguity, Distorted Messages, and Nested

Environmental Effects on Political Communication." *Journal of Politics* 60:996–1030.

Huckfeldt, Robert, Jeffrey Levine, William Morgan, and John Sprague. 1999. "Accessibility and the Political Utility of Partisan and Ideological Orientations." *American Journal of Political Science* 43:888–911.

Hurwitz, Jon, and Mark Peffley. 1997. "Public Perceptions of Race and Crime: The Role of Racial Stereotypes." *American Journal of Political Science* 41:375–401.

Inglehart, Ronald. 1977. *The Silent Revolution: Changing Values and Political Styles Among Western Publics.* Princeton, NJ: Princeton University Press.

1990. *Culture Shift in Advanced Industrial Society.* Princeton, NJ: Princeton University Press.

1997. *Modernization and Postmodernization: Cultural, Economic, and Political Change in 43 Societies.* Princeton, NJ: Princeton University Press.

Iyengar, Shanto. 1991. *Who's Responsible.* Chicago: University of Chicago Press.

Iyengar, Shanto, and Donald R. Kinder. 1987. *News that Matters.* Chicago: University of Chicago Press.

Jacobs, Lawrence R., and Robert Y. Shapiro. 1994. "Issues, Candidate Image, and Priming: The Use of Private Polls in Kennedy's 1960 Presidential Campaign." *American Political Science Review* 88:527–40.

Janis, Irving L. 1982. *Groupthink.* Boston: Houghton Mifflin.

Jervis, Robert. 1976. *Perception and Misperception in International Politics.* Princeton, NJ: Princeton University Press.

Jones, Bryan D. 1994. *Reconceiving Decision-Making in Democratic Politics.* Chicago: University of Chicago Press.

Just, Marion R., Ann N. Crigler, and W. Russell Neuman. 1996. "Cognitive and Affective Dimensions of Political Conceptualization." In Ann N. Crigler, ed., *The Psychology of Political Communication.* Ann Arbor: University of Michigan Press.

Keen, Sam. 1986. *Faces of the Enemy: Reflections of the Hostile Imagination.* San Francisco: Harper & Row.

Knutson, Jeanne N. 1972. *The Human Basis of the Polity: A Psychological Study of Political Men.* Chicago: Aldine-Atherton.

1974. "The Political Relevance of Self-Actualization." In Allen R. Wilcox, ed., *Public Opinion and Political Attitudes.* New York: Wiley.

Krosnick, Jon A. 1990. "Government Policy and Citizen Passion: A Study of Issue Publics in Contemporary America." *Political Behavior* 12:59–92.

Krosnick, Jon A., and Laura A. Brannon. 1993. "The Impact of the Gulf War on the Ingredients of Presidential Evaluations: Multidimensional Effects of Political Involvement." *American Political Science Review* 87:963–75.

Krosnick, Jon A., and Donald R. Kinder. 1990. "Altering the Foundations of Popular Support for the President through Priming." *American Political Science Review* 84:497–512.

Kuklinski, James H., Robert C. Luskin, and John Bolland. 1991. "Where Is the Schema? Going Beyond the 'S' Word in Political Psychology." *American Political Science Review* 85:1341–56.

Kuklinski, James H., Ellen Riggle, Victor Ottati, Norbert Schwarz, and Robert S. Wyer, Jr. 1991. "The Cognitive and Affective Bases of Political Tolerance Judgments." *American Journal of Political Science* 35:1–27.

Lane, Robert E. 1962. *Political Ideology: Why the American Common Man Believes What He Does.* New York: Free Press.

1969. *Political Thinking and Consciousness: The Private Life of the Political Mind.* Chicago: Markham.

Langer, Walter. 1972. *The Mind of Adolf Hitler.* New York: New American Library.

Larson, Deborah Welch. 1985. *Origins of Containment: A Psychological Explanation.* Princeton, NJ: Princeton University Press.

Lasswell, Harold. 1948. *Power and Personality.* New York: W. W. Norton.

Lau, Richard R. 1989. "Construct Accessibility and Electoral Choice." *Political Behavior* 11:5–32.

Lavine, Howard, John L. Sullivan, Eugene Borgida, and Cynthia J. Thomsen. 1996. "The Relationship of National and Personal Issue Salience to Attitude Accessibility on Foreign and Domestic Policy Issues." *Political Psychology* 17:293–316.

Lavine, Howard, Cynthia J. Thomsen, Mark P. Zanna, and Eugene Borgida. 1998. "On the Primacy of Affect in the Determination of Attitudes and Behavior: The Moderating Role of Affective-Cognitive Ambivalence." *Journal of Experimental and Social Psychology* 34:398–421.

Lodge, Milton. 1995. "Toward a Procedural Model of Candidate Evaluation." In Milton Lodge and Kathleen M. McGraw, eds., *Political Judgment.* Ann Arbor: University of Michigan Press.

Lodge, Milton, and Ruth Hamill. 1986. "A Partisan Schema for Political Information Processing." *American Political Science Review* 80:505–19.

Lodge, Milton, and Kathleen M. McGraw. 1991. "Where Is the Schema? Critiques." *American Political Science Review* 85:1355–64.

Lodge, Milton, Kathleen M. McGraw, and Patrick Stroh. 1989. "An Impression-Driven Model of Candidate Evaluation." *American Political Science Review* 87:399–419.

Lodge, Milton, Marco R. Steenbergen, and Shawn Brau. 1995. "The Responsive Voter: Campaign Information and the Dynamics of Candidate Evaluation." *American Political Science Review* 89:309–26.

Madsen, Douglas, and Peter G. Snow. 1991. *The Charismatic Bond: Political Behavior in Time of Crisis.* Cambridge, MA: Harvard University Press.

Marcus, George E. 1988. "The Structure of Emotional Response: 1984 Presidential Candidates." *American Political Science Review* 82:735–61.

Marcus, George E., and Michael B. MacKuen. 1993. "Anxiety, Enthusiasm, and the Vote: The Emotional Underpinnings of Learning and Involvement during Presidential Campaigns." *American Political Science Review* 87:688–701.

Marcus, George E., John L. Sullivan, Elizabeth Theiss-Morse, and Sandra L. Wood. 1995. *With Malice Toward Some: How People Make Civil Liberties Judgments.* New York: Cambridge University Press.

Masters, Roger, and Dennis Sullivan. 1993. "Nonverbal Behavior and Leadership: Emotion and Cognition in Political Information Processing." In Shanto Iyengar and William J. McGuire, eds., *Explorations in Political Psychology.* Durham, NC: Duke University Press.

McClosky, Herbert. 1967. "Personality and Attitude Correlates of Foreign Policy Orientation." In James N. Rosenau, ed., *Domestic Sources of Foreign Policy.* New York: Free Press.

McClosky, Herbert, and Alida Brill. 1983. *Dimensions of Tolerance.* New York: Russell Sage Foundation.

McDermott, Rose. 1998. *Risk-Taking in International Politics.* Ann Arbor: University of Michigan Press.

McGraw, Kathleen M., Milton Lodge, and Patrick Stroh. 1990. "On-line Processing in Candidate Evaluation: The Effects of Issue Order, Issue Importance, and Sophistication." *Political Behavior* 12:41–58.

McGraw, Kathleen M., and Neil Pinney. 1990. "The Effects of General and Domain-Specific Expertise on Political Memory and Judgment." *Social Cognition* 8:9–30.

McGraw, Kathleen M., and Marco Steenbergen. 1995. "Pictures in the Head: Memory Representations of Political Candidates." In Milton Lodge and Kathleen M. McGraw, eds., *Political Judgment*. Ann Arbor: University of Michigan Press.

McGuire, William J. 1993. "The Poly–Psy Relationship: Three Phases of a Long Affair." In Shanto Iyengar and William J. McGuire, eds., *Explorations in Political Psychology*. Durham, NC: Duke University Press.

Mendelsohn, Matthew. 1996. "The Media and Interpersonal Communications: The Priming of Issues, Leaders, and Party Identification." *Journal of Politics* 58:112–25.

Merelman, Richard M. 1969. "The Development of Political Ideology: A Framework for the Analysis of Political Socialization." *American Political Science Review* 63:750–67.

Miller, Arthur. 1991. "Where Is the Schema? Critiques." *American Political Science Review* 85:1369–80.

Miller, Arthur, Martin Wattenburg, and Oksana Malanchuk. 1986. "Schematic Assessments of Presidential Candidates." *American Political Science Review* 80:521–40.

Mondak, Jeffrey J. 1992. "Source Cues and Policy Approval: The Cognitive Dynamics of Public Support for the Reagan Agenda." *American Journal of Political Science* 36:186–212.

Monroe, Kristen Renwick. 1996. *The Heart of Altruism*. Princeton, NJ: Princeton University Press.

Monroe, Kristen Renwick, and Kristen Hall Maher. 1995. "Psychology and Rational Actor Theory." *Political Psychology* 16:1–21.

Mutz, Diana C. 1992. "Mass Media and the Depoliticization of Personal Experience." *American Journal of Political Science*. 36:483–508.

1998. *Impersonal Influence*. New York: Cambridge University Press.

Nadeau, Richard, Richard G. Niemi, and Timothy Amato. 1995. "Emotions, Issue Importance, and Political Learning." *American Journal of Political Science* 39:558–74.

Nelson, Thomas E. 1999. "Group Affect and Attribution in Social Policy Opinion." *Journal of Politics* 61:331–62.

Nelson, Thomas E., Rosalee A. Clawson, and Zoe M. Oxley. 1997. "Media Framing of a Civil Liberties Conflict and Its Effect on Tolerance." *American Political Science Review* 91:567–84.

Nelson, Thomas E., and Donald R. Kinder. 1996. "Issue Frames and Group-Centrism in American Public Opinion." *Journal of Politics* 58:1055–78.

Nimmo, Dan, and Charles N. Bonjean. 1972. *Political Attitudes and Public Opinion*. New York: McKay.

Noelle-Neumann, Elisabeth. 1984. *The Spiral of Silence*. Chicago: University of Chicago Press.

Oliner, Samuel, and Pearl Oliner. 1988. *The Altruistic Personality*. New York: Free Press.

45

Peffley, Mark, and Jon Hurwitz. 1992. "International Events and Foreign Policy Beliefs: Public Response to Changing Soviet–U.S. Relations." *American Journal of Political Science* 36:431–61.

Peffley, Mark, Jon Hurwitz, and Paul M. Sniderman. 1997. "Racial Stereotypes and Whites' Political Views of Blacks in the Context of Welfare and Crime." *American Journal of Political Science* 41:30–60.

Plous, Scott. 1993. *The Psychology of Judgment and Decision Making*. Philadelphia: Temple University Press.

Prentice, Deborah A., and Dale T. Miller. 1993. "Pluralistic Ignorance and Alcohol Use on Campus: Some Consequences of Misperceiving the Social Norm." *Journal of Personality and Social Psychology* 64:243–56.

Quattrone, George A., and Amos Tversky. 1988. "Contrasting Rational and Psychological Analyses of Political Choice." *American Political Science Review* 82:719–36.

Rahn, Wendy M. 1993. "The Role of Partisan Stereotypes in Information Processing about Political Candidates." *American Journal of Political Science* 37:472–96.

——— 1995. "Candidate Evaluation in Complex Information Environments: Cognitive Organization and Comparison Process." In Milton Lodge and Kathleen M. McGraw, eds., *Political Judgment*. Ann Arbor: University of Michigan Press.

Renshon, Stanley A. 1995. *High Hopes: The Clinton Presidency and the Politics of Ambition*. New York: New York University Press.

——— 1996. *The Psychological Assessment of Presidential Candidates*. New York: New York University Press.

Rosenberg, Shawn. 1988. *Reason, Ideology, and Politics*. Princeton, NJ: Princeton University Press.

——— 1995. "Against Neoclassical Political Economy: A Political Psychological Critique." *Political Psychology* 16:99–136.

Rosenberg, Shawn, Dana Ward, and Stephen Chilton. 1988. *Political Reasoning and Cognition: A Piagetian View*. Durham, NC: Duke University Press.

Scholz, John T., and Mark Lubell. 1998. "Adaptive Political Attitudes: Duty, Trust, and Fear as Monitors of Tax Policy." *American Journal of Political Science* 42:903–20.

Scholz, John T., and Neil Pinney. 1995. "Duty, Fear, and Tax Compliance: The Heuristic Basis of Citizenship Behavior." *American Journal of Political Science* 39:490–512.

Sears, David O. 1993. "Symbolic Politics: A Socio-Psychological Theory." In Shanto Iyengar and William J. McGuire, eds., *Explorations in Political Psychology*. Durham, NC: Duke University Press.

Sears, David O., C. Hensler, and L. Speer. 1979. "Whites Opposition to 'Busing': Self-Interest or Symbolic Politics." *American Political Science Review* 73:369–84.

Sears, David O., Richard Lau, Tom Tyler, and H. M. Allen, Jr. 1980. "Self-Interest vs. Symbolic Politics in Policy Attitudes and Presidential Voting." *American Political Science Review* 74:670–84.

Shaw, Daron R. 1999. "The Effect of TV Ads and Candidate Appearances on Statewide Presidential Votes, 1988–96." *American Political Science Review* 93:345–62.

Simon, Herbert. 1985. "Human Nature in Politics: The Dialogue of Psychology with Political Science." *American Political Science Review* 79:293–304.

Sniderman, Paul M. 1975. *Personality and Democratic Politics*. Berkeley: University of California Press.

Staub, Ervin. 1989. *The Roots of Evil: The Origins of Genocide and Other Group Violence*. New York: Cambridge University Press.

Sullivan, John L., James Piereson, and George E. Marcus. 1982. *Political Tolerance and American Democracy*. Chicago: University of Chicago Press.

Tetlock, Philip. 1999. "Theory-Driven Reasoning about Possible Pasts and Probable Futures in World Politics: Are We Prisoners of our Preconceptions?" *American Journal of Political Science* 43:335–66.

Theiss-Morse, Elizabeth, George E. Marcus, and John L. Sullivan. 1993. "Reason and Passion in Political Life: The Organization of Affect and Cognition in Political Tolerance." In George E. Marcus and Russell Hanson, eds., *Reconsidering the Democratic Public*. University Park: Penn State University Press.

Tyler, Tom R. 1990. *Why People Obey the Law*. New Haven, CT: Yale University Press.

Volkan, Vamik D. 1988. *The Need to Have Enemies and Allies: From Clinical Practice to International Relationships*. Northvale, NJ: Aronson.

von Hippel, William, John Jonides, James L. Hilton, and Sowmya Narayan. 1993. "The Inhibitory Effect of Schematic Processing on Perceptual Encoding." *Journal of Personality and Social Psychology* 64:921–35.

Wagner, J. 1986. "Political Tolerance and Stages of Moral Development: A Conceptual and Empirical Analysis." *Political Behavior* 8:45–80.

Wallas, Graham. 1908. *Human Nature in Politics*. New Brunswick, NJ: Transaction Books.

White, Ralph K, ed. 1986. *Psychology and the Prevention of Nuclear War*. New York: New York University Press.

Wilcox, Allen R. 1974. *Public Opinion and Political Attitudes*. New York: Wiley.

Wilson, Timothy D., and Jonathan W. Schooler. 1991. "Thinking Too Much: Introspection Can Reduce the Quality of Preferences and Decisions." *Journal of Personality and Social Psychology* 60:181–92.

Young, Jason, Cynthia Thomsen, Eugene Borgida, John L. Sullivan, and John H. Aldrich. 1991. "When Self-Interest Makes a Difference: The Role of Construct Accessibility in Political Reasoning." *Journal of Experimental Social Psychology* 27:271–96.

Zaller, John. 1996. "The Myth of Massive Media Impact Revived: New Support for a Discredited Idea." In Diana C. Mutz, Paul M. Sniderman, and Richard A. Brody, eds., *Political Persuasion and Attitude Change*. Ann Arbor: University of Michigan Press.

Part II Theory and Research

2

Who Can Persuade Whom?: Implications from the Nexus of Psychology and Rational Choice Theory

ARTHUR LUPIA

Political psychologists and rational choice theorists do not interact very much. This silence is particularly ironic when it comes to explaining political behavior, as such explanations are a core concern of both groups.

Consider, for example, the topic of persuasion, and in particular how people in political settings choose whom to believe. Voters, legislators, and jurors are but a few of the many political decision makers who have opportunities to base what they do on the written or oral statements of others. To explain the decisions that people who can learn from others make, we should understand what makes some statements more persuasive than others. An irony of extant persuasion research is that while it represents an active field of study for both political psychologists and rational choice theorists, most treatments of the topic cite the contributions of no more than one of the two scholarly traditions. It is as if political psychologists and rational choice theorists have nothing to teach each other about persuasion.

Do intellectual differences between these scholarly traditions negate the possibility of constructive dialogue? As a formal theorist who grapples with political psychology's substantive challenges, I face this question often. I have come to believe that a constructive dialogue is not only possible but also worthwhile.

I thank James Druckman, Mathew McCubbins, Sam Popkin, and Paul Sniderman for guidance offered during all stages of this project. I thank Scott Basinger, Kathleen Bawn, Henry Brady, Andrea Campbell, Christopher Den Hartog, Robert Erikson, Elisabeth Gerber, Jennifer Kuhn, Jim Kuklinski, Susanne Lohmann, Ted Miller, Jim Stimson, and Michael Thies for insightful comments. I thank Karen Garrett and the staff of the Survey Research Center at the University of California at Berkeley for administering the survey. I also acknowledge the financial support of the National Science Foundation, Grants 9309946 and 9422831.

In what follows, I first argue and then demonstrate that more frequent and serious interactions between political psychologists and rational choice theorists can generate substantial gains from trade. That is, I first offer a brief argument about what political psychologists and rational choice theorists have to offer each other. I then use a psychologically informed rational choice model and a rational choice–informed psychology experiment to construct an explanation of persuasion that is more powerful and general than other explanations that ignore at least one of the two scholarly traditions. I conclude that there are gains from trade to be had from sustained and serious interaction between political psychology and formal theory.

GAINS FROM TRADE?

The characteristic that most differentiates political psychologists and rational choice theorists is the method of inference. Political psychologists, like their methodological counterparts in social and cognitive psychology, tend to rely on experiments.[1] When these experiments show a relationship between stimulus and response, they provide evidence for psychologists' behavioral claims. Rational choice theorists, like microeconomists, rely on formal models. These models allow theorists to show how certain behavioral conclusions follow from precise assumptions.

Like all methods of inference, even the most carefully designed experiments and models have substantive limitations. These limitations can be used for different purposes. They can, for example, give members of one scholarly tradition an excuse to discount or ignore the arguments of others. This practice, while easy to justify when in a room with like-minded individuals, is seldom constructive. Alternatively, if the strengths of the political psychology approach are the foil of the rational choice approach or vice versa, then these limitations can be the source of intellectual gains from trade. To see if such gains exist, let's examine the limitations in question.

A typical psychology experiment consists of a control condition and some treatment conditions in an otherwise constant laboratory setting. Experimenters draw behavioral inferences by comparing the relations

---

1 This representation is admittedly stereotypical. Political psychologists also use quasi-experiments and nonexperimental surveys. For the argument I want to make here, however, an argument assessing the contrasts and complementarity of psychological and rational choice approaches, the focus on experiments gives sufficient representation to the main methodological difference between the two traditions.

between controlled stimuli and subjects' responses across these conditions. Since performing an experiment usually requires substantial time and money, it is usually not feasible for an experimenter to run a large number of treatment conditions – certainly less than the number it would take to identify general properties of most behaviors observed in experiments. Therefore, most experiments, *taken literally*, provide but a few isolated *examples* of reactions to selected stimuli.

Experiments, however, are not designed to be viewed literally. An experiment is supposed to be a simple, controllable analogy to a larger, uncontrollable set of circumstances.[2] Therefore, an experiment should be viewed in terms of whether scholars can use it to achieve a constructive scientific purpose.

An experiment's purpose is to demonstrate that a specific variation in a stimulus corresponds to a specific pattern of behavior. For an experiment to achieve its purpose, the audience must believe that the experimental stimuli, subjects, and environment are reasonable analogies to the stimuli, decision makers, and environments in the larger set of circumstances. In cases where the audience does not debate the analogy's quality, the experiment can achieve its purpose. However, some questions are so complex that their comprehension requires a considerable difference between what happens in and out of the laboratory. When such differences stir debate about the quality of the analogy, overcoming the literal limit of experiments requires a stronger remedy. I will describe such a remedy after briefly discussing the very similar literal limits of formal models.

A typical formal model is a set of mathematical statements. Each statement represents an assumption about human desires, opportunities, or knowledge.[3] Theorists use deductive logic to show that certain conclusions follow from these assumptions. An advantage of a formal model

2 Some people prefer to call these general sets of phenomena "reality." I resist this practice because the counterfactuals required to verify the validity of reality are beyond human comprehension (e.g., external validity is often created in the eye of the beholder).

3 *Webster's New Collegiate Dictionary* defines the term "rational" as "(a) having reason or understanding, (b) relating to, based on, or agreeable to reason." The same source defines "reason," the synonym of "intelligence," as "the proper exercise of the mind." I therefore define "rational choice theory" as an attempt to understand and explain behavior using the assumption that people do the best they can with the knowledge and skills they have. I mention this because it is common for both supporters and critics of rational choice approaches to confound rationality and omniscience. When this mistake is made, rationality ceases to be a useful concept, as the people whose behavior we seek to understand are far less than omniscient.

is generality. A simple spatial model, for example, can be used to generate predictions about behavior in an infinite number of cases. But what is the value of these predictions?

A truth of formal modeling is that analytical tractability often requires simple assumptions. As a result, a model's predictions about human behavior can also be simple. Many formal models, *taken literally*, describe *simple, logical correspondences* between assumptions and conclusions about human behavior. Since people need not be simple, a model's predictions may provide insufficient descriptions of human behavior.

Formal models, however, are not designed to be viewed literally. Like an experiment, a formal model is supposed to be a simple, controllable analogy to a larger, uncontrollable set of circumstances. Therefore, a formal model should be viewed in terms of whether scholars can use it to achieve a constructive, scientific purpose.

A formal model's purpose is to clarify correspondences that are difficult to see in the usual cacophony of social interaction. For a formal model to achieve its purpose, the audience must believe that the model's assumptions and conclusions are reasonable analogies to the stimuli, decision makers, and environments in the larger set of circumstances. In cases where the audience does not debate the analogy's quality, the model can achieve its purpose. However, some questions are so complex that relationships between assumptions, predictions, and observed behaviors can stir debate about a model's analogy. In these cases, overcoming the literal limit of formal modeling requires a stronger remedy.

The gains from trade available to political psychologists and rational choice theorists arise from the complementarity of each tradition's strengths and limitations. These gains are available when one tradition's strengths remedy the other tradition's limitations. For example, a formal model's logically valid correspondences between clearly stated premises and conclusions could make it an effective tool for demonstrating why an experimental behavior should be observed in a particular range of nonexperimental circumstances. Of course, the model must strengthen the believability of the initial experimental analogy. That is, the audience who is questioning the generality of the experiment must perceive the model to be a sufficient analogy to both the experiment and the general set of circumstances in question. Put another way, a formal model is no panacea for a badly designed experiment. However, if you

- present an audience with behavioral premises that they have difficulty refuting

- and prove the logical validity of the relationship between these assumptions and conclusions that pertain to the experiment's generality,
- and if greater interaction between political psychologists and rational choice theorists makes such models easier to design,

then greater interaction provides a remedy for the literal limit of the experiment, and participating scholars experience gains from trade.

Similarly, psychological insights and methods can clarify the validity of a formal model's analogy. In domains where many variations of a well-designed experiment reveal specific boundaries of human ability, opportunity, and information, psychology can inform rational choice theorists about where to start when making assumptions about political decision makers. Of course, the psychologists' contributions must be compelling to the theorist's audience. That is, the audience who is questioning the model's value must perceive the psychologist's data to be relevant to the model and the empirical circumstances in question – an experiment is no panacea for a badly designed model. However, if a modeler presents an audience with an experiment whose similarity to the set of relevant circumstances is difficult to refute, and if greater interaction between political psychologists and rational choice theorists makes such experiments easier to design, then greater interaction will remedy the literal limits of the formal model and participating scholars experience gains from trade.

It is one thing to claim that an explanation that combines political psychology and rational choice theory trumps explanations that ignore either or both approaches. It is quite another to show this claim to be true. What follows is one attempt to accomplish the latter.

THE PROBLEM OF PERSUASION

We know that people lack information about politics (e.g., Converse 1964; Delli Carpini and Keeter 1996). We also know that people have little incentive to acquire more information when doing so is costly (e.g., Downs 1957). When we put these two facts together, we can conclude that people who want greater knowledge have an incentive to substitute low-cost cues for the detailed information that they lack (e.g., McKelvey and Ordeshook 1985; Popkin 1991).[4]

---

4 I define "knowledge" as the ability to predict accurately the consequences of actions, "information" as the data from which knowledge may be derived, and an "attitude" as a person's general evaluation of an object (also see Lupia and McCubbins 1998).

In many situations of interest to political scientists (e.g., elections for national or state office), many low-cost cues are available.[5] For example, in the weeks before an election, television, radio, newspapers, and casual conversation contain political advertisements, endorsements, and commentaries for a wide range of candidates and causes. But no person in the midst of such a barrage can use all available cues. Each person must choose which cues to use. If we want to understand how cue usage affects behavior, then we should endeavor to explain how people sort among the many cues that are available to them. We must be precise about what differentiates a persuasive cue, one that changes attitudes, from a cue that does not persuade.

Our discipline is often vague about what makes a cue persuasive. For example, it is widely taken for granted that conservatives tend to find other conservatives' cues more credible, that African Americans tend to find other African American elites more credible, and so on. While certain cue-giver attributes sometimes correlate with cue persuasiveness, the extant persuasion literature does not reveal when these correlations are evidence of causality and when they are spurious. This literature does not provide answers to questions such as "When will a speaker's ideology affect the persuasiveness of his or her cues more than does his or her race, likability, or level of education?" Yet to explain how people behave when confronted with the many cues that political settings often proffer, we must find a way to answer such questions.

I offer an answer that comes from an integrated foundation of psychological and rational choice insights. My answer is that all cue-giver attributes – such as race, gender, ideology, partisanship, reputation, or likability – affect a cue's persuasiveness only if they are necessary to inform a cue-seeker's perceptions of a cue-giver's knowledge or interests (it need not inform the cue seeker of the cue-giver's actual knowledge or interests). If an attribute is not necessary for this effect, then any correlation between it and a cue's persuasiveness is indirect or spurious.

I support this claim in two ways. First, I derive it from a formal model of political communication. Then I use a survey experiment on over 1,400 randomly selected Americans to show that respondents' percep-

---

5 By the term "low-cost cue," I mean a statement of the form "Mr. M says 'Vote for candidate C,'" where Mr. M may himself be Candidate C. This is opposed to a higher-cost cue such as a long argument or report by Mr. M about Candidate C. In the language of social psychology, I focus on the peripheral (or heuristic) route to persuasion rather than the central (or systematic) route (Eagly and Chaiken 1993; Petty and Cacioppo 1986). As a result, I focus on the persuasive effect of cue-giver attributes (i.e., source effects) rather than on the persuasive effect of the cue-giver's argument style (i.e., message effects).

tions of a speaker's interests and knowledge explain much more about which cues they use than do cue-giver attributes such as a speaker's likability, ideology, or party.

Together, the theory and the data provide an insight that people skeptical of rational choice theory's contribution to persuasion research may regard as ironic. The insight is that, contrary to common practice, persuasion scholars should adhere to a strict interpretation of seminal psychological claims about persuasion. In particular, the claim that a cue seeker's perception of a cue-giver's knowledge and interests affects a statement's persuasiveness has famous historical antecdents, most notably Aristole (1954 translation) and Hovland, Janis, and Kelley (1953). While these antecedents are widely recognized, their substantive impact on political science is stalled by loose interpretations. As I will show, the aggregation of persuasion research that claims Hovland et al. in its lineage reveals that an incredibly large number of cue-giver attributes cause cue persuasivesness. The net effect of this research has been to bury seminal insights about persuasion so deeply that our discipline finds it hard to answer questions such as "When will a speaker's ideology affect the persuasiveness of his or her cues more than does his or her race, likability, or level of education?" Theory clarifies how the seminal insights should be interpreted, and experiments reveal that if we want to predict human behavior accurately, then careful use of the seminal insights is essential.

Next, I review seminal persuasion insights. Then I introduce a formal model of political communication and use it to clarify the determinants of persuasion. Next, I use a survey experiment on elite endorsements to test the theory's predictions. Then I offer a brief conclusion. Appendixes A and B contain more technical material pertaining to the model and the experiment.

SEMINAL FOUNDATIONS IN PERSUASION RESEARCH

I begin in the modern era with the insights offered by the Yale Communication and Attitude Change Program (e.g., Hovland et al. 1953). One of the program's most important insights is that a speaker's *credibility* determines his or her persuasive power. To evaluate this finding empirically, Hovland and his colleagues reduced credibility to a set of speaker attributes. "The Yale group stated that credibility is mainly based on two factors: expertise, which is the amount of knowledge that a communicator is assumed to possess, and trustworthiness, which is the perceived intention of the communicator to deceive" (Franzoi 1996:214).

While the claim that certain speaker attributes affect persuasion is sensible, it has a mixed legacy. On the positive side, there is a consensus that attributes such as expertise and trustworthiness can affect whose cues people use. On the negative side, the studies are therefore insufficient to answer questions about what specific role these attributes play in determining cue persuasion. One manifestation of this mixed legacy is the long list of speaker attributes that scholars have correlated with cue persuasiveness. Consider, for example, Klapper's (1960:99) summary:

In general, sources which the audience holds in high esteem appear to facilitate persuasion, while sources which the audience holds in low esteem appear to constitute at least a temporary handicap. The possible bases of such esteem are perhaps infinitely variable. Audiences have been shown, for example, to respond particularly well to specific sources because they considered them of high prestige, highly credible, expert, trustworthy, close to themselves, or just plain likable.

In another review of the persuasion literature twenty-five years later, McGuire (1985:263) could be no more precise. Not only did attractiveness join expertise and trustworthiness as causal factors, but each factor was represented empirically by its own extensive list of speaker attributes! The list of speaker attributes that scholars had correlated with cue persuasiveness now included social status, professional attainment, tallness, and erect posture.

The 1980s provided new innovations in persuasion research. These innovations, however, did not reveal what made some cues more persuasive than others. For example, Petty and Cacioppo's Elaboration Likelihood Model (ELM) defined two routes to persuasion. As the authors explain (1986:3), "The first type of persuasion was that which likely occurred as a result of a person's careful and thoughtful consideration of the true merits of the information presented in support of advocacy (central route). The other type of persuasion, however, was that which more likely occurred as a result of some simple cue in the persuasion context (e.g., an attractive source) that induced change without necessitating scrutiny of the central merits of the issue-relevant information presented (peripheral route)."

The ELM's distinction proved useful for many scholars, including political scientists. For the ELM's peripheral route resembled the cue-taking behavior that political scientists had been describing for decades (e.g., Berelson, Lazarsfeld, and McPhee 1954; Calvert 1985; Downs 1957; McKelvey and Ordeshook 1985; Popkin, Gorman, Phillips, and Smith 1976). While the ELM helped refocus political scientists' attention on persuasion, its authors recognized (1986:32) that ELM research "postponed the question of what specific qualities make arguments persuasive." Eagly and Chaiken (1993:323) gave a more direct assessment: "Because the elaboration likelihood model specifies when peripheral route persuasion should and has occurred, but not which peripheral mechanism has operated (or why), it leaves numerous mediational issues unaddressed."

In the 1990s, political psychologists became increasingly visible players in the study of cue-taking. Some of them showed that people can use cues as effective substitutes for the political information they lack.[6] However, a generalizable explanation of why only certain cues work has been absent. To be sure, there are careful arguments that suggest a strong relationship between certain attributes, such as a speaker's likability (e.g., Brady and Sniderman 1985) or ideology (e.g., Tetlock 1993), and persuasion. Still, our discipline cannot recite the conditions under which some other attribute – such as a cue-giver's race, personality, level of education, or economic interests – will overwhelm ideology or likability as determinants of persuasion. To this end, I offer the following formal model.

Formal Model

The model is that of Lupia and McCubbins (1998). Its logical lineage is most directly traceable to economic models of incomplete information (e.g., Harsanyi 1967, 1968a, 1968b), signaling models in economics and political science (e.g., Spence 1973), and economic cheap-talk models (Crawford and Sobel 1982; Farrell and Gibbons 1989). The main difference between the new framework and prior modeling efforts is in the assumptions about what cue givers and cue seekers know and in the conclusions about who can persuade whom. Most extant formal models of communication focus on the case where communicators know each other well. The new framework, by contrast, also explains cue persuasiveness when communicators know much less.

I focus on the case where cue persuasiveness is a function of *motivated choice*. I say that cue persuasiveness is a function of *choice* when cue seekers have the option of believing, ignoring, or rejecting a cue. I say that these choices are *motivated* when they are consequential from the cue-seeker's perspective (i.e., a voter may be motivated by the belief that his vote can be decisive, the belief that the mere act of participation is valuable, or something else). Put another way, I assume that cue seekers are either "motivated to hold correct attitudes" (Petty

6 See, for example, Kuklinski, Metlay, and May (1982), Kuklinski and Hurley (1994), Popkin (1991), Sniderman, Brody, and Tetlock (1991), and Lupia 1994.

and Cacioppo 1986:5) or "'economy minded souls' who wish to satisfy their goal-related needs in the most efficient ways possible" (Eagly and Chaiken 1993:330). In what follows, I describe the theory's premises and predictions. In Appendix A, I define the theory in mathematical terms.

Premises

I model communication as a game between two players, a *speaker* and a *listener*. The game begins when the speaker provides one of two cues: "x is better than y" or "x is worse than y." The listener then chooses x or y. The listener's choice of x or y ends the game and determines a payoff for each player. The model is meant to be analogous to the wide range of political situations in which one person has an opportunity to base his or her actions or opinions on the statements offered by another (e.g., the speaker runs a political campaign and the listener, who can follow the speaker's advice or ignore it, is a person whose support the speaker desires).

The speaker's attempt to persuade the listener occurs in the midst of up to four types of uncertainty. Each type of uncertainty is common to political contexts.[7] First, the listener is uncertain about the consequences of her actions. That is, the listener may not know whether choosing x or y makes her better off. Second, the listener may be uncertain about the speaker's knowledge of x and y (e.g., the listener may believe that the speaker is ignorant about which candidate is better for her). Third, the speaker may not in fact know which candidate is better for the listener.

Fourth, and finally, the listener may be uncertain about the speaker's motives. I say that the speaker and listener have *common interests* when the speaker benefits from the listener's choice only if the listener chooses what is better for her. So, if x is better than y for the listener, and if the listener and speaker have common interests, then the speaker benefits from the listener's decision only if x is chosen. Otherwise, I say that the speaker and listener have conflicting interests. Stated another way, the fourth type of uncertainty pertains to the listener's belief about whether she and the speaker have common or conflicting interests.

---

7 I treat each type of uncertainty as a probability distribution. As a result, the model allows me to describe persuasion in a broad range of contexts, including contexts in which there is no uncertainty. Note that the inclusion of these four types of uncertainty is what differentiates this chapter's model from most economic models of communication. The seminal model by Crawford and Sobel (1982), for example, includes only the first type of uncertainty.

Who Can Persuade Whom?

Predictions

I first characterize persuasion in the model with a theorem. Then I describe the theorem's main implication for the question "Who can persuade whom?" Persuasion occurs only if the speaker's statement causes the listener to change her beliefs about which alternative is better for her.

> **Theorem 1:** Perceived common interests and perceived speaker knowledge are each necessary for persuasion.[8]

Note that perceived common interests are the listener's prior belief about the probability that she and the speaker have common interests. If the listener believes that this probability is low (less than .5), then the speaker will not persuade the listener – regardless of the speaker's actual knowledge. Similarly, perceived speaker knowledge is the listener's prior belief about the probability that the speaker, in fact, knows whether x or y is better for the listener. If this probability is 0, then persuasion does not occur.[9]

> **Implication:** If a speaker attribute is not necessary to change the listener's perception of the speaker's knowledge or interests, then it is irrelevant to cue persuasiveness. Thus, perceived common interests and perceived speaker knowledge explain when all other speaker attributes affect cue persuasiveness, while the converse of this statement is not true.

The logic behind this implication is as follows. A speaker's knowledge and interests are often impossible to observe directly. When this is true, a listener's perception of a speaker's interests and knowledge will be

---

8 The sufficient condition is the satisfaction of the necessary conditions plus the listener being so uncertain about x and y that the speaker's statement, if true, will cause her to hold a correct belief about which alternative is better for her.

9 The probability of perceived common interests and perceived speaker knowledge required for persuasion varies with the listener's uncertainty. If, for example, the listener is very uncertain about which alternative is better for her, then the levels of perceived speaker knowledge and common interests necessary for persuasion approximate those described in the text. If, however, the listener is more certain, then persuasion requires stronger perceptions. So, for example, if the listener is *certain* that the speaker lacks the knowledge she desires, then persuasion is impossible. This is true even if the listener is certain that she and the speaker share common interests. By contrast, if the listener believes that the speaker *might* possess the knowledge she requires, then persuasion is *possible*.

affected by other factors. However, the fact that speaker knowledge and interests are unobservable directly does not negate the fact that each factor is necessary for persuasion. Therefore, any speaker attribute can have a nonspurious correlation with cue persusasiveness *only if* the attribute determines the listener's perception of a speaker's knowledge or interests.

Put another way, the listener's perception of the speaker's knowledge and motives is the fundamental source effect in the context of cue persuasiveness.[10] All other speaker attributes (such as a speaker's attractiveness, party, race, likability, ideology, or reputation) affect cue selection when they do because they affect the listener's perception of the speaker's knowledge or motives. If an attribute does not have this effect, then any correlation between it and cue persuasiveness is indirect or spurious.

For example, you may be Extremely Liberal, and another person who you know to be Extremely Liberal in the same way is attempting to convince you that welfare reform is a great idea. If, however, you believe that the other person knows only a subset of what you know about welfare reform, then even your shared ideology gives you an insufficient basis for following that person's cue. Put another way, a speaker's ideology makes a cue persuasive *only if* it influences the listener's assessment of the speaker's interests or knowledge. By contrast, the speaker's interests and knowledge are always relevant to a cue's persuasiveness regardless of whether or not they convey any information about a speaker's ideology. At best, a speaker attribute such as likability, ideology, race, or gender can be said to *cause* cue persuasiveness *only if* the attribute is the listener's sole means of assessing the speaker's interests or knowledge.

CUE PERSUASION IN MASS COMMUNICATION CONTEXTS

In some political contexts, one person attempts to convince another about what he or she should do. More commonly, however, attempts at political persuasion often involve more people. In particular, when we

10 Neither *actual* speaker knowledge nor *actual* common interests is necessary or sufficient for the cue to be persuasive. This implies that a speaker can persuade a listener even if the speaker actually knows nothing. This occurs when the listener mistakenly perceives the speaker to be knowledgeable. More generally, a speaker's actual knowledge may have *absolutely nothing* to do with his ability to persuade. As a result, and as Hovland et al. (1953:21) recognized, knowledge is not necessarily (persuasive) power. For similar reasons, *a knowledgeable speaker who shares common interests with a listener will fail to persuade* if the listener does not perceive these interests accurately.

think of the persuasive attempts of candidates, campaigns, or advertisers, it is a case of one or more people attempting to persuade a large audience. A simple extension of the model just described reveals how people choose whom to believe in mass communication settings.

When a persuasive attempt involves only one speaker and one listener, as described earlier, persuasion is impossible when the speaker and listener have conflicting interests.[11] For when the listener perceives a speaker to have conflicting interests, her best response is to ignore the cue.[12] However, this claim contradicts a common experience – sometimes a cue is persuasive because a speaker has conflicting interests. For example, a person may oppose environmental regulation but might have her attitude changed by the claims of a pro-environment group; she may learn from their claims which way not to vote. I call this outcome "negative third-party persuasion."

To derive the conditions for third-party persuasion, it is sufficient to add third parties, called "observers," to the original model. The only difference between observers and the (original) listener is that the observers cannot directly affect the speaker's utility. Examples of observers include individuals at a mass rally or people watching a nationally televised political speech.

Amending the theory in this way allows me to revise Theorem 1 in the following way:

> **Theorem 1′:** If the observer believes that her interests conflict with both the listener's and the speaker's and that the speaker has an incentive to make truthful, knowledgeable statements to the listener, then the speaker can persuade.

11 Lupia and McCubbins (1998) extend the model described here in a different way to identify conditions under which certain external forces – inherent in common political institutions – substitute for common interests as a determinant of persuasion.

12 Formal models of communication, such as the one presented here, reveal why this is so. For example, a listener should not follow the advice of a speaker who she believes wants to deceive her. If she did, the speaker's best response would be to make a false statement. However, it is reasonable to ask why the listener might not then do the opposite of what the speaker recommends. The answer to this question is that the speaker in the model can anticipate such behavior and would adapt by making a true statement (which, if the listener did the opposite of what this statement recommends, would make her worse off). In equilibrium, the listener's best response is to make her choice of x or y independently of what the speaker says. In the case where the listener perceives the speaker to have conflicting interests, this strategy is the only one that prevents the speaker from deceiving her.

So, when an observer comes across a speaker in such a situation, she has an incentive to take the speaker's advice and do the opposite. For example, suppose that you are a Democrat who observes a prominent politician addressing an important group of Republican supporters. If you believe that the politician is knowledgeable, that he and the group perceive themselves to have common interests, and that your interests conflict with both, then you ought to do the opposite of what he recommends. *Positive third-party persuasion* occurs when an observer perceives that she shares common interests with both the listener and the speaker and that the speaker has an incentive to make truthful statements to the listener. In this case, the observer should follow the speaker's advice.

SURVEY EXPERIMENT

Of course, Theorem 1 and its implication are, at the moment, mere logical implications from a theory about how listeners who are either "motivated to hold correct attitudes" or "economy-minded souls" should process cues. To see whether people actually process cues in this way, I designed a simple experiment.

My experiment was part of the Multi-Investigator Study on Political Persuasion and Attitude Change. The study contained twelve separate and independently conceived experiments along with a set of core questions. The University of California's Survey Research Center conducted the study. The survey population consisted of all English-speaking adults eighteen years of age or older, residing in households with telephones, within the forty-eight contiguous U.S. states. Professional interviewers conducted all interviews between June 15 and November 4, 1994. The interviewers randomly contacted 2,234 households using computer-assisted telephone interviewing technology. In these households, 686 persons refused to participate, 68 were never at home, and 16 were unable to participate. The remaining 1,464 households constitute the sample.

The experiment consisted of three questions. It began with respondents hearing one version of the Attitude Question.

> **Attitude Question with No Cue:** *"Now I am going to ask you a couple of questions about a new issue in American politics – spending money to build prisons. What do you think? Is spending money to build prisons a good idea or a bad idea?"*

> **Attitude Question with Cue:** *"Now I am going to ask you a couple of questions about a new issue in American*

> *politics – spending money to build prisons. It's been*
> *reported that talk show host [SPEAKER] [POSITION]*
> *spending money to build more prisons. What do you think?*
> *Is spending money to build prisons a good idea or a bad*
> *idea?"*

The Attitude Question elicited data on the dependent variable of interest: respondent attitudes. It also contained the experimental variation, which had two components. The variation's first component, [SPEAKER], determined the speaker's identity. Respondents in the treatment group heard a version of the Attitude Question with a cue by Rush Limbaugh or Phil Donahue. Respondents in the control group heard a version of the Attitude Question with no cue. The variation's second component, [POSITION], determined the cue's content. Some respondents in the treatment group heard a cue (by either Limbaugh or Donahue) that supported spending on prison construction; others heard a cue that opposed it. Random assignment determined which version of the question each respondent heard.[13]

Although the Attitude Question contained the sole experimental intervention, the purpose of the experiment was to evaluate the relationship between cue persuasiveness and respondent perceptions. I designed the Interest Question and Knowledge Question to elicit measures of perceived speaker interests and knowledge, respectively.

> **Interest Question:** *"Now I am going to ask you a couple*
> *of questions about [SPEAKER]. On most political issues*
> *would you say that you and [SPEAKER] agree all of*
> *the time, most of the time, only some of the time, or*
> *never?"*

13 Each respondent had a 10% chance of hearing the Attitude Question without a cue and a 22.5% chance of hearing the Attitude Question with each of the four possible cues: "Rush Limbaugh supports," "Rush Limbaugh opposes," "Phil Donahue supports," and "Phil Donahue opposes." Note that this experiment employs a "posttest only" design. I can draw inferences about persuasion in such an experiment when the random assignment of respondents across experimental conditions results in each condition-specific subsample having roughly comparable initial attitudes. Note also that respondents had the option of responding "a very good idea" or "a very bad idea." To simplify the presentation, we collapsed such responses into the categories "a good idea," and "a bad idea" respectively. Only eleven respondents replied "don't know" to the Attitude Question. Each of them was then asked a similarly worded question in an attempt to elicit an opinion. Only three respondents subsequently replied "don't know." I dropped their interviews from the analysis.

Knowledge Question: *"How much would you say that [SPEAKER] knows about what will happen if this country spends money to build more prisons – a lot, some, a little, or nothing?"*

Since the Interest and Knowledge Questions offer only crude measures (as opposed to precise point estimates) of respondent perceptions, Theorem 1 implies that respondent attitudes are most likely to match the speaker's cue when respondents perceive the speaker to agree with them "all of the time" and to know "a lot." It also implies that the incidence of such matches should decrease as *either* of these perceptions becomes less favorable.[14]

Motivation for Choice of Issue and Speakers

I chose prison spending as the experiment's issue for three reasons. First, I expected it to be salient for many respondents; indeed, many public opinion polls showed crime to be a primary concern for many Americans at the time of the study. Second, I expected subjects to be unclear about what side to take on this issue. While building prisons is consistent with the law-and-order caricature of contemporary conservatism, spending money to solve problems fits better with the contemporary liberal stereotype of supporting government intervention. In other words, I chose the issue so that we could represent each of our speakers as either a supporter or an opponent. Third, I expected that many respondents would be uncertain about the effect of such a policy change. By contrast, had we chosen an issue whose consequences were transparent, we would

---

14 Some critics have questioned the experimental design on the grounds that respondents' answers to the Interest and Knowledge Questions are affected by the experimental manipulation in the Attitude Question rather than mediating the effects, as I argue. I concur that prior survey questions can affect answers to later ones, so this critique affects any ordering of the questions – not just this one. I chose this ordering, as it was *the least likely* to contaminate the experiment. That is, asking the Interest and Knowledge Questions first suggests that something approximating the Attitude Question is forthcoming, while the converse of this statement is not true. Moreover, if the critics are correct, then why did so few people who agreed with the speaker give him the highest ranking on the *Agrees* or *Knows* scales? Table 2.2 indicates that nothing of the sort occurred. And when we asked the respondent feeling thermometer questions about the same speaker, why did so few who agreed (disagreed) with the speaker offer a score of 100 (0)? Table 2.6 indicates that nothing of the sort occurred. The critics' complaint is, at best, a curious speculation and, at worst, unsupported by the data and theoretically baseless.

Who Can Persuade Whom?

Table 2.1. *Responses to Opinion Question*

Category	% Replying "Good Idea"	N
All respondents	60	1427
Heard "supports" from either source	60	639
Heard "opposes" from either source	59	666
Heard no endorsement	61	122
Heard Phil Donahue supports	59	339
Heard Phil Donahue opposes	61	344
Heard Rush Limbaugh supports	61	300
Heard Rush Limbaugh opposes	57	322

expect, and Theorem 1 predicts, no persuasion – as it is difficult to persuade people of something they think they know.

I chose Rush Limbaugh and Phil Donahue as speakers for similar reasons. First, I wanted speakers with whom most respondents were likely to be familiar. In fact, only three respondents volunteered that they had never heard of the speaker whose cue we presented to them. Second, I wanted speakers for whom it was reasonable to expect variance in responses to the Interest and Knowledge Questions. Instead of choosing speakers who were likely to be universally trusted or reviled, I chose talk show hosts who were not widely recognized experts on crime-related issues.[15]

Analysis

In this section, I analyze the data. First, I present summary statistics about the responses of the 1,464 participants (Tables 2.1 and 2.2). Then I describe the relationship between perceived speaker knowledge, perceived speaker interests, and persuasion (Tables 2.3 and 2.4). Next, I examine the cue–persuasion relationship in the context of two alternative explanations – ideological similarity and the likability heuristic (Tables 2.5 and 2.6). Then I present a regression analysis that allows me to evaluate a broader range of explanations (Table 2.7).

Table 2.1 contains summary statistics of attitudes on prison spending. Overall, just under 60% of the respondents responded "good idea" to

---

15 Of course, I would have preferred to run many variations of this experiment combining many more issues and speakers. However, in a collaborative effort, such as the Multi-Investigator Study, the time available for questions is both valuable and scarce. I am happy to have run even this variation.

Table 2.2. *Responses to Agrees and Knows Questions*

	Rush Limbaugh			
	Knows = a Lot	Knows = Some	Knows = a Little	Knows = Nothing
Agrees = all	8	1	0	0
Agrees = most	48	43	5	0
Agrees = some	30	155	90	26
Agrees = never	4	17	45	52
	Phil Donahue			
	Knows = a Lot	Knows = Some	Knows = a Little	Knows = Nothing
Agrees = all	3	0	0	0
Agrees = most	19	28	4	0
Agrees = some	56	191	121	27
Agrees = never	4	16	34	31

the Attitude Question. To see that the experimental intervention alone did not create this division, notice that the level of support for prison spending in the control group (61%) was about the same as the level of support in the entire sample (60%).

These summary statistics also suggest that neither speaker was persuasive. For example, respondents who heard "Limbaugh supports" were only a little more likely (3.3 percentage points) to respond "good idea" than were those who heard "Limbaugh opposes." Respondents who heard "Donahue supports" were slightly less likely to support the issue than were those who heard "Donahue opposes."

Hidden beneath these statistics, however, is substantial variance in respondents' perceptions of speaker interests and knowledge. Theorem 1 implies that this variance is the key to identifying when the cues are most (and least) likely to persuade. Table 2.2 shows the distribution of respondents' perceptions.[16] For simplicity, I henceforth refer to responses to the Interest Question (perceived speaker interests) and responses to the Knowledge Question (perceived speaker knowledge) as the variables *Agrees* and *Knows*, respectively.

16 Tables 2.2 through 2.6 refer exclusively to respondents in the treatment group who answered the Attitude, Interest, and Knowledge questions. Comparisons with the control group are straightforward – 61.4% of the respondents in the control group responded "good idea."

Two elements of Table 2.2 merit attention. First, almost no respondents (12/1,058) reported agreeing with the speaker "all of the time." So, to clarify the tables that follow, I collapse the top two categories of *Agrees* into a single category labeled "*Agrees* = all or some." Second, respondents varied in their perceptions of the speaker. While the modal pair of responses was "*Agrees* = some" and "*Knows* = some," fewer than 35% (346/1,058) of the sample gave this response. This variance is important, as it gives us the opportunity to identify the correspondence between respondent perceptions and cue persuasiveness.

In Tables 2.3 and 2.4, I examine two predictions from Theorem 1. The predictions are "an increase in *Agrees* increases the incidence of persuasion when it has an effect" and "an increase in *Knows* increases the incidence of persuasion when it has an effect."[17]

I evaluate these predictions by looking at the correspondence between *Agrees* or *Knows* and respondent attitudes. Table 2.3 separates respondents by their choice of *Agrees* or *Knows*. For example, in the parts of Table 2.3 that pertain to the variable *Agrees*, I separate respondents who reported that they agree with Limbaugh "all or most" of the time from respondents who said they agree with him "some" of the time.

I further separate respondents who heard "supports" from those who heard "opposes." Then I report the percentage of these respondents who replied "good idea." For example, the top of Table 2.3 shows that, of the respondents who agreed with Limbaugh "all or most" of the time and heard that Limbaugh supports prison spending, 76% responded "good idea." By contrast, only 54% of the respondents who agreed with Limbaugh "all or most" of the time and heard that Limbaugh opposes prison spending responded "good idea."

The column labeled *Effect of Treatment* contains my measure of persuasion. *Effect of Treatment* measures how often the response to the Attitude Question ("good idea" or "bad idea") matches the speaker's cue. I computed *Effect of Treatment* by subtracting the percentage of respondents who heard "opposes" and replied "good idea" from the percentage of respondents who heard "supports" and replied "good idea." As the share of respondents whose attitudes match the speaker statements increases, so does *Effect of Treatment*. So, if all respondent attitudes match speaker statements, then *Effect of Treatment* = 100; if all respondent attitudes are contrary to speaker statements, then *Effect of*

---

17 *Agrees* and *Knows* are too blunt to allow reasonable interpretation of their lowest values as a 0% chance of common interests or knowledge, respectively. Therefore, the prediction from Theorem 1's implication is that for every category of *Agrees* (*Knows*), an increase in *Knows* (*Agrees*) will either increase or not change the incidence of persuasion.

Table 2.3. *Responses to Opinion Question, Separated by Agrees or Knows*

	Rush Limbaugh			
Response to "Agrees" or "Knows" Question	Of Those Who Heard "Supports," % Replying "Good Idea"	Of Those Who Heard "Opposes," % Replying "Good Idea"	Effect of Treatment	N (Total, Heard "Supports," Heard "Opposes")
Agrees = all or most	76	54	22	(105, 51, 54)
Agrees = some	66	60	6	(306, 150, 156)
Agrees = never	33	55	−22	(123, 60, 63)
Knows = a lot	72	45	27	(90, 50, 40)
Knows = some	76	65	11	(222, 106, 116)
Knows = a little	46	60	−14	(142, 70, 72)
Knows = nothing	27	48	−21	(81, 37, 44)

	Phil Donahue			
Response to "Agrees" or "Knows" Question	Of Those Who Heard "Supports," % Replying "Good Idea"	Of Those Who Heard "Opposes," % Replying "Good Idea"	Effect of Treatment	N (Total, Heard "Supports," Heard "Opposes")
Agrees = all or most	76	43	33	(54, 33, 21)
Agrees = some	59	59	0	(401, 191, 210)
Agrees = never	53	77	−24	(85, 38, 47)
Knows = a lot	74	51	23	(89, 46, 43)
Knows = some	62	53	9	(243, 125, 118)
Knows = a little	49	74	−25	(179, 83, 96)
Knows = nothing	48	65	−17	(64, 27, 37)

Treatment = −100, and if the number of respondent attitudes that match the speaker statements equals the number of respondent attitudes that are contrary to the speaker statements, then *Effect of Treatment* = 0.[18]

Theorem 1 predicts that *Effect of Treatment* should increase as we move from a lower category of *Agrees* or *Knows* to a higher category. Table 2.3 reveals that higher values of *Agrees* or *Knows* were associated with increases in *Effect of Treatment*. For example, respondents who agreed with Rush Limbaugh "all or most of the time" and who were

18 The final column gives the total number of respondents for each category, as well as the total number of respondents who heard "supports," and "opposes," respectively.

randomly assigned to hearing "Rush Limbaugh supports" were 22% more likely to respond "good idea" than were subjects with the same attribute who were randomly assigned to hearing "Rush Limbaugh opposes." As the model predicts, our experimental intervention ("supports" or "opposes") had a sizable persuasive effect on this subset of the sample. By contrast, respondents who agreed with Limbaugh "some of the time" were less affected by the cue (*Effect of Treatment* = 6). Moreover, respondents who never agreed with Limbaugh showed a tendency to take his advice and do the opposite (*Effect of Treatment* = −22); these reactions are evidence of *negative third-party persuasion*. With one exception, the relationship between *Agrees*, *Knows*, and *Effect of Treatment* in the Phil Donahue treatment conditions have the same direction and magnitude.

Next, I focus on the combined impact of *Agrees* <u>and</u> *Knows* on *Effect of Treatment*. It is this combined effect about which Theorem 1 is most explicit. It predicts the highest incidence of persuasion when both *Agrees* <u>and</u> *Knows* take on high values. It also predicts a decrease in the incidence of persuasion when <u>either</u> *Agrees* or *Knows* falls.

In Table 2.4, I separate respondents by *Agrees* <u>and</u> *Knows*. To simplify the presentation, I henceforth collapse *Knows* into a binary variable of "a lot or some" or "a little or nothing." I do this because the within-group variance of these combined categories was low relative to the between-group variance, as can be seen in Table 2.3.[19]

As predicted, at every level of *Agrees*, *Effect of Treatment* increases as *Knows* increases. Similarly, at every level of *Knows*, *Effect of Treatment* increases as *Agrees* increases. Moreover, for *Effect of Treatment* to take on positive values (i.e., for the speaker's cue to elicit matching respondent attitudes), <u>both</u> *Agrees* and *Knows* require high values. This is also consistent with the model's predictions, which is quite remarkable given the crudeness of the *Agrees* and *Knows* measures.

---

19 I exclude from Table 2.4 the category *Agrees* = "all or most" and *Knows* = "a little or nothing" because almost no respondents were in this category. Their behaviors were as follows: of the three respondents who heard Rush Limbaugh supports, none responded "good idea"; of the three respondents who heard that Rush Limbaugh opposes, both responded "good idea" (therefore *Effect of Treatment* for this group = −100); the one respondent who heard that Phil Donahue supports did not respond "good idea"; and of the three respondents who heard that Phil Donahue opposes, two responded "good idea" (therefore *Effect of Treatment* for this group = −67). Note also that in the top and bottom halves of Table 2.4 I switch the order of the category *Agrees* = "some" and *Knows* = "a little or nothing" and the category *Agrees* = "never" and *Knows* = "a lot or some." The theorem implies no prediction about which of these two categories should have a higher *Effect of Treatment*.

Table 2.4. *Responses to Opinion Question, Separated by Agrees __and__ Knows*

Rush Limbaugh					
Response to "Agrees" Question	Response to "Knows" Question	Of Those Who Heard "Supports," % Replying "Good Idea"	Of Those Who Heard "Opposes," % Replying "Good Idea"	Effect of Treatment	N (Total, Heard "Supports," Heard "Opposes")
All or most	A lot or some	81	52	29	(100, 48, 52)
Some	A lot or some	76	63	13	(185, 93, 92)
Some	A little or nothing	49	56	−7	(116, 55, 61)
Never	A lot or some	46	62	−16	(21, 13, 8)
Never	A little or nothing	30	54	−24	(97, 47, 50)
Phil Donahue					
Response to "Agrees" Question	Response to "Knows" Question	Of Those Who Heard "Supports," % Replying "Good Idea"	Of Those Who Heard "Opposes," % Replying "Good Idea"	Effect of Treatment	N (Total, Heard "Supports," Heard "Opposes")
All or most	A lot or some	78	39	39	(50, 32, 18)
Some	A lot or some	63	52	11	(247, 119, 128)
Never	A lot or some	67	75	−8	(20, 12, 8)
Some	A little or nothing	52	68	−16	(148, 71, 77)
Never	A little or nothing	46	77	−31	(65, 26, 39)

Moreover, recall that Theorem 1 implies that actual speaker interests, knowledge, or attributes, such as ideology, are neither necessary nor sufficient for persuasion. Now note that neither Rush Limbaugh's nor Phil Donahue's *actual* knowledge, interests, ideology, personality, or reputation varied within the experiment – they were exogenous constants. As a result, these attributes cannot possibly be the source of the systematic variation in the data.

Table 2.5. *Responses to Opinion Question, Separated by Ideological Similarity, Agrees, and Knows*

Speaker-Respondent Ideology	Agrees Knows Category	Of Those Who Heard "Supports," % Replying "Good Idea"	Of Those Who Heard "Opposes," % Replying "Good Idea"	Effect of Treatment	N (Total, Heard "Supports," Heard "Opposes")
Same		61	59	2	(399, 188, 211)
Different		55	64	−9	(423, 211, 212)
Same	High	79	54	25	(95, 47, 48)
	Medium	61	57	4	(147, 64, 83)
	Low	52	68	−16	(101, 44, 57)
Different	High	73	25	48	(19, 15, 4)
	Medium	62	60	9	(123, 61, 62)
	Low	45	68	−23	(207, 100, 107)

Alternative Explanations

In Tables 2.5 through 2.7, I continue to examine the relationship between *Agrees*, *Knows*, and *Effect of Treatment*. However, I now do so in the context of other well-known cue persuasiveness explanations. I will demonstrate that Theorem 1 adds to and clarifies, as opposed to merely restates, these explanations.

To simplify the presentation in these analyses, I group respondents into three self-selected categories: *AK High*, *AK Medium*, and *AK Low*. Respondents classified themselves as *AK High* if *Agrees* = "all or most" and *Knows* = "a lot or some." Respondents classified themselves as *AK Medium* if *Agrees* = "some" and *Knows* = "a lot or some." Otherwise, respondents who answered the *Agrees* and *Knowledge Questions* classified themselves as *AK Low*. Tables 2.3 and 2.4 suggest that these groupings are relatively homogeneous for the purpose of our analysis (i.e., with respect to observed behavior, there is low within-group variance and high between-group variance).

In Table 2.5, I first consider ideological similarity as an alternative explanation of cue persuasiveness. This explanation is manifest in beliefs such as "people who share my ideology usually have correct attitudes."[20] Using ideological similarity to explain cue persuasiveness implies that,

---

20 In this analysis, I classify Phil Donahue as a liberal and Rush Limbaugh as a conservative and use responses to the standard ideology survey question to measure respondent ideologies. The ideology question is "Generally speaking, do you usually think of yourself as a liberal, a conservative, or what?"

regardless of the value of *Agrees* and *Knows, Effect of Treatment* should increase as we move from the case where the speaker and respondent have different ideologies to the case where they share ideology. This prediction finds little support in Table 2.5. In the top part of the table, *Effect of Treatment* is slightly higher for respondents who shared the speaker's ideology (+2) than for those who did not (−9). However, the bottom part of the table reveals that this correspondence is heavily conditioned by *Agrees* and *Knows*. In fact, *Effect of Treatment* was greatest (+48) for the subset of the sample who heard cues by speaker *with different ideologies* for whom *Agrees* and *Knows* were both high.

By contrast, Theorem 1 predicts that, regardless of ideological similarity, *Effect of Treatment* should increase as we move from *AK Low* to *AK Medium* to *AK High*. The data strongly support this prediction. When *Agrees* and *Knows* were high, so was *Effect of Treatment*, regardless of ideological similarity. As *Agrees* and *Knows* decreased, so did *Effect of Treatment*, regardless of ideological similarity.

Table 2.5 shows that claims such as "*Agrees* and *Knows* are mere restatements of the effect of ideology" are plainly false. As Theorem 1 predicts, when *Agrees* and *Knows* were high, respondents were persuaded by speakers with different ideologies, and when *Agrees* and *Knows* were low, ideological similarity was not sufficient for persuasion. This evidence makes clear the primacy of perceived common interests and perceived speaker knowledge as determinants of cue persuasiveness. Put another way, our respondents were far more likely to be persuaded by someone they regarded as knowledgeable and as having common interests than by someone they perceived to be a common ideologue.

I next consider a common measure of affect as an alternative explanation of cue persuasiveness. The "likability heuristic" is expressed by beliefs such as "People should agree with people they like" or "People I like usually have correct opinions." In his review of the relevant social psychology literature, O'Keefe (1990:107) states, "Where this heuristic is invoked, liked sources should prove more persuasive than disliked sources."

Feeling thermometers are the conventional measure of "liking." If feeling thermometers are a good measure of liking, and if the likability heuristic is a good predictor of persuasion, then an increase in the speaker's thermometer should correspond to an increase in *Effect of Treatment*.[21] In Table 2.6, I use feeling thermometers to reevaluate the

---

21 The Multi-Investigator Study's feeling thermometer question was: "I'll read a name and ask you to rate the person on a thermometer that runs from zero to one hundred. The higher the number, the warmer or more favorable you feel toward that person. The lower the number, the colder or less favorable you feel. If you feel neither warm nor cold toward them, rate that person a fifty."

Table 2.6. *Responses to Opinion Question, Separated by Feeling Thermometer, Agrees, and Knows*

Therm	Agrees Knows Category	Of Those Who Heard "Supports," % Replying "Good Idea"	Of Those Who Heard "Opposes," % Replying "Good Idea"	Effect of Treatment	N (Total, Heard "Supports," Heard "Opposes")
0 to 10		45	63	−18	(234, 114, 120)
11 to 20		57	50	7	(62, 28, 34)
21 to 30		49	52	−3	(113, 51, 62)
31 to 40		63	77	−14	(98, 54, 44)
41 to 49		56	89	−33	(18, 9, 9)
50		66	59	7	(355, 163, 192)
51 to 60		56	62	−6	(111, 61, 50)
61 to 70		66	53	13	(87, 47, 40)
71 to 80		71	51	20	(86, 45, 41)
81 to 90		53	41	12	(32, 15, 17)
91 to 100		100	67	33	(16, 7, 9)
Under 50	High	100	67	33	(15, 7, 6)
	Medium	65	59	6	(131, 63, 68)
	Low	45	63	−18	(302, 146, 156)
Over 50	High	78	47	31	(116, 63, 53)
	Medium	64	52	8	(144, 77, 67)
	Low	31	70	−39	(56, 26, 30)

experimental data. The likability heuristic implies that, regardless of the value of *Agrees* and *Knows*, *Effect of Treatment* should increase as we move from low thermometer scores to high ones. The top and bottom parts of Table 2.6 reveal this prediction's limited success.

By contrast, Theorem 1 predicts that, regardless of the value of the feeling thermometer score, *Effect of Treatment* should increase as we move from *AK Low* to *AK Medium* to *AK High*. The bottom part of Table 2.6 shows that when *Agrees* and *Knows* are high, people can indeed be persuaded by speakers they do not like. Similarly, when *Agrees* and *Knows* are low enough, even liked speakers cannot persuade.

Table 2.6 supports my general conclusion about attribute-based explanations of cue-taking behavior. When people like others because of their knowledge or interests, then liking may well be correlated with cue persuasiveness. However, if a listener likes a speaker but regards the speaker as either lacking knowledge or having conflicting interests, then likability will not affect persuasiveness. Consequently, my explanation for the failure of this affect-driven variable is that feeling thermometers are a terrible measure of the factors that cause persuasion; they do not allow for a speaker's perceived knowledge or interests to mediate the manner in which a respondent's feelings affect attitudes.[22]

Of course, it is possible that the preceding analysis obscures the fact that some people use the likability heuristic, others condition their willingness to follow a cue on ideological similarity, and still others use other well-known explanations of cue persuasiveness as ways to choose whom to believe. I explore this possibility, and conclude my analysis, by conducting logit analyses that simultaneously incorporate a broad range of alternative explanations of cue persuasiveness. In each logit analysis, the dependent variable is the response to the Attitude Question. The dependent variable equals 1 if the respondent's answer to the Attitude Question was "good idea" and 0 if the response was "bad idea." To simplify the interpretation of the logit coefficients, I scaled *all* independent variables to the range [0,1].

The most important explanatory variables, from the perspective of Theorem 1, are those representing the interaction between *Agrees*, *Knows*, and cue's content. So, for example, the variable *Supports AK High* equals 1 if and only if *Agrees* = "all or most," *Knows* = "a lot or some," and the respondent heard a cue supporting prison spending. Similarly, *Opposes AK Medium* equals 1 if and only if *Agrees* = "some," *Knows* = "a lot or some," and the respondent heard a statement opposing prison spending. The other AK variables have equivalent definitions.

Theorem 1 predicts that *Supports AK High* will have a large positive coefficient, that *Supports AK Medium* will have a smaller positive coefficient, that *Opposes AK High* will have a large negative coefficient, and

22 I have also considered process-based explanations of cue persuasiveness. For example, Petty and Cacioppo (1986) argue that a person's "need for cognition" affects whether he or she will pursue the central or peripheral route to persuasion and, therefore, partially explains cue usage. As O'Keefe (1990:101) summarizes: "it appears that persons low in need for cognition are relatively more influenced by peripheral persuasion cues [e.g., speaker attributes] than are those in high need for cognition; and, correspondingly, those in high need for cognition appear to be more influenced by the quality of the message's arguments than are those low in need for cognition." My analysis of the effect of need for cognition parallels that of the analysis of feeling thermometers in Table 2.6 – both in construct and in consequence. As was true with feeling thermometers, what I draw from the relative failure of the need for cognition variable is that need for cognition explanations of cue persuasiveness should be founded on the premise that people who use the peripheral route to persuasion are not passive recipients of all cues – even people on the peripheral route make systematic choices about whose cues to use.

that *Opposes AK Medium* will have a smaller negative coefficient. If we allow for the possibility of negative third-party persuasion, then Theorem 1′ implies that *Supports AK Low* will have a negative coefficient and that *Opposes AK Low* will have a positive coefficient. That is, Theorem 1 implies that if *Agrees* or *Knows* increases, then so does the likelihood that the respondent's attitude matches the speaker's cue.

The remaining independent variables represent either alternative explanations of cue-taking or demographic variables that could affect the preferences on prison spending. Since most of these variables are secondary to my argument and have small and insignificant coefficients, I defer their descriptions to Appendix B.

Table 2.7 contains the results. The table describes three logistic regressions. The first logit includes only variables derived from responses to the Interest and Knowledge Questions. The second and third logits add variables representing alternative explanations and demographic variables that, independent of persuasion, could affect attitudes on prison spending.

The signs on the AK coefficients correspond precisely to the model's predictions. Our experimental treatment had its greatest effect on attitudes when *Agrees* and *Knows* were *High*, and its effect decreased as we moved to *AK Medium* and *AK Low*. Moreover, the impact of the AK variables did not vary much across the logits. The consistent impact of the AK variables is evidence that *Agrees* and *Knows* were not merely restatements of the alternative explanations. By contrast, the performance of independent variables derived from alternate explanations of cue persuasiveness was uniformly weak. In sum, the experiment reveals that over 1,000 randomly selected survey respondents made systematic, and seemingly motivated, choices about whose cues to use.

CONCLUSION

Formal models of persuasion demonstrate systematic relationships between simple assumptions about speakers and listeners and clear conclusions about when persuasion occurs. Persuasion experiments generate examples of how certain types of cues affect behavior. Yet many formal models of persuasion are based on premises about human cognition that few psychologists recognize as reasonable, and many persuasion experiments are not attached to clearly stated theory. Fortunately, there are remedies to these ills.

Attention to the empirical foundations of modern psychology can alert modelers to more reasonable assumptions about human decision makers. Attention to the logical requirements of rational choice theory can reveal ways to draw a logically consistent lesson from the wealth of extant

Table 2.7. *Multivariate Analyses of Experimental Data*

Position	Independent Variable	Pred. Sign	Agrees and Knows Only	With *Ideology* Controls	With *Party* Controls
	Constant		0.42[a]	−0.36	−0.38
			(0.10)	(0.55)	(0.56)
Supports	AK High	+, big	0.97[a]	1.26[a]	1.13[a]
			(0.30)	(0.38)	(0.38)
Supports	AK Medium	+	0.38[a]	0.74[a]	0.68[a]
			(0.18)	(0.25)	(0.26)
Supports	AK Low		−0.59[a]	−0.05	−0.11
			(0.17)	(0.25)	(0.25)
Opposes	AK High	−, big	−0.60[a]	−0.81[a]	−0.73[a]
			(0.28)	(0.35)	(0.35)
Opposes	AK Medium	−	−0.14	−0.33	−0.19
			(0.17)	(0.24)	(0.24)
Opposes	AK Low		0.13	−0.05	0.06
			(0.17)	(0.24)	(0.24)
Supports	Need for cognition	−		−0.39	−0.59
				(0.32)	(0.32)
Opposes	Need for cognition	+		0.11	0.28
				(0.30)	(0.31)
Supports	Low involvement	+		−0.16	−0.14
				(0.19)	(0.19)
Opposes	Low involvement	−		−0.53[a]	−0.50[a]
				(0.19)	(0.19)
	Conservative/ Republican			0.29	0.19
				(0.23)	(0.29)
	Liberal/ Democrat			−0.24	−0.08
				(0.24)	(0.28)
	Moderate			−1.60[a]	
				(0.63)	
Supports	Same Ideology/Party	+		−0.47	0.23
				(0.31)	(0.36)
Supports	Different Ideology/Party	−		−0.38	0.33
				(0.30)	(0.36)
Opposes	Different Ideology/Party	+		0.03	0.12
				(0.22)	(0.19)
Supports	Thermometer	+		0.67	0.74
				(0.43)	(0.43)
Opposes	Thermometer	−		0.36	0.29
				(0.41)	(0.41)
	African American			−0.62[a]	−0.53[a]
				(0.21)	(0.22)
	Age			1.22[a]	1.28[a]
				(0.32)	(0.32)
	Education			0.07	−0.07
				(0.18)	(0.17)
	Observations		1427	1190	1190
	Initial Log Likelihood		−989.12	−824.85	−824.85
	End Log Likelihood		−938.72	−751.33	−759.49

Dependent Variable: = 1; if response to the Opinion question was "good idea."
= 0; if response to the Opinion question was "bad idea."
[a] Indicates that the coefficient is significant at the .05 level.

experiments. The research presented in this chapter is but one modest attempt to attend to both sets of lessons simultaneously. While rational choice theory and political psychology often proceed as though the other tradition has nothing to contribute, for behavioral questions in which each tradition's methods provide insufficient analogies, both traditions are worse off for their lack of interaction. There are important questions about politics that do not allow the luxury of simple argument. For scholars whose goal is the pursuit of clear and reliable explanation, logically organized and empirically grounded analyses are the only path to success. Together, the logic of rational choice theory and the empirical foundations of political psychology provide the foundations for achieving such success.

APPENDIX A: THE FORMAL MODEL

The purpose of this appendix is to supply the notation necessary to present a precise statement of the model's equilibrium. Readers who are interested in knowing more about this theoretical framework should consult Lupia and McCubbins (1998).

The sequence of events begins with three probabilistic choices by nature. These choices are the source of the four types of uncertainty described in the text. I denote these choices $n = \{\beta, A, K\}$. The order of these choices is irrelevant. Unless otherwise stated, all elements of the model are common knowledge.

The choice $\beta \in \{better, worse\}$ determines whether x is better or worse than y for the listener. Nature chooses the state $\beta = better$ (for the listener) with probability $b \in [0,1]$ and the state $\beta = worse$ with probability $1 - b$. The listener knows b, but not β. If $\beta = better$ and the listener chooses x, then the listener earns utility $U \geq 0$. If $\beta = worse$ and if the listener chooses x, then she earns utility $\underline{U} \leq 0$. If the listener chooses y, then she earns utility 0.

The choice $K \in \{0,1\}$ determines whether or not the speaker knows the true value of β. Nature allows the speaker to know β ($K = 1$) with probability $k \in [0,1]$ and makes no such revelation (chooses $K = 0$), with probability $1 - k$. The speaker knows K, while the listener does not. Both players know k.

The choice $A \in \{0,1\}$ determines whether the speaker and listener have common or conflicting interests. If $A = 1$ (common interests), then the speaker receives utility $Z \geq 0$ when the listener receives utility $U \geq 0$ and receives utility $\underline{Z} \leq 0$ when the listener receives utility $\underline{U} \leq 0$. If $A = 0$ (conflicting interests), then the speaker receives utility $\underline{Z} \leq 0$ when the listener receives utility $U \geq 0$ and receives utility $Z \geq 0$ when the listener receives utility $\underline{U} \leq 0$. If the listener chooses y, then the speaker earns utility o. Nature chooses $A = 1$ with probability $a \in [0,1]$ and $A = 0$ with probability $1 - a$. The speaker knows A and knows that the listener does not. Both players know a.

After nature makes its three choices, the speaker sends a signal $s \in \{B,W\}$ to the listener. $s = B$ is the signal "I assert that x is better than y for the listener." $s = W$ is the signal "I assert that x is worse than y for the listener." Next the listener chooses x or y. Then the game ends and both players receive a utility payoff.

I use the perfect Bayesian equilibrium to derive the theoretical results (see Fudenburg and Tirole 1991). Let the vector π be a typical strategy profile, the scalar h a typical information set, and the vector μ a typical system of beliefs. So, $\mu(h)$ is a player's beliefs about which of several <u>unobservable</u> events – the decision nodes within information set h – has led to his present <u>observable</u> situation – the information set h. Formally, μ is a function from $d \in D$, the set of decision nodes, to $[0,1]$, such that for every information set h, $\Sigma_{d \in h} \, \mu(d) = 1$. I make the usual assumption that the game's information sets collectively partition D.

Let π_s denote the speaker's component of strategy profile π. π_s has six scalar elements, one for each speaker information set $h_s \in \{h_1, \ldots, h_6\}$. Let $N = \{\beta,K,A\}$ be the vector of moves by nature. Then at h_1, $N = \{1,1,1\}$, at h_2, $N = \{0,1,1\}$, at h_3, $N = \{1,1,0\}$, at h_4, $N = \{0,1,0\}$, at h_5, $N \in \{\{0,1\}, 0,1\}$, and at h_6, $N \in \{\{0,1\}, 0,0\}$. Speaker information sets are completely determined by nature's choice vector N. Each element, $\pi_s(s;h_j)$, $j = 1$, $\ldots 6$, is the probability that the speaker signals $s \in \{B,W\}$ if he or she is at information set h_j. These probabilities sum to 1 for each information set.

I use the vector π_r to denote the listener's component of strategy profile π. This vector has two scalar elements, one for each listener information set $h_r = \{h_B, h_W\}$. Note that the listener's information sets are completely determined by the speaker's signal. Each element, $\pi_r(x;s)$, is the probability that the listener chooses x after having heard the signal $s \in \{B,W\}$. $1 - \pi_r(x;s)$ is the probability that the listener chooses y given the same signal. A signal s is "along the path of play" if there exists an information set at which $\pi_s(s;h_s) > 0$.

Definition

A pair of strategy profiles (π_r, π_s) is a perfect Bayesian equilibrium if (1) for each h_s, $\pi_s(s;h_s)$ maximizes the speaker's expected utility given $\pi_r(x;s)$ for all $s \in \{B,W\}$; (2) for each s that is along the path of play, $\pi_r(x;s)$ maximizes the listener's expected utility given $\mu(\text{better}|s)$ and $\mu(\text{worse}|s)$, where μ is computed from π_s by Bayes's rule; and (3) for any s that is not along the path of play, $\pi_r(x;s)$ maximizes the listener's expected utility given $\mu(\text{better}|s) = b$ and $\mu(\text{worse}|s) = 1 - b$.

I identify the set of nonbabbling perfect Bayesian equilibria. A babbling equilibrium requires either a listener who ignores all signals or a speaker who sends only uninformative signals. In this model, a babbling equilibrium is an equilibrium in which either the speaker does not base his signal on n_b or the listener does not base her response on s. I focus on nonbabbling equilibria because we are interested in determining the conditions under which people *can* persuade each other when they attempt to communicate with each other. I also focus on nonneologistic equilibra. In our model, a neologistic equilibrium *requires* the speaker and listener to agree that the signal B means "worse" and not "better" and that the signal W means "better" and not "worse." Focusing on nonneologistic equilibria is equivalent to assuming that words have focal meanings. Since the speaker can lie, focusing on nonneologistic equilibria is not restrictive. For notational simplicity, let $\pi = (\pi_r, \pi_s)$, $\pi_{14} = (\pi_s(B;h_1), \pi_s(B;h_2), \pi_s(B;h_3), \pi_s(B;h_4))$, $\pi_5 = \pi_s(B;h_5)$, $\pi_6 = \pi_s(B;h_6)$, and $\pi_r = (\pi_r(x;B), \pi_r(x;W))$.

Equilibrium

The only nonbabbling, nonneologistic perfect Bayesian equilibrium in the basic model is $\pi_{14} = (1,0,0,1)$; $\pi_5 = 1$; if $bZ + (1 - b)\underline{Z} \geq 0$ and $\pi_5 = 0$ otherwise; $\pi_6 = 1$; if $b\underline{Z} + (1 - b)Z \geq 0$ and $\pi_6 = 0$ otherwise; $\pi_r = (1,0)$. This equilibrium requires Condition A:

$$\frac{[(1-a)k + [(1-k) \times [\pi_s(B;h_5)a + \pi_s(B;h_6)(1-a)]]]}{[ak + [(1-k) \times [\pi_s(B;h_5)a + \pi_s(B;h_6)(1-a)]]]} \leq bU/(b-1)\underline{U}$$

and Condition B:

$$\frac{[ak + [(1-k) \times [(1-\pi_s(B;h_5))a + (1-\pi_s(B;h_6))(1-a)]]]}{[(1-a)k + [(1-k) \times [(1-\pi_s(B;h_5))a + (1-\pi_s(B;h_6))(1-a)]]]} \geq bU/(b-1)\underline{U}$$

where at least one of the inequalities is strict.

Proof

I proceed as follows. First, I define the expected value of every pure strategy at every speaker information set. Second, I identify the boundaries of the set of potential nonbabbling, nonneologistic perfect Bayesian equilibria. Third, I identify the sequentially rational strategy profiles within this set. I find that the named equilibrium is this set's only member.

Finally, I evaluate the consistency of the sequentially rational strategy profiles.

To see the expected value of every pure strategy at every speaker information set, consider the following relationships. At h_1, the expected utility from $\pi_s(B;h_1) = 1$ is $\pi_r(x;B)Z$. The expected utility from $\pi_s(B;h_1) = 0$ is $\pi_r(x;W)Z$. If $\pi_r(x;B) \geq \pi_r(x;W)$, then $\pi_s(B;h_1) = 1$ is the best response. At h_2, the expected utility from $\pi_s(W;h_2) = 1$ is $\pi_r(x;B)\underline{Z}$. The expected utility from $\pi_s(W;h_2) = 0$ is $\pi_r(x;W)\underline{Z}$. If $\pi_r(x;B) \geq \pi_r(x;W)$, then $\pi_s(B;h_2) = 0$ is the best response. At h_3, the expected utility from $\pi_s(B;h_3) = 1$ is $\pi_r(x;B)\underline{Z}$. The expected utility from $\pi_s(B;h_3) = 0$ is $\pi_r(x;W)\underline{Z}$. If $\pi_r(x;B) \geq \pi_r(x;W)$, then $\pi_s(B;h_3) = 0$ is the best response. At h_4, the expected utility from $\pi_s(W;h_4) = 1$ is $\pi_r(x;B)Z$. The expected utility from $\pi_s(W;h_2) = 0$ is $\pi_r(x;W)Z$. If $\pi_r(x;B) \geq \pi_r(x;W) = 0$, then $\pi_s(B;h_4) = 1$ is the best response. At h_5, the expected utility from $\pi_s(B;h_5) = 1$ is $b\pi_r(x;B)Z + (1 - b)\ \pi_r(x;B)\underline{Z}$. The expected utility from $\pi_s(W;h_5) = 0$ is $b\pi_r(x;W)Z + (1 - b)\ \pi_r(x;W)\underline{Z}$. If $\pi_r(x;B) \geq \pi_r(x;W)$ and $bZ + (1 - b)\underline{Z} \leq 0$, then $\pi_s(B;h_5) = 0$ is the best response. At h_6, the expected utility from $\pi_s(B;h_6) = 1$ is $b\pi_r(x;B)\underline{Z} + (1 - b)\pi_r(x;B)Z$. The expected utility from $\pi_s(W;h_6) = 0$ is $b\pi_r(x;W)\underline{Z} + (1 - b)\pi_r(x;W)Z$. If $\pi_r(x;B) \geq \pi_r(x;W)$ and $b\underline{Z} + (1 - b)Z \leq 0$, then $\pi_s(B;h_6) = 0$ is the best response.

> **Lemma 1:** All mixed-strategy perfect Bayesian equilibria in the model are babbling equilibria.

Proof of Lemma 1. A mixed-strategy equilibrium requires that each player choose a strategy that makes the other player indifferent between their two pure strategies. A necessary and sufficient condition for rendering the speaker indifferent between his pure strategies at information sets h_1 through h_4 is to set $\pi_r(x;B) = \pi_r(x;W)$. Setting $\pi_r(x;B) = \pi_r(x;W)$ is also necessary and sufficient to make the speaker indifferent between her two strategies at h_5 if $bZ + (1 - b)\underline{Z} \equiv 0$ and at h_6 if $b\underline{Z} + (1 - b)Z \equiv 0$. Setting $\pi_r(x;B) = \pi_r(x;W)$ implies that the listener is not conditioning her strategy on the signal. Anticipating such behavior, the speaker can choose any strategy he likes. These speaker strategies will either make the listener indifferent between her pure strategies, in which case we have a babbling equilibrium, or they will not, in which case we do not have an equilibrium.

If $bZ + (1 - b)\underline{Z} = 0$ or $b\underline{Z} + (1 - b)Z = 0$, then any listener strategy, including $\pi_r(x;B) = \pi_r(x;W)$, makes the speakers at h_5 and h_6 indifferent. Note, however, that the listener has an incentive to choose a mixed strategy other than $0 < \pi_r(x;B) = \pi_r(x;W) < 1$ only if she can induce the speaker at h_5 and h_6 to take distinct and knowledge transferring actions. Since the speaker at h_5 and h_6 has no useful private information at either of these information sets, by definition, the requirement cannot be met. Therefore, only an equilibrium that could result from such an adaptation is a babbling equilibrium. QED.

From similar logic, it follows that all equilibria for which $\pi_r(x;B) = \pi_r(x;W)$ are babbling equilibria. Moreover, any nonbabbling equilibrium for which $\pi_r(x;B) = 0$ and $\pi_r(x;W) = 1$ requires neologisms (i.e., both players know that B means "worse" and W means "better"). Therefore, nonbabbling, nonneologistic perfect Bayesian equilibria must include $\pi_r = (1,0)$.

Since nonbabbling, nonneologistic perfect Bayesian equilibria must include $\pi_r = (1,0)$, they must also include $\pi_{14} = (1,0,0,1)$. The reason for this is that the expected speaker utility at h_1 through h_4 reveals $\pi_{14} = (1,0,0,1)$ to be the unique profile of best responses when $\pi_r(x;B) > \pi_r(x;W)$. Therefore, the set of nonbabbling, nonneologistic perfect Bayesian equilibria must be contained *within* $\pi = (1,0,0,1, \{0,1\}, \{0,1\}, 1,0)$, where $\{0,1\}$ within strategy profile π is read as "either 0 or 1." First, one must identify the sequentially rational strategy profiles within this set and then evaluate these profiles' consistency.

At h_B, the expected utility from $\pi_r(x;B) = 1$ is

$$[akb\pi_S(B;h_1)U + ak(1-b)\pi_S(B;h_2)U + (1-a)kb\pi_S(B;h_3)U + (1-a)k(1-b)\pi_S(B;h_4)U + a(1-k)b\pi_S(B;h_5)U + a(1-k)(1-b)\pi_S(B;h_5)U + (1-a)(1-k)b\pi_S(B;h_6)U + (1-a)(1-k)(1-b)\pi_S(B;h_6)U]/[akb\pi_S(B;h_1) + ak(1-b)\pi_S(B;h_2) + (1-a)kb\pi_S(B;h_3) + (1-a)k(1-b)\pi_S(B;h_4) + a(1-k)b\pi_S(B;h_5) + a(1-k)(1-b)\pi_S(B;h_5) + (1-a)(1-k)b\pi_S(B;h_6) + (1-a)(1-k)(1-b)\pi_S(B;h_6)]$$

At h_W, the expected utility from $\pi_r(x;W) = 1$ is

$$[akb(1-\pi_S(B;h_1))U + ak(1-b)(1-\pi_S(B;h_2))U + (1-a)kb(1-\pi_S(B;h_3))U + (1-a)k(1-b)(1-\pi_S(B;h_4))U + a(1-k)b(1-\pi_S(B;h_5))U + a(1-k)(1-b)(1-\pi_S(B;h_5))U + (1-a)(1-k)b(1-\pi_S(B;h_6))U + (1-a)(1-k)(1-b)(1-\pi_S(B;h_6))U]/[akb(1-\pi_S(B;h_1)) + ak(1-b)(1-\pi_S(B;h_2)) + (1-a)kb(1-\pi_S(B;h_3)) + (1-a)k(1-b)(1-\pi_S(B;h_4)) + a(1-k)b(1-\pi_S(B;h_5)) + a(1-k)(1-b)(1-\pi_S(B;h_5)) + (1-a)(1-k)b(1-\pi_S(B;h_6)) + (1-a)(1-k)(1-b)(1-\pi_S(B;h_6))]$$

Recall that the listener earns utility zero for choosing y. Therefore, $\pi_r(x;B) = 1$ is the best response only if the expected utility from $\pi_r(x;B) = 1$ is ≥ 0 and $\pi_r(x;W) = 0$ is the best response only if the expected utility from $\pi_r(x;W) = 1$ is ≤ 0. Since a nonbabbling equilibrium requires that the expected utility from $\pi_r(x;B) = 1$ is ≥ 0, that the expected utility from $\pi_r(x;W) = 1$ is ≤ 0, and that one of these inequalities is strict, it requires that one of the inequalities in Conditions A or B be strict.

We can now prove that $\pi = (1,0,0,1,0,0,1,0)$ is a perfect Bayesian equilibrium under the conditions of the equilibrium. The other cases — $\pi = (1,0,0,1,0,1,1,0)$, $\pi = (1,0,0,1,1,0,1,0)$, and $\pi = (1,0,0,1,1,1,1,0)$ — follow equivalent logic. From the expected utility at information sets h_5 and h_6, we know that this equilibrium holds only if $bZ + (1 - b)\underline{Z} \leq 0$ and $b\underline{Z} + (1 - b)Z \leq 0$. This requirement matches the related requirement of the equilibrium. From the expected utility at information sets h_1 through h_4, we know that this equilibrium requires the expected utility of $\pi_r(x;B) = 1 \geq 0 \geq$ the expected utility of $\pi_r(x;W) = 1$. We evaluate the conditions under which this inequality holds subsequently.

If $\pi_s = (1,0,0,1,0,0)$, then the numerator of the expected utility from $\pi_r(x;W) = 1$ reduces to $ak(1 - b)U + (1 - a)kbU + a(1 - k)bU + a(1 - k)(1 - b)U + (1 - a)(1 - k)bU + (1 - a)(1 - k)(1 - b)U$. It is trivial to show that this quantity is ≤ 0 iff $[1 - k + ak]/[1 - ak] \geq bU/(b - 1)U$, which is true iff Condition B is true. Similarly, if $\pi_s = (1,0,0,1,0,0)$, then the numerator of the expected utility from $\pi_r(x;B) = 1$ reduces to $akbU + (1 - a)k(1 - b)U$. It is trivial to show that this quantity is ≥ 0 iff $bU/(b - 1)\underline{U} \geq [1 - a]/a$, which is true iff Condition A is true. Therefore, $\pi = (1,0,0,1,0,0,1,0)$ is sequentially rational under the conditions of the equilibrium.

If the beliefs required to support this profile are consistent, then the profile and beliefs together constitute a perfect Bayesian equilibrium. Beliefs are consistent iff

$$\mu(better|B) = (b \times probability\ that\ s = B\ if\ B = better)$$

$$[(b \times probability\ that\ s = B\ if\ B = better) + ((1 - b) \times probability\ that\ s = W\ if\ B = better)]$$

In the proposed equilibrium $\mu(better|B) = 1$, the probability that $s = W$ if $B = better$ is zero and the probability that $s = B$ if $B = better$ is nonzero. Therefore, beliefs are consistent. Equivalent logic proves consistency for $\mu(better|W)$, $\mu(worse|B)$, and $\mu(worse|W)$. QED.

Lemma: The equilibrium exists only if $a > .5$ and $k > 0$.

Theorem: Perceived common interests and perceived speaker knowledge are necessary, but not sufficient, for persuasion. The sufficient condition is the satisfaction of both necessary conditions plus the listener's uncertainty about x and y leading her to believe that she can benefit from the speaker's knowledge.

APPENDIX B: OTHER INDEPENDENT VARIABLES

Like the *AK* variables, I introduce likability, ideological similarity, and partisan similarity (another popular attribute-based explanation of cue-taking that is analogous to ideological similarity) into the empirical model by interacting them with the content of the cue. The alternative explanations that generate these three sets of variables imply that each set will affect the dependent variable in the same way.

Affect-driven explanations of cue-taking imply that *Supports Thermometer* will have a large positive coefficient and that *Opposes Thermometer* will have a large negative coefficient. For respondents who heard a "supports" cue, I set *Opposes Thermometer* = .5. I used an equivalent transformation for respondents who heard an "opposes" cue. This transformation is consistent with the wording of the thermometer questions; respondents were instructed to rate the person as a 50 if they feel neither warm nor cold toward the person.

The variables *Supports/Same Ideology*, *Supports/Different Ideology*, and *Opposes/Different Ideology* account for the ideological similarity between respondent and speaker. For example, the variable *Supports/Same Ideology* equals 1 if either a conservative respondent hears "Rush Limbaugh supports" or a liberal respondent hears "Phil Donahue supports." It equals 0 otherwise. I use partisan similarity variables in an analogous manner. Ideological similarity-based explanations imply that *Supports/Same Ideology* will have a large positive coefficient, *Opposes/Different Ideology* will have a large positive coefficient, and *Supports/Different Ideology* may have a negative coefficient. Partisan-based similarity explanations of persuasion suggest analogous implications for the variables *Supports/Same Party*, *Opposes/Different Party*, and *Supports/Different Party*, respectively. I ran separate logit analyses for party and ideology because the two factors were too highly correlated to allow their simultaneous inclusion.

The need for cognition variables is analogous to the need for the variables just described. However, this set of variables is hypothesized to have a different coefficient. Petty and Cacioppo (1986), among others, argue that a person's need for cognition affects whether he or she will take the central or peripheral route to persuasion. To evaluate the claim that need for cognition affects cue persuasiveness, I use the Multi-Investigator Study's four "need for cognition" questions. These questions began with the query "How well would you say that the following statement describes you?" where the four statements in question were "I only think as hard as I have to;" "It's enough for me that something gets the job done; I don't care how or why it works"; "I really enjoy a task that involves coming up with new solutions to problems"; and "I like tasks that require only a little thought once I've learned them." I follow the standard practice in need for cognition studies and use the answers to the four questions to form a need for cognition scale. The scale ranges from 0 to 4, with 4 implying highest in need for cognition and 0 implying lowest in need for cognition. Need for cognition–based explanations imply that as need for cognition increases, the effect of the cue will decrease. That is, high need for cognition will drive the coefficient to 0. Therefore, it implies that *Supports/Need for Cognition* will have a negative sign and *Opposes/Need for Cognition* will have a positive sign.

I also include a variable representing the respondent's prior involvement with prison spending. The "prior involvement" hypothesis that "Source credibility has more impact under low than under high involvement" is common in persuasion research (e.g., Chaiken 1980; Petty, Cacioppo, and Goldman 1981). To measure prior involvement, I used responses to the question "How often would you say that you had thought about this issue before today – often, sometimes, rarely, or never?" In an analysis analogous to that of Table 2.7, the prior involvement prediction fared poorly, while the theorem's prediction performed well regardless of the subject's prior involvement with prison spending. Prior involvement–based explanations imply that the variable *Supports/Low Involvement* will have a positive coefficient and that *Opposes/Low Involvement* will have a high coefficient.

The other independent variables represent additional factors that could affect respondent attitudes on prison spending. Each is drawn from standard survey questions. These factors are the respondent's partisanship, ideology, education, race, and age. *Democrat* = 1 for self-identified Democrats and 0 otherwise. I code *Republican, Conservative, Liberal, Moderate,* and *African American* analogously. *Age* is based on the numerical response to the question "How old were you on your last birthday?" *Education* is based on the response to the question "What is the highest grade or year of school you completed?"

In the analysis, *Opposes/Low Involvement* and *Supports Thermometer* were relatively good performers. Both were large, the former statistically significant, and both had the signs predicted by the alternative explanations. By contrast, the coefficients of *Supports/Low Involvement* and *Opposes Thermometer* had the wrong sign and were not significant. Also of interest is the fact that African Americans were significantly less likely to support prison spending and older people were significantly more likely to support it, all else constant. All other variables performed far worse. While *Age* also had a large coefficient, note that the underlying range of *Age* is eighteen to ninety-six years. Therefore, an age increase of seventy-eight years was required to get the large effect seen in Table 2.7.

References

Aristotle. 1954. *Rhetoric*. New York: Modern Library.

Berelson, Bernard, Paul F. Lazarsfeld, and William N. McPhee. 1954. *Voting: a Study of Opinion Formation in a Presidential Campaign*. Chicago: University of Chicago Press.

Brady, Henry E., and Paul M. Sniderman. 1985. "Attitude Attribution: A Group Basis for Political Reasoning." *American Political Science Review* 79: 1061–78.

Calvert, Randall L. 1985. "The Value of Biased Information: A Rational Choice Model of Political Advice." *Journal of Politics* 47:530–55.

Chaiken, Shelly. 1980. "Heuristic versus Systematic Information Processing and the Use of Source versus Message Cues in Persuasion." *Journal of Personality and Social Psychology* 39:752–66.

Converse, Philip E. 1964. "The Nature of Belief Systems in Mass Publics." In David E. Apter, ed., *Ideology and Discontent*. New York: Free Press.

Crawford, Vincent, and Joel Sobel. 1982. "Strategic Information Transmission." *Econometrica* 50:1431–51.

Delli Carpini, Michael X., and Scott Keeter. 1996. *What Americans Know About Politics and Why It Matters*. New Haven, CT: Yale University Press.

Downs, Anthony. 1957. *An Economic Theory of Democracy*. New York: Harper & Row.

Eagly, Alice H., and Shelly Chaiken. 1993. *The Psychology of Attitudes*. Fort Worth, TX: Harcourt Brace Jovanovich.

Farrell, Joseph, and Robert Gibbons. 1989. "Cheap Talk with Two Audiences." *American Economic Review* 79:1214–23.

Franzoi, Stephen L. 1996. *Social Psychology*. Madison, WI: Brown & Benchmark.

Fudenberg, Drew, and Jean Tirole. 1991. "Perfect Bayesian Equilbrium and Sequential Equilibrium." *Journal of Economic Theory* 53:236–60.

Harsanyi, John. 1967. "Games with Incomplete Information Played by 'Bayesian' Players, I: The Basic Model." *Management Science* 14:159–82.

    1968a. "Games with Incomplete Information Played by 'Bayesian' Players, II: Bayesian Equilibrium Points." *Management Science* 14:320–34.

    1968b. "Games with Incomplete Information Played by 'Bayesian' Players, III: The Basic Probability Distribution of the Game." *Management Science* 14:486–502.

Hovland, Carl I., Irving L. Janis, and Harold H. Kelley. 1953. *Communication and Persuasion: Psychological Studies of Opinion Change*. New Haven, CT: Yale University Press.

Klapper, Joseph T. 1960. *The Effects of Mass Communication*. New York: Free Press.

Kuklinski, James H., and Norman L. Hurley. 1994. "On Hearing and Interpreting Political Messages: A Cautionary Tale of Citizen Cue-Taking." *Journal of Politics* 56:729–51.

Kuklinski, James H., Daniel S. Metlay, and W. D. May. 1982. "Citizen Knowledge and Choice on the Complex Issue of Nuclear Energy." *American Journal of Political Science* 26:615–42.

Lupia, Arthur. 1994. "Shortcuts versus Encyclopedias: Information and Voting Behavior in California Insurance Reform Elections." *American Political Science Review* 88:63–76.

Lupia, Arthur, and Mathew D. McCubbins. 1998. *The Democratic Dilemma: Can Citizens Learn What They Need to Know?* New York: Cambridge University Press.

McGuire, William J. 1985. "Attitudes and Attitude Change." In Gardner Lindzey and Elliot Aronson, eds., *Handbook of Social Psychology*, 3rd ed. New York: Random House.

McKelvey, Richard D., and Peter C. Ordeshook. 1985. "Elections with Limited Information: A Fulfilled Expectations Model Using Contemporaneous Poll and Endorsement Data as Information Sources." *Journal of Economic Theory* 36:55–85.

O'Keefe, Daniel J. 1990. *Persuasion: Theory and Research*. Newbury Park, CA: Sage Publications.

Petty, Richard E., and John T. Cacioppo. 1986. *Communication and Persuasion: Central and Peripheral Routes to Attitude Change*. New York: Springer-Verlag.

Petty, Richard E., John T. Cacioppo, and R. Goldman. 1981. "Personal Involvement as a Determinant of Argument-Based Persuasion." *Journal of Personality and Social Psychology* 41:847–55.

Popkin, Samuel L. 1991. *The Reasoning Voter: Communication and Persuasion in Presidential Campaigns*. Chicago: University of Chicago Press.

Popkin, Samuel L., John W. Gorman, Charles Phillips, and Jeffrey A. Smith. 1976. "Comment: What Have You Done for Me Lately? Toward an Investment Theory of Voting." *American Political Science Review* 70:779–805.

Sniderman, Paul M., Richard A. Brody, and Philip E. Tetlock. 1991. *Reasoning and Choice: Explorations in Political Psychology*. Cambridge: Cambridge University Press.

Spence, A. Michael. 1973. "Job Market Signaling." *Quarterly Journal of Economics* 87:355–74.

Tetlock, Philip E. 1993. "Cognitive Structural Analysis of Political Rhetoric: Methodological and Theoretical Issues." In Shanto Iyengar and William J. McGuire, eds., *Explorations in Political Psychology*. Durham, NC: Duke University Press.

3

Expanding the Envelope:
Citizenship, Contextual Methodologies, and
Comparative Political Psychology

PAMELA JOHNSTON CONOVER
DONALD D. SEARING

We construct here an argument for expanding the envelope of political psychology to encompass new topics for investigation and new methodologies with which to investigate them. The topics are associated with the civic side of citizenship. The methods are associated with contextual analysis. Because both citizenship and contextual analysis are so closely associated with other subfields of our discipline (political philosophy and comparative politics, respectively), their relevance has rarely been appreciated for the type of political psychology that is done within the research paradigm of political behavior. We have, however, become increasingly aware of their importance in the course of pursuing our current research program on the meaning of citizenship in modern liberal democratic states and, in particular, in the United States and Great Britain.

First, we shall review briefly the breadth and current political relevance of the topic of citizenship and the general conceptual framework that we have created for studying it. Then we shall discuss at greater length the utility of contextual methodologies for investigating this subject.

CITIZENSHIP: OLD WINE IN NEW BOTTLES

Throughout the world, intellectuals and politicians are asking, "What does it mean to be a citizen?" This perennial political question has been explored by philosophers from Aristotle to Rawls and debated by politicians from ancient Greece to contemporary Russia. Unfortunately, such discussions have never been properly informed by social scientific knowledge about the political psychology of citizenship, about what citizenship means to citizens – for such knowledge hardly exists. This situation is not a minor matter, because the understandings and actions of citizens define the practice of citizenship. And this practice of citizenship determines the nature of our public lives, the vitality of our civil society, and the stability of our democratic regimes.

Throughout much of the post–World War II era, the topic of citizenship has been in eclipse, and even political philosophers have had little new to say on the subject. Recently, however, that has changed, and citizenship is now a topic of vigorous public discussion and philosophic inquiry. Dramatic changes in the global political context have drawn the question of what it means to be a citizen back into view. In particular, the sovereignty of the nation-state, which has been the locus of our modern citizenship, has come under fire from both "above" and "below" (see Hall and Held 1989). From above, the forces of globalization and growing economic interdependence make people wonder whether "citizen of the world" is a concept whose time has come. From below, regional patriotism challenges citizenship's conceptual locus in the nation state (Hood 1988). But it is the world's lurch toward democracy that has done the most to bring citizenship back into our public discourse. Thus, the 1980s saw a resurgence of democratic government in Latin America, while in 1989, the fall of the Berlin Wall and the dismantling of Communist rule across the Soviet bloc states reinvigorated the democratic spirit. All across the world, it suddenly seems that people are struggling to establish democratic traditions.

To succeed, they need models that suggest what forms of citizenship nurture vital civil societies and sustain democratic governments in different institutional circumstances. Surprisingly, the established democracies are unable to offer anything like reliable social scientific knowledge about this critical subject. Western intellectuals and politicians have some answers, many of them contradictory, about what it *should* mean to be a democratic citizen and what role the practice of citizenship *should* play in democratic societies. Yet the embarrassing truth is that we do not understand how we do it ourselves, for there is no sound empirical evidence about most of the established patterns that are involved. Of course, we do know a good deal about electoral participation, although we have not unraveled its motivational core. But the electoral dimension is only half the story; we have not studied nearly enough of the other side – the civic side of citizenship (but see Verba, Scholzman, and Brady 1995). We simply do not know how people in contemporary liberal democratic states like the United States and Great Britain actually understand their citizenship, let alone the causal role that their practice of citizenship plays in sustaining their civil societies and democratic regimes.[1]

---

1 There have been surprisingly few empirical studies of the meaning of citizenship per se. The landmark study remains Gabriel Almond and Sidney Verba's *The Civic*

Expanding the Envelope

The Elements of Citizenship

It is still true, as Aristotle pointed out long ago, that "there is no general agreement on a single definition" of citizenship (quoted in Heater 1990:vii; also see Riesenberg 1992). But however citizenship is defined, the definition must address the meaning of membership in a political community (Hall and Held 1989; Oliver 1991). This is the basis upon which people answer the fundamental questions about their public lives: Who are we? What can we do? What must we do? (van Gunsteren 1991:732).

Two sets of answers to such questions, two fundamental conceptions of citizenship, have persisted throughout the history of political philosophy (see Daggar 1981; Heater 1990; Riesenberg 1992; Walzer 1989). The first, and oldest, view of citizenship originated in the civic republicanism of Aristotle and other political philosophers of classical antiquity. It was further shaped by medieval and Renaissance thought (Pocock 1975) and found its modern voice in eighteenth-century theorists like Rousseau (Vernon 1986). At its core, this communal perspective entails an active citizenry and depicts citizenship as grounded in relationships among friends and neighbors who are bound together by common activities and traditions (Barber 1984). Politics is, from this viewpoint, a fundamentally public activity through which people pursue the collective good. Moreover, since people usually identify their personal good with this collective good, civic activity also serves as a source of personal development (Daggar 1981).

The second view of citizenship, and the dominant one in recent centuries, is the contractual vision that is rooted in liberal political philosophy. John Locke and Thomas Hobbes crafted this viewpoint, and John Rawls (1971) has forged its contemporary interpretation. The contractual version of citizenship is, at its core, a legalistic account that places minimal demands on the public and thus anticipates a passive citizenry (Ackerman 1980; Daggar 1981; Heater 1990; Portis 1985; Riesenberg 1992; Sullivan 1986). Citizens are seen as separate individuals bound together by a "social contract" rather than as friends and neighbors united by common activity (Barber 1984; Sullivan 1986; Wolin 1986). Within this context, political activity is essentially private in nature, for it is regarded "principally as a means of protecting and furthering one's private interests" (Daggar 1981:720).

Culture (1963), now thirty years old. Since then, there have been only a few direct examinations of citizenship and citizen identities (e.g., Dryzek and Berejikian 1993; Theiss-Moore 1993). The topic of political tolerance is the major exception here: it has been investigated carefully and creatively.

From these descriptions of citizenship's two major strains, it is evident that the concept is multifaceted; it encompasses a wide variety of elements, some legal, some psychological, and some behavioral. Yet most of them remain unexamined by contemporary research in political psychology and political behavior. They need to be distinguished from one another and investigated empirically if we are to develop a full understanding of the role of citizenship in contemporary liberal democratic states. Here is our map of the conceptual terrain.

Membership. The most basic element of citizenship is "membership" in the political community, as signified by legal status or "standing" (Shklar 1991). And the concepts of "citizen" and "citizenship," which are built around this element by publics and politicians, have wide-ranging political consequences. These concepts structure the creation, revision, and interpretation of the polity's legal definition of citizenship.

In the modern world, the focal point of citizenship has been membership in nation-states (Shklar 1991). But one can also talk of membership in political communities within nations – regions, states, cities – and membership in political communities that combine nations, such as the European Union. Thus the concepts of citizen and citizenship may define and structure multiple levels of citizenship nested within each other (Wolin 1989). The definitional politics of citizenship focuses on questions of membership: Who should be allowed to belong to the political community? and What will be the legal responsibilities and privileges of these members (Fierlbeck 1991; van Gunsteren 1991; Walzer 1993)? When the formal political community is a subset of society, as it is in those liberal democratic states that make it difficult for guest workers and immigrants to become citizens, then citizenship becomes an important means of ranking, with citizens inevitably enjoying higher status (Riesenberg 1992; Shklar 1991). In such societies, membership per se assumes a special significance. Moreover, it is to guarantee equal citizenship to minorities, especially cultural minorities, that liberal theorists urge the citizens of liberal states to think of citizenship as an abstract status rather than as a set of cultural attributes. For when citizenship is understood as membership in culturally defined national and local communities, then members of cultural minorities find that acceptance as equal citizens may require assimilation to the majority's practices and erosion of the distinctiveness of their preferred ways of life.

Sense of Citizenship. The second element of citizenship is its psychological meaning for the individual citizen, which we shall refer to as "sense of citizenship." Two distinct components contribute to an individual's sense of citizenship: identity and understanding.

"Identity" refers to the affective significance that people attach to their membership in a particular political community (for a more general discussion of identity, see Conover 1984, 1988). The character of a person's sense of citizenship is defined by the interplay between its communal and contractual components. In communal citizenship, the individual's relationship to her political community becomes imbued with psychological meaning through the development of a communal identity, a sense of attachment, and positive affect for the community. Some also develop a sense of communal consciousness, the recognition that others share one's communal identity and that, through this sharing, a civic bond exists that binds members to one another and to the community as a whole (see Barber 1984; Gusfield 1975; Janowitz 1983). "Contractual citizenship", by contrast, involves the individual's psychological relationship to a category or label rather than to a specific community (for a related discussion, see Wolin 1986). People are simply aware of their legal status as citizens of a political entity. Some of them develop a sense of civic identity such that this status acquires additional psychological meaning: the label "citizen" becomes part of their personal identity. Not all people who belong to a political community develop an identity based on that membership. And among those who do, there is considerable variation in its strength.

Two other politically important concepts are typically associated with the development of citizen identities: civic memory and loyalty or patriotism. "Civic memory" refers to the individual's recollection of the "events, characters and developments that make up the history" of one's community (Dagger 1981:729). Civic memory fosters a sense of citizenship by making the political community seem familiar and understandable. "Loyalty," which at the national level has become synonymous with patriotism, is also today automatically associated with nationalism. The meaning of loyalty therefore requires some reconstruction before it can be investigated empirically, perhaps by building on Tocqueville's (1969:234–235) "reflective patriotism," an attachment to shared lands, traditions, and symbols.

"Understanding" is the other component that defines an individual's psychological sense of citizenship. This denotes the framework of beliefs that people develop about their relationship to the political community and to other citizens. Thus, understanding constitutes the cognitive side of a sense of citizenship, while identity comprises the affective side. The legal specification of citizens' rights and duties contributes much to this understanding but by no means defines it. Thus we have found that Americans seem to focus their attention on civil rights like freedom of speech and religion, whereas the British are more likely to emphasize social rights like housing and health care (Conover, Crewe, and Searing 1991).

Understanding also encompasses tolerance and civic virtue. Tolerance is the willingness to endure those whose attitudes, traditions, race, religion, or other attributes differ from one's own. Unlike most of our other key concepts, tolerance has been the focus of considerable empirical research in political science. There is, for instance, a rich survey tradition extending from Stouffer's (1955) work in the 1950s to a great deal of research in the 1980s (Gibson and Bingham 1985; McClosky and Brill 1983; McClosky and Zaller 1984; Sullivan, Piereson, and Marcus 1982). Civic virtue is if anything more difficult to instill than is tolerance, but in the history of democratic theory it is no less important. "Civic virtue" refers to the willingness to subordinate one's personal interests to the public good; it suggests a public-minded spirit that checks egoism by inspiring people to consider placing the welfare of their community ahead of their own (see Burtt 1993; Dagger 1981; Diggins 1984; Gill 1987; Landy and McWilliams 1985; Murphy 1983).

Practice. The final element of citizenship is "practice," the behaviors that people engage in as part of their public lives. The practice of citizenship encompasses two broad categories of behavior: political participation and civic activity. "Political participation" refers to "acts that aim at influencing the government, either by affecting the choice of government personnel or by affecting the choices made by government personnel" (Verba and Nie 1972:2). It encompasses the performance of instrumental political acts (e.g., voting, signing a petition, marching in protest) as well as participation in political organizations (e.g., political parties, interest groups) that directly engage in efforts to influence public policy. This, the electoral side of citizenship, has been investigated very thoroughly and remains the predominant concern of research in political psychology and political behavior.

By contrast, civic activity has received far less attention from political scientists, but it nonetheless has very important implications for individual citizens and for regimes. Many political philosophers believe that its significance is at least as great as that of the electoral side. "Civic activity" encompasses a variety of practices, including civility, military service, civic engagement, public discourse, and participation in civic rituals. Such activities define the fundamental nature of civil society: they shape the kinds of political communities that we live in and the quality of life that they inspire (Janowitz 1983; Putnam 1993; Rosenblum 1998; Verba et al. 1995; Walzer 1976, 1992).

Civility encompasses both obedience to the law and the disposition to respect the informal social norms that govern interactions among people, and particularly with strangers. Civility is essential to democratic societies, for when it deteriorates, governments are compelled to pass increasing numbers of laws that bring the state into the business of regulating everyday life (Carter 1998; Janowitz 1983).

Military service and civic engagement are both forms of public service broadly understood. Military service is one of the most agreed-upon and also one of the most demanding tests of the obligations of citizens. "Civic engagement" refers to involvement in social networks, in the groups, organizations, and voluntary associations that connect citizens with the life of their communities. Such voluntary public service is at the heart of communal visions of citizenship, for volunteerism is regarded as one of the principal means of exercising civic virtue and enhancing self-development (Barber 1984; Rosenblum 1998; Sullivan 1986). Robert Putnam (1993) has demonstrated its powerful effects on the propensity to engage in both electoral and civil activities. And there is evidence that many of these same effects are associated with the discussion of public affairs, of topics ranging from party-political issues to community concerns, to discussions that occur in private as well as public settings, to discussions that range from casual conversations to serious deliberations (Conover, Crewe, and Searing 1992). Civic rituals have not been investigated much at all. And indeed, many of the citizens in the American and British communities we have been studying complain about their decline, for they believe that this decline is not just a marker of the withdrawal from civil society, but also a factor that contributes to it.

Membership, a sense of citizenship, and practice – these, the principal elements of citizenship, encompass a wide range of politically significant topics that invite study by students of political psychology. Such topics are at the political center of the intellectual debates of our era. And we believe that they can best be examined empirically by supplementing our established survey and experimental methods with some of the qualitative, case-oriented methodologies that are usually associated with contextual analysis.

CONTEXTUAL EXPLANATION

In pursuing our own research program on these topics, we have been increasingly impressed with the utility of a viewpoint that has been articulated best by cultural psychologists like Richard Schweder (1991:Chapter 2), who begin with the fundamental presumption that there are no context-free thinking processes and that the content of thinking, including political thinking, is therefore best studied in the cultural and political contexts of meaning in which it occurs. If there are no context-free thinking processes, then there are no social vacuums in which, as microeconomists claim, we can theorize about thinking, or as we ourselves used to assume, discover universal laws of political behavior. The patterns and regularities that we investigate are not universal because they are constructed by particular citizens thinking and behaving in particular times and places, thinking particular thoughts, and applying particular decision rules (Fay 1994:100). When taken seriously, this search for persistent regularities as opposed to universal laws enriches our theories and explanations by highlighting the importance of meaning and context. To construct convincing explanations of the political thinking of particular citizens, then, it is necessary to study *their* concepts carefully, to listen to *their* language, and to take account of the contexts of meaning in which they are doing what we wish to study. And this suggests that we should pay greater attention in political psychology than we have before to political culture, focus groups, and, perhaps surprisingly, to macro-level variables.

Rethinking Political Culture

For political psychology, the study of political culture is not an option – it is a necessity. For without the study of political culture, political thinking and behavior cannot be explained satisfactorily. Such explanations are, at their core, interpretive, because they require that the explanatory desires and beliefs of the subjects be understood as the subjects themselves understand them. To understand how the subjects themselves understand them, we need to study the relevant vocabulary and language of their political culture. The concept of political culture has long been associated with the subfield of comparative politics, where, from our perspective, it has been misconceived, and from which it needs to be rescued and restructured. In comparative politics, political culture has been mismeasured to build universal taxonomies and misconstrued as a set of explanatory variables for predicting-explaining political behavior.

The roots of both misconceptions can be seen in the anthropological-sociological definitions of the general term "culture," from which the "political culture" concept was drawn. It was Kroeber's theory of culture patterns, and his work with Kluckhohn, that had the greatest influence on the emergence of the concept of political culture in comparative politics. The essence of culture in this view is psychological: systems of ideas, values, and norms, which are distinguished from and partitioned off from the behavior that they may condition. This is more or less the basis of the definition of political culture that was developed in comparative politics: "The political culture of a society consists of the system of empirical beliefs, expressive symbols and values which define the situation in which political action takes place" (Verba 1965:515). Although it was believed at the time to be a great advantage to have linked this political concept to the study of culture in anthropology and sociology (Verba 1965:515), this was, in retrospect, the source of our taxonomic and explanatory misconceptions.

An important feature of these anthropological culture and personality studies was their search for global culture and personality traits that could be measured uniformly and used to construct global inventories (Schweder 1991:Chapter 1). The political culture concept was created with these kinds of taxonomic goals in mind. At the same time, the development of a reliable quantitative methodology for survey research seemed to make it all possible. This was the era of Parsonian structural-functional analysis when taxonomy and "theory" were confounded in images of periodic tables of the basic political elements. We would create a universalistic inventory of concepts for the construction of cross-national data sets that could be used to investigate the general laws of political behavior.

These were the goals that led us to develop theoretically defined, standardized concepts and measures with which to study attitudes cross-nationally. Thus, in *The Civic Culture*, Almond and Verba (1963) constructed measures of theoretically defined concepts that were drawn from the work of Weber and Parsons (e.g., parochial, subject, and participant orientations) to describe and compare the views of citizens in five different countries with five different institutional and cultural contexts. More recently, Inglehart (1990) constructed and applied, across a still larger number of countries, a set of standardized measures of postmaterialist values that are inspired by the psychodynamic theories of Abraham Maslow. And much the same approach is currently being pursued in studies of political culture in Eastern Europe and the former Soviet Union, where scales originally developed in the United States have been translated into the languages of the nations where they are to be used (Gibson, Duch, and Tedin 1992; Hahn 1991).

There is among today's comparativists a growing uneasiness about the results of such studies, a feeling that, although they produce important and often path-breaking data where we otherwise would have no data at all, they cannot, in the end, produce the convincing descriptions and explanations that, as scientists, we must seek. They seem peculiarly detached from the worlds of the people they are investigating precisely because they use academically defined concepts and standardized language rather than the concepts and language of the people whose worlds are being investigated. In the natural sciences, advances have often been made by realizing that everyday descriptive categories, like those that citizens use to talk about their citizenship, are impediments to discovering generalizations and need to be replaced by more theoretically standardized terms. But in the social sciences, we must work, at least initially, with the descriptive categories that we find in everyday life, because these concepts are part of the motivational structure of the actors whose behavior we are trying to explain (Fay 1994). Indeed, *they are often the most important part of the explanation*. If we as observers wish to use other concepts for theoretical purposes, including reasons of cross-national comparability, we must somehow relate our role concepts to theirs; otherwise, we may miss the phenomena that are actually doing the explanatory work (Rosenberg 1988).

Again, there is no context-free political thinking. Citizens think about public affairs in the contexts of meaning that are familiar to them and to their associates. Beginning with their concepts and language suggests the desirability of beginning our inquiries with qualitative methods such as focus groups, Q-sorts, and in-depth interviews that will allow us to listen and build what we hear into our measures. It also suggests the desirability of ending our inquiries with some of these same qualitative methods in order to explore more fully, after we have been in the field, the meaning that some of our more complex topics have for our subjects so that we can better interpret their responses to our survey items.

The other fundamental misconception in the original formulation of political culture was to construct it as a variable, or as a set of variables, that would predict-explain or causally explain a wide range of political behavior. These expectations were, in fact, the reason why behavior was deliberately excluded from the concept's definition. Political culture was important because it would in some sense be used to explain behaviors like political participation, discussion, influence, and conduct in institutions (Verba 1965:514–17). It was that "in some sense" that caused the difficulty, because at the same time that the subfield of comparative politics was taking political culture on board, it was learning new rules of navigation with which to chart its course in the search for universal laws. The first and most consequential of these rules was to treat explanation as prediction. For political culture, this was a setup for a fall.

Particular behaviors are usually best predicted by the specific desires and beliefs that are associated with them – not by the general cultural concepts and variables in which these desires and beliefs are embedded and that give them meaning. This was emphasized early on by Sidney Verba (1965:518) in the most thoughtful and influential essay on the subject. But it wasn't emphasized enough. Let us say, for example, that the specific act of electoral turnout can be predicted by the interactions between two particular desires and two particular beliefs with which it is intertwined: the desire to influence the outcome of the election and the desire to do one's duty as a citizen, and the belief that voting will influence this outcome and the belief that voting will fulfill this duty. Now, in the context of contemporary American politics, these desires and beliefs cannot be properly understood without understanding something about the rights-oriented citizen identities, and perhaps also the liberal individualism, of the people who hold them. Indeed, it is this understanding that provides the explanatory account of *why* the interactions between these particular desires and beliefs predict the dependent variable of electoral turnout. It may be the case that to predict electoral turnout we would add nothing at all by adding to the model additional variables that measured those citizen identities or that liberal individualism. To predict in this case, there may be nothing at all about the political culture background that we need to know.

In fact, the political culture approach was eventually discredited in comparative politics because, it was said, the attitudes that it contained were too general and diffusely formulated to provide good explanations (sic) of political behavior (Rogowski 1976). This depreciation of political culture was, however, based on a wholly inappropriate test: its potential contribution to the *prediction* of specific acts of political behavior. To be fair, many researchers who study political culture accept this test – and find themselves hoisted on their own petards (Almond 1980:26; Inglehart 1988). Yet there is no reason to believe that political culture could or should generate many predictions at the micro level of particular acts of political behavior. That is not its principal utility – and its dismissal on these grounds is as unwarranted as it is unwelcome, for this negative experience has made us wary of bringing the concept of political culture into the center of the study of political psychology. The principal utility of political culture is instead to help us understand the interactions among more specific beliefs and behaviors. And, in the social sciences, such accounts are critical to constructing convincing causal explanations (Fay 1994:106).

The utility that political culture offers the study of political psychology is its provision of interpretative contexts of meaning and political significance. Thus, the study of political culture has far more to do with the contextual study of political thinking than with explanations of particular political actions, however much such explanations may rely on the contextual information that it provides. Political culture is basic because there is no context-free political thinking – and because unless we investigate political thinking in the political contexts that give it meaning, our micro analyses are threatened by a myopia that misses much of the political relevance of the topics that we study.

This view is consistent with Verba's (1965:518) original suggestion that political culture should be defined quite generally to focus on the basic categories and values that structure our political thinking. That is why political identities, which are organizing and motivating principles for much of our thinking about citizenship, have from the beginning of political culture research been recognized as central to the subject (Verba 1965:519). The character and salience of political identities have a great deal to do with how we conceive of ourselves as citizens, with how we understand our relationships to public life, to other citizens, and to governmental authority. Political identities have been said to be as fundamental to our experience as are our beliefs about the nature of physical reality (Verba 1965:519). And their investigation is, first and foremost, a study of meaning: a qualitative as well as quantitative investigation of the meaning of such identities to the subjects involved. Thus, it was through our preliminary work with focus groups that we discovered that many Americans tend to merge their national identity with their identity as citizens into a single identity or self-schema that emphasizes liberal rights more than duties, whereas many Britons distinguish in their minds between a comparatively communitarian schema of national identity and a comparatively liberal understanding of citizenship (Conover et al. 1991:821–23).

Focus Groups

As political psychologists, we are well advised to resist the temptation to speak for citizens; whenever possible, we should try instead to use methods that allow citizens to speak for themselves. Thus, our interest in focus group methodology began with the classroom exercises that we conducted, at the very beginning of our study, in junior and senior high schools. Our aim was to get a sense of how students conceptualized (or didn't) the topics that we wished to investigate, topics that had thus far been defined largely by philosophical and political literatures. We read aloud our questions and concepts and asked the students to write out their responses and definitions. Then, as a matter of politeness to their teachers, we led general discussions on these topics before heading home to study the written materials. As it turned out, we unexpectedly learned much more from the general discussions than from the written materials, so much more that we began to look into the methodology of focus groups and decided to try to formulate the questions for the surveys that we were planning by making citizens themselves participants in the research process, much as they are already participants in citizenship's ongoing public dialogues.

Focus group discussions are planned group conversations that are tape-recorded and in some cases video-taped as well (Just et al. 1996; Krueger 1988; Morgan 1997, 1998). They are particularly useful in the context of discovery and are therefore valuable supplements to survey interviews. The "mildly-directive" nature of focus groups offers an opportunity to listen to citizen's discussions about citizenship, to listen to the sorts of exchanges through which political meaning is constructed and disseminated in democracies (Barber 1984; Gamson 1992:192; Just et al. 1996). Equally important, focus groups are fertile sources of new hypotheses about the mechanisms through which the participants' sense of citizenship has been formed. These results are created mainly by the group character of the discussion: participants talk with one another about their experiences in their communities, and talk in their own language rather than simply reacting to the questions and language of an interviewer in a one-on-one situation (compare Zaller and Feldman 1992). Focus groups also provide the opportunity for group influence and, in so doing, offer further insights into the social context within which citizenship is typically experienced (Krueger 1988; Morgan 1998).

We conducted one set of discussions at the beginning of our study's data collection phase to facilitate our subsequent questionnaire design. These involved nineteen different groups of students and parents in seven different communities in the United States and Great Britain. A second set of discussions was conducted at the end of the data collection process to facilitate interpretations of our respondents' reactions to some of the key concepts in our surveys. These involved thirteen different groups of adults in the American and British communities where we had conducted our research. Most groups had, besides the moderator, eight participants. The groups were stratified for different research tasks by combinations of the following selection criteria: residence (urban vs. rural), gender, age, familiarity (strangers, acquaintances, friends), and length of time in the community. The moderator asked each focus group approximately a dozen questions accompanied by specific probes. Some of these questions presented hypothetical problems to be solved, while the remainder were more abstract inquiries about topics related to citizenship. The discussions lasted for one and a half to two hours, with a short break in the middle for refreshments (which facilitated conversation by making the exercise more of a friendly social occasion than it might otherwise have been).

These discussions each produced an average of thirty to forty-five pages of transcribed text, which were analyzed in three stages. First, the transcript was read through in order to identify descriptive and inferential codes for classifying the concepts and themes in participants' statements. The aim was to allow the language and concepts of the participants to guide, as much as possible, the development of the coding scheme – to let the "voices" of citizens emerge. Next, the transcript was reread to code each statement according to the scheme developed on the basis of the first reading. Various software programs are available to organize this process to enable the researcher to recover efficiently statements on particular topics made by people with particular characteristics. Finally, the coded statements were subjected to a pattern analysis to identify common themes in the understanding of concepts and relationships among concepts (see Strauss 1987, and Miles and Huberman 1984 for discussions of the development of coding schemes for qualitative data analysis).

There are, of course, drawbacks to this kind of qualitative research. The principal problem is that the participants are not representative of any particular population, and therefore the results are not generalizable in a statistical sense. Still, the purpose of the exercise has more to do with discovery than with verification, and particularly with clarifying language and meaning, with discovering insights and clues that can bring us closer to the citizens' experiences that we are trying to explain. The most useful focus groups work much like a successful "mildly directive" seminar: beyond introducing questions and interjecting occasional probes, the leader fades into the background as the participants become animated and begin to talk with one another directly.

Other problems arise from social desirability effects and structural effects of the focus group's seminar-like format, which inject elements of artificiality into the discussions. William Gamson's (1992:193) alternative format of peer group conversations avoids this problem in part by removing the researcher from the group and by constituting more natural groups of friends. But without guidance from the researcher, much of the talk strays into irrelevant topics, and one or several participants may dominate the discussions, while others never put forward their views at all. Moreover, there is much to be learned from listening to people react to one another's views when these people are *not* friends, perhaps not even acquaintances, when they are simply citizens from different backgrounds who have been brought together for particular theoretical reasons. Structuring the composition of the groups is one of the few semiexperimental controls that the researcher possesses. It is also true that the open-ended, discursive nature of these discussions makes coding and analysis difficult. Nonetheless, if we are seriously to understand how people in liberal polities think about citizenship, it seems desirable to begin by listening to how they talk about it, and to analyze the language that they themselves use. By allowing them to articulate their own sense of citizenship in their own words, we allow ourselves to tailor our more quantitative methods of study to their understandings – a first exploratory step for designing questionnaires and a last interpretive step for explaining the results.

Expanding the Envelope

Let us now move from these microworlds of meaning to the macrocontexts within which they are constructed.

Microexplanations in Macrocontexts

Cross-national studies of political psychology and behavior have taken their cues more from the subfield of political behavior than from the subfield of comparative politics; for one of the defining features of comparative politics is its concentration on explaining *macro*phenomena that are politically, historically, and culturally important, phenomena like the creation of the European Union or transitions to democracy in Latin America. Political psychology and behavior have never quite fit in.

Thus, when we think of classic research in comparative politics, we think of studies that concentrate on macro-units like party systems, religious cleavages, or revolutions. This is because comparative politics has taken its lead from sociologists like Marx, Weber, Durkheim, Barrington Moore, and Theda Skocpol, who construct grand theories about the impact of macroindependent variables on macrodependent variables. What gets left out is precisely what interests us most: convincing accounts of the political behavior involved – accounts of how, for instance, particular economic or political conditions structure the learning of attitudes that shape the actions of individuals that trigger the change in the macrodependent variable (Taylor 1989).

Comparative political psychology investigates these microlevel stepping stones. But once the study of political psychology moves into this comparative world, the case for adding qualitative and historical analysis to its strategies of inquiry becomes compelling, since qualitative case-oriented studies are, for good reason, the dominant tradition in comparative politics. The good reason is that they provide the most convincing explanations of important political phenomena – not of revolutions in general, but of the Russian Revolution; not of political participation in general, but of political participation in Britain (Parry, Moyser, and Day 1992); not of civic behavior in general, but of civic behavior in Italy (Putnam 1993).

This is no small virtue because, lacking genuine laws from which to derive our explanations, the general models that we construct typically do not turn out to be very powerful explanations of any important political phenomena "in particular." However valuable such general models may be in guiding and informing our explanations, they usually do not themselves explain important political phenomena convincingly – for there is no such thing as context-free political thinking and behavior. Hence, qualitative, case-oriented, macro-level studies are valued in comparative politics because they are sensitive to the fact that, in different times and places, different combinations of conditions can produce the same outcome, and because they regularly produce more convincing explanations of important political phenomena than do variable-oriented studies of larger numbers of cases (see Ragin 1987). But how can comparative political psychology and behavior (a variable-oriented enterprise) be fitted into this case-oriented tradition?

The linkages between interpretive microexplanations and causal macroexplanations are poorly understood and rarely studied systematically. Braybrooke (1987:31–2) characterizes them as connections between "person facts," on the one hand, and "group facts," on the other, and argues that the two go hand in hand since each raises causal questions that can only be answered by the other. Our micromodels of political thinking constitute person facts whose causal and political significance lies, in large part, in the institutional and systemic contexts through which our subjects learn to interpret the world as they do. Thus, it is through their experiences and relationships in institutions like families, schools, media, and voluntary associations that people learn the concepts that constitute their citizen identities. And if these institutions emphasize rights more than duties, for instance, or deference more than participation, this in turn is a consequence of the cultural and constitutional traditions, and perhaps also of the demographic and social structural constraints, by which the institutions have been shaped.

Contextual explanations are, then, causal explanations for interpretive explanations in that they seek to provide an account of how a set of independent contextual variables affects the learning of concepts, schemas, or ideologies. They address the question of why particular people in particular times and places tend to have the political understandings that they do. The goal here is not so much to explain political behavior as it is to explain political thinking, indeed to explain our experience as citizens in contemporary liberal states. And this explanation can best be achieved by putting political thinking in context. Earlier we made the case for analyzing (at the micro level) political thinking in the conceptual contexts of its political culture. Now we want to make the case for analyzing it (at the macro level) in social contexts. It is not enough to know, for instance, that citizens in one sort of community are more tolerant than citizens in another. We want to know why they are more tolerant so that we can better understand the constraints on tolerance and the means by which it might most effectively be promoted. The answers to such "why" questions lie in the institutional and systemic contexts through which our subjects learn to interpret the world as they do. It is in the links between micromodels and their macroinstitutional and systemic origins that the political significance of political thinking is to be found.

The actions of individuals are the pivots of most political explanations. The desires and beliefs of individuals explain these actions. And the concepts, schemas, or ideologies within which the desires and beliefs are constructed are essential parts of those explanations. We need to consider the impact of contextual variables on these patterns of political thinking because the explanation of why particular people in particular times and places hold particular attitudes is essential to understanding the politics of these particular times and places. It would not do, for example, to explain Auschwitz by studying only the attitudes of the Nazis involved without inquiring further into the institutional contexts in which their attitudes were formed and also into the more important cultural, political, economic, or social conditions that shaped this learning (Staub 1989).

The type of explanation that we need is captured in Appleby's (1992:332) powerful metaphor "the taproots of human thought," which she uses to suggest what is missing in the approaches of some of the new ideological historians who act as though there is nothing to explain beyond interpretive explanations of systems or symbols; they neglect, according to Appleby, important political, economic, and social factors that help explain why particular types of political thinking are characteristic of particular times and places. The principal taproots are the institutions through which society passes on established patterns of thinking and teaches new ones.

We may never explain in fully satisfactory accounts how or why anyone holds a particular desire or belief. Most political attitudes are learned incrementally, over considerable periods of time, in a wide variety of formal and informal settings and through happenstance as much as formal teaching. Nonetheless, we can learn a great deal from studying political learning in institutions, because institutions are the principal connections between human thought and the social, economic, and political contexts that constrain and condition it. Institutions are the main contexts within which information is transmitted. Institutional learning connects the thinking of the individual citizen with the experience of the collectivity.

Political culture shapes this institutional learning in two ways. First, as a macrocontextual factor, that is to say alongside political, economic, and social factors, culture helps explain why particular institutions are structured in particular ways – why, for instance, American families and schools are organized more democratically than British families and schools. Then, as a microphenomenon, culture constitutes much of the content of that institutional learning. Political culture defines the contexts of citizen identities and the contexts of citizen choices because it frames the construction of those identities and choices. It serves as a frame of reference for the perception, interpretation, evaluation and storage of information.

Thus, the explanation of institutional learning requires: (1) accounts of why particular institutions are teaching particular information at particular places and times – causal historical-contextual explanations in terms of cultural, political, economic, and social factors; (2) interpretive explanations of the information that is being taught, of desires, beliefs, concepts, schemas, and ideological paradigms; and (3) models of some of the principal learning processes through which these attitudes are being shaped in these institutions.

Macrolevel causal explanations treat the institutions as the units of analysis and ask why they are structured as they are and why they teach what they do. As we move our research enterprise within these institutions, however, we address microlevel puzzles through interviews with individuals, through survey instruments, focus groups and depth interviews. We move, in other words, from case-oriented studies to variable-oriented studies in order to describe and explain the political learning, thinking, and behavior of individual citizens.

This is what needs to be done in the study of institutional learning. Here we will be using quantitative methodology not to test general models, but instead to identify the institutional contexts in which key attitudes are learned, and to identify particular learning situations and processes that are involved, with special attention to processes that can, from the perspective of amelioration, be changed to modify the content of what is being taught. For learning the attitudes of citizenship, the principal institutional contexts are likely to include (1) family, (2) school, (3) media, (4) voluntary associations, and (5) civic rituals. And within the contexts of these institutions we need to identify, first, the characteristic situations and relationships through which learning occurs and, second, the characteristic learning processes that are involved in the formation and change of attitudes. Fortunately, social psychologists have a cupboard full of models of attitude development and change that can facilitate sorting out particular learning processes in particular institutions. These models are organized into four "families" (Eagly and Chaiken 1993:671–2): (1) simple affective processes (e.g., classical conditioning); (2) persuasion (e.g., social judgment theory); (3) impact of behavior (e.g., dissonance theory); and (4) social influence (e.g., conformity research).

A Comparative Method for Political Psychology

Thus, the political relevance of micro variables can only be understood in their macro contexts. And macro case-study work at both community and national levels takes its cues from the comparative method. The "comparative method" refers to techniques in comparative politics derived from John Stuart Mill's method of agreement and indirect method of difference (Ragin 1987:11–16). These are logical procedures for comparing configurations of explanatory variables in different cases in order to assess causes. Mill offered the comparative method as a quasi-experimental method for testing hypotheses in nonexperimental research. It is attractive to social scientists because we regard experimental designs as the ideal research strategies. They allow investigators to test for causality by comparing an experimental group, which receives a particular treatment, to a control group, which does not.

Some of the comparative method's advocates in comparative politics would like to think that, by following its rules, careful cross-national case selection can create the promised quasi-experimental conditions that permit quasi-testing of hypotheses about causal relationships. This would be done by selecting cases for comparison that are very similar except that one has experienced a particular event or institution, while the other has not. In fact, in comparative politics, the comparative method is rather hopeless as a convincing methodology for testing causal relationships – almost hopeless at the community level and absolutely hopeless at the national level.

Three difficulties in comparative politics render the comparative method deficient as a serious exercise in verification, and a fourth difficulty suggests its alternative uses and true utility: (1) Comparable control variables: it is difficult to find control variables that are genuinely equivalent across communities and truly unusual to find such variables that are genuinely equivalent cross-nationally. (2) Other variables: there are usually many important additional variables that should be controlled but cannot be controlled because we are in the field rather than the laboratory. (3) Indefinite universe of cases: experimental testing requires data on all relevant cases; but in comparative politics we are typically unclear about the relevant universe of cases – and therefore we cannot know whether our research set is the whole or any sort of sample of the whole. The difficulty is that the addition of a few cases with different results can completely undermine our conclusions about causality in the existing set. This is very serious. We know it is very serious because this is exactly the way that theories rise and fall and rise again in comparative politics until we tire of them and turn to new topics (Geddes 1991). (4) "Multiple conjunctural causation": this is the difficulty that turns the comparative method on its head (Ragin 1987:20–6).

Ragin's notion of multiple conjunctural causation draws attention to indeterminacy at the macro level. The point is that similar outcomes (e.g., contractual or communal citizen identities) can be caused in different times and places by different combinations of conditions.[2] Multiple conjunctural causation's claim is not that each outcome is caused by a unique set of conditions, but rather that various, and sometimes quite different, combinations of conditions seem able to produce what most of us would regard as similar outcomes. Interaction effects that differ across cases create a situation in which apparently different conditions have the same effects and apparently similar conditions have different effects – depending on the national or community context in which they are operating (Ragin 1987:48–9). Multiple conjunctural causation finishes off the comparative method as a method of verification, but it also leads to reconsideration of its utility in a different scientific context – the context of discovery. In the context of discovery, the comparative method functions as a logic with which to guide the selection and comparison of cases for purposes of constructing descriptions and explanations. The comparative method provides rules of thumb that can make "soaking and poking" in political psychology far more systematic and productive than it might otherwise be.

The context of discovery is a context of creativity. And the comparative method's systematic selection and comparison of cases can (1) sharpen the focus of our descriptions; (2) alert us to potential causes and combinations of causes that will improve the power of our explanations; and (3) suggest, on the basis of these explanations, general models that fit similar circumstances in other times and places (Ragin 1987:45–9). To illustrate how the comparative method can be used as a set of rules of thumb in the context of discovery, let us consider once again our own research program. Following the comparative method's logic, we have at the national level constructed a "similar nation" design – a design that compares similar cases (the United States and Great Britain) that have different outcomes (contractual and communal citizen identities). By comparing these similar cases that have different outcomes, the design facilitates description of the contrasting citizen identities (by suggesting what each is not) and, more effectively still, facilitates the construction of explanations for them by directing our search, in the first instance, beyond similar potentially causal conditions (e.g., electoral and economic systems) to different potentially causal conditions (e.g., political cultures and constitutional traditions).

Likewise, at the community level we have followed the comparative method in constructing a "different community" design – a design that compares different cases (suburban, urban, and rural communities in each

2 For a clear example, see Barnum and Sullivan's (1990) account of how quite different processes within the American and British constitutional traditions have promoted the learning of similar attitudes toward tolerance.

nation) that have similar outcomes (e.g., modest variations in common citizen identities). Within each nation we are, of course, comparing communities that are more similar than are the nations themselves. What makes these communities different are the conditions of urbanization, social structure, and mobility. Comparisons across these communities are helping us to describe the character of citizen identities by drawing attention to distinctions that are more subtle than the distinctions across nations. But they are also helping us to explain the character of these similar outcomes by focusing our attention on the independent contextual variables that the communities share despite their obvious structural differences. And this exercise, like the most similar nations design, at the same time suggests patterns and regularities that provide the basis for more general models with wider applications.

This design for our case selection and for "soaking and poking" looks like a typical quasi-experimental design. The difference is that we are not using it for vigorous hypothesis testing. Nonetheless, in the context of discovery, the same logic of comparison draws our attention to descriptive categories and characteristics, and to potential causal variables, that we would not otherwise have noticed or interpreted in the same way without the comparison. Such a systematic focusing of attention does not, however, bring us to the end of the exercise but rather to the beginning: the comparative method produces a geological map that suggests where to dig. For each key descriptive feature and for each putative cause, it is then up to the investigators to build a convincing case by combining qualitative case-oriented analyses at the macro level with quantitative variable-oriented analyses at the micro level.

COMPARATIVE POLITICAL PSYCHOLOGY AS A POLICY SCIENCE

Citizenship has become the key political topic of our times, a central concern for contemporary philosophers, politicians, and citizens. To understand how we can contribute to contemporary dialogues about citizenship, we must first recognize that the most fundamental questions in such dialogues are questions for political psychology: the autonomy and embeddedness of citizen identities and, more generally, the principal motivations, beliefs, and behaviors that constitute the practices of citizenship (see Elster 1993; Rosenberg 1988). As political psychologists, our contribution is to describe these phenomena, explain the relationships among them, and investigate the mechanisms through which they are learned and modified.

Indeed, contributions from political psychologists are essential. These contributions begin with research on the views of citizens, for it is only by articulating, probing, and publicizing their views that we can help philosophers think about the empirical assumptions and contextual constraints that bound prescriptions. How much political participation, for example, is it realistic to expect? Similarly, it is only by explaining the mechanisms that structure citizens' political learning that we can help politicians identify key educational and institutional levers for reform. What types of community service, for instance, best teach sensitivity to the interests of other citizens?

To think clearly what kind of citizenship ought to exist and how best to achieve it, we need to know first what actually does exist. In short, we need to know a great deal more than we do at present about how citizens themselves understand their conduct as citizens and about the causal mechanisms that connect this practice to its contexts. The mechanisms are critical, for they lead us to look beyond political psychology to the systemic and institutional contexts that both structure these learning mechanisms and are restructured by their effects. These are the pathways that connect political psychology to matters of political relevance and to the broad concerns of philosophers, politicians, and citizens.

Whether in the context of verification or in the context of discovery, political psychology is best understood as a comparative enterprise. And research in comparative political psychology is done most effectively when it melds variable-oriented investigations of political behavior at the micro-level with case-oriented explanations of this behavior at the macro-level, that is to say, with contextual studies of institutions, communities, and nations. Yet this contextual description and explanation is itself done most effectively when it concentrates on small numbers of cases, or on single cases analyzed from comparative viewpoints (e.g., Converse and Pierce 1986; Parry et al. 1992; Putnam 1993). If our principal aim is not to chase after chimerical universal laws but rather to explain important political phenomena convincingly, then it is undesirable to increase the number of cases automatically, because there is little to be gained and much to be lost by doing so. The larger the number of cases, the more the qualitative case-oriented work gets squeezed out of the quantitative variable-oriented investigations. And this degrades significantly the quality of descriptions, the power of explanations, and the utility of both for normative recommendations.

Furthermore, we need not restrict ourselves to the roles of analysts and advisors who facilitate dialogues about citizenship but do not participate in them. It is perfectly appropriate, as political psychologists, for us to seek to shape the ongoing dialogues about such problems by using our own normative judgments to structure systematically the conduct of our inquiries. Thus, in defining political relevance, identifying problems for study, formulating concepts, and even selecting data, we may follow the priorities of contemporary philosophers, politicians, citizens, or professional colleagues – or we may follow our own. It is perfectly appropriate for social scientists, as social scientists, to focus their research on particular models of democracy that they think deserve attention, to formulate concepts so as to emphasize aspects of these models that they believe have been neglected, or to treat data in a way that brings out the views of particular groups that they feel need attention (Braybrooke 1987).

From this viewpoint, it is important to recognize that, although the study of citizenship cannot be value free, it can be free of bias. Even where, for instance, we characterize racial or religious minorities as disadvantaged and seek to see things from their point of view, our research need not be error laden, nor need we buy into misperceptions in description or into attributing unwarranted validity to generalizations. Confusion about these matters arises from the muddled thinking that confounds value judgments in research with bias and blurs the distinction between cases where values actually do lead to distortions in results and cases where value judgments are made without such distortions (Searing 1970). There is, of course, a relationship between how passionately we pursue political causes through our research and the likelihood that errors favoring our most passionate concerns will occur. But the difficulty lies more with the excessive passion than with the normative judgments. Thus, without checking their values at the door, political psychologists can join philosophers, politicians, and citizens in addressing some of the most fundamental questions of our era and forging new conceptions of citizenship.

References

Ackerman, Bruce. 1980. *Social Justice in the Liberal State*. New Haven, CT: Yale University Press.

Almond, Gabriel. 1980. "The Intellectual History of the Political Culture Concept." In Gabriel Almond and Sidney Verba, eds., *The Civic Culture Revisited*. Boston: Little, Brown.

Almond, Gabriel, and Sidney Verba. 1963. *The Civic Culture*. Princeton, NJ: Princeton University Press.

Appleby, Joyce. 1992. *Liberalism and Republicanism in the Historical Imagination*. Cambridge, MA: Harvard University Press.

Barber, Benjamin. 1984. *Strong Democracy: Participatory Politics for a New Age*. Berkeley: University of California Press.

Barnum, David G., and John L. Sullivan. 1990. "The Elusive Foundations of Political Freedom in Britain and the United States." *Journal of Politics* 52:719–39.

Braybrooke, David. 1987. *Philosophy of Social Science.* Englewood Cliffs, NJ: Prentice-Hall.

Burtt, Shelley. 1993. "The Politics of Virtue Today: A Critique and a Proposal." *American Political Science Review* 87:360–88.

Carter, Stephen L. 1998. *Civility: Manners, Morals and the Etiquette of Democracy.* New York: Basic Books.

Conover, Pamela Johnston. 1984. "The Influence of Group Identifications on Political Perception and Evaluation." *Journal of Politics* 46:760–85.

1988. "The Role of Social Groups in Political Thinking." *British Journal of Political Science* 18:51–76.

Conover, Pamela Johnston, Ivor M. Crewe, and Donald D. Searing. 1991. "The Nature of Citizenship in the United States and Great Britain: Empirical Comments on Theoretical Themes." *Journal of Politics* 53:800–32.

1992. "Does Democratic Discussion Make Better Citizens?" Paper presented at the annual meeting of the American Political Science Association, Chicago, September 3–6.

Converse, Philip E., and Roy Pierce. 1986. *Political Representation in France.* Cambridge, MA: Harvard University Press.

Daggar, Richard. 1981. "Metropolis, Memory, and Citizenship." *American Journal of Political Science* 25:715–37.

Diggins, John P. 1984. *The Lost Soul of American Politics: Virtue, Self-Interest, and the Foundations of Liberalism.* Chicago: University of Chicago Press.

Dryzek, John S., and Jeffrey Berejikian. 1993. "Reconstructive Democratic Theory." *American Political Science Review* 87:48–61.

Eagly, Alice H., and Shelly Chaiken. 1993. *The Psychology of Attitudes.* New York: Harcourt Brace Jovanovich.

Elster, Jon. 1993. *Political Psychology.* New York: Cambridge University Press.

Fay, Brian. 1994. "General Laws and Explaining Human Behavior." In Michael Martin and Lee C. McIntyre, eds., *Readings in the Philosophy of Social Science.* Cambridge, MA: MIT Press.

Fierlbeck, Katherine. 1991. "Redefining Responsibility: The Politics of Citizenship in the United Kingdom." *Canadian Journal of Political Science* 24:575–93.

Gamson, William A. 1992. *Talking Politics.* Cambridge: Cambridge University Press.

Geddes, Barbara. 1991. "Paradigms and Sand Castles in the Comparative Politics of Developing Areas." In William Crotty, ed., *Political Science: Looking to the Future,* vol. 2, *Comparative Politics, Policy and International Relations.* Evanston, IL: Northwestern University Press.

Gibson, James L., and Richard D. Bingham. 1985. *Civil Liberties and Nazis: The Skokie Free Speech Controversy.* New York: Praeger.

Gibson, James L., Raymond M. Duch, and Kent L. Tedin. 1992. "Democratic Values and the Transformation of the Soviet Union." *Journal of Politics* 54:329–71.

Gill, Emily R. 1987. "Virtue, Commerce, and Liberty: Or, Civic Republicanism, the Moral Sentiments, and Publius." Paper presented at the annual meeting of the Midwest Political Science Association, Chicago, April 21–4.

Gusfield, Joseph R. 1975. *Community: A Critical Response.* New York: Harper & Row.

Hahn, Jeffrey. 1991. "Continuity and Change in Russian Political Culture." *British Journal of Political Science* 21:393–421.

Hall, Stuart, and David Held. 1989. "Left and Rights." *Marxism Today* 16–23.

Heater, Derek. 1990. *Citizenship: The Civic Ideal in World History, Politics and Education*. New York: Longman.

Hood, Stuart. 1988. "The Couthy Feeling." *New Statesman and Society*, Aug. 12, pp. 29–31.

Howard, John A. 1984. "Reopening the Books on Ethics: The Role of Education in a Free Society." *American Education* 20:6–11.

Inglehart, Ronald. 1988. "The Renaissance of Political Culture." *American Political Science Review* 82:1203–30.

1990. *Culture Shift in Advanced Industrial Society*. Princeton, NJ: Princeton University Press.

Janowitz, Morris. 1983. *The Reconstruction of Patriotism: Education for Civic Consciousness*. Chicago: University of Chicago Press.

Just, Marion R., Ann N. Cigler, Dean E. Alger, Timothy E. Cook, Montague Kern, and Darrell A. West. 1996. *Crosstalk: Citizens, Candidates and the Media in a Presidential Campaign*. Chicago: University of Chicago Press.

Kreuger, Richard A. 1988. *Focus Groups: A Practical Guide for Applied Research*. Beverly Hills, CA: Sage.

Landy, Marc, and Wilson Carey McWilliams. 1985. "Civic Education in an Uncivil Culture." *Society* 22:52–5.

McClosky, Herbert, and Alida Brill. 1983. *Dimensions of Tolerance: What Americans Believe about Civil Liberties*. New York: Russell Sage Foundation.

McClosky, Herbert, and John Zaller. 1984. *The American Ethos: Public Attitudes toward Capitalism and Democracy*. Cambridge, MA: Harvard University Press.

Miles, Matthew B., and A. Michael Huberman. 1984. *Qualitative Data Analysis: A Sourcebook of Methods*. Beverly Hills, CA: Sage.

Morgan, David L. 1997. *Focus Groups as Qualitative Research*, 2nd ed. Beverly Hills, CA: Sage.

1998. *The Focus Group Guidebook*. Beverly Hills, CA: Sage.

Murphy, Paul L. 1983. "The Obligations of American Citizenship: A Historical Perspective." *Journal of Teacher Education* 34:6–10.

Oliver, Dawn. 1991. "Active Citizenship in the 1990's." *Parliamentary Affairs* 44:157–71.

Parry, Geraint, George Moyser, and Neil Day. 1992. *Political Participation and Democracy in Britain*. Cambridge: Cambridge University Press.

Pocock, J. G. A. 1975. *The Machiavellian Moment: Florentine Political Thought and the Atlantic Republican Tradition*. Princeton, NJ: Princeton University Press.

Portis, Edward B. 1985. "Citizenship and Personal Identity." *Polity* 18:457–72.

Putnam, Robert D. 1993. *Making Democracy Work: Civic Traditions in Modern Italy*. Princeton, NJ: Princeton University Press.

Ragin, Charles C. 1987. *The Comparative Method*. Berkeley: University of California Press.

Rawls, John. 1971. *A Theory of Justice*. Cambridge, MA: Harvard University Press.

Riesenberg, Peter. 1992. *Citizenship in the Western Tradition*, Chapel Hill: University of North Carolina Press.

Rogowski, Ronald. 1976. *A Rational Theory of Legitimacy*. Princeton, NJ: Princeton University Press.

Rosenberg, Alexander. 1988. *Philosophy of Social Science*. Oxford: Oxford University Press.

Rosenblum, Nancy. 1998. *The Personal Uses of Pluralism in America*. Princeton, NJ: Princeton University Press.

Schweder, Richard A. 1991. *Thinking Through Cultures: Expeditions in Cultural Psychology*. Cambridge, MA: Harvard University Press.

Searing, Donald D. 1970. "Values in Empirical Research: A Behavioral Response." *American Journal of Political Science* 14:71–104.

Shklar, Judith. 1991. *American Citizenship: The Quest for Inclusion*. Cambridge, MA: Harvard University Press.

Staub, Ervin. 1989. *The Roots of Evil*. New York: Cambridge University Press.

Stouffer, Samuel A. 1955. *Communism, Conformity, and Civil Liberties: A Cross-Section of the Nation Speaks Its Mind*. New York: J Wiley.

Strauss, Anselm L. 1987. *Qualitative Analysis for Social Scientists*. Cambridge: Cambridge University Press.

Sullivan, John L., James Piereson, and George E. Marcus. 1982. *Political Tolerance and American Democracy*. Chicago: University of Chicago Press.

Sullivan, William M. 1986. *Reconstructing Public Philosophy*. Berkeley: University of California Press.

Taylor, Michael. 1989. "Structure, Culture and Action in the Explanation of Social Change." *Politics and Society* 17:115–62.

Theiss-Moore, Elizabeth. 1993. "Conceptualizations of Good Citizenship and Political Participation." *Political Behavior* 15:355–80.

Tocqueville, Alexis de. 1969. *Democracy in America*, trans. George Lawrence, ed. J. P. Mayer. New York: Doubleday Anchor Books.

van Gunsteren, Herman R. 1991. "Admission to Citizenship." *Ethics* 98:731–41.

Verba, Sidney. 1965. "Comparative Political Culture." In Lucian Pye and Sidney Verba, eds., *Political Culture and Political Development*. Princeton, NJ: Princeton University Press.

Verba, Sidney, and Norman H. Nie. 1972. *Participation in America: Political Democracy and Social Equality*. New York: Harper & Row.

Verba, Sidney, Kay Lehman Schlozman, and Henry E. Brady. 1995. *Civic Volunteerism in American Politics*. Cambridge, MA: Harvard University Press.

Vernon, Richard. 1986. *Citizenship and Order: Studies in French Political Thought*. Toronto: University of Toronto Press.

Walzer, Michael. 1976. "Civility and Civic Virtue in Contemporary America." *Social Research* 41:593–611.

⸻ 1989. "Citizenship." In Terence Ball, James Farr, and Russell L. Hanson, eds., *Political Innovation and Conceptual Change*. Cambridge: Cambridge University Press.

⸻ 1992. "The Civil Society Argument." In Chantal Mouffe, ed., *Dimensions of Radical Democracy: Pluralism, Citizenship, Community*. London: Verso.

⸻ 1993. "Exclusion, Injustice and the Democratic State." *Dissent* (Winter): 55–64.

Wolin, Sheldon. 1986. "Contract and Birthright." *Political Theory* 14:179–93.

⸻ 1989. *The Presence of the Past: Essays on the State and Constitution*. Baltimore, MD: Johns Hopkins University Press.

Zaller, John, and Stanley Feldman. 1992. "A Simple Theory of the Survey Response: Answering Questions versus Revealing Preferences." *American Journal of Political Science* 36:579–616.

4

The Challenges of Political Psychology: Lessons to Be Learned from Research on Attitude Perception

JON A. KROSNICK

Political psychology is a relatively young empirical enterprise. As dated by research involving quantitative techniques such as sample surveys and laboratory experiments, political psychology does not begin to approach the long histories of chemistry, physics, and astronomy. And even considering the application of typically qualitative analytic methods such as case studies and historical document analysis, our enterprise is in its relative youth (see, e.g., Hermann 1986).

Partly as a result of our youth and partly as a reflection of it, we have not experienced the dramatic paradigm shifts that other sciences have (see, e.g., Kuhn 1970). Whereas other disciplines have seen the rise and fall of major organizing theoretical perspectives, we have shown no signs yet of rejecting old overarching perspectives in favor of new ones. There have also been no dramatic shifts during the history of political psychology in terms of the methods we employ to evaluate our hypotheses empirically. This is not to say that methods are uniformly employed by investigators across the subfield; clearly, this is not the case. But the current state of affairs seems to be one of tolerance of a multiplicity of methods, rather than a universal sense that some methods have proven not to be useful while others are.

Yet a close look at the history of studies in some areas of political psychology suggests that there might be some useful lessons to be learned about the value of certain methods over others. A few prominent political psychology hypotheses have been the focus of many empirical studies over a relatively long time period, and the testing approaches employed have shifted in interesting, systematic ways. In each case, the methods initially used were found to be inadequate in retrospect, and more appropriate approaches were employed in later stages of investigation.

The author wishes to thank Lee Jussim, Donald R. Kinder, Donald Granberg, Gregory Markus, and Richard Petty for helpful comments on an earlier draft of this chapter.

Yet when new hypotheses are tested for the first time these days, the same initial methods of inquiry are employed again and again, only to set the stage for more informative analyses using different approaches later. Instead of skipping over the uninformative methods and going right to the more useful ones, we continue to start in the same place each time. In this light, it seems useful to chronicle the common progression, as a way to accelerate progress from less informative approaches to more informative ones in future work.

This chapter offers such a chronicling of research on one particularly prominent hypothesis in political psychology: the projection hypothesis. In short, it proposes that democratic citizens systematically distort their perceptions of competing candidates' positions on controversial issues of public policy. The roots of this idea are in psychological theories of the late 1950s, and it has inspired an unusually large number of tests in the political psychology literature. After first addressing the political significance of candidate perceptions, I will outline the theoretical basis of the projection hypothesis and review and critique the evidence generated to test it over the years.

THE POLITICAL SIGNIFICANCE OF CANDIDATE PERCEPTIONS

Theories of electoral behavior view citizens' perceptions of candidates' stands on public policy issues as playing important roles in voters' decision making. According to this view, voters evaluate candidates by assessing the match between their own policy attitudes and those of each candidate. The candidate whose positions most closely match those of a given voter is most likely to receive that voter's support. Obviously, such calculations cannot be performed unless voters are able to discern which policies each candidate favors and which each candidate opposes.

Election analysts have long recognized that candidates might be better off making it difficult for citizens to discern their issue positions. Downs (1957), Page (1976, 1978), Shepsle (1972), and Bartels (1988) have asserted that candidates have incentives to be ambiguous and that they win more votes through vagueness than they do by taking clear stands on policy issues (but see Macdonald, Listhaug, and Rabinowitz 1991; Patton and Smith 1980; Rabinowitz and Macdonald 1989). And indeed, ambiguity is more the norm than the exception because candidates rarely state their positions on issues (Page 1978). Candidates frequently endorse the "end states" they find desirable, such as peace and prosperity, but they rarely describe the policy *means* by which they would achieve those end states (McGinniss 1969).

Challenges of Political Psychology

The ambiguity inherent in candidate behavior represents a challenge to voters. Citizens who wish to evaluate candidates on the basis of their stands on policy issues are likely to be frustrated if they search for direct information about candidates. These voters must therefore assess those stands through self-generated or cue-guided inferences. That is, candidate perception is likely to be a task in which voters "go beyond the information given" (Bruner 1957). Psychologists' theories of social cognition suggest a wide variety of inference procedures that citizens might employ to make such inferences, and the projection hypothesis is one of them.

THEORETICAL BACKGROUND

The Projection Hypothesis

According to cognitive dissonance theory (Festinger 1957), balance theory (Heider 1958), and congruity theory (Osgood and Tannenbaum 1955), people prefer to maintain psychological consistency (Abelson and Rosenberg 1958) among their cognitions. Cognitive inconsistency occurs when two cognitions do not fit together, that is, when one does not follow from the other. Salient inconsistencies between cognitions are uncomfortable, and this discomfort presumably motivates individuals to instigate repair strategies. The magnitude of the discomfort is a function of the personal importance of the two cognitions to the individual (Festinger 1957; Newcomb 1961; Singer 1968). The more important both are, the more discomfort will be experienced, and the more similar the two are in terms of importance, the more discomfort will be experienced. The most straightforward approach to resolving cognitive inconsistency is to change one of the inconsistent cognitions, though if both cognitions are strongly supported by other cognitions, strategies such as bolstering, differentiation, or transcendence may be implemented (Abelson 1959; Festinger, Riecken, and Schachter 1956).

This reasoning can be readily applied in an analysis of political candidate perception. Consider three cognitive elements: a voter's attitude toward a particular government policy, his or her attitude toward a particular candidate, and his or her perception of the candidate's attitude toward the policy. Cognitive consistency exists when the voter's attitude toward the policy agrees with the perceived policy attitude of a liked candidate. Cognitive consistency also exists when the voter's own policy attitude disagrees with the perceived policy attitude of a disliked candidate. If the voter believes he or she disagrees with a liked candidate or agrees with a disliked candidate, inconsistency exists. An inconsistency will presumably become salient (1) if an individual is induced to think about an existing inconsistency in his or her cognitions about a candidate's policy stand, (2) if an individual's attitude toward a candidate or policy changes, thus inducing inconsistency, or (3) if an individual encounters a piece of information that reveals a candidate's attitude on a policy issue and thus induces inconsistency.

Such an inconsistency can be most easily resolved in one of three ways. First, sentiment toward the candidate can be changed, a process called "policy-based evaluation." That is, sentiment can become more positive when agreement exists, and sentiment can become more negative when disagreement exists. Second, the voter's own attitude toward the policy can change through persuasion. That is, a voter may come to adopt the policy attitude of a liked candidate or to reject the policy attitude of a disliked candidate. If a voter's sentiment toward the candidate is firmly established on other grounds, the voter's own policy attitude is highly resistant to change, and the voter has relatively little direct information about the candidate's policy attitude, inconsistency can be resolved by altering the voter's perception of the candidate's policy attitude, a process called "projection." That is, the voter may come to believe that a liked candidate shares his or her attitude toward the policy (a process I will call "positive projection") or that a disliked candidate disagrees with him or her regarding the merits of the policy (a process I will call "negative projection").[1]

Projection is not only regulated by sentiment toward candidates. According to Heider's balance theory, projection is also regulated by "unit relations" with candidates. A unit relation specifies the degree to which a voter is linked to or associated with a candidate, regardless of liking. One possible unit relation between a candidate and a voter would be determined by the voter's belief about the likelihood that the candidate will be elected (Kinder 1978). Voters who see a candidate as likely to be elected will have a unit relation and will be disposed toward positive projection of that candidate's policy attitudes. Voters who see a candidate as unlikely to be elected will not have a unit relation and may be likely to displace that candidate's attitude away from their own (see Heider 1958:202). Alternatively, a unit relation might be established by

1 Some authors have used the terms "assimilation" and "contrast" to refer to the processes I call "positive projection." and "negative projection." However, I prefer to use these alternative terms to differentiate the projection hypothesis from the predictions derived from social judgment theory that are described later. Of course, one might shy away from using the term "projection" here because it has been used in psychoanalytic theory to refer to the process of denying one's own undesirable thoughts and actions and attributing them to others (e.g., Freud 1938). But this use of the term is so different that confusion in the current context is unlikely.

shared political party affiliation, shared racial or ethnic identity, or some other shared characteristic.

According to cognitive dissonance theory, projection is also regulated by *choices* such as voting decisions (Festinger 1957). Once a voter has decided to vote for a given candidate, the likelihood of positive projection is increased in order to reduce any postdecisional dissonance that might be experienced. Similarly, voters presumably displace away candidates whom they decide not to vote for.

Mechanisms of Projection

There are a number of mechanisms by which projection may occur (see Kinder 1978). First, it may occur by "selective attention" during encoding when individuals are exposed to new information about a candidate. Voters may pay close attention to and devote extensive thought to statements that reinforce their preferred view of a candidate's attitude. And voters may devote relatively little attention or thought to statements that challenge their preferred views of candidates. Second, projection may occur as the result of "selective retention." Citizens may strategically forget pieces of information that challenge their preferred perceptions of a candidate's attitude, and they may remember information that reinforces preferred perceptions of candidate attitudes well. Third, projection may occur through selective "rationalization." When a voter acquires a piece of information that is inconsistent with his or her beliefs regarding where a candidate stands on an issue, the voter may spend an unusually large amount of time and cognitive effort reinterpreting the information so that it is consistent with the voter's preference (Hastie and Kumar 1979).

Asymmetry

Early research on the cognitive consistency theories' predictions found evidence of a possible asymmetry in the effects of sentiment toward others. Laboratory and field studies of agreement and attraction revealed that, although people clearly prefer to agree rather than disagree with others they like, they are not as concerned about disagreeing with others they dislike. Newcomb (1953, 1968) argued that this occurs because people disengage from others they dislike and are therefore less aware of and bothered by cognitive inconsistencies involving attitudes toward and perceptions of these individuals. This is the theoretical justification for the "asymmetry hypothesis" in candidate perception, which states that positive projection onto liked candidates will be a stronger and more common process than negative projection onto disliked candidates.

TESTS OF THESE HYPOTHESES

Studies Using Cross-Sectional Data

Nearly every causal hypothesis of significance in political psychology is tested initially using cross-sectional data. Such data are easily available to investigators, especially through such mechanisms as the National Election Study (NES) surveys. Although we all know that a correlation does not document causality, there is a tendency at times to describe a correlational result as documenting causality, especially when it is based on a multivariate regression in which the association of interest is a partial correlation (see, e.g., the literature on symbolic racism: Kinder and Sears 1981; Sears, Lau, Tyler, and Allen 1980). Nonetheless, demonstrating that a suspected cause is correlated with its supposed consequence is a necessary step in providing scientific evidence on behalf of the hypothesized influence process.

The literature on the projection hypothesis is typical of political psychology in that its initial tests were nearly exclusively based on cross-sectional data.[2] However, it took quite a while for the ambiguities of this sort of evidence to be recognized, and indeed, the results of cross-sectional studies are still sometimes reported and interpreted as documenting the hypothesized process. Yet as we shall see, there are numerous alternative interpretations for this sort of evidence, some of which have been recognized and others not.

Some cross-sectional tests of projection have examined the relation between sentiment toward a candidate and agreement between a respondent's issue position and his or her perception of the candidate's position (Berelson, Lazarsfeld, and McPhee 1954; Brent and Granberg 1982; Shaffer 1981; Sherrod 1972). In these studies, agreement was assessed by computing the difference between a voter's self-placement on an attitude dimension and his or her placement of a candidate on that dimension. Relative to voters who did not favor a candidate, voters who favored the candidate were found to perceive greater agreement between their own attitudes and the candidate's. As would be expected, this tendency was greater among voters who had stronger candidate preferences.

---

2 A number of studies have explored projection effects on perceptions of the policy attitudes of political parties and of the federal government (Granberg 1985b; Granberg and Robertson 1982) and on the perception of others' voting behavior (Granberg 1987b; Granberg and Brent 1983). Because the dynamics of these perceptions are likely to vary significantly from the dynamics of perceptions of candidates' issue positions, these studies are not considered in this chapter.

Consistent with the asymmetry hypothesis, the departure of level of agreement from what would be expected on the basis of chance alone was greater for liked candidates than for disliked candidates.

The majority of cross-sectional projection studies, however, have computed measures of linear association between voters' own policy attitudes and their perceptions of a candidate's position separately for groups of voters differing in sentiment toward or unit relations with the candidate (Conover and Feldman 1982; Enelow and Hinich 1985; Franklin 1991; Granberg 1985a; Granberg and Brent 1974, 1980; Granberg, Harris, and King 1981; Granberg and Holmberg 1986b; Granberg and Jenks 1977; Granberg, Kasmer, and Nanneman 1988; Granberg and Seidel 1976; Kinder 1978; King 1977–8; Page 1978:184–91; Page and Brody 1972; Shaffer 1981). These studies consistently found strong positive associations between respondents' own positions and their perceptions of liked candidates' positions, a result that has been viewed as supportive of the positive projection hypothesis. Also consistent with this hypothesis, this positive association was enhanced among voters who considered an issue to be highly important personally (Granberg and Seidel 1976). Furthermore, the positive association (measured near the election) between voters' policy attitudes and their perceptions of liked candidates' attitudes were stronger among voters who had decided for whom to vote *early* in the campaign, as compared to those who decided late. This result is consistent with the claim that the positive association is the result of projection that evolves gradually over time. Contrary to the unit relation hypothesis, the positive relation was no stronger after an election than before (Granberg and Jenks 1977).

Consistent with expectations, these studies discovered negative correlations between voters' attitudes and their perceptions of disliked or non-preferred candidates' attitudes. However, these negative correlations were smaller in absolute value than the positive correlations found in perceptions of liked or preferred candidates. Furthermore, the magnitudes of the negative correlations were found to be unrelated to the personal importance of the policy issue to the voter. These findings have been interpreted as evidence that negative projection with disliked candidates is a weaker process than positive projection onto liked candidates, consistent with the asymmetry hypothesis.

Critiques of Cross-Sectional Data Analyses

Although the results of these studies are consistent with the projection and asymmetry hypotheses, there are compelling alternative explanations for these results as well: (1) perspective effects, (2) policy-based evaluation and persuasion, (3) variation in candidates' attitude statements, and (4) the agreement principle. Because these effects are likely to cause problems in many other cross-sectional studies of public opinion and political attitudes, it is useful to review them here.

Perspective Effects. Perspective effects on attitude reports occur because different people define the endpoints of attitude rating scales differently (e.g., Judd and DePaulo 1979; Ostrom and Upshaw 1968). Consider, for example, a 7-point rating scale ranging from "strongly pro-abortion" to "strongly anti-abortion." When survey respondents rate themselves on such a scale, they must conceptually define each of the scale points in order to decide which best matches their own attitudes. According to the large literature on perspective effects, an important component of this defining process is deciding just how extreme the endpoints are. These definitions are what this literature calls respondents' "perspectives."

This body of research has made it clear that different respondents bring different perspectives to each attitude-reporting task; that is, they reach different conclusions about the extremity of the scale endpoints. Some respondents feel that one must take a very extreme stand on an issue in order to fall at one of the endpoints of a scale, whereas other respondents see the scale endpoints as corresponding to more moderate stands on the issue. Even if two individuals have identical attitudes, they will rate themselves differently if they have different interpretations of the meanings of the response scale points. The more extreme an individual views the endpoints as being, the more moderate his or her ratings on the scale will be.

Perspective effects can affect only one of the scale endpoints, thus shifting some perceivers' ratings in one direction. In such cases, a group of people would all assign the same meaning to one end of the rating scale but differ in their interpretations of the other end. For example, people might all agree on what it means to favor pulling U.S. troops out of Bosnia immediately and completely, but they might have varying views about what it means to favor continued involvement strongly. The more extreme the "continued involvement" endpoint is perceived to be, the more toward the "pull out" end of the scale will be a perceiver's ratings of others' attitudes.

Perspective effects induce correlations between attitude reports made on a single response scale by the same individual. Consider, for example, a respondent who indicates his attitude toward increased defense spending on a 7-point scale, as well as his perceptions of various presidential candidates' attitudes toward increased defense spending. Respondents who define the endpoints as representing very extreme attitudes will tend to cluster their ratings near the scale midpoint. In contrast, respondents who define the endpoints as representing more moderate attitudes will tend to cluster their ratings more near the endpoints. This will induce a positive correlation between ratings across individuals. Thus, variation across respondents in terms of perspective causes positively correlated errors of measurement to appear in two attitude reports made on the same response scale.

This has important implications for the study of projection (see Judd, Kenny, and Krosnick 1983). All past studies have asked voters to report their own attitudes and their candidate perceptions on the same scale. Therefore, the positive correlation between self-ratings and candidate ratings induced by perspective effects will combine with other, substantively induced correlations between these ratings. Consequently, perspective effects can enhance the appearance of asymmetry of positive and negative projection if both processes occurred. That is, perspective effects would enhance the expected positive correlation among people who like a candidate, depress the expected negative correlation among dislikers, and induce a positive correlation among people neutral toward the candidate. Or perspective effects can create the appearance of positive projection among all respondents, even if none actually occurred.[3]

Policy-Based Evaluation and Persuasion. A second alternative explanation for previous results involves the effects of candidate perceptions on voters' own attitudes (Brody and Page 1972; Judd et al. 1983). Voters derive their evaluations of presidential candidates partly from how much they agree with the candidates on policy issues (e.g., Krosnick 1988b; Nie, Verba, and Petrocik 1979; Pomper 1972; Rosenstone 1983). This process is called "policy-based evaluation" or "policy voting." Also, numerous psychological experiments suggest that persuasion is likely to be a common phenomenon in daily life generally (see, e.g., Petty and Cacioppo 1986), and persuasion of voters by political candidates, by presidents, and by government is well documented (e.g., Abramowitz 1978; Jacoby 1988; Jordan 1993; Lorge 1936; Page and Shapiro 1983, 1984, 1987; Shaffer 1981; c.f. Anderson and Avery 1978; Markus 1982; see also Carmines and Stimson 1989; Gerber and Jackson 1993; Markus

---

3 Granberg and Holmberg (1986a) have argued that the use of verbally labeled response categories overcomes the problem of perspective effects. It does seem likely that verbally labeled response categories are less ambiguous than numerically labeled ones, so perspective effects may be somewhat reduced in the case of the former. However, Ostrom and Upshaw's (1968) theoretical account of perspective effects suggests that they are unlikely to disappear completely in the case of verbally labeled response categories.

and Converse 1979; Zaller 1992). Via such persuasion, citizens are led to adopt the policy positions advocated by liked candidates and presidents and to adopt policy positions opposite to those advocated by disliked political figures. In cross-sectional data, projection is confounded with policy-based evaluation and persuasion. Therefore, it seems most sensible to consider policy voting and persuasion to be possible confounds in any study of projection and to use analytic methods that take them into account.

Policy-based evaluation and persuasion each produce a positive association between voters' attitudes on an issue and the position they perceive a liked candidate to hold. Similarly, policy-based evaluation and persuasion increase the strength of the negative association between voters' attitudes and their perceptions of disliked candidates' attitudes. To infer that an increase in the positivity of this correlation with increasing sentiment is the result of projection may therefore be inappropriate.

The magnitudes of policy-based evaluation and persuasion are likely to vary, depending partly on the personal importance of the policy issue to the voter. Policy attitudes that voters consider personally important are especially resistant to change, so persuasion is most likely to occur when a policy attitude is unimportant to a voter (Krosnick 1988a). On the other hand, policy-based evaluation is most likely to occur when a voter considers his or her policy attitude to be highly important (Krosnick 1988b). Therefore, the observed increase in the correlation between voters' policy attitudes and their candidate perceptions under conditions of high importance may reflect an increase in policy-based evaluation instead of an increase in projection.

Furthermore, the evidence for asymmetry could be due to persuasion. Theorists (e.g., Festinger 1954) have argued and empirical evidence (Osgood and Tannenbaum 1955) has shown that persuasion toward liked people is more potent than persuasion away from disliked people. Therefore, the association between voters' attitudes and their candidate perceptions in traditional tests of projection may have appeared larger in the case of liked candidates because persuasion is stronger.

Variation in Candidates' Attitude Statements. A third possible explanation for prior findings is variation in candidates' attitude statements (Judd et al. 1983). A variety of observers have asserted that candidates express different attitudes to different voters, perhaps to maximize their public appeal (Graber 1976:181; Mueller 1969:189). Anecdotal evidence indicates that, for example, Ronald Reagan's 1980 campaign involved fine-tuning his statements of his policy attitudes to suit audiences' proclivities (Williams 1980). Furthermore, Miller and Sigelman (1978) found that Lyndon Johnson varied the stand he took on U.S. involvement in Vietnam, depending upon the attitude of the audience to which he was speaking. He expressed more dovish attitudes to dovish audiences and more hawkish attitudes to hawkish audiences. Googin (1984) found the same pattern across a range of issues for Johnson and documented such variation for Ronald Reagan as well. Page (1978:143–9) found evidence of similar shadings in various presidential election campaigns, as did Wright and Berkman (1986) among senators. Also, laboratory studies of attitude expression indicate that people routinely tailor statements of their attitudes to be consistent with the attitude of their audience (Manis, Cornell, and Moore 1974; McCann, Higgins, and Fondacaro 1991; Newtson and Czerlinsky 1974).

If candidates do state different policy attitudes when speaking to different audiences in ways that maximize their appeal, a positive correlation between expressed attitude and the attitude of the audience would be induced. And this would produce a positive correlation between voters' attitudes and their perceptions of a candidate's attitude. This correlation would enhance the apparent strength of positive correlations in the case of liked candidates, and it would suppress the apparent strength of negative correlations in the case of disliked candidates. Thus, traditional tests of projection could be distorted so as to produce the appearance of asymmetry.

In fact, this sort of distortion can result from another mechanism as well: de facto selective exposure (see, e.g., Freedman and Sears 1965). Even if candidates do not strategically shade their attitude statements, voters are nonetheless especially likely to encounter statements made by a candidate with whom they agree. By the same token, voters are especially unlikely to encounter statements made by a candidate with whom they disagree. This sort of selective exposure is not driven by voters' desire to avoid attitude-challenging information, but instead is a by-product of many other determinants of information exposure. The result of this would again be a positive correlation between voters' own policy attitudes and their perceptions of candidates' policy attitudes, though this correlation would not be evidence of projection.

The False Consensus Effect. A fourth possible explanation for the results of previous projection studies is the false consensus effect. When asked to describe the attitudes of a group of people, individuals tend to believe that they agree with others, regardless of their sentiment toward the group (see, e.g., Marks and Miller 1987; Mullen et al. 1985; Ross, Greene, and House 1977). This exaggerated perception of the commonness of one's views has been dubbed the "false consensus" effect. Some of the possible reasons for this tendency are motivational in character.

For example, people may enjoy agreeing with others more than dis-agreeing because agreement validates one's own views, whereas disagreement challenges the wisdom of one's views (Festinger 1954; Zajonc 1968). Purely cognitive explanations have also been offered, one of which involves de facto selective exposure. People tend to affiliate with those who share their views and tend to avoid affiliating with those who have very different views (Berscheid and Walster 1978; Newcomb 1961). Therefore, it is presumably easier for people to bring to mind instances of others with whom they agree than images of others with whom they disagree.

All this suggests that voters will be biased toward assuming that all candidates share their own attitudes, *regardless* of whether they like or dislike the candidates. If this is true, it would bias projection estimates just as correlated measurement error and variation in candidates' atti-tude statements would. That is, it would cause conventional cross-sectional estimates of positive projection to be biased upward, and it would make conventional estimates of negative projection appear to be more negative.

Overcoming These Problems with Cross-Sectional Data

Correcting for Correlated Measurement Error. In order to overcome the problem of correlated measurement error, Judd et al. (1983) specified a multiple-indicator structural equation model that permitted extrac-tion of correlated measurement error from estimates of the association between voters' attitudes and candidate perceptions. This model was applied to cross-sectional data from the 1968 election. As expected, Judd et al. found significant and substantial correlated measurement error in the NES survey data they examined. Consistent with positive projection, they found significant positive associations between voters' attitudes and perceptions of liked candidates' attitudes. And consistent with negative projection, Judd et al. found significant though a bit weaker negative associations between voters' attitudes and perceptions of disliked candi-dates' attitudes.

Judd et al. argued that the effect of variability in candidates' attitude statements can be overcome by not examining the absolute magnitudes of the regression coefficients. Instead, they argued, researchers should examine the linearity of the relation between sentiment and an unstan-dardized regression coefficient estimating the effect of voters' attitudes on perceptions of candidates' attitudes. A positively accelerating relation, they claimed, would confirm the asymmetry hypothesis. Because the rela-tion was linear, Judd et al. (1983) concluded that the asymmetry hypoth-esis was disconfirmed.

Judd et al.'s methods have some advantages over the traditional, simpler correlational approach. However, Judd et al.'s approach confounded projection with persuasion, policy-based evaluation, and false consensus. Consequently, although their evidence is consistent with positive and negative projection and inconsistent with the asymmetry hypothesis, there remained important confounds yet to be eliminated. Second, Judd et al. (1983) ignored the potential impact of variation in candidates' attitude statements. Had this been controlled for, the positive associations they viewed as evidence of positive projection might have dropped substantially. Furthermore, Judd et al. did not examine voters' perceptions of candidates' stands on issues per se. Rather, these investigators examined latent perceptions of candidates' ideological orientations by treating attitudes toward U.S. involvement in Vietnam and toward methods of reducing urban unrest as indicators of ideology. A great deal of evidence suggests that ideological orientations are generally only very weakly related to specific issue stands (see Kinder 1983), so Judd et al.'s findings may not be directly applicable to perceptions of candidates' issue stands per se.

Correcting for False Consensus and Candidates' True Attitudes. Ottati, Fishbein, and Middlestadt (1988) and Bartels (1988) both recognized the potential bias caused by the false consensus effect in studies of projection. They therefore incorporated estimates of this effect in their statistical analyses of cross-sectional data. As expected, both studies revealed evidence of a false consensus bias presuming agreement with candidates regardless of sentiment toward them. Even after correcting for this effect, both studies yielded significant evidence of projection.

In Ottati et al.'s (1988) analysis, the expected asymmetry in positive and negative projection appeared even when false consensus was controlled for. However, Ottati et al. took a step further and attempted to gauge asymmetry by comparing voters' perceptions to the candidates' actual positions on the issues in question. This was done by treating the average perception of a candidate across voters (controlling for attitudes toward the candidate and toward the policy) as the candidate's true attitude. When this was done, the previously apparent asymmetry effect disappeared.

Because this approach ignores many potential biases in such perceptions that were not controlled, and because it ignores potential variation in candidates' expressed attitudes across voters, it may not be fully effective in accomplishing its intended goal. Furthermore, both Ottati et al. (1988) and Bartels (1988) failed to adjust for the impact of correlated measurement error, persuasion, and policy-based evaluation.

Correcting for Persuasion and Policy-Based Evaluation. A few studies attempted to eliminate the confounding of projection with persuasion and policy-based evaluation. For example, Page and Jones (1979) specified an extensive, nonrecursive structural equation model of the relations among a host of variables thought to be antecedents of vote choice. This model hypothesized that having a more positive evaluation of one candidate than the other leads voters to perceive that their preferred candidate's policy attitudes are more similar to their own than are the nonpreferred candidate's policy attitudes. As the notion of policy-based evaluation anticipates, attitudes toward the candidates appeared to be derived importantly from voter–candidate similarity in terms of issue stands. And as the projection hypothesis predicts, the effect of sentiment on perceived relative proximity was large, positive, and statistically significant.

This analysis was potentially problematic, however, partly because conclusions about the directions of causal relations between variables are always difficult to derive from cross-sectional data with any confidence. In Page and Jones's case, the validity of their conclusions depends on the validity of assumptions made about the instrumental variables included in their analytic model. Unfortunately, these assumptions seem quite tenuous (see also Asher 1983). The most important and questionable of these assumptions is the claim that demographic variables, including education, income, age, race, and gender, as well as ideological orientations, did not have any direct influence on candidate preferences. Instead, Page and Jones assumed, these variables only affected candidate evaluations indirectly by shaping perceptions of similarity between voters' and candidates' policy attitudes and by shaping voters' political party identifications.

This seems highly unlikely. In some of the earliest quantitative research on voting, Lazarsfeld, Berelson, and Gaudet (1948; see also Berelson et al. 1954) demonstrated that demographic variables are powerful proximate determinants of candidate preferences. Furthermore, regression equations predicting candidate preferences with numerous psychological variables (including party identification, policy preferences, and assessments of the national economy), as well as ideology and demographics, show significant independent direct effects of these latter variables (e.g., Kinder, Adams, and Gronke 1989). Therefore, because the most important assumptions underlying Page and Jones's analyses seem implausible, the validity of their conclusions regarding projection seems questionable.

Even if Page and Jones's (1979) assumptions were more reasonable than they appear to be, the effect of sentiment on perceived similarity they documented could have reflected persuasion instead of projection.

Consequently, there is still a confound present that prevents clear interpretation.

An attempt to unconfound projection from both policy-based evaluation *and* persuasion in cross-sectional data was reported by Granberg and Holmberg (1986b, 1988; Granberg 1987a). Their analyses focused on two correlations. The first is the usual estimate of positive projection: the correlation between voters' own attitudes on a policy issue and their perceptions of a liked candidate's attitude on the issue. Granberg and Holmberg recognized that in addition to projection, this correlation (which they called the "subjective agreement coefficient") reflects policy-based evaluation and persuasion. The second correlation is between voters' own policy attitudes and their overall evaluations of the candidate. Granberg and Holmberg argued that this second correlation (which they called the "rational democratic coefficient") is only a reflection of policy-based evaluation and persuasion. Further, they asserted that what remains after subtracting the second correlation from the first is an indication of the amount of projection. Granberg and Holmberg (1986b, 1988; Granberg 1987a) found positive residuals after this subtraction process, which they took to be evidence of projection.

This approach may be misleading for three primary reasons. First, the subjective agreement coefficient is calculated using data only from voters who like a candidate. In contrast, the rational democratic coefficient is calculated using data from all voters. If the asymmetry hypothesis is correct in predicting less projection among voters who dislike a candidate than among those who like him or her, the subjective agreement coefficient would be an overestimate of the amount of projection taking place for likers and dislikers combined. Therefore, the positive difference between the subjective agreement coefficient and the rational democratic coefficient may be a result of this overestimation.

A second possible problem with this approach is that, as Judd et al. (1983) pointed out, the subjective agreement coefficient reflects perspective effects and variation in candidates' attitude statements, in addition to projection, persuasion, and policy-based evaluation. Therefore, what is left over after Granberg and Holmberg's (1986b, 1988; Granberg 1987a) subtraction exercise may represent perspective effects or variation in candidates' attitude statements instead of projection.

Third, the rational democratic coefficient may underestimate the amount of policy-based evaluation that has occurred. According to spatial modeling theories of voting (e.g., Enelow and Hinich 1984), a voter's attitude toward a candidate is a function of the amount of distance between the voter's own attitude on a policy issue and his or her perception of the candidate's attitude on that issue. Given that

candidates' policy attitudes are almost never at the extreme of the dimension (Page 1978), this view predicts a nonmonotonic relation between
voters' own policy attitudes and their evaluations of a candidate. Compared to the voters who are extremely opposed to the policy option,
increases in positivity toward the policy option should be associated with
increased liking for the candidate up to the point at which voters' attitudes toward the policy match the candidate's attitude toward it. At this
point, liking should reach a maximum. Beyond that point, increases in
voters' positivity toward the policy should be associated with *decreased*
liking of the candidate.

Instead of estimating the strength of this nonmonotonic relation,
Granberg and Holmberg's rational democratic coefficient simply estimates the linear relation between voters' own policy attitudes and their
candidate evaluations. Therefore, this coefficient probably does not fully
capture the amount of policy-based evaluation present.[4] Consequently,
what is left over after Granberg and Holmberg's (1986b, 1988; Granberg
1987a) subtraction exercise may represent policy-based evaluation
instead of projection.

Granberg and Holmberg (1986b, 1988) conducted another set of
cross-sectional analyses that is similarly problematic. They compared
two sets of regressions, one that regressed voters' candidate evaluations
on perceived similarity between voters' policy attitudes and the candidate's, and the other that regressed perceived similarity between voters'
policy attitudes and the candidate's on voters' candidate evaluations.
Granberg and Holmberg (1986b) viewed these two analyses as allowing
them to assess the strength of the two causal processes. However, because
the data being analyzed were cross-sectional, simply altering which variable is specified as the dependent variable and which is specified as the
independent variable does not permit the differentiation of the reciprocal causal effects between pairs of variables (Kenny 1979). Furthermore,
any apparent effects on voter–candidate similarity could reflect adjustments of either voters' own attitudes or of their candidate perceptions.
Therefore, these analyses are not informative about the sizes of projection effects per se.

The efforts made by Page and Jones (1979) and Granberg and Holmberg (1986b, 1988; Granberg 1987a) are admirable attempts to use
sophisticated analytic approaches in efforts to overcome the confounding of various causal processes in yielding cross-sectional data. But unfortunately, both undertakings yielded results that are easy to counterargue

---

4 Although this argument has been phrased with regard to the case of voters attitudes toward a single candidate, it applies equally well to the case in which voters
express a preference for one candidate over another (see Krosnick 1988b:198).

and consequently are not as clear as one might hope. Consequently, researchers in this area turned their attention to longitudinal data in the hope that time sequencing could allow them to get a better handle on what causes what in the minds of voters (see, e.g., Kessler and Greenberg 1981).

Summary. The four principal critiques of cross-sectional tests of projection have been recognized by various investigators, and various studies have attempted to eliminate one or more confounds in traditional analyses. All of these studies demonstrated that the confounds are real and therefore threatening to any projection analysis, but no single study eliminated all confounds. This is presumably so partly because it is very difficult to separate projection from persuasion and policy-based evaluation with cross-sectional data. However, as a number of other investigators have recognized, this can be accomplished using longitudinal data.

Analyses of Longitudinal Data

The Logic of Longitudinal Analysis. Longitudinal analysis is valuable because it offers an opportunity to get an empirical handle on particular causal processes. Specifically, one tracks the dependent variable of interest over time and attempts to predict changes in it based upon values of independent variables assessed at prior time points. As long as the independent variables are measured prior to the changes in the dependent variable, it is unlikely that the latter caused the former (see Kessler and Greenberg 1981; Markus 1979). In research on projection, this approach allows one to overcome persuasion, policy-based evaluation, and correlated measurement error (assuming that such error is uncorrelated over time) by using initial measurements of voters' candidate preferences (and perhaps issue preferences) to predict later shifts in perceptions of candidates' issue stands or voter–candidate similarity.

Predicting Candidate Stands. Although the value of longitudinal data thus lies in the study of change over time, Markus and Converse (1979) employed such data in an attempt to unconfound projection and persuasion, but they did not study change per se. Rather, these investigators proposed a nonrecursive structural equation model of electoral choice that modeled perceptions of candidates' position as follows:

$$\text{Perceived Cand. Stand}_t = \text{Actual Cand. Stand}_t + b_1(\text{R's Stand}_{(t-1)} \\ - \text{Actual Cand. Stand}_t)\text{Eval}_t + e_t \qquad (1)$$

This equation views perceptions of a candidate's attitude as adjusted perceptions of the candidate's actual attitude. Candidate perceptions are presumably adjusted so as to minimize the distance between a voter's policy attitude and his or her perception of the candidate's. Furthermore, this adjustment is proposed to be greater as sentiment toward the candidate becomes more positive.

Markus and Converse found b_1 to be small but statistically significant for each of five policy issues they examined and interpreted this as evidence in support of the projection hypothesis. However, because candidate evaluations were measured at time t instead of at time $t - 1$, b_1 may reflect either changes in perceptions of candidates resulting from projection or changes in attitudes toward candidates resulting from policy-based evaluation. That is, voters may have adjusted their candidate evaluations between time $t - 1$ and time t in order to maximize liking of candidates with whom they agreed and to minimize liking of candidates with whom they disagreed. This process would produce a significant b_1 coefficient, just as adjustments of candidate perceptions between time $t - 1$ and time t would. Had candidate evaluations been measured at time $t - 1$ instead, this alternative explanation could have been ruled out.

Markus and Converse (1979) treated candidate evaluations measured at time t as endogenous in their system of equations. This might at first appear to eliminate any problem with the fact that these evaluations were measured at time t instead of time $t - 1$. However, all of the causes of candidate evaluations at time t were also measured at time t. Thus, it seems quite plausible that this approach did not fully resolve the simultaneity problem as effectively as would have been the case had candidate evaluations at time $t - 1$ been used instead.

Predicting Voter–Candidate Similarity. Granberg and King (1980) conducted just such analyses testing the hypothesis that positive sentiment leads to perceived similarity. Regressions of perceived policy stand similarity (averaged across five political issues) at time t on perceived policy stand similarity and sentiment toward the candidate measured at time $t - 1$ indicated that sentiment caused changes in perceived similarity, such that liked candidates were perceived as becoming more similar to voters over time.

Swindel and Miller (1986) did a similar analysis and reached similar conclusions. They found that respondents who voted for a candidate perceived that candidate's attitude as closer to their own than did respondents who did not vote for the candidate. This pattern was stronger among respondents who decided early in the campaign for whom to vote, which is consistent with the hypothesis that the pattern is due to projection. During the campaign, respondents' attitudes became closer to their perceptions of their preferred candidates' attitudes, and respondents' attitudes became more different from their perceptions of nonpreferred candidates' attitudes. Contrary to the asymmetry hypothesis, though, the increase in closeness between voters and preferred candidates was equal in magnitude to the decrease in closeness between voters and nonpreferred candidates. These shifts were found to be greatest for individuals with the least exposure to campaign news, which supports the claim that this movement is reduced by a voter's having more direct information about candidates' attitudes.

Granberg and King's (1980) and Swindel and Miller's (1986) evidence is consistent with the projection hypothesis. However, the changes they documented in voter–candidate proximity could reflect persuasion instead. That is, voters' own attitudes might have changed, while candidate perceptions remained constant. Therefore, these studies are again ambiguous with regard to the projection hypothesis.

Predicting Changes in Candidate Perceptions. The most effective way to overcome the problems caused by persuasion and policy-based evaluation is to examine the effect of voters' attitudes on changes in perceived candidates' attitudes using longitudinal data collected from a panel of respondents over time. Evidence that changes in candidate perceptions can be predicted by prior measurements of voters' policy attitudes and candidate evaluations cannot be explained by persuasion or policy-based evaluation. Furthermore, the effect of voters' attitudes measured at time $t - 1$ on candidate perceptions at time t does not reflect correlated measurement error if one controls for candidate perceptions at time $t - 1$. This is so because any correlated measurement error between voters' attitudes at time $t - 1$ and their candidate perceptions at time t is likely to be mediated by candidate perceptions at time $t - 1$. Thus, analysis of longitudinal data in this fashion permits an investigator to overcome this drawback of the traditional method as well.

One investigation that attempted this type of analysis of panel data was reported by Feldman and Conover (1983). They estimated equations of the following form:

$$\text{Perceived Cand. Stand}_t = a + b_1(\text{Perceived Cand. Stand})_{(t-1)}$$
$$+ b_2(\text{R's Stand}_{t-1})(\text{Eval}_{t-1}) + e_t \qquad (2)$$

Here b_2 estimates the effect of a respondent's attitude on changes in his or her perception of a candidate's attitude between time $t - 1$ and time t. If b_2 is positive and statistically significant, that would suggest that as sentiment toward a candidate becomes more positive, respondents' attitudes cause changes in perceptions of the candidate's attitudes that increase their correspondence. In all of Feldman and Conover's analyses, b_2 was substantial and statistically significant, which they interpreted as evidence of projection.

In another study, Conover and Feldman (1986) used a similar approach to test the asymmetry hypothesis by examining perceptions of liked and disliked candidates separately (see also Conover and Feldman 1989). For this study, they estimated equations of the following general form:

Perceived Cand. Stand$_t$ = a + b_1(Perceived Cand. Stand)$_{(t-1)}$
$\qquad$ + b_2(R's Stand$_{t-1}$)(Pos Eval$_{t-1}$)
$\qquad$ + b_3(R's Stand$_{t-1}$)(Neg Eval$_{t-1}$) + e_t $\qquad$ (3)

These analyses produced strong and statistically significant estimates of b_2, indicating positive projection. And consistent with the asymmetry hypothesis, estimates of b_3 were negative but relatively weak.

Martinez (1988) estimated an equation that was equivalent to Feldman and Conover's (1983), with one exception. Instead of using measured candidate evaluation at time $t - 1$ as an independent variable, Martinez created an estimated "true" candidate evaluation at time t using respondents' demographics and party identification as instrumental variables. Contrary to Feldman and Conover's (1983) evidence, Martinez's estimates of b_2 were all zero for respondents low in political involvement, and, among respondents high in political involvement, they were positive but weak for two issues and zero for two other issues. When Martinez included an additional interaction term to assess asymmetry, he found it to be sizable for only one of the four issues. Thus, Martinez's findings are very different from Feldman and Conover's (1983; Conover and Feldman 1986, 1989). However, as is true of Page and Jones's (1979) study, Martinez's assumption that demographics and party identification do not have direct effects on other variables in his equation (particularly voters' own policy attitudes) seems tenuous. This may explain the discrepancy in findings to some degree.

More important, however, Feldman and Conover's analyses (1983; Conover and Feldman 1986, 1989) and Martinez's (1988) all suffer from a drawback that renders their interpretation ambiguous. In order for the estimates of b_2 in Equation (2) and of b_2 and b_3 in Equation (3) to represent the interactions of respondents' stands and candidate evaluations, lower-order main effect terms for respondents' stands and candidate evaluations must be included in the predictive equations (see Arnold 1982; Arnold and Evans 1979; Cohen 1978; Cohen and Cohen 1975; Evans 1991; Judd and McClelland 1989; Schmidt 1973; Schmidt and Wilson 1975). Omitting these terms, as was done in all these studies, causes the main effects to be confounded with the interaction. Thus, instead of reflecting projection, the observed b_2 and b_3 values may reflect either or both of these main effects. Even though the main effects are not theoretically directly relevant to the study of projection, it is statistically necessary to include them in the equation. Therefore, this evidence, though in some cases consistent with projection, may be due to this confound instead.

If all of the main effects in equations such as Equation (3) are zero, omitting them is not a problem for estimating the projection interactions. However, Feldman and Conover (1983; Conover and Feldman 1986) and Martinez (1988) reported no evidence to indicate that this was the case. In their 1989 article, Conover and Feldman did include main effects for respondents' stands in their regressions, and they offered a justification for omitting candidate evaluations (see footnote 9, p. 927). They argued that when they reestimated their equations including main effects for candidate evaluations, those main effects were never statistically significant at $p < .05$.

Unfortunately, simply presenting tests of the statistical significance of the individual main effects may not be sufficient to validate omitting them when estimating interactions. First, if the main effects are tested in equations that also included the interactions, the full main effects are not being tested correctly (see Arnold 1982; Arnold and Evans 1979; Cohen 1978; Cohen and Cohen 1975; Evans 1991; Judd and McClelland 1989; Schmidt 1973; Schmidt and Wilson 1975). In such an equation, a main effect term simply indicates the variable's effect at one particular level of each interacting variable. In Conover and Feldman's (1989) case, their main effect tests apply only to the respondents whose candidate evaluations were neutral. Obviously, testing the main effect under this limited condition cannot serve as a basis for concluding that the main effect is not significant when combining across all levels of candidate evaluation.

Even if the main effects had been tested in an equation including no interaction terms, relying only upon tests of statistical significance may be problematic. Consider the case in which a set of variables each has relatively weak main effects, not strong enough to be detected at $p < .05$ with typical survey sample sizes. Nonetheless, these main effects can be real, and when confounded together, they can yield a statistically significant and substantial distorting confound. Similarly, a small and nonsignificant omitted main effect, when confounded with a small and nonsignificant interaction, could yield an apparently significant overall effect that would be attributed to the interaction. Therefore, the most appropriate approach to testing projection using longitudinal data is to include all of the main effects in any equation estimated. This point has been made numerous times by data analysis specialists in recent years (see Arnold 1982; Arnold and Evans 1979; Cohen 1978; Cohen and Cohen 1975; Evans 1991; Judd and McClelland 1989; Schmidt 1973; Schmidt and Wilson 1975) because investigators so often make mistakes in this regard in published papers.

In footnote 9 on page 927, Conover and Feldman (1989) indicated that including the main effects in their equations caused their standard errors to increase. This may imply that some of their previously statistically significant projection effects were no longer significant, which might explain their preference for omitting the main effects from the equation. But the preceding argument makes it clear that this increase in standard errors is unlikely to be problematic; instead, it reflects the fact that more effects are being estimated, all of them necessary. Thus, the possibly reduced number of statistically significant projection effects may have constituted a more accurate estimate of the presence or absence of these effects.

A similar investigation by Markus (1982) using panel data overcame all of the problems associated with Feldman and Conover's (1983; Conover and Feldman 1986, 1989) and Martinez's (1988) analyses. Separately for liked and disliked candidates, Markus regressed candidate perceptions at time t on candidate perceptions at time $t - 1$ and voters' own attitudes at time $t - 1$. This analysis included the necessary lower-order main effects, and candidate evaluations were measured at time $t - 1$, so policy-based evaluation was not a confound. Furthermore, because Markus examined changes in candidate perceptions from the very beginning of the 1980 presidential election campaign (January) to the very end (October), he was unlikely to have missed any substantial amount of projection that might have occurred outside of his time frame.

Markus found some evidence of projection. Of the thirty-two projection coefficients he estimated, eight were statistically significant and all were relatively small. Three of the significant coefficients reflected positive effects of voters' attitudes on perceptions of liked candidates, and five reflected negative effects of voters' attitudes on perceptions of disliked candidates. Thus, a negative effect for disliked candidates appeared to be more common than a positive effect for liked candidates, disconfirming the asymmetry hypothesis. In general, though, these analyses indicated some positive projection and some negative projection.

One problem with Markus's analytic approach is that it did not take into account variability in candidates' attitude statements. As Judd et al. (1983) argued, such variability is likely to enhance the appearance of positive projection and mask the appearance of negative projection. Thus, negative projection may have been stronger than Markus's evidence indicated, and positive projection may have been even weaker than his evidence suggested. However, as we shall consider next, his method and those used in every other longitudinal study suffer from additional methodological problems.

Problems with Linear Association Measures

Given that Markus's (1982) study and nearly all other past studies of projection effects have used measures of the linear association between voters' attitudes and candidate perceptions, the value of these studies hinges on the degree to which linear associations represent the causal processes of interest. And unfortunately, careful consideration of the properties of linear association measures and of the projection hypothesis reveals that these measures are inappropriate for testing this hypothesis. Although measures of linear association are well suited to estimating the magnitude of positive projection onto liked candidates, assessing negative projection with a measure of linear association is wholly inappropriate.

First, consider why the linear association method is appropriate for testing positive projection.[5] Assume that a respondent's own position on some issue and his or her perception of a candidate's position on that issue are both measured on the same 7-point scale, as has usually been the case. If complete positive projection were to occur, each respondent would perceive a liked candidate to hold the same position he or she holds. Therefore, as long as there is some variation in respondents' own attitudes, the correlation between the two variables would be +1. If positive projection is not perfect, but each unit that a respondent is away from the candidate's true position is associated with a constant fraction of a unit of positive projection, the correlation will still be +1. An unstandardized regression coefficient would reflect the incompleteness of positive projection in this situation by taking a value less than 1. Thus, a large positive measure of linear association validly indicates positive projection as it is conceived theoretically.

Next, consider negative projection. In all the research reviewed previously that involved computation of linear association measures, it has generally been assumed that a negative correlation between the respondent's own position and his or her perception of a disliked candidate's position indicates negative projection. This is true at a very general level: for negative projection to occur, respondents who are in favor of some piece of legislation would perceive the candidate to be opposed to it. However, because attitudes and perceptions are most often measured on

---

5 All of the arguments in this section apply equally well to monotonic, nonlinear measures of association for use with ordinal data, such as tau-b (used by Brent and Granberg 1982) or eta (used by Granberg and Holmberg 1988).

7-point scales, a negative correlation indicates a more refined relation. It indicates that respondents who are further away from a candidate's true position distort the candidate *more* than do respondents close to the candidate's true position. An unstandardized regression coefficient of −1 would indicate that respondents at the extremes of the scale see the candidate at the opposite extreme, and moderates see the candidate at moderate positions.

However, cognitive consistency theories anticipate no such relation but rather make a very different prediction. People who dislike a candidate are presumably uncomfortable if they perceive themselves to agree with him or her. Consequently, people who dislike a candidate and perceive that they agree with him or her would be expected to displace his or her position away from their own. People who dislike a candidate and disagree with his or her true attitude would have no reason to distort his or her position at all. The further one's own policy attitude is from the true attitude of a disliked candidate, the less one would be expected to distort his or her position. Thus, among people at a given level of sentiment for the candidate, those whose positions are close to a candidate's true position would feel more motivated to displace the candidate away than would respondents whose positions are further from the candidate. These latter individuals already disagree sufficiently with the candidate's true attitude in order to maintain cognitive consistency and have no need to distort perceptions of him or her. This suggests that negative projection would not produce a negative linear relation between the two variables among people who dislike a candidate. Instead, we should expect to observe a discontinuous relation, the shape of which depends in part on the candidate's true attitude.

According to cognitive consistency theory, the expected relation among people who dislike a candidate when the candidate's true position is at the midpoint of the scale is depicted in Curve #1 in Figure 4.1. Respondents at position 2 are closer to the candidate's true position than are respondents at position 1 and would therefore be expected to distort the candidate's position more. Similarly, respondents at position 3 are closer than are respondents at position 2, so the former should distort more. A similar argument explains the predictions for respondents at positions 5, 6, and 7.

It might appear that this curve implies that respondents at position 4 do not distort the candidate's position at all. But, of course, it is these people who are closest to the candidate's true position and who would be expected to distort his or her position the most. However, the direction in which they should distort is not clear a priori. If we assume that about half of these respondents displace the candidate toward position 1 and half distort him or her toward position 7, the resulting average

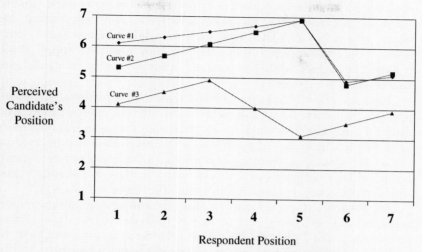

Figure 4.1. Negative projection onto a disliked candidate.

across these respondents is near the midpoint of the scale, the candidate's true position.[6]

If the candidate's true position departs substantially from the scale's midpoint, a differently shaped curve should occur. An example for a candidate whose true position lies between 5 and 6 appears in Curve #2 of Figure 1. The closer respondents' positions are to the disliked candidate's true position, the more they should be motivated to distort it away from themselves: respondents at 2 more than those at 1; respondents at 3 more than those at 2; respondents at 4 more than those at 3; and respondents at 5 more than those at 4. Respondents at positions 6 and 7 must displace the candidate in the opposite direction from the distortions of the other respondents so as to increase the discrepancy between their own positions and the candidate's true position. The shape of the curve is essentially the same as that in Curve #1, but its center is displaced to the right.

If candidates' true positions are variables that are correlated with respondents' own positions, the predictions embodied in Curve #2 are not drastically altered. Curve #3 in Figure 4.1 is a translation of Curve #2 treating the candidate's true position as a variable that is positively

6 Note that this reasoning suggests that, among people who dislike a candidate and whose own attitude on an issue matches the candidate's true attitude, there should be increased variance in candidate perceptions.

correlated with the respondent's position. The shape of the curve remains the same, but the two sections with positive slopes are more steep. No matter where the candidate's true position is, however, a negative correlation should not appear. If a nonzero correlation were to appear at all, it should be slightly positive and should occur only when the candidate's true position is extreme.

Thus, the evidence reported by most past cross-sectional studies of negative projection (i.e., weak negative correlations among people who dislike a candidate) is actually inconsistent with the cognitive consistency view of projection. So why have such negative relations appeared so often? The most likely explanations are that other processes are operating in addition to projection, or that some artifact is present, or that negative projection is occurring in some other form.

One possible explanation involves the relations among attitude importance, attitude extremity, and sensitivity to cognitive imbalance. Theoretical expositions of cognitive consistency theories proposed that the more important an attitude is for a person, the more he or she will be sensitive to inconsistency and motivated to resolve it (Zajonc 1968). Empirical evidence examining positive projection effects (Granberg and Seidel 1976), judgments of attitude position statements (e.g., Judd and Harackiewicz 1980), and perceptions of others' attitudes (Judd and Johnson 1981) is all consistent with this notion. Furthermore, because individuals for whom an attitude is highly important tend to endorse extreme attitude positions more often than individuals for whom it is less important (e.g., Judd and Krosnick 1982), extreme respondents should displace a disliked candidate disproportionately more than moderate respondents do.

A tendency of individuals who endorse extreme positions to displace disliked candidates more would produce the weak negative correlation researchers have discovered in the past. Figure 4.2 displays how this would occur. Curve #1 here is Curve #1 from Figure 4.1 after adjusting the degree of negative projection for attitude importance, assuming a positive correlation between extremity and importance. On average, the predictions of respondents at position 4 would not change. But respondents at the other positions would displace the candidate more for each unit closer to the extreme of the scale where their own position is located. These adjustments produce a curve with a negative slope. If the correlation between extremity and importance is less strong than is assumed here, the curves connecting the perceptions will become more horizontal, as is shown in Curve #2 of Figure 4.2. The correlation between the respondent's position and the perceived candidate's position implicit in this curve is slightly negative, if not zero.

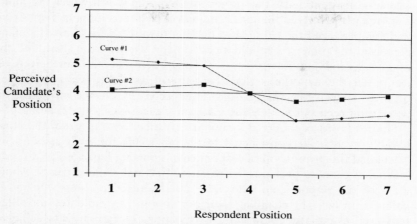

Figure 4.2. Negative projection with high importance at the scale extremes.

In summary, then, a measure of linear association between a citizen's position on an issue and his or her perception of a candidate's position is appropriate for testing positive projection but is inappropriate for testing negative projection. The weak negative correlation among people who dislike a candidate that is typically found and interpreted as evidence for asymmetry probably results from the tendency of people at the scale extremes to displace candidates more. Therefore, previous studies of negative projection using measures of linear association between voters' attitudes and candidate perceptions provide at best ambiguous information about the validity of the negative projection hypothesis. In fact, the negative correlations usually taken to be evidence of negative projection are not conceptually consistent with this hypothesis.

Longitudinal Studies Using Nonlinear Measures

Only three studies have examined changes in candidate perceptions over time without using measures of linear association; remarkably, none of them yielded compelling evidence of projection. In Anderson and Avery's (1978) four-wave longitudinal study, respondents' policy attitudes and their candidate preferences remained quite stable, so persuasion and policy-based evaluation did not occur to any substantial degree. For almost 37% of the sample, perceptions of the preferred candidate's position moved closer to the respondent's, and perceptions of the opposing candidate's position moved further away. This pattern of movement is clearly consistent with the projection hypothesis. However, as many respondents perceived the two candidates' positions moving away from them as perceived the candidates moving toward them. Similarly, many perceived the preferred candidate as moving farther from them and the opposing candidate moving closer. Thus, these data do not permit rejection of the hypothesis that the pattern associated with projection occurred more often than would be expected by chance movement in perception reports (due, e.g., to random measurement error) alone.[7]

Shaffer (1981) conducted a similar investigation and produced comparable results. He constructed Heiderian triads for each respondent, calculated the proportion of respondents reporting balanced triads, and examined changes over time in balanced and unbalanced triads. About 40% of the respondents who were not balanced at time 1 achieved balance at time 2 by changing their perceptions of candidates' attitudes. However, essentially comparable proportions of respondents achieved balance through persuasion or policy-based evaluation. And most importantly, the proportion of respondents reporting balanced triads did *not* increase over time. Thus, it appears, there was no systematic movement toward balanced states via projection over and above what would be expected by chance alone.

Krosnick (1990) conducted multiple regressions with longitudinal data predicting changes in voters' perceptions of candidates using prior assessments of voters' own attitudes toward the candidates. As is appropriate, positive projection was modeled as a linear association, and negative projection was modeled as a linear association based upon the deviation of a respondent's perceptions of a candidate from his likely true position on the issue.[8] Remarkably, Krosnick found essentially no evidence of either positive or negative projection across two candidates (Reagan and Mondale in 1984) and three issues (government spending, U.S. involvement in Central America, and federally guaranteed jobs).

Krosnick's (1990) analyses focused only on changes in candidate perceptions between preelection interviews and postelection interviews, the

---

7 One might argue that controlling for schema-based inferences would interfere with the assessment of the *total* effect of voters' own attitudes on candidate perceptions via projection (i.e., the sum of direct and indirect effects). However, it would be a mistake to characterize total effects on candidate perceptions as summarizing only distortions in those perceptions per se motivated by the desire to maintain cognitive consistency.

8 One particular challenge for Krosnick (1990) was to determine the candidate's true positions. He experimented with a variety of possibilities and found no change in the substantive implications of his analyses. Thus, his conclusions do not seem to be especially dependent on this aspect of the analysis.

average time between them being forty-seven days in his study. This is a relatively short time period, and one might argue that it was too short to detect the effects of interest. Perhaps as well, projection effects occur relatively early in a campaign, and candidate perceptions become fixed midway through. Consequently, Krosnick's (1990) focus on the latter part of the campaign may have missed projection that occurred earlier.

Another potential problem with Krosnick's (1990) approach is that he ignored the likely positive correlations between candidate-expressed positions and respondents' own positions. If such correlations evolved during the period of his study's focus, they may have masked negative projection effects occurring simultaneously. However, if systematic variation in candidates' expressed attitudes changed voters' perceptions of them, one would also expect to see positive correlations appearing in longitudinal tests of positive projection. The fact that they did not appear in Krosnick's (1990) study suggests that such correlated error was not evolving and did not mask evidence of negative projection.

Thus, the three studies that succeeded in separating projection from persuasion and policy-based evaluation and that avoided measures of linear association provided no compelling evidence of positive or negative projection.

CONCLUSION

General Implications

If we are simply in the business of generating evidence consistent with hypotheses, then the literature on projection clearly stands as a solid accomplishment. Working simultaneously, political scientists and psychologists have produced a great many findings consistent with the projection hypothesis. Unfortunately, however, most of this evidence is also just as consistent with other hypotheses that are based on equally compelling theory. And when these alternative hypotheses – or processes – have been tested cleanly, they have been supported handsomely. Consequently, eliminating the impact of *all* such processes *simultaneously* is necessary in order to provide a compelling test of projection. And this has yet to be done.

Why has no such unconfounding work been done to date? First, it took a while for investigators in this arena to recognize the various confounding processes. Diffusion of knowledge is not as fast as we all would like, and work in progress gets published even when doubt is cast on its informativeness by recent insights of other investigators. Second, unconfounding these various processes poses a great conceptual challenge. If this unconfounding were easy to do, investigators would undoubtedly have done it already. Third, although panel data seem to hold the promise of solving major problems here, such data are harder to access and harder to analyze than cross-sectional data. Finally, the projection idea is so conceptually compelling that people may be disinclined to be skeptical about empirical support for it: such a good idea *must* be right, some observers might presume.

Another impediment to useful projection tests has been the failure to represent the theoretical hypotheses appropriately in mathematical terms. This is no doubt partly a function of the habitual reliance of social scientists on statistical techniques presuming linear relations among variables. Because so much software is available for linear analysis, and because we are all so practiced at using it, our first inclination is to stick with what we know. And when early studies produced results that seemed sensible, analysts were presumably even less motivated to scrutinize the correspondence of hypotheses being tested to mathematical representations being employed.

If we are to generate convincing evidence about projection or any other psychological processes in politics, the pitfalls identified here must be avoided. Most obviously, when we propose and test causal hypotheses, it makes little sense to assert that cross-sectional data (even when analyzed with multivariate techniques) yield compelling support. Many causal hypotheses in the political psychology literature are currently being treated as empirically validated, despite the fact that only cross-sectional evidence is available to date. These all-too-strong assertions are likely to cause substantial delays for the field if they are taken to be definitive.

There is no doubt that cross-sectional data can be informative regarding the validity of a causal hypothesis. If an expected correlation fails to appear, this certainly casts doubt on the causal process that implied it. But even a supportive correlation is not very informative if the impact of correlated measurement error has not been eliminated. And once an initial convincing demonstration of correlational support is provided, it seems essential to move quickly on to employing either longitudinal data analysis methods (Kessler and Greenberg 1981) or experimental methods (Kinder and Palfrey 1993) in order to determine the hypothesis's plausibility more effectively. Furthermore, evidence on mediators and moderators makes the generated case all the more compelling. With regard to the projection literature and many other areas of political psychology, it seems fair to say that not nearly enough such work has been done.

Implications Regarding Projection

With regard to the notion of projection, it is probably most appropriate to conclude that although this hypothesized process may well occur in the perception of political candidates, it has yet to be demonstrated in a sufficiently convincing manner. Despite the tone of this conclusion, however, it is not my intention to discourage the field from carrying out research on projection in the future. Furthermore, it makes no sense to erect such a high standard for clarity of interpretation that we can never hope to achieve it. But it does seem clear that we can do a much better job at analyzing currently available data in order to increase confidence in the conclusions of projection research.

Projection may never be conclusively demonstrated in any single study, because plausible alternative interpretations might exist for any given empirical demonstration. However, evidence varies in the degree to which it convinces readers, so future studies that attempt to rule out the many obvious and plausible alternative explanations for the observed effects can leave readers quite a bit more certain about the meaning of their results. This will certainly be a more desirable state of affairs, even though possible alternative explanations may never completely disappear.

Rather than being discouraging, I hope that this chapter will reinvigorate projection research. Research in this area has all but died out in recent years, presumably because political scientists view the projection hypothesis as having been conclusively validated. What recent work exists has usually involved application of the same analytic methods over and over again to new data sets without questioning their validity. Instead, we should be approaching old data sets with new analytic methods. I hope this chapter highlights the challenges that might attract researchers to this area to do work that is useful and constructive.

It may be somewhat unfulfilling to read a chapter filled with criticisms that does not conclude with more concrete, constructive suggestions regarding solutions to the outlined problems. However, the problems to be addressed are exceedingly complex, and will require substantial conceptual and analytical advancements. In order to spur researchers to recognize and address these many problems, it seems most appropriate at this point to clarify their details, to highlight their significance, and to make clear that a hypothesis many have long taken for granted as valid now deserves closer scrutiny.

Most importantly, however, we must not lose a sense of the forest for the trees with regard to candidate perception. Perhaps the most significant substantive/normative question here is how accurate such perceptions are. If projection exerts a dominant influence, then we would not expect to see high levels of accuracy, and voters are ill-equipped to function as democratic citizens according to the ideals of political theorists.

But as Krosnick (1990) showed, representative samples of American adults were remarkably accurate in their perceptions of the stands the candidates took on major issues in 1984. Furthermore, perceptions were especially accurate among people who are highly involved in politics, presumably because of their regular exposure to useful information about the candidates through the media and through interpersonal interactions. Larson (1990) reported a similar result and demonstrated as well that voters can accurately learn the positions of candidates if they are conveyed by the media. Thus, it seems, the responsibility for inaccuracy in candidate perception may lie with inadequate media coverage of issues (Patterson and McClure 1976) rather than with the handicapping psychodynamics of projection generated within the human mind.

References

Abelson, Robert P. 1959. "Modes of Resolution of Belief Dilemmas." *Journal of Conflict Resolution* 3:343–52.

Abelson, Robert P., and Milton J. Rosenberg. 1958. "Symbolic Psycho-logic: A Model of Attitudinal Cognition." *Behavioral Science* 3:1–8.

Abramowitz, Alan I. 1978. "The Impact of a Presidential Debate on Voter Rationality." *American Journal of Political Science* 22:680–90.

Anderson, J. A., and R. K. Avery. 1978. "An Analysis of Changes in Voter Perceptions of Candidates' Positions." *Communication Monographs* 45:354–61.

Arnold, H. J. 1982. "Moderator Variables: A Clarification of Conceptual, Analytic, and Psychometric Issues." *Organizational Behavior and Human Performance* 29:143–74.

Arnold, H. J., and M. G. Evans. 1979. "Testing Multiplicative Models Does Not Require Ratio Scales." *Organizational Behavior and Human Performance* 24:41–59.

Asher, Herbert B. 1983. "Voting Behavior Research in the 1980s: An Examination of Some Old and New Problem Areas." In Ada Finifter, ed., *Political Science: The State of the Discipline.* Washington, DC: American Political Science Association.

Bartels, Larry M. 1988. *Presidential Primaries and the Dynamics of Public Choice.* Princeton, NJ: Princeton University Press.

Berelson, Bernard R., Paul R. Lazarsfeld, and M. N. McPhee. 1954. *Voting: A Study of Opinion Formation in a Presidential Election Campaign.* Chicago: University of Chicago Press.

Berscheid, Ellen, and Elaine H. Walster. 1978. *Interpersonal Attraction.* Reading, MA: Addison-Wesley.

Brent, E., and Donald Granberg. 1982. "Subjective Agreement with the Presidential Candidates of 1976 and 1980." *Journal of Personality and Social Psychology* 42:393–403.

Brody, Richard A., and Benjamin I. Page. 1972. "Comment: The Assessment of Policy Voting." *American Political Science Review* 66:450–8.

Bruner, J. S. 1957. "Going Beyond the Information Given." In H. Gulber et al., *Contemporary Approaches to Cognition.* Cambridge, MA: Harvard University Press.

Carmines, Edward C., and James A. Stimson. 1989. *Issue Evolution: Race and the Transformation of American Politics*. Princeton, NJ: Princeton University Press.

Cohen, Jacob. 1978. "Partialled Products *Are* Interactions: Partialled Powers *Are* Curve Components." *Psychological Bulletin* 85:858–66.

Cohen, Jacob, and Patricia Cohen. 1975. *Applied Multiple Regression/Correlation Analysis for the Behavioral Sciences*. Hillsdale, NJ: Erlbaum.

Conover, Pamela J., and Stanley Feldman. 1982. "Projection and the Perception of Candidates' Issue Positions." *Western Political Quarterly* 35:228–44.

1986. "The Role of Inference in the Perception of Political Candidates." In Richard R. Lau and David O. Sears, eds., *Political Cognition*. Hillsdale, NJ: Erlbaum.

1989. "Candidate Perception in an Ambiguous World: Campaigns, Cues, and Inference Processes." *American Journal of Political Science* 33:912–40.

Downs, Anthony. 1957. *An Economic Theory of Democracy*. New York: Harper & Row.

Enelow, James M., and Meluin J. Hinich. 1984. *The Spatial Theory of Voting: An Introduction*. Cambridge: Cambridge University Press.

1985. "Estimating the Parameters of a Spatial Model of Elections: An Empirical Test Based on the 1980 National Election Study." *Political Methodology* 11:249–68.

Evans, Martin G. 1991. "The Problem of Analyzing Multiplicative Composites: Interactions Revisited." *American Psychologist* 46:6–15.

Feldman, Stanley, and Pamela J. Conover. 1983. "Candidates, Issues, and Voters: The Role of Inference in Political Perception." *Journal of Politics* 45:810–39.

Festinger, Leon. 1954. "A Theory of Social Comparison Processes." *Human Relations* 7:117–40.

1957. *A Theory of Cognitive Dissonance*. Evanston, IL: Row, Peterson.

Festinger, Leon, H. Riecken, and Stanley Schachter. 1956. *When Prophecy Fails*. Minneapolis: University of Minnesota Press.

Franklin, Charles H. 1991. "Eschewing Obfuscation? Campaigns and the Perception of U.S. Senate Incumbents." *American Political Science Review* 85:1193–214.

Freedman, J. L., and David O. Sears. 1965. "Selective Exposure." In Leonard Berkowitz, ed., *Advances in Experimental Social Psychology*, Vol. 2. New York: Academic Press.

Freud, Sigmund. 1938. *The Basic Writings of Sigmund Freud*. New York: Modern Library.

Gerber, Elizabeth R., and John E. Jackson. 1993. "Endogenous Preferences and the Study of Institutions." *American Political Science Review* 87:639–56.

Googin, Malcolm L. 1984. "The Ideological Content of Presidential Communications: The Message-Tailoring Hypothesis Revisited." *American Politics Quarterly* 12:361–84.

Graber, Doris A. 1976. *Verbal Behavior and Politics*. Urbana: University of Illinois Press.

Granberg, Donald. 1985a. "An Anomaly in Political Perception." *Public Opinion Quarterly* 49:504–16.

1985b. "An Assimilation Effect in Perceptions of Sweden's Political Parties on the Left–Right Dimension." *Scandinavian Journal of Psychology* 26:88–91.

1987a. "A Contextual Effect in Political Perception and Self-Placement on an Ideology Scale: Comparative Analyses of Sweden and the U.S." *Scandinavian Political Studies* 10:39–60.

1987b. "Candidate Preference, Membership Group, and Estimates of Voting Behavior." *Social Cognition* 5:323–35.

Granberg, Donald, and Edward E. Brent. 1974. "Dove–Hawk Placements in the 1968 Election: Applications of Social Judgment and Balance Theories." *Journal of Personality and Social Psychology* 29:687–95.

1980. "Perceptions of Issue Positions of Presidential Candidates." *American Scientist* 68:617–25.

1983. "When Prophecy Binds: The Preference–Expectation Link in U.S. Presidential Elections, 1952–1980." *Journal of Personality and Social Psychology* 45:477–91.

Granberg, Donald, W. Harris, and M. King. 1981. "Assimilation But Little Contrast in the 1976 U.S. Presidential Election." *Journal of Social Psychology* 108:241–7.

Granberg, Donald, and S. Holmberg. 1986a. "Political Perception Among Voters in Sweden and the U.S.: Analyses of Issues with Explicit Alternatives." *Western Political Quarterly* 39:7–28.

1986b. "Subjective Ideology in Sweden and the U.S." *Research on Political Sociology* 2:107–43.

1988. *The Political System Matters: Social Psychology and Voting Behavior in Sweden and the United States.* New York: Cambridge University Press.

Granberg, Donald, and R. Jenks. 1977. "Assimilation and Contrast Effects in the 1972 Election." *Human Relations* 30:623–40.

Granberg, Donald, Jeff Kasmer, and T. Nanneman. 1988. "An Empirical Examination of Two Theories of Political Perception." *Western Political Quarterly* 41:29–46.

Granberg, Donald, and M. King. 1980. "Cross-Lagged Panel Analysis of the Relation Between Attraction and Perceived Similarity." *Journal of Experimental Social Psychology* 16:573–81.

Granberg, Donald, and C. Robertson. 1982. "Contrast Effects in Estimating Policies of the Federal Government." *Public Opinion Quarterly* 46:43–53.

Granberg, Donald, and J. Seidel. 1976. "Social Judgments of the Urban Unrest and Vietnam Issues in 1968 and 1972." *Social Forces* 55:1–15.

Hastie, Reid, and P. A. Kumar. 1979. "Person Memory: Personality Traits as Organizing Principles in Memory for Behaviors." *Journal of Personality and Social Psychology* 37:25–38.

Heider, Fritz. 1958. *The Psychology of Interpersonal Relations.* New York: Wiley.

Hermann, Margaret G. 1986. *Political Psychology.* San Francisco: Jossey-Bass.

Jacoby, William G. 1988. "The Impact of Party Identification on Issue Attitudes." *American Journal of Political Science* 32:643–61.

Jordan, Donald L. 1993. "Newspaper Effects on Policy Preferences." *Public Opinion Quarterly* 57:191–204.

Judd, Charles M., and Bella M. DePaulo. 1979. "The Effect of Perspective Differences on the Measurement of Involving Attitudes." *Social Psychology Quarterly* 42:185–9.

Judd, Charles M., and Judith M. Harackiewicz. 1980. "Contrast Effects in Attitude Judgment: An Examination of the Accentuation Hypothesis." *Journal of Personality and Social Psychology* 38:390–8.

Judd, Charles M., and Joel T. Johnson. 1981. "Attitudes, Polarization, and Diagnosticity: Exploring the Effect of Affect." *Journal of Personality and Social Psychology* 41:26–36.

Judd, Charles M., David A. Kenny, and Jon A. Krosnick. 1983. "Judging the Positions of Presidential Candidates: Models of Assimilation and Contrast." *Journal of Personality and Social Psychology* 44:952–63.

Judd, Charles M., and Jon A. Krosnick. 1982. "Attitude Centrality, Organization, and Measurement." *Journal of Personality and Social Psychology* 42:436–47.

Judd, Charles M., and Gary H. McClelland. 1989. *Data Analysis: A Model-Comparison Approach.* San Diego: Harcourt Brace Jovanovich.

Kenny, David A. 1979. *Correlation and Causality.* New York: Wiley.

Kessler, Roland C., and D. F. Greenberg. 1981. *Linear Panel Analysis: Models of Quantitative Change.* New York: Academic Press.

Kinder, Donald R. 1978. "Political Person Perception: The Asymmetrical Influence of Sentiment and Choice on Perceptions of Presidential Candidates." *Journal of Personality and Social Psychology* 36:859–71.

    1983. "Diversity and Complexity in American Public Opinion." In A. Finifter, ed., *Political Science: The State of the Discipline.* Washington, DC: American Political Science Association.

Kinder, Donald R., Gordon S. Adams, and Paul W. Gronke. 1989. "Economics and Politics in the 1984 American Presidential Election." *American Journal of Political Science* 33:491–515.

Kinder, Donald R., and Thomas R. Palfrey. 1993. *Experimental Foundations of Political Science.* Ann Arbor: University of Michigan Press.

Kinder, Donald R., and David O. Sears. 1981. "Prejudice and Politics: Symbolic Racism versus Racial Threats to the Good Life." *Journal of Personality and Social Psychology* 40:414–31.

King, M. 1977–8. "Assimilation and Contrast of Presidential Candidates' Issue Positions, 1972." *Public Opinion Quarterly* 41:515–22.

Krosnick, Jon A. 1988a. "Attitude Importance and Attitude Change." *Journal of Experimental Social Psychology* 24:240–55.

    1988b. "The Role of Attitude Importance in Social Evaluation: A Study of Policy Preferences, Presidential Candidate Evaluations, and Voting Behavior." *Journal of Personality and Social Psychology* 55:196–210.

    1990. "Americans' Perceptions of Presidential Candidates: A Test of the Projection Hypothesis." *Journal of Social Issues* 46:159–82.

Kuhn, Thomas S. 1970. *The Structure of Scientific Revolutions.* Chicago: University of Chicago Press.

Larson, Stephanie G. 1990. "Information and Learning in a Congressional District: A Social Experiment." *American Journal of Political Science* 34:1102–18.

Lazarsfeld, Paul F., Bernard Berelson, and H. Gaudet. 1948. *The People's Choice.* New York: Columbia University Press.

Lorge, Irving. 1936. "Prestige, Suggestion, and Attitudes." *Journal of Social Psychology* 7:386–402.

Macdonald, Stuart Elaine, Ola Listhaug, and George Rabinowitz. 1991. "Issues and Party Support in Multiparty Systems." *American Political Science Review* 85:1107–31.

Manis, Melvin, S. D. Cornell, and J. C. Moore. 1974. "Transmission of Attitude-Relevant Information Through a Communication Chain." *Journal of Personality and Social Psychology* 30:81–94.

Marks, G., and Norman Miller. 1987. "Ten Years of Research on the False-Consensus Effect: An Empirical and Theoretical Review." *Psychological Bulletin* 102:72–90.

Markus, Gregory B. 1979. *Analyzing Panel Data*. Beverly Hills, CA: Sage.

    1982. "Political Attitudes During an Election Year: A Report on the 1980 NES Panel Study." *American Political Science Review* 76:538–60.

Markus, Gregory B., and Philip E. Converse. 1979. "A Dynamic Simultaneous Equation Model of Electoral Choice." *American Political Science Review* 73:1055–77.

Martinez, Michael D. 1988. "Political Involvement and the Projection Process." *Political Behavior* 10:151–67.

McCann, C. Douglas, E. Tory Higgins, and Rocco A. Fondacaro. 1991. "Primacy and Recency in Communication and Self-Persuasion: How Successive Audiences and Multiple Encodings Influence Subsequent Evaluative Judgments." *Social Cognition* 9:47–66.

McGinniss, Joseph. 1969. *The Selling of the President 1968*. New York: Trident Press.

Miller, L. W., and Lee Sigelman. 1978. "Is the Audience the Message? A Note on LBJ's Vietnam Statements." *Public Opinion Quarterly* 42:71–80.

Mueller, J. E. 1969. "The Use of Content Analysis in International Relations." In George Gerbner, Ole R. Holsti, K. Krippendorff, and P. Stone, eds., *The Analysis of Communication Content*. New York: Wiley.

Mullen, Brian, J. L. Atkins, D. S. Champion, C. Edwards, D. Hardy, J. E. Story, and M. Vanderklok. 1985. "The False Consensus Effect: A Meta-Analysis of 155 Hypothesis Tests." *Journal of Experimental Social Psychology* 21:262–83.

Newcomb, Theodore M. 1953. "An Approach to the Study of Communicative Acts." *Psychological Review* 60:393–404.

    1961. *The Acquaintance Process*. New York: Holt.

    1968. "Interpersonal Balance." In R. P. Abelson, E. Aronson, W. J. McGuire, T. M. Newcomb, M. J. Rosenberg, and P. H. Tannenbaum, eds., *Theories of Cognitive Consistency: A Sourcebook*. Chicago: Rand McNally.

Newtson, D., and T. Czerlinsky. 1974. "Adjustment of Attitude Communications for Contrasts by Extreme Audiences." *Journal of Personality and Social Psychology* 30:829–37.

Nie, Norman H., Sidney Verba, and John R. Petrocik. 1979. *The Changing American Voter*. Cambridge, MA: Harvard University Press.

Osgood, Charles E., and Percy Tannenbaum. 1955. "The Principle of Congruity and the Prediction of Attitude Change." *Psychological Review* 62:42–55.

Ostrom, Thomas M., and Harry S. Upshaw. 1968. "Psychological Perspective and Attitude Change." In Anthony G. Greenwald, Timothy C. Brock, and Thomas M. Ostrom, eds., *Psychological Foundations of Attitudes*. New York: Academic Press.

Ottati, Victor, Martin Fishbein, and Susan E. Middlestadt. 1988. "Determinants of Voters' Beliefs About the Candidates' Stands on the Issues: The Role of Evaluative Bias Heuristics and the Candidates' Expressed Message." *Journal of Personality and Social Psychology* 55:517–29.

Page, Benjamin I. 1976. "The Theory of Political Ambiguity." *American Political Science Review* 70:742–52.

    1978. *Choices and Echoes in Presidential Elections*. Chicago: University of Chicago Press.

Page, Benjamin I., and Richard A. Brody. 1972. "Policy Voting and the Electoral Process: The Vietnam War Issue." *American Political Science Review* 66: 979–95.

Page, Benjamin I., and C. C. Jones. 1979. "Reciprocal Effects of Policy Preferences, Party Loyalties, and the Vote." *American Political Science Review* 73: 1071–89.

Page, Benjamin I., and Robert Y. Shapiro. 1983. "Effects of Public Opinion on Policy." *American Political Science Review* 77:175–90.

1984. "Presidents as Opinion Leaders: Some New Evidence." *Policy Studies Journal* 12:649–61.

1987. "Educating and Manipulating the Public." Paper presented at the annual meetings of the Midwest Political Science Association, Chicago, April 21–4.

Patterson, Thomas E., and Robert D. McClure. 1976. *The Unseeing Eye: The Myth of Television Power in National Elections.* New York: G. P. Putnam's Sons.

Patton, G. W. R., and B. Smith. 1980. "The Effect of Taking Issue Positions on Ratings of Political Candidates." *Political Psychology* 1:20–34.

Petty, Richard E., and John T. Cacioppo. 1986. *Communication and Persuasion: Central and Peripheral Routes to Attitude Change.* New York: Springer-Verlag.

Pomper, Gerald M. 1972. "From Confusion to Clarity: Issues and American Voters, 1956–78." *American Political Science Review* 66:415–28.

Rabinowitz, George, and Stuart Elaine Macdonald. 1989. "A Directional Theory of Issue Voting." *American Political Science Review* 83:93–121.

Rosenstone, S. J. 1983. *Forecasting Presidential Elections.* New Haven, CT: Yale University Press.

Ross, Lee, D. Greene, and P. House. 1977. "The 'False Consensus Effect': An Egocentric Bias in Social Perception and Attribution Processes." *Journal of Experimental and Social Psychology* 13:279–301.

Schmidt, F. L. 1973. "Implications of a Measurement Problem for Expectancy Theory Research." *Organizational Behavior and Human Performance* 10:243–51.

Schmidt, F. L., and T. C. Wilson. 1975. "Expectancy Value Models of Attitude Measurement: A Measurement Problem." *Journal of Marketing Research* 12:366–8.

Sears, David O., Richard R. Lau, Tom R. Tyler, and Harris M. Allen. 1980. "Self-Interest vs. Symbolic Politics in Policy Attitudes and Presidential Voting." *American Political Science Review* 74:670–84.

Shaffer, S. D. 1981. "Balance Theory and Political Cognitions." *American Politics Quarterly* 9:291–320.

Shepsle, Kenneth A. 1972. "The Strategy of Ambiguity: Uncertainty and Electoral Competition." *American Political Science Review* 66:555–68.

Sherrod, D. R. 1972. "Selective Perception of Political Candidates." *Public Opinion Quarterly* 35:554–62.

Singer, J. E. 1968. "The Bothersomeness of Inconsistency." In Robert P. Abelson, E. Aronson, W. J. McGuire, T. M. Newcomb, M. J. Rosenberg, and P. H. Tannenbaum, eds., *Theories of Cognitive Consistency: A Sourcebook.* Chicago: Rand McNally.

Swindel, S. H., and M. M. Miller. 1986. "Mass Media and Political Decision Making: Application of the Accumulated Information Model to the 1980 Presidential Election." In M. McLaughlin, ed. *Communication Yearbook 9.* Beverly Hills, CA: Sage.

Williams, D. 1980. "Reagan's Strategy." *Newsweek*, July 28, 32.

Wright, G. C., and M. B. Berkman. 1986. "Candidates and Policy in U.S. Senate Elections." *American Political Science Review* 80:567–90.

Zajonc, Robert B. 1968. "Cognitive Theories in Social Psychology." In Gardner Lindzey and Eliot Aronson, eds., *The Handbook of Social Psychology*, 2nd ed., Vol. 1. Reading, MA: Addison-Wesley.

Zaller, John R. 1992. *The Nature and Origins of Mass Opinion*. New York: Cambridge University Press.

Part III   The Psychology–Politics Nexus

5

Political Psychology and Political Science

WENDY M. RAHN
JOHN L. SULLIVAN
THOMAS J. RUDOLPH

In our other chapter in this volume, we discussed the history of the subfield of political psychology, tracing the rise, fall, and continuity of certain themes and theoretical approaches within it. In this chapter, we attempt to situate political psychology in the wider discipline of political science. We begin by documenting its growing influence. We then offer several speculations about the causes of its increasing regard within political science. We further demonstrate how political psychology, in its current form, is relevant to the core concerns of the wider discipline.

THE GROWTH OF POLITICAL PSYCHOLOGY

We can assess the visibility of political psychology in political science by examining the content of articles published in the discipline's three most prestigious general journals: the *American Political Science Review*, the *American Journal of Political Science*, and *The Journal of Politics*. We reviewed articles published in these journals for three time periods: 1981 to 1983 ($n = 310$), 1991 to 1993 ($n = 326$), and 1997 to 1999:3 ($n = 312$). We excluded research notes, workshop articles, review essays, and controversies from our tabulations. We coded each article as falling into one of four categories: rational choice, political psychology, political behavior, or something else. The "something else" category includes a variety of different types of work, including political philosophy, public policy analysis, some kinds of comparative politics, and some kinds of international relations scholarship. Given that we were attempting to document the vitality of political psychology, we followed a conservative coding strategy. For example, Bartels's (1993) article, "Messages Received," was placed in the rational choice category simply because of

We thank Laura Olson for her research assistance of this chapter.

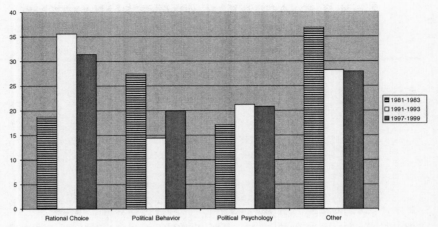

Figure 5.1. Types of articles published in political science journals, by time periods.

his assumption that "respondents use new information from the mass media and elsewhere to update their political opinions *rationally* in accordance to Bayes' Rule" (Bartels 1993:268, emphasis added), even though the content of the article draws on psychological theories about media effects. Articles that are essentially criticisms of rational choice theories, such as MacDonald, Listhaug, and Rabinowitz (1991) or Searing (1991), were also coded as rational choice articles. Political behavior articles were separated from political psychology articles according to whether the explanations offered for the phenomenon emphasized institutional, contextual, or cultural variables (for the former) or individual-level psychological processes such as opinion formation and change (for the latter). Because of these coding rules, we view our content analysis as a stringent test of the salience of political psychology to the wider discipline.

Figure 5.1 presents the results of our analysis, collapsing across journals. The strongest message the figure sends is the dramatic growth of rational choice in the discipline. The percentage of articles devoted to rational choice approaches nearly doubled from the early 1980s to the early 1990s, although it appears to have stabilized at the end of the decade. While this trend is somewhat overstated given our generous rule for inclusion in the rational choice category, the growth of rational choice is unmistakable (see also Green and Shapiro 1994).

Political psychology also increased its share during the time period studied, although its growth is not nearly as dramatic as that of rational choice. Given our conservative coding rules with respect to political

Table 5.1. *Percentages of Articles by Journal, Category, and Time Period*

	APSR	AJPS	JOP	All Three Journals
Rational Choice				
1981–3	23.1%	25.0%	7.2%	18.7%
1991–3	45.5%	40.3%	16.5%	35.6%
1997–9	40.4%	34.7%	18.9%	31.4%
Political Behavior				
1981–3	19.7%	34.4%	30.0%	27.4%
1991–3	12.4%	14.0%	17.6%	14.4%
1997–9	17.2%	16.9%	27.4%	19.9%
Political Psychology				
1981–3	13.7%	16.7%	21.6%	17.1%
1991–3	14.0%	25.4%	27.5%	21.2%
1997–9	16.2%	21.2%	23.2%	20.8%
Other				
1981–3	43.6%	24.0%	41.2%	36.8%
1991–3	28.1%	20.2%	38.5%	28.2%
1997–9	26.3%	27.1%	30.5%	27.9%

psychology, we are inclined to view the increase presented in Figure 5.1 as real and probably understated to some degree. The other clear message in Figure 5.1 is that the growth of the two interdisciplinary subfields – rational choice and political psychology – has largely come at the expense of political behavior and, to a lesser degree, the residual "other" category.

Table 5.1 presents our analysis broken down by journal. Inspection of this table reveals a more nuanced account than the aggregated results of Figure 5.1. From the early 1980s to the early 1990s, political psychology became increasingly visible in two of the three journals, but its share in the discipline's leading journal remained virtually unchanged. By the late 1990s, the percentage of articles in political psychology remained or moved above its 1980s levels in all three journals. We conclude, then, based on this content analysis, that political psychology has garnered greater exposure in the last two decades, at least as gauged by our measure of scholarly visibility. While there are clear differences among the three journals – political psychology remains least well represented in the premier journal – its presence in the discipline has clearly increased over the last twenty years.[1]

---

1 It is the authors' impression that contemporary political psychology also reflects a more sophisticated understanding of psychological theory than does work from the early 1980s.

Visibility of research publications is one way to measure the influence of a subfield. We can also point to other developments in the last few years that strengthen our claim about the growth of the subfield. The establishment within the American Political Science Association of an organized political psychology section and consistent increases in membership in the International Society of Political Psychology both point to vigorous interest in the subfield. Several major presses have launched or are launching book series in political psychology, suggesting that the imprimatur of the subfield now comes with enough value added that it will sell books. Some of the books published in these series even carry "political psychology" in the title or subtitle (Iyengar and McGuire 1993; Sniderman, Brody, and Tetlock 1991). One of these (Sniderman et al. 1991) went on to win the discipline's Woodrow Wilson Award for best book on American politics. Other indicators of political psychology's growing regard within the discipline include several formal graduate training programs in political psychology at major universities and the Summer Institute in Political Psychology at Ohio State University (see also Sears and Funk 1991).

Why is political psychology growing now? Is this excitement a passing fad or something more substantial (see Hermann 1989 for another answer to this question)? In an insightful article about intellectual fads in political science, using the histories of political socialization and community power studies as examples, Yali Peng (1994) suggests several reasons why academic disciplines in general and political science in particular are prone to faddishness. Clearly, the reflowering of political psychology in the last decade is at least partially attributable to the causes Peng notes, such as the fragmentation of the discipline and the need of younger scholars to publish and make a name for themselves in the "repute system" (Ricci 1984). Some of the incentives for doing political psychology surely owe something to its being political science's soup du jour, but there have also been larger societal, intellectual, and generational changes that have opened up a window of opportunity for those who are trained in the theories and methods of the subfield. Furthermore, the rapid institutionalization of political psychology in the last few years suggests that the trend evinced in the publication data is not simply due to current fancy. The movement may have more staying power and vitality than is characteristic of mere fads.

We have some speculations about "why now" for political psychology. At the most general level, the problems facing the world in the late 1980s changed from a preoccupation with superpower confrontation to age-old conflicts of race, ethnicity, and nation-building. Prevailing theories seemed inadequate for explaining these new tensions; psychologically informed models may hold out more promise for coming to grips with the new face of the world.

At the same time, the United States began a collective reconstruction in the 1980s. The entrepreneurial spirit championed in popular culture during that time is now portrayed as an excess of greed and selfishness. Community and public good are challenging unbridled individualism as important values. Culture is as important as economics (see Putnam 1993). This collective memory process has created a climate more receptive to political psychological accounts of behavior. While rational choice models continue to occupy a privileged position in the discipline as a whole, there are clear trends that, to borrow the title of a book representative of this new era, we have moved *Beyond Self Interest* (Mansbridge 1990) in our accounts of human motivation.

Of course, there have always been critics of the rational actor, self-interest model of political behavior. The symbolic politics tradition (Edelman 1964; Sears 1993), for example, sought to show how political behavior is less often moved by practical, utilitarian calculations of cost and benefit than by long-standing, emotionally charged predispositions and leadership manipulation of cultural icons. While this perspective has always had quite a few adherents, the symbolic manipulation of the 1988 election and the political problems of a post–Cold War world have given these ideas added relevance. Oddly enough, the symbolic politics idea has even received recognition within a more purely economic framework. For example, Green's (1992) article on the "price elasticity" of mass preferences, one that we placed in our rational choice category, ends with the conclusion that the public's preferences for political goods are extremely unresponsive to price considerations in comparison to economic goods. "Microeconomic reasoning is not inapplicable to mass political preferences; but neither is it especially powerful" (Green 1992:137).

Straightforward application of economic models may prove to be less and less tenable, even for enthusiasts of rational choice. Political economists Brennen and Lomasky (1993), for example, argue that "although homo economicus may be a useful abstraction in explaining market behavior, he is unlikely to be as useful in a theory of electoral politics. Voters cannot properly be modeled as choosing the electoral option that would, if it prevailed, best satisfy their interests, and in this critical respect the standard public choice account of democratic political process is flawed" (17). They then go on to construct a public choice theory based on the notion that people's behavior is primarily motivated by expressive (as opposed to instrumental) concerns, which winds up bearing a strong resemblance to a mathematical version of symbolic politics theory.

There are other ways in which our data are misleading about the pre-eminence of rational choice. One of the trends we noticed is that even quite formal rational choice models are increasingly building in "psychological" assumptions of limited information and/or cognitive biases. Our coding scheme does not detect this more subtle way in which political psychology has infiltrated the way the discipline thinks about political behavior. We point to several articles that serve to illustrate this type of penetration. Lupia (1992) presents a formal theory of agenda control (complete with lemmas, with proofs in the appendix, sure signs of the article's pedigree) that incorporates the idea of "incompletely informed voters." This assumption drives the results of the various models, and because of it, Lupia derives conclusions at odds with those of more traditional (read: nonpsychological) rational choice models. Another formal model, that of Orbell and Dawes (1991), also explicitly takes into account psychological concepts, and in doing so, it revises the standard pessimistic conclusion about the failure of cooperation in prisoner's dilemma situations. The article even acknowledges in the title that it draws inspiration from recent psychological theorizing: "A 'Cognitive Miser' Theory of Cooperators' Advantage." More recently, in "A Behavioral Approach to the Rational Choice Theory of Collective Action," Ostrom (1998) acknowledges the contributions of cognitive scientists and explicitly incorporates their ideas about heuristics into her model of collective action. Additionally, Chong (1996) presents a formal model of how people develop common frames of reference to political issues. Though clearly formal in nature, Chong's model is grounded in the psychological processes of framing and association.

Not just rational choice models, but popular culture too has become increasingly "psychologized." Bellah and his colleagues (1985) write of the "culture of therapy" that now pervades modern American life, a tendency surely abetted by the explosion of talk show programs that occurred in the 1990s. These shows typically feature guests and experts who emphasize pop psychological interpretations of both everyday problems and extraordinary life situations. Increasingly, social problems and tragedies are treated psychologically, as evidenced by the psychologizing that took place soon after the shootings at Columbine High School. These wider cultural forces undoubtedly influence the interests of students and the approaches they find appealing. Student interest in political psychology has probably never been higher.

In addition to cultural influences, there are scholarly reasons for the renewed interest in political psychology. As we note in our other chapter in this volume, political psychological approaches have provided new leverage on old problems and have furnished successful explanations for contemporary phenomena of concern to political scientists. The political behavior research of the 1950s and 1960s focused on distal, long-term socialization processes in accounting for political behavior. These explanations seemed increasingly less applicable to a more candidate-centered, television-mediated politics. Political science researchers were drawn to psychological work that emphasized the *contemporary* information environment as an important influence on behavior. For example, the role of the mass media in politics was underplayed and minimized to the point where most political scientists routinely told their students that the media had little effect on citizens or on political outcomes (and perhaps some still do; see Finkel 1993; Gelman and King 1993). Research on agenda setting, priming, and framing turned all that on its head, and demonstrated the value of using concepts and methods from political psychology to obtain stronger insights into media effects (see the discussion of media effects in our other chapter in this volume). These efforts suggested that other verities might be overturned and stimulated new research programs in political psychology.

Generational change within the discipline has also aided the growth of political psychology. The scholars at the forefront of the behavioral revolution, who were often wedded to the large sample survey as the hallmark of science, have been replaced by a new cohort more eclectic in its methodological tastes and more tolerant of nontraditional approaches. Experimental methods, focus groups, in-depth interviewing, and Q-methodological studies are routinely published now in the discipline's most prestigious journals. Increasingly, political psychologists are taking seriously the methodological desiderata of multimethod approaches and triangulation urged upon them by Campbell and Fiske (1959) and Greenstein (1969). For example, random sample surveys have been paired with Q-methodology (Sullivan, Fried, and Dietz 1992; Theiss-Morse 1993), and focus groups have been joined with surveys (Conover, Crewe, and Searing 1991; Delli Carpini and Keeter 1993, 1996; Hibbing and Theiss-Morse 1995). Many of the "softer" methods employed by political psychologists would not have been acceptable fifteen years ago. The tolerance displayed by the current generation of scholars has enhanced the acceptance of political psychology as a separate subfield with unique subject matter and approaches.

IS POLITICAL PSYCHOLOGY SUFFICIENTLY POLITICAL?

As a subfield matures, both the producers and consumers of the knowledge in that domain reflect on its progress. Where has it come from? Where is it going? Is the scholarship worthwhile, or is it old coffee in new cups? As we demonstrated earlier, political psychology is growing more visible. The wider discipline, therefore, has to take it seriously. It is no surprise, then, that we would begin to hear from detractors. The most serious charge that seems to be leveled against the "new" political psychology is that it is "insufficiently political" (see Kuklinski, Luskin, and Bolland 1991; Luskin this volume; Luttbeg 1991).

The very act of addressing the question of whether research in political psychology is sufficiently political requires us to draw on psychological concepts. The answer to this question, of course, depends on where one sits on the political-to-psychological continuum. As in most cases, our perceptions are influenced by psychological tendencies – in this case, the biasing effects of assimilation and contrast.

Assuming that most scholarship in political psychology has an actual location on this continuum, those of us near that particular location will assimilate it and perceive it as closer to ourselves than it actually is. And since "where we are" is obviously sufficiently political, so too will the field be sufficiently political. Those of us far from the location of political psychology on this continuum will contrast it, and perceive it as further away from ourselves than it actually is. And, since things "less political" or "more psychological" than our preferred position are insufficiently political, so too will the field be insufficiently political – by a considerable margin. Or so the theory says. According to this theory, then, the authors of this chapter will see the balance between political and psychological analysis in the field of political psychology as about right, while critics of the subfield will believe there is far too little political analysis and far too much psychology in the field.

Perhaps social judgment theory is simply wrong or inappropriate to this example. We hope our canvas of the scope of political psychology in our other chapter reduced this potential distortion through its focus on the diversity of the field as a whole. Our review should have made it clear that it is difficult to characterize the extent to which a typical or modal example of research in political psychology is sufficiently or insufficiently political in its orientation. In the remainder of this chapter we will discuss what constitutes the "political" in political analysis, and then we will focus more specifically on several potential objections to the lack of "politics" in political psychology. We will examine these objections further by creating a typology of work in political psychology and treating at greater length several exemplars of each type, to illuminate how they fall short and how they measure up to the desideratum that work in political psychology be sufficiently political as well as sufficiently psychological. Then we provide a summary of the deeply political problems that have been addressed in political psychology, and the way political analysis has been combined with psychology to provide important explanations and insights. Finally, we present an argument in favor of interdisciplinary approaches such as that of political psychology, and argue that they characterize some of the best contemporary research and are likely to do so for some time to come.

THE "POLITICAL" IN POLITICAL PSYCHOLOGY

In this section we take up more explicitly the task of defending the field against charges that it is insufficiently political. We first attempt to elucidate what the charge may mean. We then illustrate with recent political psychological research that much of the field deals with issues that may be deemed political by various definitions of the word.

What Do the Naysayers Mean?

First, one complaint may be that political psychology is insufficiently political because it spends too much effort studying the mass public and not enough examining the role of political elites or, more precisely, does not pay enough attention to the role of elites in mass political behavior. Another objection might be that political psychology may be insufficiently political because it is too focused on the individual as the unit of analysis. Finally, and related to the foregoing, there may be concern that when psychological theories and methods are applied to political science content, political theories are not integrated with the psychological models, and the implications of this research for larger political questions are not explicitly addressed.

Let us take up the first objection, that of the role of elites. A number of prominent books on public opinion have in fact placed elite discourse and political leadership cues at the center of theories of political attitude formation and change. Richard Brody (1991) argues in his book on presidential popularity that the vicissitudes of presidents' approval ratings depend heavily on the messages citizens pick up in the mass media about policy outcomes. If political elites are critical of these outcomes, information presumably picked up by the mass media, so too will be the public. This dynamic even seems to be at work during "rally events," events usually considered exceptional in other theories of presidential popularity: "When opposition elites avoid criticizing foreign policy failures, the public appears to ignore manifestly bad outcomes and increases its support for the president. International crises in which the opposition elite performs its usual role of criticizing presidential policy-making fail to produce rallies" (Brody 1991:169–70).

Page and Shapiro (1992), in their mammoth analysis of a half-century of public opinion trends, also argue that change in public opinion is often driven by the information about events that is carried in the news media. People respond to interpretations of these events by various elites, including news commentators, experts, and public officials, as reported by the mass media, rather than to the events themselves.

The evolution in Americans' racial attitudes and party images charted by Carmines and Stimson (1989) is also driven largely by elite behavior. In their model, citizens pick up cues about what the parties stand for by observing party activists. Activist polarization around some issue helps clarify it for the less politically interested mass electorate, and should people find that they care about this new cleavage, a new policy alignment may emerge around the issue.

Political competition among elites also emerges as an important variable in John Zaller's (1992) book on public opinion. Individual predispositions and levels of political involvement interact with the information environment to produce highly variegated response patterns on various issues. Whether elites are polarized on some topic and how intense the message flow is on the issue are two important variables in explaining the distribution of opinion across different issue areas in his model.

Is the role accorded political elites in these just-reviewed books "sufficiently political" political psychology? We, of course, think so, and critics of the subfield, we suspect, would be hard pressed to disagree. However, it is also important to note that while political elites are indeed central to these works, there is nothing particularly political about their role in mass opinion. Rather, elites figure conspicuously in these analyses because their actions and behavior provide the mass public with cues and information that shape individuals' attitudes toward political objects such as the parties or public policies. The importance of political elites is thus largely informational, not primarily theoretical. Indeed, a close look at the mechanisms driving the processes described in these books reveals that the explanations are for the most part psychological theories that have been heavily politicized, that is, placed in political context. For example, Page and Shapiro resort to "communicator credibility," a persuasion variable long studied in psychology, to explain their findings that news commentary and expert opinion both have hefty effects on aggregate mass opinion change. Zaller is more explicit in acknowledging that there is nothing inherently political in the theoretical engine that drives his model:

[S]trictly speaking, one cannot use the results of my modeling to support even a weak argument for elite influence. The reason is that the RAS model, as formulated, is entirely agnostic about the sources of the political communications that move public opinion. Thus, it is consistent with the model that elites, including even the media, have no influence whatsoever on public opinion, and that all political communications diffuse through the population by personal contact, like germs. (Zaller 1992:272)

We would be happy to claim all of these books as exemplars of political psychology, even if some of the authors might be reluctant to identify themselves as political psychologists. The explanations that are offered for the phenomena under study in these books are clearly psychological, but when they are wedded to ideas about political processes, new insights are gained about politics. This appears to us to be characteristic of a good deal of work in political psychology.

Perhaps the critics have something else in mind: political psychology may be insufficiently political because it concentrates too much on the individual as the unit of analysis, even though political outcomes are the result of aggregate processes. In similar ways, Page and Shapiro (1992), Stimson (1991), and Stimson, MacKuen, and Erikson (1995) have argued that individual attitudes and opinions are most appropriately studied as aggregate phenomena, in part because politicians respond primarily to aggregations: "Useful, and therefore, consequential, opinion is aggregate. Politicians care about the views of states, districts, areas, cities, what-have-you. Individual opinion is useful only as an indicator of the aggregate. For a politician to pay attention to individual views is to miss the main game" (Stimson 1991:12). In addition, "the public," as opposed to an individual's political opinions, appears to behave consistently and coherently; its policy preferences seem sensible.

While this may be true to some degree, we can think of examples of politicians responding to the views not of aggregates but of individuals. Ronald Reagan's obsession with the families of the hostages in Iran is legendary, playing a much larger role in dictating U.S. foreign policy than the general views of the American public. In any case, simply because politicians may respond to aggregate opinion does not mean that political psychologists must be interested in it. Furthermore, while aggregation is an important mechanism that accounts for many of the puzzles of political behavior – in particular, why uninterested, not very sophisticated individuals as a collectivity can behave in ways that may seem quite wise (see Converse 1990; MacKuen, Erikson and Stimson 1992; Neuman 1986; Page and Shapiro 1992; but cf. Althaus 1998; Bartels 1996) – by itself it is not a *theory*, but rather an analyst's perspective on which side of the micromacro divide to work. The theory in the books and articles written from a macroperspective is actually as much *psychological* as political. The question is not whether we will rely on psychological models to explain both individual and aggregate phenomena, but whether we will rely explicitly or implicitly, naively or with expertise, on such models.

We suspect that the charges of depoliticization may not be aimed at political psychology generally. Rather, the slings and arrows may be directed at a particular research program that has become increasingly prominent. We will use the term "Stony Brook School" to refer to this work. While somewhat caricatured, this program of research can be distinguished by its strong reliance on experimental methods and its concern with memory and other intrapsychic processes.

Of course, many political scientists use experimentation in their research (see, e.g., the chapters in Kinder and Palfrey 1993). All such work is vulnerable to concerns about the external validity of the results, except, perhaps, the experimental manipulations of question wording and the like that have been built into large-sample surveys. What may bother other political scientists about the Stony Brook program of research is that it looks – well, so psychological. The stimulus materials that are used are highly artificial, some of their studies feature the dreaded college sophomore (Sears 1986), and the principal dependent measures are not the familiar attitudes and opinions of political psychology, but more microscopic, highly cognitive measures of memory, typically the recognition or recall of the information presented. So much of it, the critics might inveigh, looks like a psychological experiment that just happened to use political objects (e.g., political candidates or public policies) as stimulus materials.

These features of the research program would not be so nettlesome to critics if the research remained obscure. But because much of it has appeared in the discipline's flagship journals such as the *American Political Science Review* (Lodge and Hamill 1986; Lodge, McGraw, and Stroh 1989; Lodge, Steenbergen, and Brau 1995; McGraw 1991) or the *American Journal of Political Science* (Hamill, Lodge and Blake 1985; Huddy and Terkildsen 1993; Terkildsen 1994), often with conclusions that challenge prevailing views, the discipline is forced to take it seriously, much as it had to confront the Rochester School two decades ago. For example, the notion of on-line processing undermines the extensive use in models of vote choice of the National Election Studies' open-ended questions about the presidential candidates (Lodge et al. 1989; Rahn, Krosnick, and Breuning 1994). In addition, the fact that experiments generally can often be conducted with considerably less expense than a major national survey and are increasingly published in good places challenges the preeminence of the National Election Studies and the scholars who have built their careers on these data. Some might worry that the prominence of the Stony Brook School will prompt outsiders to identify political psychology with the research questions, methods, and theories of this approach to political psychology, much as political psychology used to be identified with psychoanalysis and the methodologies of Lasswell and Lane. When psychoanalysis fell out of favor in the 1970s, so did political psychology. Perhaps the same could happen again when the political cognition rage has run its course.

Political Psychology and Political Science

Political psychology, and the Stony Brook School is a good recent example, has been and continues to be reductionist. This by itself may lead some to see it as insufficiently political, particularly those who prefer to work on higher levels of analysis. Although most political psychologists of all stripes are committed to methodological individualism as an epistemology, there is still something unsettling about seeing the traditional concerns of behavioral political science, like vote choice or political ideology, reduced to such jargon-laden metaphors as "judgment operators" or "schemas." It is worth noting that there are other parts of the discipline even more reductionist than that reviewed here – for example, the work in biopolitics. No doubt this type of work too is viewed in some quarters as reductionist and therefore not sufficiently political. We see reductionism as an inherent and unavoidable feature of doing work in political psychology and therefore will not apologize for it (see also Elster 1989). Furthermore, the translation of these micro psychological ideas into political science may have payoffs for more traditional concerns in the discipline. We illustrate this positive role in the next section.

The political content of political psychology is murky in large measure because the definition of "politics" and the scope of political science are themselves so contested. Political scientists in general are a little defensive about the nature of our discipline because most of us recognize that many of the important ideas in our field were originally inspired somewhere else, typically in psychology and economics. This sensitivity is heightened by the existence of what is, in some respects, a "theoretical trade deficit" between disciplines in which political scientists tend to import more theoretical ideas than they export. This is not to say that political science is an applied discipline; rather, it is to say that some political scientists appear to be defensive when theories from other fields are brought to bear too directly on political phenomena. It does seem to be true that many of the problems that typically preoccupy political scientists are not at a level of analysis that encourages basic *political* theory. For example, a proper psychologist might be interested in theories of persuasion for their own sake. Typically, the political scientist is drawn to theories of attitude change because they help elucidate some political phenomenon, such as the effects of campaign expenditures on vote choice.

The belief that modern political psychology has drifted away from the traditional concerns of the discipline perhaps has fueled some of the recent questioning of political psychology's utility. It is clear that some of the detractors are prepared to see recent work as so much applied psychology rather than as contributions to the long-standing concerns of political science (Kuklinski et al. 1991). We agree that political psychology should strive to be more than applied psychology. But we also argue that by almost any definition of the term "political," there is much in political psychology that deals with the traditional preoccupations of the parent discipline.

THE "POLITICAL" AND POLITICAL PSYCHOLOGY

There are many definitions of the "political." Each of us in teaching undergraduates probably offers our own favorite quote or paraphrase regarding the scope of the discipline, whether it is from Easton, Dahl, Lasswell, or other founding scholars. While we may disagree about the best definition of politics, there is probably a rough consensus that politics involves at least one of the following: power, conflict, or governing. For example, one introductory political science text defines politics as "a struggle between actors pursuing conflicting desires on issues that may result in an authoritative allocation of values" (Winter and Bellows 1992:11).

Thus, to be political, political psychology should have something to say about power, conflict, or governing. Let's begin with the easiest and most studied of the three: conflict. In politics, people disagree, sometimes violently. More often than not, the disagreements political psychologists study take the form of differences of opinion about some object in the political world – say, a public policy or a president or a group of people. Sometimes opinion conflict takes on heightened importance because individuals need to choose, as in electoral choice.

Many of the works we reviewed to prepare this chapter have something to say about conflict. The role of elite conflict plays prominently in the books on public opinion reviewed earlier. But conflict is also central to many other topics in political psychology, in part because we as a field seem to have rediscovered the role of groups in political cognition and behavior, and the importance of affect and emotions in political reasoning. Both groups and emotions were at the core of the early political psychology of Wallas, Freud, and Lasswell. However, the behavioral revolution, the large sample survey, the temporary ascendance of the rational choice school, and the cognitive focus of social psychology conspired to delegitimate these traditional concerns. In interesting but more modern theoretical ways, political psychology seems to have returned to its roots.

Some of this reawakening is due to "indigenous" theories such as Brady and Sniderman's (1985) likability heuristic, a concept that puts together affect and political group conflict (see the subsequent discussion). But our understanding of political conflict is also due to work of political psychologists who took emerging developments in social cognition and made them relevant to the concerns of political scientists. For example, Conover and Feldman (1986), Marcus (1988), and Nelson (1999) drew on social psychological ideas about the role of emotions, applying these notions to people's judgments about the economy, presidential candidates, and social policy opinions, respectively. Rahn and her colleagues (Rahn, Kroeger, and Kite 1996) have developed an individual-level measure of "public mood," demonstrating its role in the formation of a variety of judgments commonly studied by political scientists, including economic expectations, external efficacy, and global attitudes about the United States. Sullivan and Masters (1988) argue that emotional bonding between leaders and followers is at the heart of the leadership relationship. Emotions appear to be powerful components of people's political experiences, and simply on pragmatic grounds, non-political psychologists would be well advised to include affect in their models, for it seems to improve substantially our ability to predict commonly studied political behavior variables. Emotions may also affect the way people make their political choices, and they also appear to have consequences for *political behaviors* such as political learning and campaign involvement (Marcus and MacKuen 1993; Nadeau, Niemi, and Amato 1995).

Similarly, our understanding of political tolerance judgments has become considerably more complex with the work of Kuklinski and his colleagues (1991) and Marcus, Sullivan, Theiss-Morse, and Wood (1995), where we see how affect and cognition intersect in individuals' group assessments. It thus appears to us that political psychology has become "repoliticized" not in spite of these psychological ideas, but because of them.

Power has been a central preoccupation for political analysis, whether it appears in one, two, three, or now four faces (Digeser 1992). Some forms of power are not subtle – threats of coercion or the use of force, for example. But as Riker (1986) argues in his book on "heresthetics," the inescapability of Arrovian problems of social choice offers less blatant opportunities to get what you want. As Riker's recounting of Senator Warren Magnuson's efforts to stop the shipment of nerve gas through the port of Seattle illustrates, framing an issue around a new evaluative dimension can, in effect, change people's expressed preferences. Political psychologists are well equipped to demonstrate framing effects, and, more importantly, explain why framing works in the way it does (see Druckman 1999; Gamson 1992; Iyengar 1991; Kinder and Sanders 1990; Lau, Smith, and Fiske 1991; Nelson, Clawson, and Oxley 1997; Nelson and Kinder 1996; Quattrone and Tversky 1988).

Political psychology has contributed in important ways to a third area of politics, that of governing. There are at least two separable literatures in political psychology that deal with aspects of governing: the study of elite decision making and the research on legitimacy. Both of these areas have been heavily influenced by psychological theories and, increasingly in the elite area, by cognitive psychological methods such as simulation as well (see Sylvan, Goel, and Chandrasekaran 1990; Tabor 1992).

An important part of political psychology has been devoted to the study of political elites. The study of elites is an enduring legacy of Lasswell's influence on the development of the field. While the early "personality and politics" literature was often criticized for ignoring political context, more recent work in this area has been more explicit about incorporating environmental and organizational variables (see, e.g., Burke and Greenstein 1989; Hermann and Hermann 1989). Furthermore, the impact of Jervis (1976) and Janis (1982) on the study of elite decision making can hardly be overstated. Their ideas persist as wellsprings for scholarly research both in political science (McCalla 1992) and in psychology (Tetlock, Peterson, McGuire, Chang, and Feld 1992; Turner, Pratkanis, Probasco, and Leve 1992).

As systems theory told us decades ago, the stability of political regimes depends importantly on perceptions of its legitimacy. The bases for legitimacy have been investigated in a spate of recent studies we would classify as political psychological in orientation. Tom Tyler (1990, 1994b, 1997), for example, studies people's interactions in legal, political, educational, and family settings, developing a model of the psychology of legitimacy that puts perceptions of procedural fairness ahead of self-regarding interests in people's calculations about whether to trust authorities (see also Weatherford 1992). Kelman and Hamilton (1989), drawing on Milgram's (1974) classic social psychology of authority, stand the problem of legitimacy on its head: How can we encourage citizens to be more challenging of authorities? Hamilton and Sanders (1992) extend this work through a cross-cultural study of responsibility attributions in the United States and Japan.

Conflict, power, and legitimacy are enduring themes of political theory. We have found numerous examples in recent political psychology that deal explicitly with these profoundly political topics. In our final section we compare three different modes of doing political psychology, each of which, we argue, contributes to our understanding of political processes and institutions.

TYPOLOGY OF WORK IN POLITICAL PSYCHOLOGY

In this section, we distinguish three different ways of doing political psychology. We briefly review exemplars of work in each category and discuss the contributions that each category makes to the field of political psychology. In doing so, we refer back to our review of approaches to the field of political psychology in our other chapter in this volume.

Our typology includes the following categories: works that represent direct applications of psychological models to political science topics and concerns; works that represent applications of psychological models to politics, but do so in a more or less contextualized way; and works that actually contextualize psychological theory by applying it to political situations and, in so doing, modify the theory itself.

The aim underlying most research in the first category is not to reformulate psychological models or to test political or psychological theories, but rather to apply them to a political science concern such as international bargaining and conflict, vote choice, public opinion, or elite decision making. Perhaps the prototype of this approach is psychologist Stuart Oskamp's (1991) textbook on attitudes and opinions. Oskamp devotes the first two-thirds of his book to an analysis of theory, methods, and research on attitudes and opinions. The last third of his book, however, applies social psychological theory and research to political subject matter such as civil liberties, voting, international attitudes, and racism and prejudice. A second and equally prototypical example of a straightforward application of psychological theory to political content is Larson's (1985) analysis of the origins of containment theory, noted in our other chapter.

Finally, most of the burgeoning "mass political cognition" literature falls into this category. We discussed in chapter 1 the various types of political cognition research. The "schema theory" variety of this literature has been subject to some very pointed criticism (Kuklinski et al. 1991) and some very spirited defenses (Conover and Feldman 1991; Lodge and McGraw 1991; Miller 1991). The debate between schema theory detractors and defenders need not be reviewed here, for it has already become passé. Interest in schema "theory" may have peaked both in political and in social cognition. While schema theory itself may be out of vogue, the ideas that were once packaged together under that appellation are still alive and well, only refashioned in more innocuous terminology such as "cognitive representations" or cognitive "categories" or "stereotypes" (see, e.g., Conover and Feldman 1989; Huddy and Terkildsen 1993; Hurwitz and Peffley 1997; Peffley, Hurwitz, and Sniderman 1997; Rahn 1993).

In both political and social cognition, researchers are focusing on questions not of knowledge structure, but of knowledge use. Hurwitz and Peffley (1997) show that the use of racial stereotypes in judgment situations is conditional on contextual information such as the nature of the criminal, crime, and policy involved. Huckfeldt, Leoine, Morgan, and Sprague (1999) suggest that the utility of partisan and ideological orientations is conditional on their accessibility. The shift in emphasis from knowledge structures to knowledge use is particularly evident in Conover and Feldman's (1989) analysis of candidate perception. In this piece of research they begin with a long-standing concern of political behavior analysts: how do citizens come to know what the candidates' positions are on issues? Their answer, it turns out, is quite nuanced. The sources of these inferences turn out to be varied and *variable* across the campaign and across candidates. Voters, for example, can rely on their knowledge about the political parties (partisan categories or schemas) or their own issue positions. The relative influence of these two sources changes over the course of the campaign. In Conover and Feldman's study of the origins of inferences, we as political scientists learn something interesting about the dynamics of candidate evaluation, not just about cognitive categories and information processing.

Even if one were to concede that some of the earliest applications of social cognition ideas to politics smacked more of applied psychology than of an explicitly political psychology, these works nevertheless played a tremendously important role in introducing political scientists to a field of research (and a vocabulary) that had the potential to illuminate many political questions. The application of the next "imported" idea that we review – the on-line model – has played a similar role in translating a set of ideas to an untutored audience.

The on-line processing idea has been around in political science in various guises. Fiorina's conceptualization of party identification as a running tally of retrospective evaluations is one example cited by Stony Brook scholars. An example they don't cite, but one that also has a strong flavor of on-line processing, is Brady and Sniderman's (1985, note 9) exposition of the "likability heuristic." Their model builds in assumptions that sound very much like on-line processing: "True feelings (about a group) may represent the residue of cognitions as an individual repeatedly encounters information about a group, makes judgments about the group from the information, and then forgets the facts on which the judgment was based . . . the results of these cognitive processes are economically stored in our feelings."

Simply because the intuition was present in the pre–Stony Brook School era does not mean that the on-line/memory-based distinction introduced by Lodge et al. (1989) is "old wine in new bottles." Quite the contrary. In these earlier studies, the on-line intuition was an "armchair" psychological assumption (to borrow from Herbert Simon 1985) built into a statistical operationalization of interesting theoretical ideas. As we know from critiques of rational action models, assumptions are not tests. The studies of political cognition by Lodge and his colleagues are important both for convincingly demonstrating the operation of on-line processing *and* for establishing some important contingencies involved in its use. Not all voters process information on-line in every circumstance. On-line processing requires both motivation to process and ability to process. It appears that neither memory-based nor on-line assumptions are generally applicable to all types of citizens.

The on-line model of information processing has been criticized as inappropriate in the domain of political attitude reports (see Zaller 1992:278–9). Certainly Zaller is correct in pointing out that most citizens do not have the industry to do the kind of continual updating of evaluations postulated in the on-line model for all issues. Lavine and Lodge (in press) suggest that we can better understand the determinants of processing mode by attending to individuals' motivation and ability. These "conditions under which" discussions we view as very productive for the field, something that we would not expect if the on-line/memory-based distinction was a mere demonstration of applied psychology. In addition, subsequent research has demonstrated that the on-line model is not merely an artifact of the types of stimulus materials employed in the Stony Brook paradigm (typically, written descriptions about a hypothetical candidate). For example, one of the authors and her colleagues (Rahn, Krosnick, and Breuning 1994), using panel survey data collected during the 1990 gubernatorial election, presented evidence that voters' evaluations of candidates appear to be more on-line than memory-based. There appear to be, however, interesting differences in the balance of these two processes for different subgroups of voters. For example, voters who decide late in the campaign appear to be more memory-based in their evaluations than those who decide early. Voters highly involved in politics, on the other hand, are much more likely to process information on-line (once we take into account the relationship between political involvement and media exposure), confirming a laboratory finding of McGraw, Lodge, and Stroh (1990; but see Rahn, Aldrich, and Borgida 1994).

More traditional political behavior scholars have found the on-line/memory-based distinction productive for their concerns. For example, Wright (1993) examines the winner bias in self-reported vote choice measures used in the National Election Studies. He argues that the overstating of support for winning candidates may be due to voters who process information about candidates in memory-based rather than on-line fashion. When an interviewer queries these voters after Election Day, they may not be able to remember their previous decision, having not been motivated enough during the campaign to be on-line processors. "The problem is that the respondent's evaluation at the time of the interview is based on information and impressions that have changed since the election, and moreover, the interview itself can influence the relative accessibility of different bits of information in memory . . . losers fade from view" (Wright 1993:293). The "reconstruction" of the vote choice for memory-based processors thus biases them toward misremembering their decision as one for the winner.

We would conclude that even in the worst-case scenario – instances of rather direct applications of psychological models or research agendas to political science – a great deal of political knowledge is gained by political scientists who aim to understand rather narrow political phenomena. Understanding how citizens process political information allows us to make realistic and valid assumptions upon which to build models of voting, for example.

Our next category in the typology contains examples of research that are less straightforward in their applications of psychological ideas. Typically, the application of psychology in this type of work is "looser" than in the previous category, and the *context* of politics plays a larger role in the derivation of hypotheses. Brady and Sniderman's (1985; Sniderman et al. 1991) likability heuristic, mentioned earlier, is one such example. Bringing together psychological notions of judgmental shortcuts, or heuristics, and the conflict-ridden nature of politics, they specify a calculus, the likability heuristic, that allows individuals to estimate the policy positions of various politically important groups. They argue that the calculus is made possible by the nature of political conflict:

What allows citizens to simplify political calculations efficiently is this two-sided, "us versus them" character of politics; the more attached they are to their side – and the more opposed they are to the other – the more they appreciate the differences between the issue positions of the two sides. What counts, then, is not how people feel toward groups, one by one; rather it is how they feel toward *pairs* of opposing groups (Sniderman et al. 1991:114–15; emphasis in the original).

In our model of candidate evaluation (Rahn, Aldrich, Borgida, and Sullivan 1990), we attempted to situate the development of candidate impressions in a specifically political context. Our understanding of the structure of the political information environment led us to formulate two specific hypotheses about the process of candidate evaluation. First, we argued that the task of choosing and the comparative nature of political information lead voters to adopt a particular comparison strategy, one that compares the candidates along policy dimensions, ideology, partisanship, and trait assessments. Second, we postulated that in certain kinds of informational configurations, conditions that are typically met in presidential elections, the importance of political sophistication differences among citizens will be diminished. Later, we carried our ideas about the role of context into the primary setting (Sullivan, Aldrich,

Borgida, and Rahn 1990), arguing that different comparison processes may be operating. We would view John Zaller's (1992) work on processes of opinion formation and change as falling into our second category as well. His model of "question-answering" is based loosely on the work of McGuire and Converse on attitude stability and change and on more recent cognitive theories of the survey response. When wedded to ideas about the informational importance of elite discourse about politics, the basic model cuts a swath exceedingly wide, covering areas as diverse as Vietnam, acquired immune deficiency syndrome (AIDS), and primary election campaigns as special cases of these more general processes.

Other examples – reviewed at length in our other chapter – of research in political psychology that incorporate the political context include Barber's work on presidents and Staub's work on genocide. Barber (1992), for example, emphasizes the importance of character, which develops during early childhood. But he also incorporates in his analysis the individual's world view, which develops during adolescence, and his style, which evolves during the first independent political successes. Further, the importance of the "climate of expectations" in interacting with the more personal elements of the individual president further incorporates the political context with individual psychological analysis.

Staub (1989), as noted earlier, explicitly consolidates political and economic conditions in his psychological analysis of how genocide occurs, using Germany, Turkey, Argentina, and Cambodia as examples. While political and economic forces create the broader preconditions for genocidal actions, the psychology of perpetration and victimization explains the more immediate preconditions and illuminate how it can (and does) actually happen.

Our last category in the typology includes works that we believe contribute to political psychology by contextualizing even more fully psychological theory, and in doing so add insight into political phenomena at the same time that they reformulate psychological theory. We should be explicit in our belief that this genre of work does not grow out of the aggrandizing impulses of our colleagues in psychology; it is not merely "applied political science." Rather, the context of application matters in important ways for theory development.

One example is Lusk and Judd's (1988) research on the structural mediators of political expertise. In social psychological theory, the relationship between individuals' knowledge about stimulus objects and the evaluations they make of these same objects has been disputed. Some research suggests that more thought about an object results in more polarized evaluations, while other research has found that more thought tends to moderate judgments. Judd and Lusk (1984) suggested a resolution in which evaluative extremity depends on both the number of dimensions used to differentiate among stimuli and the degree to which these dimensions are correlated. In their initial studies, they found that support for their hypothesis was domain-specific. In judgments of rock bands, there was a slightly negative relationship between the number of dimensions used to differentiate the bands and the average correlation between dimensions. As the number of dimensions increased, the average correlation decreased. In the case of judgments about sororities, however, the opposite relationship obtained. The number of dimensions used to discriminate among the sororities was positively related to the average correlation – the more dimensions used, the higher their correlation.

To explore further how the domain of judgment affects the relationship between the number of dimensions used to represent stimulus objects and the intercorrelation of those dimensions, Lusk and Judd (1988) turned to the domain of political candidate judgments. They found that the relationship between the number of dimensions and their evaluative redundancy is positive. Moreover, political expertise was associated with both more differentiation and higher redundancy, resulting in more extreme candidate judgments. By contextualizing psychological theory in this way, not only did this research illuminate an ongoing controversy in the social cognition literature, but we learned something new about how political sophistication might affect the processes by which individuals cognitively organize and generate their candidate judgments.

Another excellent example of a study in political psychology that takes both psychological theory and political context seriously enough to incorporate and modify both is Granberg and Holmberg's (1988) study of voting behavior in Sweden and the United States. They identify a number of general findings about public opinion and voting behavior among the U.S. electorate and some of the social psychological explanations that have been provided to account for these findings. Then, using Swedish data, they examine whether these theories and findings also apply in a very different political context with a totally different electoral and party system. They find that "the system matters" – many of the findings about Swedish public opinion and voting are quite different from those in the United States, and the same psychological theory cannot be used to explain both sets of findings without modifications and without taking political theory into account. For example, levels of ideological constraint are much higher in Sweden than in the United States, and one must rely on more than attitude theory to explain this – political theory must modify and complement psychological theory. Granberg and Holmberg also find higher levels of issue voting in Sweden and lower levels of projection. Overall, they conclude that the democratic process in Sweden is more rational, while that in the United States is more irrational and characterized by a greater degree of misperception, including the distortions induced by psychological projection, assimilation, and contrast effects. This is true not because U.S. citizens are inherently less sophisticated than Swedes but because of the way the party system structures information, cues, and choices for citizens. The Swedish party system offers clearer and more abundant information and choices to its citizens. One interesting consequence of this difference is that while the most volatile voters in U.S. elections are the least interested and informed citizens, in Swedish elections volatile voters are those who are highest in interest and knowledge. This the authors take as additional evidence that the party system structures choices in ways that enhance irrational campaigns and voting in the United States but more rational political campaigns and voting in Sweden. On page 218 of their study, they conclude that Swedish citizens "have ideological convictions, understand the meaning of the left–right dimension, and are quite capable of relating this dimension to the parties."

Kluegel and Smith's (1986) work on beliefs about inequality also falls into this category. They apply principles of social cognition and attribution theory to the analysis of beliefs about economic opportunity, outcomes, inequality, and policy. Their approach, however, is not merely a straightforward application of these theories and principles, but also includes explicit modification of these theories to incorporate concepts from social stratification, political belief systems, and the dominant national ideology. In the end, perceptions about economic inequality are not merely straightforward applications of attribution theory, as the fundamental attribution error cannot explain Americans' beliefs about economic success, failure, and opportunity. An understanding of the independent role of cultural and individual political ideology is also required, which suggests modifications in cognitive theories such as attribution theory.

Hamilton and Sanders (1992), like Kluegel and Smith, are also interested in attributions of responsibility, but in their case the attributions of concern are more legalistic in origin, specifically attributions of wrongdoing. They conclude that "culture matters": while attributions in both the United States and Japan are influenced by information about the deed, the context, and the roles of the actors, the weight attached to each of these ingredients varies across the two countries. Americans and Japanese have different conceptions of the responsible actor, differences that are related to the way the self is conceptualized in the two societies. These more micropsychological and microsociological differences are reflected in the legal cultures of the two societies. These legal cultures, in turn, constrain how ordinary citizens process information related to judgments of wrongdoing and justice. The authors' cross-cultural study not only has implications for the way psychologists think about attributional processes, but also contributes to important political questions concerning the interplay between institutions and actors.

We would also place Janis's work on groupthink (1982), reviewed earlier, in this category. Janis, for example, takes theory and research about small group behavior and contextualizes it deeply, applying it to elite foreign policy decision-making groups in a way that incorporates understandings of individual psychological processes, group dynamics, and policy decision-making processes. The theory of groupthink is, in the end, both political and psychological in profound ways.

The work on symbolic politics is another example of work that speaks compellingly to both political scientists and psychologists. As developed by Sears (1993) and his many collaborators over the years, symbolic politics theory is both a theory of certain kinds of attitudes and a theory of mass politics. It intersects many debates in political science – for example, the determinants of vote choice and the role of self-interest in political motivation – and in psychology – for example, the nature of prejudice. Work in symbolic politics has influenced how political scientists think about the role of race – even critics of the symbolic politics approach have to consider it before offering an alternative (e.g., Sniderman and Piazza 1993) – and has influenced how social psychologists think about ethnocentrism (see Esses, Haddock, and Zanna 1992).

Tom Tyler's (1997) work on the psychology of legitimacy informs both psychologists' and political scientists' research on individuals' compliance with authorities. Analyzing voluntary deference to authorities across a variety of settings, Tyler concludes that resource-based or instrumental perspectives do not provide a complete account of legitimacy. He demonstrates that the psychology of legitimacy is grounded in identification-based or relational elements as well. As noted by Tyler, his results speak directly to several literatures in psychology, including analyses of how authorities shape group behavior and studies on obedience to authority. The relational component of legitimacy has distinctly political implications as well, as it influences perceptions of Congress (Tyler 1994a) and the Supreme Court (Tyler and Mitchell 1994).

Tetlock's (1993; Tetlock and Belkin 1996) research on integrative complexity is another interdisciplinary research program that has contributed equally to political science and psychology. Originally applied to the study of the complexity of political elites' reasoning processes, the integrative complexity idea ultimately led to the development of the value pluralism model and a theory of the role of accountability in the process of reasoning. Tetlock's many studies have implications for enduring issues in political behavior, such as the nature of political belief systems and political sophistication and the role of personality in political reasoning. His work also fits squarely into dual-process models of social cognition. Under what conditions do people use complex, resource-demanding strategies of information processing? Tetlock's research spotlights accountability as an essential determinant of strategy choice. But there are also clear individual differences involved in the selection of complex or simple reasoning styles. Political conservatives generally have more internally consistent value systems, and thus most policy issues do not force them to make complex trade-offs between competing value orientations. Liberals, on the other hand, are more likely to face value conflict and, therefore, have to resort to more complicated strategies in order to resolve the tension between competing concerns, such as freedom and equality. More recently, Tetlock (1999) has employed dual-process models of information processing to study the counterfactual reasoning abilities of political elites. If they accept an alternative antecedent condition in history, Tetlock argues, professional political observers exhibit the belief-system defenses associated with "theory-driven" processing. When judging the plausibility of such alternative antecedent conditions, however, political elites are more likely to engage in "data-driven" processing.

Even though we have spent considerable space discussing examples in this third category, it is, in fact, the least populated cell in our typology. The examples of research that truly integrate politics and psychology, and thus are capable of speaking authoritatively to practitioners in each discipline, are rare. We would be surprised if it were otherwise, for bridging is probably harder than borrowing. There is clearly room for both bridgers and borrowers under the umbrella of political psychology, and each of the three types of work we have illustrated contributes to our understanding of things political.

THE PRESENT AND FUTURE OF INTERDISCIPLINARY RESEARCH

A great deal of intellectual cross-fertilization is now occurring between and among academic disciplines. Many new and revamped cross-disciplinary fields are emerging in both the natural and the social sciences, taking institutional form as research centers, joint graduate programs, interdisciplinary concentrations within single graduate program, Ph.D. minor programs, and so on. Research funding seems to be following this trend as well. These developments seems to reflect an increasing recognition that disciplinary boundaries are no longer as relevant to the advancement of knowledge as we once thought. These boundaries were always somewhat artificial, and hyperconcern with disciplinary purity extracted great costs that can no longer be justified.

In the social sciences, recent examples of change include graduate, research, and training programs in cognitive science, conflict and change, political economy, political psychology, interpersonal relations, and so on. Major goals of social science include the understanding of human behavior; social, economic, and political institutions; and the interactions among them. Narrow disciplinary understandings and foci may actually impede the achievement of these goals. For example, the view that political scientists will attempt only to understand political behavior and institutions, economists will focus only on economic behavior and institutions, psychologists will focus only on individual behavior and psychological processes quite devoid of content and context, and so on, leads to compartmentalized specialization that in all probability creates intellectual understandings that are untenable. Humans do not compartmentalize their lives in ways that coincide with academic specialties. Instead, most people live seamless lives in which they engage simultaneously in thoughts and behaviors that connect their rich psychological inner lives, their political attitudes and behaviors, their religious beliefs and practices, and their economic activities, to mention but a few. There is little reason to expect that scholars who focus on but a few of these phenomena will gain much insight into the whole human being and how he or she operates within a particular social and institutional culture and environment. Instead, one might expect the greatest understanding from a focus on the ways in which these analytically distinct but subjectively and objectively interrelated spheres of thought and activity intersect.

References

Althaus, Scott L. 1998. "Information Effects in Collective Preferences." *American Political Science Review* 92:545–58.

Barber, James David. 1992. *The Presidential Character: Predicting Performance in the White House*, 4th ed. Englewood Cliffs, NJ: Prentice-Hall.

Bartels, Larry M. 1993. "Messages Received: The Political Impact of Media Exposure." *American Political Science Review* 87:267–85.

——— 1996. "Uninformed Votes: Information Effects in Presidential Elections." *American Journal of Political Science* 40:194–230.

Bellah, Robert N., Richard Madsen, William M. Sullivan, Ann Swidler, and Steven M. Tipton. 1985. *Habits of the Heart*. Berkeley: University of California Press.

Brady, Henry E., and Paul M. Sniderman. 1985. "Attitude Attribution: A Group Basis for Political Reasoning." *American Political Science Review* 79: 1061–78.

Brennen, Geoffrey, and Loren Lomasky. 1993. *Democracy and Decision: The Pure Theory of Electoral Preference*. Cambridge: Cambridge University Press.

Brody, Richard A. 1991. *Assessing the President*. Stanford, CA: Stanford University Press.

Burke, John P., and Fred I. Greenstein. 1989. "Presidential Personality and National Security Leadership: A Comparative Analysis of Vietnam Decision-Making." *International Political Science Review* 10:73–92.

Campbell, Donald T., and D. T. Fiske. 1959. "Convergent and Discriminant Validation by the Multitrait-Multimethod Matrix." *Psychological Bulletin* 56:81–105.

Carmines, Edward G., and James A. Stimson. 1989. *Issue Evolution: Race and the Transformation of American Politics*. Princeton, NJ: Princeton University Press.

Chong, Dennis. 1996. "Creating Common Frames of Reference on Political Issues." In Diana C. Mutz, Paul M. Sniderman, and Richard A. Brody, eds., *Political Persuasion and Attitude Change*. Ann Arbor: University of Michigan Press.

Conover, Pamela J., Ivor M. Crewe, and Donald D. Searing. 1991. "The Nature of Citizenship in the United States and Great Britain: Empirical Comments on Theoretical Themes." *The Journal of Politics* 53:800–32.

Conover, Pamela J., and Stanley Feldman. 1986. "Emotional Reactions to the State of the Economy: I'm Mad as Hell and I'm Not Going to Take It Anymore." *American Journal of Political Science* 30:50–78.

   1989. "Candidate Perception in an Ambiguous World." *American Journal of Political Science* 33:912–40.

   1991. "Where Is the Schema? Critiques." *American Political Science Review* 85:1364–69.

Converse, Philip E. 1990. "Popular Representation and the Distribution of Information." In John A. Ferejohn and James H. Kuklinski, eds., *Information and Democratic Processes*. Urbana: University of Illinois Press.

Delli Carpini, Michael X., and Scott Keeter. 1993. "Measuring Political Knowledge: Putting First Things First." *American Journal of Political Science* 37:1179–206.

   1996. *What Americans Know About Politics and Why It Matters*. New Haven, CT: Yale University Press.

Digeser, Peter. 1992. "The Fourth Face of Power." *The Journal of Politics* 54:977–1007.

Druckman, James N. 1999. "Do Party Cues Limit Framing Effects?" Paper presented at the Annual Meeting of the American Political Science Association, Atlanta, September 2–5, 1999.

Edelman, Murray. 1964. *The Symbolic Uses of Politics*. Urbana: University of Illinois Press.

Elster, Jon. 1989. *Nuts and Bolts for the Social Sciences*. Cambridge: Cambridge University Press.

Esses, Victoria M., Geoffrey Haddock, and Mark P. Zanna. 1992. "Values, Stereotypes, and Emotions as Determinants of Intergroup Attitudes." In Diane M. Mackie and David L. Hamilton, eds., *Affect, Cognition, and Stereotyping*. New York: Academic Press.

Finkel, Steven E. 1993. "Reexamining the 'Minimal Effects' Model in Recent Presidential Campaigns." *The Journal of Politics* 55:1–21.

Gamson, William A. 1992. *Talking Politics*. Cambridge: Cambridge University Press.

Granberg, Donald, and Soren Holmberg. 1988. *The Political System Matters: Social Psychology and Voting Behavior in Sweden and the United States*. Cambridge: Cambridge University Press.

Gelman, Andrew, and Gary King. 1993. "Why Are American Presidential Election Campaign Polls So Variable When Votes Are So Predictable?" *British Journal of Political Science* 23:409–51.

Green, Donald Philip. 1992. "The Price Elasticity of Mass Preferences." *American Political Science Review* 86:128–48.

Green, Donald P., and Ian Shapiro. 1994. *Pathologies of Rational Choice Theory: A Critique of Applications in Political Science*. New Haven, CT: Yale University Press.

Greenstein, Fred I. 1969. *Personality and Politics: Problems of Evidence, Inference, and Conceptualization*. Chicago: Markham.

Hamill, Ruth C., Milton Lodge, and Frederick Blake. 1985. "The Breadth, Depth, and Utility of Class, Partisan, and Ideological Schemata." *American Journal of Political Science* 29:850–70.

Hamilton, V. Lee, and Joseph Sanders. 1992. *Everyday Justice*. New Haven, CT: Yale University Press.

Hermann, Margaret G. 1989. "Political Psychology: Fad, Fantasy or Field?" Manuscript. Columbus: The Ohio State University.

Hermann, Margaret G., and Charles F. Hermann. 1989. "Who Makes Foreign Policy" *International Studies Quarterly* 33:361–87.

Hibbing, John R., and Elizabeth Theiss-Morse. 1995. *Congress as Public Enemy: Public Attitudes Toward American Political Institutions*. Cambridge: Cambridge University Press.

Huckfeldt, Robert, Jeffrey Leoine, William Morgan, and John Sprague. 1999. "Accessibility and the Political Utility of Partisan and Ideological Orientations." *American Journal of Political Science* 43:898–911.

Huddy, Leonie, and Nayda Terkildsen. 1993. "Gender Stereotypes and the Perceptions of Male and Female Candidates." *American Journal of Political Science* 37:119–47.

Hurwitz, Jon, and Mark Peffley. 1997. "Public Perceptions of Race and Crime: The Role of Racial Stereotypes." *American Journal of Political Science* 41: 375–401.

Iyengar, Shanto. 1991. *Is Anyone Responsible?* Chicago: University of Chicago Press.

Iyengar, Shanto, and Donald R. Kinder. 1987. *News that Matters*. Chicago: University of Chicago Press.

Iyengar, Shanto, and William G. McGuire, eds. 1993. *Explorations in Political Psychology*. Durham, NC: Duke University Press.

Janis, Irving L. 1982. *Groupthink*. Boston: Houghton Mifflin.

Jervis, Robert. 1976. *Perception and Misperception in International Politics*. Princeton, NJ: Princeton University Press.

Judd, Charles M., and Cynthia M. Lusk. 1984. "Knowledge Structures and Evaluative Judgments: Effects of Structural Variables on Judgmental Extremity." *Journal of Personality and Social Psychology* 46:1193–207.

Kelman, Herbert C., and V. Lee Hamilton. 1989. *Crimes of Obedience*. New Haven, CT: Yale University Press.

Kinder, Donald R., and Thomas R. Palfrey, eds. 1993. *Experimental Foundations of Political Science*. Ann Arbor: University of Michigan Press.

Kinder, Donald R., and Lynn Sanders. 1990. "Mimicking Debate with Survey Questions: The Case of White Opinion on Affirmative Action for Blacks." *Social Cognition* 8:73–108.

Kluegel, James R., and Eliot R. Smith. 1986. *Beliefs About Inequality: Americans' Views of What Is and What Ought to Be.* New York: Aldine De Gruyter.

Kuklinski, James H., Robert C. Luskin, and John Bolland. 1991. "Where Is the Schema? Going Beyond the 'S' Work in Political Psychology." *American Political Science Review* 85:1341–56.

Kuklinski, James H., Ellen Riggle, Victor Ottati, Norbert Schwarz, and Robert S. Wyer, Jr. 1991. "The Cognitive and Affective Bases of Political Tolerance Judgments." *American Journal of Political Science* 35:1–27.

Larson, Deborah Welch. 1985. *Origins of Containment: A Psychological Explanation.* Princeton, NJ: Princeton University Press.

Lau, Richard R., Richard A. Smith, and Susan T. Fiske. 1991. "Political Beliefs, Policy Interpretations, and Political Persuasion." *The Journal of Politics* 53:644–75.

Lavine, Howard, and Milton Lodge. In press. "On-Line vs. Memory-Based Process Models of Political Evaluation." *Political Psychology.*

Lodge, Milton, and Ruth Hamill. 1986. "A Partisan Schema for Political Information Processing." *American Political Science Review* 80:505–19.

Lodge, Milton, and Kathleen M. McGraw. 1991. "Where Is the Schema? Critiques." *American Political Science Review* 85:1355–64.

Lodge, Milton, Kathleen M. McGraw, and Patrick Stroh. 1989. "An Impression-Driven Model of Candidate Evaluation." *American Political Science Review* 87:399–419.

Lodge, Milton, Marco R. Steenbergen, and Shawn Brau. 1995. "The Responsive Voter: Campaign Information and the Dynamics of Candidate Evaluation." *American Political Science Review* 89:309–26.

Lupia, Arthur. 1992. "Busy Voters, Agenda Control, and the Power of Information." *American Political Science Review* 86:390–403.

Lusk, Cynthia M., and Charles M. Judd. 1988. "Political Expertise and the Structural Mediators of Candidate Evaluation." *Journal of Experimental Social Psychology* 24:105–26.

Luttbeg, Norman R. 1991. "Political Attitudes: A Historical Artifact or a Concept of Continuing Importance in Political Science?" In William Crotty, ed., *Political Science: Looking to the Future,* Vol. 3. Evanston, IL: Northwestern University Press.

MacDonald, Stuart Elain, Ola Listhaug, and George Rabinowitz. 1991. "Issues and Party Support in Multiparty Systems." *American Political Science Review* 85:1107–32.

MacKuen, Michael B., Robert S. Erikson and James A. Stimson. 1992. "Peasants of Bankers? The American Electorate and the U.S. Economy." *American Political Science Review* 86:597–611.

Mansbridge, Jane J. 1990. *Beyond Self-Interest.* Chicago: University of Chicago Press.

Marcus, George E. 1988. "The Structure of Emotional Response: 1984 Presidential Candidates." *American Political Science Review* 82:735–61.

Marcus, George E., and Michael MacKuen. 1993. "Anxiety, Enthusiasm, and the Vote: The Emotional Underpinnings of Learning and Involvement During Presidential Campaigns." *American Political Science Review* 87:672–85.

Marcus, George E., John L. Sullivan, Elizabeth Theiss-Morse, and Sandra L. Wood. 1995. *With Malice Toward Some: How People Make Civil Liberties Judgments.* Cambridge: Cambridge University Press.

McCalla, Robert. 1992. *Uncertain Perceptions.* Ann Arbor: University of Michigan Press.

McGraw, Kathleen M. 1991. "Managing Blame: An Experimental Test of the Effects of Political Accounts." *American Political Science Review* 85:1133–58.

McGraw, Kathleen M., Milton Lodge, and Patrick Stroh. 1990. "On-line Processing in Candidate Evaluation: The Effects of Issue Order, Issue Importance and Sophistication." *Political Behavior* 12:41–58.

Milgram, Stanley. 1974. *Obedience to Authority.* New York: Harper & Row.

Miller, Arthur. 1991. "Where Is the Schema? Critiques." *American Political Science Review* 85:1369–80.

Nadeau, Richard, Richard G. Niemi, and Timothy Amato. 1995. "Emotions, Issue Importance, and Political Learning." *American Journal of Political Science* 39:558–74.

Nelson, Thomas E. 1999. "Group Affect and Attribution in Social Policy Opinion." *The Journal of Politics* 61:331–62.

Nelson, Thomas E., Rosalee A. Clawson, and Zoe M. Oxley. 1997. "Media Framing of a Civil Liberties Conflict and Its Effect on Tolerance." *American Political Science Review* 91:567–84.

Nelson, Thomas E., and Donald R. Kinder. 1996. "Issue Frames and Group-Centrism in American Public Opinion." *The Journal of Politics* 58:1055–78.

Neuman, Russell W. 1986. *The Paradox of Mass Politics.* Cambridge, MA: Harvard University Press.

Orbell, John, and Robyn M. Dawes. 1991. "A 'Cognitive Miser' Theory of Cooperators' Advantage." *American Political Science Review* 85:515–28.

Oskamp, Stuart. 1991. *Attitudes and Opinions,* 2nd ed. Englewood Cliffs, NJ: Prentice-Hall.

Ostrom, Elinor. 1998. "A Behavioral Approach to the Rational Choice Theory of Collective Action." *American Political Science Review* 92:1–22.

Page, Benjamin I., and Robert Y. Shapiro. 1992. *The Rational Public.* Chicago: University of Chicago Press.

Peffley, Mark, Jon Hurwitz, and Paul M. Sniderman. 1997. "Racial Stereotypes and Whites' Political Views of Blacks in the Context of Welfare and Crime." *American Journal of Political Science* 41:30–60.

Peng, Yali. 1994. "Intellectual Fads in Political Science: The Cases of Political Socialization and Community Power Studies." *PS: Political Science and Politics* 27:100–8.

Putnam, Robert D. 1993. *Making Democracy Work: Civic Traditions in Modern Italy.* Princeton, NJ: Princeton University Press.

Quattrone, George A., and Amos Tversky. 1988. "Contrasting Rational and Psychological Analyses of Political Choice." *American Political Science Review* 82:719–36.

Rahn, Wendy M. 1993. "The Role of Partisan Stereotypes in Information Processing About Political Candidates." *American Journal of Political Science* 37:472–96.

Rahn, Wendy M., John H. Aldrich, and Eugene Borgida. 1994. "Individual and Contextual Variations in the Process of Candidate Evaluation." *American Political Science Review* 88:193–99.

Rahn, Wendy M., John H. Aldrich, Eugene Borgida, and John L. Sullivan. 1990. "A Social-Cognitive Model of Candidate Appraisal." In John A. Ferejohn and James H. Kuklinski, eds., *Information and Democratic Processes*. Urbana: University of Illinois Press.

Rahn, Wendy M., Brian Kroeger, and Cynthia M. Kite. 1996. "A Framework for the Study of Public Mood." *Political Psychology* 17:29–58.

Rahn, Wendy M., Jon A. Krosnick, and Marijke Breuning. 1994. "Rationalization and Derivation Processes in Survey Studies of Political Candidate Evaluation." *American Journal of Political Science* 38:582–600.

Ricci, David. 1984. *The Tragedy of Political Science: Politics, Scholarship, and Democracy*. New Haven, CT: Yale University Press.

Riker, William H. 1986. *The Art of Political Manipulation*. New Haven, CT: Yale University Press.

Searing, Donald D. 1991. "Roles, Rules, and Rationality in the New Institutionalism." *American Political Science Review* 85:1239–60.

Sears, David O. 1986. "College Sophomores in the Laboratory: Influences of a Narrow Data Base on Psychology's View of Human Nature." *Journal of Personality and Social Psychology* 51:515–30.

1993. "Symbolic Politics: A Socio-Psychological Theory." In Shanto Iyengar and William J. McGuire, eds., *Explorations in Political Psychology*. Durham, NC: Duke University Press.

Sears, David O., and Carolyn Funk. 1991. "Graduate Education in Political Psychology." *Political Psychology* 12:345–62.

Simon, Herbert. 1985. "Human Nature in Politics: The Dialogue of Psychology with Political Science." *American Political Science Review* 79:293–304.

Sniderman, Paul M., Richard A. Brody, and Philip E. Tetlock. 1991. *Reasoning and Choice: Explorations in Political Psychology*. Cambridge: Cambridge University Press.

Sniderman, Paul M., and Thomas Piazza. 1993. *The Scar of Race*. Cambridge, MA: Belknap Press of Harvard University Press.

Staub, Ervin. 1989. *The Roots of Evil: The Origins of Genocide and Other Group Violence*. Cambridge: Cambridge University Press.

Stimson, James A. 1991. *Public Opinion in America: Moods, Cycles and Swings*. Boulder, CO: Westview Press.

Stimson, James A., Michael B. MacKuen, and Robert S. Erikson. 1995. "Dynamic Representation." *American Political Science Review* 89:543–65.

Sullivan, Denis G., and Roger D. Masters. 1988. "'Happy Warriors': Leaders' Facial Displays, Viewers' Emotions, and Political Support." *American Journal of Political Science* 32:345–68.

Sullivan, John L., John H. Aldrich, Eugene Borgida, and Wendy Rahn. 1990. "Candidate Appraisal and Human Nature: Man and Superman in the 1984 Election." *Political Psychology* 11:459–84.

Sullivan, John L., Amy Fried, and Mary G. Dietz. 1992. "Patriotism, Politics, and the Presidential Election of 1988." *American Journal of Political Science* 36:200–34.

Sylvan, Donald A., Ashok Goel, and B. Chandrasekaran. 1990. "Analyzing Political Decision Making from an Information-Processing Perspective." *American Journal of Political Science* 34:74–123.

Tabor, Charles S. 1992. "POLI: An Expert System Model of U.S. Foreign Policy Belief Systems." *American Political Science Review* 86:888–904.

Terkildsen, Nayda. 1993. "When White Voters Evaluate Black Candidates: The Processing Implications of Candidate Skin Color, Prejudice, and Self-Monitoring." *American Journal of Political Science* 37:1032–53.

Tetlock, Philip E. 1993. "Cognitive Structural Analysis of Political Rhetoric: Methodological and Theoretical Issues." In Shanto Iyengar and William J. McGuire, eds., *Explorations in Political Psychology*. Durham, NC: Duke University Press.

——. 1999. "Theory-Driven Reasoning about Possible Pasts and Probable Futures in World Politics: Are We Prisoners of our Preconceptions?" *American Journal of Political Science* 43:335–66.

Tetlock, Philip E., and Aaron Belkin. 1996. *Counterfactual Thought Experiments in World Politics: Logical, Methodological, and Psychological Perspectives*. Princeton, NJ: Princeton University Press.

Tetlock, Philip E., Randall S. Peterson, Charles McGuire, Shi-jie Chang, and Peter Feld. 1992. "Assessing Political Group Dynamics: A Test of the Group Think Model." *Journal of Personality and Social Psychology* 63:403–25.

Theiss-Morse, Elizabeth. 1993. "Conceptualizations of Good Citizenship and Political Participation." *Political Behavior* 15:355–80.

Turner, Marlene E., Anthony Pratkanis, Preston Probasco, and Craig Leve. 1992. "Threat, Cohesion, and Group Effectiveness: Testing a Social Identity Maintenance Perspective on Group Think." *Journal of Personality and Social Psychology* 63:781–96.

Tyler, Tom R. 1990. *Why People Obey the Law*. New Haven, CT: Yale University Press.

——. 1994a. "Governing Amid Diversity: Can Fair Decision-Making Procedures Bridge Competing Public Interests and Values." *Law and Society Review* 28:701–22.

——. 1994b. "Psychological Models of the Justice Motive: Antecedents of Distributive and Procedural Justice." *Journal of Personality and Social Psychology* 67:850–63.

——. 1997. "The Psychology of Legitimacy: A Relational Perspective on Voluntary Deference to Authorities." *Personality and Social Psychology Review* 1:323–45.

Tyler, Tom R., and G. Mitchell. 1994. "Legitimacy and the Empowerment of Discretionary Legal Authority: The United States Supreme Court and Abortion Rights." *Duke Law Journal* 43:703–815.

Weatherford, M. Stephen. 1992. "Measuring Political Legitimacy." *American Political Science Review* 86:149–66.

Winter, Herbert R., and Thomas J. Bellows. 1992. *Conflict and Compromise: An Introduction to Political Science*. New York: HarperCollins.

Wright, Gerald C. 1993. "Errors in Measuring Vote Choice in the National Election Studies, 1952–88." *American Journal of Political Science* 37:291–316.

Zaller, John R. 1992. *The Nature and Origins of Mass Opinion*. Cambridge: Cambridge University Press.

6

Is Political Psychology Sufficiently Psychological? Distinguishing Political Psychology from Psychological Political Science

JON A. KROSNICK

During the last thirty years or so, political psychologists have turned out a great deal of empirical research and theory of which we can be quite proud. In the midst of this productive enterprise, we have occasionally taken time out to lobby other scholars outside our circles to make use of the theories and methods that we find most useful (e.g., Kinder and Palfrey 1993). Less often, we have taken a step back from our empirical work to don a self-critical hat and ask whether we are going about our enterprise in as constructive a fashion as we might (see, e.g., Kuklinski, Luskin, and Bolland 1991).

One purpose of this book is to do so quite deliberately. Other chapters address the questions of whether political psychology is sufficiently theoretical and whether it is sufficiently political, two matters on which we have been criticized by political scientists who take different approaches. In this chapter, I will address a different question, asking whether political psychology is sufficiently psychological.

My goal is to be controversial in raising philosophical issues about political psychology as an enterprise that may deserve more explicit consideration than they currently receive. In short, I will suggest that two very different sorts of political psychology are being carried on, sometimes within the same research project or even within the same paper. I will clarify the distinction between the two, illustrate that one seems to be far more common than the other, and argue that it would be useful to reduce this imbalance by doing a more psychological version of political psychology more often.

The author wishes to thank Margaret Hermann, Marilynn Brewer, Tom Nelson, and Ewa Golobiowska for very helpful comments on an earlier draft.

POLITICAL PSYCHOLOGY VERSUS PSYCHOLOGICAL
POLITICAL SCIENCE

Is political psychology sufficiently psychological? "A preposterous question to ask!" you might say. "Of *course* it is sufficiently psychological! Everything we do uses psychological concepts!" But merely using psychological concepts is not what I mean by psychological.

To clarify what I do mean, consider a linguistic analysis of the term "political psychology." This reigning label for our joint enterprise, given its ordering of the two constituent disciplines within it, makes politics a modifier or qualifier of the type of psychology being done. That is, the label can be viewed as suggesting that we are doing *psychology*, but in a particular context, the political one. Thus, the name we have settled on for our enterprise might seem to place the priority on the goals of *psychology* and suggest that political psychology is a subtype of the larger discipline of psychology generally. So to understand what the principal aim of such an enterprise would be, we must establish what psychology is.

According to Zimbardo (1988), psychology seeks to answer one fundamental question: "What is the nature of human nature?" (5). Stated more concretely, psychology is "the scientific study of behavioral and mental processes . . . [with an interest] in discovering . . . general laws" (5). Because psychology seeks to identify *generalizations* about the mind, a person doing political psychology true to its name would not be interested in identifying patterns that hold *only* in the political context. Rather, he or she would study the political context in a search for more general principles of thought and action that are pan-contextual. This would be political psychology true to its name, and it would be comparable to "social psychology" or "cognitive psychology" or "consumer psychology" or "health psychology," all terms routinely used to describe currently active subfields seeking to identify generalizations by detailed studies of particular contexts.

To anyone knowledgeable about the history of political psychology, it is immediately apparent that this conception of our field falls quite short of effectively describing most of what we do. If one were to gather up all the political psychology studies published during the last thirty years, "psychological political science" would most certainly seem to be the more apt descriptor in most cases. That is, we usually have a primary interest in serving the core goals of political science.

What is political science? According to Easton (1953), it is the study of "activity that influences significantly the kind of authoritative policy adopted for a society and the way it is put into practice" (128). Put more succinctly, politics may be said to be activities "of or concerned with government" (*Webster's New World Dictionary*, 1988). Stated in more detail, according to Lane (1963), the central questions of political science include:

How shall government power be organized so as to achieve a "just" distribution of benefits? How can government be made both efficient and responsible, and what are the relationships between these two goals? What is the relationship between majority rule and minority rights? How do nations relate to one another, in what terms, through what channels, with what results? What is the nature of law, and how does law develop, how is it interpreted? (583–4).

Thus, political science attempts to understand how and why the processes of politics unfold as they do, with no special interest in understanding whether these principles apply to other domains of behavior. Indeed, political science concepts are often defined in ways that inhibit easy and direct applications to domains such as health or consumer behavior.

Of course, what distinguishes political psychology from other sorts of political science is that we explain political phenomena by taking a *psychological* perspective. We could instead, for example, adopt an economic perspective, attributing significant political events to economic forces, which are typically more easily observable via purchase behavior, interest rates, unemployment rates, and the like (e.g., Alt and Chrystal 1983). But instead, we place our emphasis on unobservable psychological processes unfolding in the minds of political actors. Thus, the modifier structure of "psychological political science," though more linguistically cumbersome, might more appropriately emphasize that we are doing a particular type of political science, to be distinguished from other types of political science.

In fact, two somewhat different forms of psychological political science seem to be practiced. The first ignores the psychological literature and focuses its explanations of political phenomena on psychological concepts. The second begins with a particular theory or finding in psychology and attempts to apply it to an analysis of political events. These two sorts of work have rarely yielded *new* psychological theories. Instead, they tend to apply existing, more general theories of the mind in the specific context of politics, or they develop a new set of psychologically tinged ideas so tailored to the political context that exporting them is difficult to envision.

To illustrate the first of these forms, consider Kinder's (1981) idea of sociotropic politics. The starting point for this work was the finding that presidential popularity shifts with the state of the national economy: as economic conditions improve and decline, so does presidential approval (Kernell 1978). The most popular interpretation of this result was the notion of "pocketbook voting" (e.g., Neustadt 1960). According to this perspective, citizens who are doing well financially support the president (to whom they partly attribute their own successes), and citizens suffering financially partly blame the president and consequently withhold their support. The more people are in the latter category, the lower a president's level of popular support supposedly falls. Thus, this view portrays the American citizen as focused on his or her own personal welfare, selfish rather than collectivist in orientation.

Kinder (1981) offered a very different interpretation, one that provided a more appealing portrait of ordinary Americans. According to his view, people distinguish between their personal economic circumstances and the economic state of the nation as a whole. And Kinder's data demonstrated that people base their presidential approval primarily on judgments of the national economy, not of their own personal circumstances. Thus, it seems, people want what is best for the country as a whole, not necessarily what is best for them personally.

This conclusion cast an optimistic light on an empirical relation that might otherwise have raised troubling questions about the motives of democratic citizens. And to rescue the promise of democracy in this small way, Kinder offered a psychological analysis. Yet he did so without citing a single theory or research finding from psychology. The distinction he drew between individually focused and collectively focused economic judgments was one developed specifically for this purpose. The finding that collective judgments are more consequential than self-focused judgments has not been cited especially often by mainstream psychologists since then, but it was very valuable indeed to political science.

The second sort of psychological political science I mentioned is illustrated by research by Lodge, McGraw, and Stroh (1989) on processes of candidate evaluation. Some years before Lodge and colleagues embarked on their enterprise, Hastie and Park (1986), two social psychologists, had published a paper in *Psychological Review* drawing the distinction between memory-based and on-line decision-making. Memory-based evaluation occurs when a person is prompted to make a new evaluation of an object, such as when a survey interviewer asks a respondent a question about which he or she has not previously formed an opinion. In this case, the respondent presumably digs into his or her memory to retrieve whatever relevant information would be useful to make this judgment and constructs it on the spot. In contrast, when on-line evaluation occurs, a person forms an overall evaluation of an object and updates it as each new piece of relevant information about the object is acquired in the course of daily life. So, when he or she is asked about this overall evaluation, it is simply retrieved from memory and reported. The distinction between memory-based and on-line evaluation was very helpful for a number of reasons, by making sense of apparently contradictory results regarding the relation of judgments to recollections.[1]

Lodge et al. (1989) built a bridge from Hastie and Park's general theoretical assertions to the world of politics. Evaluation processes apparent in psychologists' decision-making studies in the laboratory should also be apparent in the thinking of voters operating in the real world, said Lodge et al. (1989). Their study was a contrived experiment as well, rather than an investigation of a naturally occurring election. But it did involve uniquely political stimuli, uniquely political judgments, and a cross section of adults (rather than the typical college student sample).

Lodge et al.'s (1989) study challenged the reigning presumption in political science that voters evaluate candidates in a memory-based fashion (Kelley 1983) and offered compelling evidence that voters are at least sometimes on-line evaluators instead. Their work also motivated subsequent research by others that has made further use of this conceptual distinction and has offered additional evidence in support of the on-line view of voters (e.g., Rahn, Krosnick, and Breuning 1994). And Lodge et al.'s (1989) article illustrates a very common form of psychological political science: taking an existing psychological theory or idea and applying it to understand a political phenomenon.

Many other examples of this sort of psychological political science have appeared over the years. For example, Converse's (1964) landmark work on belief systems grew directly out of reigning psychological theories of cognitive consistency (Festinger 1957; Heider 1958). Zaller's (1993) work on the diffusion of political attitudes was inspired by McGuire's (1968) two-factor notion of exposure and acceptance as regulators of attitude change. And numerous studies of voters' perceptions of political candidates' stands on issues have brought to bear psychological theories of cognitive consistency (Kinder 1978), social judgment (Granberg and Brent 1974), schemas (Conover and Feldman 1986), expression structures (Ottati, Fishbein, and Middlestadt 1988), and more. In all of this latter work, the goal has been to understand the striking diversity among citizens in their perceptions of a single object (i.e., a candidate). And to do so, preexisting, well-developed psychological theories were used to derive predictions that could then be tested in the political context, with the primary goal of understanding *that* context more fully.

---

1 The seeds of this distinction were quite apparent in a number of earlier psychological works. For example, Lingle and Ostrom (1979) had developed the idea of forming a judgment that is retained in memory while the ingredients are lost, which is the very notion of on-line evaluation. Nonetheless, Hastie and Park's (1986) article was a cogent and compelling statement of the distinction.

Table 6.1. *Enrollment in the Ohio State University Summer Institute in Political Psychology by Discipline*

Discipline	Year						
	1991	1992	1993	1994	1995	1996	1997
Political science	38	36	33	33	45	29	33
Psychology	14	11	18	11	18	11	4
Other	11	2	9	1	1	6	2

ASYMMETRIC INTEREST IN THE TWO APPROACHES

During the last couple of decades, these forms of psychological political science have dominated political psychology true to its name. That is, political science and political scientists have placed much more value on political psychology than have psychologists. This is revealed by a variety of different indicators, one of which is enrollment rates in the Ohio State University Summer Institute in Political Psychology, a one-month intensive training program we have run for the past seven years. Each summer, we host about fifty participants, mostly graduate students from as many as fifteen different countries, all interested in learning about political psychology. And in each of the first seven years, enrollment has been strikingly out of balance (see Table 6.1). We hosted more political scientists (presumably interested in doing psychological political science) than psychologists (interested in doing political psychology) by a wide margin.

Greater interest in psychological political science is also apparent in hiring practices at major research universities. Political science departments have often hired faculty members with Ph.D.s in psychology, including Donald Kinder (initially at Yale University and now at the University of Michigan), Margaret Hermann and Tom Nelson (at Ohio State University), Rick Lau (initially at Carnegie-Mellon University and now at Rutgers), Victor Ottati and Leoni Huddie (formerly and currently at the State University of New York at Stony Brook, respectively), and Kathleen McGraw (initially at the State University of New York at Stoney Brook and now at Ohio State). But it is much more difficult to think of individuals with primary appointments on psychology faculties whose Ph.D.s are in political science. So the asymmetry apparent in our Summer Institute participants is apparent as well in their faculty mentors' departmental affiliations. Thus, one could view these affiliations as reinforcing the notion that psychology has much to offer political science, but political science has little if anything to offer psychology.

This asymmetry is reflected in journal publication patterns as well. It is not uncommon at all for psychology Ph.D.s to publish articles in political science journals. And indeed, the creative application of psychological notions in the study of politics often gets significant and prominent attention, as evidenced by prominent publications in the *American Political Science Review* in recent years. In contrast, it is much harder to come up with prominent publications in major psychology journals written solely by political science Ph.D.s. One notable exception is John Zaller, who has published work on attitude change in the *Journal of Personality and Social Psychology* and in *Social Cognition*. But generally, journal publication patterns also suggest that psychology seems not especially interested in political science, and certainly much less so than political science is interested in psychology.

This portrait is further reinforced when one examines the book publishing area. A growing number of publishers are producing books on the psychology of politics, some explicitly titled as such and others clearly addressing relevant subject matter without the label. Although there are a few examples of such work being handled by psychology editors at the presses and marketed primarily to psychologists (e.g., Milburn 1991), it is far more common for them to be handled by political science editors and marketed accordingly (e.g., Cambridge University Press, the University of Chicago Press, the University of Michigan Press). Thus, it seems that political psychology again falls under the disciplinary umbrella of political science much more often than under psychology.

If anything, this perspective is likely to be reinforced still further by a smattering of recent publications in social psychology on the value of basic psychological research for understanding "applied," real-world phenomena. In the face of shrinking federal budget allocations for basic psychological research and rising skepticism about the value of such research (in contrast with basic research in chemistry and physics), social psychologists seem to feel the need to demonstrate that their work is valuable for helping to solve significant social problems.

For example, a book edited by Ruble, Costanzo, and Oliveri (1992) offers numerous chapters illustrating how basic social psychological theories (regarding, e.g., social cognition and attitudes) can be useful for understanding mental health. Fazio (1990) edited a special issue of *Personality and Social Psychology Bulletin* entitled "Illustrating the Value of Basic Research." It contained articles addressing aggression among children, depression, jury decision making, eyewitness memory, desegregation, energy conservation, acquired immune deficiency syndrome (AIDS), and other phenomena. More recently, Mark Snyder's (1993) presidential address to the Society for Personality and Social

Psychology illustrated how basic personality and motivational theories can be useful for understanding when and why people volunteer to help others. As psychologists make the case that their research has valuable potential for application in general, this campaign will undoubtedly reinforce the notion that political science in particular stands to benefit from careful attention to the literature of psychology. Yet the notion that psychology can benefit from exporting its insights and reading the literatures of other fields is rarely expressed.

REASONS TO DO POLITICAL PSYCHOLOGY
TRUE TO ITS NAME

I want to challenge this presumption: to suggest that complementing psychological political science should be a genuine political psychology that is true to its name. But why, one might ask, should a discipline focus intensely on a single context (i.e., the political one) if the goal is to describe cross-context consistencies? As counterintuitive as this may seem, there are at least three reasons why explicitly context-focused research has the potential for great payoffs for psychology. The first reason grows from the observation that there is in fact no such thing as context-free psychological research.

Although psychologists might hope to set up novel and unfamiliar information environments in their laboratories to study "basic" psychological processes as they occur *across* social contexts, it is impossible to prevent people from bringing to these situations the experiences they have had in the outside world. And in doing so, experimental subjects diagnose the sort of situation they face in the laboratory and draw on their previous experiences with similar situations in order to decide how to think and act. Therefore, every laboratory finding seems likely to be conditional, specific to the nature of the context involved.

A few years ago, my colleagues and I produced one illustration of this notion (Krosnick, Li, and Lehman 1990). Our focus in this investigation was Kahneman and Tversky's (1973) famous demonstration that people underutilize base-rate information and overweight individuating, vivid, case-based information when making social judgments. In particular, these scholars showed that when laboratory subjects were asked how likely a randomly selected man was to be a lawyer or an engineer, people overweighted the implications of a brief personality sketch of him and underweighted the proportions of lawyers and engineers in the sample from which he was selected.

We demonstrated that this occurred because the base rate was presented to subjects before the personality sketch. Based on the norms of conventional conversation in everyday life, subjects presumed that the information presented last by the experimenter was the information he or she considered most informative. Although Kahneman and Tversky (1973) had presumed that subjects would simply take in the information and make a judgment with it, regardless of presentation order, subjects interpreted the incoming flow of information in light of their previous real-world experiences and yielded a result that was misinterpreted as being a general tendency in human social judgment.

If the objects and interactions being explored in a psychological study are inherently political in nature (as in the numerous attitude change studies that have focused on political objects, such as politicians and controversial social policies), it would be narrow-minded for a researcher not to consider the role played by subjects' previous real-world experiences with such phenomena. To ignore those experiences would be to attempt to understand what happened in the laboratory without attributing proper responsibility to these prior experiences. Therefore, understanding politics (by consulting the political science literature when it touches on relevant topics) will allow one to interpret and perhaps even to design psychological laboratory experiments more effectively and to avoid attributing outcomes to the wrong causes.

But even more importantly, careful attention to the political context can help psychologists, because many of them study explicitly political phenomena, not merely psychological processes in a political context. For example, consider the following core topics in social psychology: aggression, altruism, intergroup relations, stereotyping, prejudice, cooperation and competition, and group decision making. These topics are all clearly, inherently, and unavoidably political and have been studied extensively by political scientists. In fact, their political nature is most obvious when considered at the level of international relations: nearly all the interesting questions about how nations interact with one another involve each of these processes: aggression, altruism, intergroup relations, stereotyping, prejudice, cooperation and competition, and group decision making. And to discuss these processes at an intergroup or an interindividual level is to discuss politics.

Yet remarkably, when one reads any of the numerous introductory social psychology textbooks on the market these days, citations of research done by political scientists on these topics are essentially invisible. Although a great deal of work has been done examining just these "psychological" processes and phenomena by political scientists, psychologists seem either unaware of or uninterested in it. I believe that psychologists can do our business better by becoming acquainted with studies that have explored precisely the same topics that are of interest to us in other disciplines.

Most important of all, however, there is an even greater potential value of political psychology true to its name for psychology as a whole, even for psychologists who are not necessarily studying inherently political phenomena: careful attention to the political context will help to inspire new directions for theory development. The idea here is that thinking about real political events will push psychologists to develop new constructs, to focus on new variables, and especially to identify new interactions: conditions under which effects occur, and classes of people among which effects are most likely to occur.

To illustrate this notion, consider the basic work in psychology on priming. Early studies of this phenomenon demonstrated that if people were exposed to words signifying a particular attribute (e.g., hostility), they were subsequently likely to interpret ambiguous behavior by a target person as being consistent with the attribute. So, for example, exposure to words like "nasty" and "rude" increased the likelihood that subsequently observed actions would be interpreted as hostile. The presumption here was that the initial exposure made the concept of hostility more accessible in memory and thereby more likely to be used in subsequent thinking.

Once a psychologist has identified a process like this, where does he or she go from there in theory development? Some factions of psychology tend to presume that the phenomenon demonstrated holds in all situations for all people until proven otherwise. Therefore, part of the value of a new psychological theory or insight is its generality – the fact that it presumably occurs everywhere for everyone. For example, Bargh, Chaiken, Govender, and Pratto (1992) asserted that automatic activation processes like priming are quite general. Given the appropriate stimulus, they said, a priming effect will appear in essentially everyone, because these effects are automatic results of the structure of knowledge in memory (see also Bargh and Pietromonaco 1982). But most psychological effects are unlikely to occur identically for all people in all situations.

Why would this implicit view of generality be so prevalent among psychologists? Undoubtedly, some of the basis for this presumption is psychologists' reliance on college sophomores as research subjects and laboratory settings. To acknowledge that different sorts of people may be more or less susceptible to a certain effect is to acknowledge that a very homogeneous, limited subject population may be inadequate for studying it. So psychologists may be drawn to the view that their effects are quite general as a way to feel comfortable with their anything-but-representative subject populations. Similarly, it is quite conceivable that effects observed in contrived laboratory settings might not occur in the more rich and complex real-world settings in which significant social behaviors occur. To acknowledge the possibility that situational factors may turn on or off the effects that are observed in the laboratory may also threaten the apparent value of the work.

These two hallmarks of psychological research (i.e., collecting data from college sophomores in laboratory settings) are not fatal flaws in the approach. Every research method has its potential weak spots, whether it is a survey study or a content analysis or a participant observation. Laboratory studies, of course, have the unique virtue of being able to demonstrate causality compellingly. Thus, when conducted in a contrived setting with college sophomore subjects, such a study can demonstrate that a causal effect *can* happen under those particular circumstances and among those particular people. Then, subsequent studies could presumably attempt to pursue those conditions and demonstrate the generalizability of the result.

Furthermore, science will almost certainly progress more quickly and efficiently if we place the burden of proof on the critic of laboratory studies rather than on the investigator in one particular sense. It is very easy for critics to charge that all laboratory studies are uninformative because of limited subject populations and artificial circumstances. Similarly, it is easy for qualitative researchers to reject all traditional survey research out of hand because of its tendency to place respondents in artificially structured categories and prevent people from expressing the richness and fullness of their views in their own words, including essential qualifications and elaborations. And yet because every research method is subject to such criticisms, the fields of psychology and political science alike will be left with no believed evidence at all if we accept this blanket rejecting approach.

Instead, we should embrace all research methods as potentially informative, and each set of results should be subjected to careful scrutiny, in an attempt to identify plausible alternative processes that may be responsible for the observed results. And if such processes can be identified, one should be appropriately skeptical of the observed results. But in the absence of such plausible alternative mechanisms for observed results, we are best off accepting the results from laboratory and survey studies alike as useful elements in the progress of science. But because many psychologists have elevated the laboratory experiment to the level of "most desirable method," they are likely to be invested in the belief that their findings are quite generalizable.

There is another, more interesting and significant reason for psychologists' view regarding generalizability as well: it is hard to identify interacting variables within a context-free framework. Consider, for example, the priming case: What variables should interact with priming stimuli? In what contexts should priming be most effective? Among which sorts of people should it be most powerful? These are not easy questions to answer in the abstract. So it is no surprise that most of the initial psychological research on priming presumed that it was quite a general phenomenon across people and situations.

To identify regulating variables, it is useful to refer to specific real-world social contexts, and this is where the literature of political science and the political context more generally have something to offer psychologists. It is much easier to begin by selecting such a context (e.g., the case of news media coverage of issues and its impact on presidential evaluations) and then speculate about when and among whom the effect should be most pronounced. With the context in hand, one can phrase one's hypotheses about interactions in ways that are pancontextual. But the inspiration for the idea comes from the inherent parameters of the context itself, as I will illustrate with a review of politically inspired research on priming. As it will illustrate, a benefit of doing political psychology true to its name is that it may help psychologists to expand their theories by identifying more, and more interesting, interactions.

Paying close attention to political contexts helps one to spot new potential causal processes as well. Certainly, if we begin an investigation focused on a theoretically derived effect of an independent variable on a dependent variable (as psychologists tend to do), our attention is likely to turn first to variables likely to interact with the independent variable. But as we continue to think about a rich social context, we are likely to recognize other independent variables that are also likely to influence the dependent variable of interest. Thus, the potential value of political psychology is not limited to interactions, though it may initially begin that way for any given investigation.

These benefits of political psychology cannot accrue if one remains at the surface of political science. In order for truly new ideas to emerge in psychological research as the result of attention to the political context, a theorist must become immersed in that context. An afternoon's reading of a few key political science references (or even a few days' reading) is at best likely to function as a Rorschach inkblot, providing an opportunity for the psychologist to see what he or she already believes and is comfortable identifying and understanding. Only when one gets deeply into the literature of political science can one truly adopt a new perspective thoroughly enough to push theory in truly new directions. In this sense, I am suggesting that the enterprise of psychology should become more politically sophisticated in order to permit more effective political psychology true to its name.

Is Political Psychology Sufficiently Psychological?

Is the political context a particularly valuable one for psychological research? Is there some reason why doing political psychology will be more useful to psychology than doing consumer psychology or health psychology? I suspect not. Each domain of behavior is likely to be rich and interesting, and different domains may be useful for investigation of psychological processes in different ways. But I see no reason why the political arena is better or richer or more interesting than any other context in which social cognition and action unfold. I am suggesting the value of context-specific investigation in general, and the political context is clearly no less interesting or potentially fruitful than these others.

ILLUSTRATIONS OF POLITICAL PSYCHOLOGY TRUE TO ITS NAME

In an effort to complement the strong interest in psychology among political scientists, I want to encourage political scientists and psychologists alike to see that psychology has much to gain from careful attention to political science. And to do so, I will point to a few examples illustrating how research in political psychology has yielded useful payoffs for psychology in the pursuit of its core goals. These examples are from my own work, because they are the ones I know best and can discuss most easily. But the work of others could easily be substituted. My intention here is simply to illustrate the types of benefits that can be accrued from political psychology true to its name.

Interestingly, the three examples of work I will discuss are cases in which we set out to do psychological political science – to apply empirically validated psychological theories to understand a political phenomenon. And in each case, we presumed that our hypotheses would be confirmed, an expectation that was met in some cases and not in others. But in each instance, a useful yield for psychology as a discipline was produced.

Branching and Labeling in Political Attitude Measurement

The first and simplest example involves attitude measurement (Krosnick and Berent 1993). Our investigation was inspired by the predominant view in the political behavior literature, offered especially clearly in *The American Voter* (Campbell, Converse, Miller, and Stokes 1960), that American citizens' identifications with political parties are highly crystallized and are powerful determinants of people's political decisions, whereas their attitudes on matters of government policy are highly flexible and relatively inconsequential. This view has been supported in numerous investigations that documented the superiority of party identification measures over policy attitude measures in terms of over-time consistency and in terms of correlations with criterion judgments such as candidate preferences in elections.

Although all this seemed quite reasonable to us, we had also been aware of a methodological confound inherent in nearly all prior investigations of these matters. Most past studies had relied on the National Election Study (NES) surveys, and many of the other studies in this literature had collected original data using questions taken from the NES. And in the NES, the two sorts of variables of interest had been measured in notably different ways.

Party identification was measured by branching respondents through a sequence of questions involving fully verbally labeled response options. All respondents were asked initially whether they considered themselves a Republican, a Democrat, an independent, and so on. Then, people who reported identifying with a party were asked whether they did so strongly or weakly. And self-proclaimed independents were asked whether they leaned toward one party or the other. In contrast, policy attitudes were measured in one step by asking respondents to place themselves on a 7-point scale, with verbal labels on only the endpoints.

It seemed to us that two differences between these measurement approaches might have contributed to the relatively low apparent stability and consequentiality of policy attitudes. First, decomposing the attitude-reporting task into two component parts, one reporting direction and the other reporting extremity, might reduce the cognitive demands of the task and might improve precision, especially among respondents for whom the cognitive demands of the task were most burdensome. Second, it seemed that simply numbering some attitude-rating scale points leaves their meaning relatively ambiguous and requires that respondents infer the meanings of those points. Providing verbal labels to all respondents for all scale points seemed to us again to reduce the cognitive burden of the task and thereby possibly to improve the precision of attitude reports.

Some previous studies in psychology suggested that verbal labeling enhances measurement reliability (Peters and McCormick 1966), though other such studies failed to document this relation (Finn 1972). No previous psychological studies had examined whether decomposition could improve the reliability of attitude reports. However, a variety of studies had illustrated how decomposition could help people to answer quiz questions such as "How many families were living in the United States in 1970?" more accurately (see, e.g., Armstrong, Denniston, and Gordon 1975; Einhorn 1972).

To test these ideas with regard to the measurement of political attitudes, we conducted eight experiments, two in the laboratory and six in typical survey settings. Some of our studies involved face-to-face interviewing, some involved telephone interviews, and some involved self-administered questionnaires. Some studies involved college student subjects, and others involved regional or national general population samples. Across all these instances, we found support for our two hypotheses. Furthermore, our general population studies indicated that branching and labeling are the greatest help to respondents with the least amount of formal education, whose cognitive ability at abstract manipulation of verbal concepts was presumably relatively low on average.

This finding seems clearly useful to political science. A widely accepted truism and a central pillar of the American politics literature was discredited, at least a bit, by this evidence. Our findings did not completely refute this central idea, because the gap between party identification and policy preferences in terms of stability and consequentiality remained even after we equated the measurement approaches. But what had initially appeared to be a very large gap was significantly reduced by this action.

Thus, our work on this topic was clearly "psychological political science," because it was a psychologically informed investigation of a political question that yielded a useful new insight for political science. Furthermore, this work set an example by illustrating the need for careful attention to measurement approaches (for another example, see Green 1988). Perhaps other findings in political science will be similarly reinterpreted when measurement problems are solved, and thus the field will progress forward.

At the same time, our study of branching and labeling is valuable for psychology as well. Our demonstration regarding decomposition helps to establish the validity of this notion by documenting it in a new domain: attitude measurement. And we demonstrated that decomposition is especially important among a subset of people: those for whom effortful cognitive exercises are the most difficult. Furthermore, our evidence documents a general principle for attitude measurement that is useful for researchers across the social sciences: that data quality can be enhanced via sequences of fully verbally labeled branching questions measuring attitude direction and extremity separately. Thus, our work appears to have been political psychology at the same time that it was psychological political science.

News Media Priming

The next example again began explicitly as psychological political science and ended up yielding surprising insights for psychology. When

Shanto Iyengar, Don Kinder, and I began our work on news media priming, we borrowed the term and the notion of "priming" from psychology. Our inspiration came from research done in psychological laboratories demonstrating that activating a body of knowledge in a person's memory led that knowledge to have enhanced impact on subsequent relevant judgments (Higgins and King 1981; Wyer and Hartwick 1980). This work, as well as other related laboratory studies in psychology, contributed to the rising popularity of an associative network model of memory processes (Anderson 1983; Collins and Loftus 1975). Within this conceptual framework, activating any given node in memory yields spreading activation to other linked nodes, which enhances the likelihood that they will have an impact on relevant judgments as well.

It seemed to us relatively straightforward to apply these notions in an analysis of news media effects on political cognition. By repeatedly addressing a certain issue day after day, the news media seemed capable of activating the body of relevant knowledge in viewers' memories, thereby making that knowledge more accessible and causing it to have greater impact on a variety of relevant political judgments, such as evaluations of a president's job performance. This hypothesis offered the promise of a new understanding of the types of effects the news media could have on the conduct of politics: by focusing on some issues and not others, we suspected, the news media might shape the public's approval of the president and thereby determine in part his ability to shape policy making in Washington.

We conducted a series of studies testing the viability of this idea, initially in the laboratory and later in real-world settings via surveys (for a review, see Miller and Krosnick 1996). Our first studies exposed laboratory subjects (general population samples in some cases and college students in others) to different sets of television news stories, varying across individuals the extent to which particular issues received attention. And as we expected, greater coverage of an issue led subjects to base their overall evaluations of the U.S. president's overall job performance more on his handling of that issue (see Iyengar, Kinder, Peters, and Krosnick 1984).

Later survey studies showed similarly that when news coverage of a particular issue increased, the weight citizens attached to that issue in forming presidential evaluations also increased. Specifically, we showed first that news coverage of the Iran/Contra affair increased the weight attached to President Reagan's handling of relations with Central America (Krosnick and Kinder 1990). And subsequently, we demonstrated that news coverage of the 1991 Gulf War increased the weight attached to President Bush's handling of it (Krosnick and Brannon 1993).

These findings, in and of themselves, were not groundbreaking for psychology, despite the fact that the initial work was published in the *Journal of Personality and Social Psychology*. Psychologists could legitimately have responded to the work by saying: "Of course! Why *wouldn't* our priming effects replicate?" Yet it was nonetheless useful to demonstrate first that the effects could be observed in the laboratory with more real-world-like stimuli (i.e., television news programs) and judgments (of presidential performance) that were likely to be based significantly on information obtained previously, outside the laboratory. And second, it was useful to demonstrate that real-world shifts in news media coverage were associated with shifts in the bases of citizens' consequential political judgments. Of course, this latter evidence alone does not definitively document the causal process(es) responsible for the observed associations. But coupled with the laboratory studies that did demonstrate the causal impact of news media coverage, the survey studies seem informative about media influence as it occurs in the course of ordinary daily life. And the survey studies demonstrated the social significance of an effect that could conceivably have been limited to the laboratory setting, with its relatively impoverished judgment conditions and the experimental demand characteristics that could conceivably have lurked within.

The more useful contribution to psychology, however, came as we explored interactions in this work. We began by speculating that resistance to priming effects might be a function of political expertise. This suspicion was not driven by any explicit research on expertise and priming within psychology. In fact, the psychological literature in the mid-1980s did not point to any interacting variables that might regulate priming effects. It seemed taken for granted that notions such as "spreading activation" were relatively universal processes that were inevitable results of the architecture of knowledge structures in memory.

We suspected instead that political experts might be especially resistant to priming effects for a variety of reasons. Principally, individuals with little knowledge have only a minimal ability to see flaws or distortions in new information, and they have few other bases from which to derive political judgments. And just as we anticipated, our laboratory studies revealed that priming effects were strongest among political novices, a result that was replicated in our first survey study, of the Iran/Contra affair (Krosnick and Kinder 1990).

But when we set out to do the Gulf War study, it seemed that simply demonstrating the priming effect and the expertise interaction again would not be especially valuable. We therefore decided to pursue an idea that had been lurking in the backs of our minds for some time, inspired by the writings of McGuire (1968), Converse (1962), and Zaller (1987,

1989). The idea was to differentiate factors that regulate the dosage of media coverage a person receives from factors that regulate his or her resistance to the media's influence.

In our previous studies, we had thought of expertise as a basis for resistance, and we had identified political experts by their performance on political knowledge quizzes (Iyengar et al. 1984; Krosnick and Kinder 1990). When asked a series of open-ended or multiple-choice questions about factual matters, some individuals provided much more accurate information than others, and we labeled these two groups "political experts" and "novices," respectively. But at the same time, we had always been aware that in the world outside the laboratory, political knowledge is positively correlated with two other relevant factors: interest in politics and exposure to political information through the news media (e.g., Krosnick and Milburn 1990).

In designing our Gulf War study, it seemed useful to think of these two factors as related to dosage: the more a person was exposed to political news, and the more he or she was interested in it, the stronger the priming manipulation and the more pronounced the effect should be. Because interest and exposure are positively correlated with knowledge and yet were expected to have oppositely signed effects on the magnitude of priming, we suspected that a multivariate analysis looking at the effects of all three factors simultaneously might eliminate suppression and thereby reveal an even stronger effect of knowledge than we had thus far observed.

In fact, our results were quite the opposite (see Krosnick and Brannon 1993). We found plenty of effects of knowledge, interest, and exposure, but they each regulated priming in ways precisely opposite to what we had anticipated. Rather than high knowledge being associated with resistance, high knowledge *enhanced* priming effects when all other variables were controlled. And rather than high levels of exposure and interest strengthening priming, it was actually weakened by them, controlling for all other variables. Interestingly, when we returned to the Iran/Contra data and repeated the same multivariate analyses, we found the same pattern of relations, thus suggesting that it was not specific to the Gulf War context.

These findings were quite startling to us, yet they make sense in light of the entire literature on cognitive social psychology (see Krosnick and Brannon 1993). First, consider knowledge. Although we originally thought of knowledge as a basis for counterarguing or scrutinizing incoming information, our results are consistent with two alternative possibilities instead. First, more knowledge could be associated with more elaborate storage structures in memory, which would allow priming stimuli to be remembered better and thereby to have effects over longer periods of time. Alternatively, more structured knowledge in memory means that more links exist among knowledge bits, which would therefore facilitate more spreading activation. Among people with few political knowledge structures, there is little stored in memory that news coverage of an issue could activate, so there would be no cognitive mechanism by which any effect could occur.

With regard to interest and exposure, our results made sense in light of notions involving cognitive overload and interference. Even people with low levels of exposure and interest probably can't help but receive the big message of the news media, which was the Iran/Contra affair in late 1985 and the Gulf War in early 1991. But people with higher levels of exposure and interest undoubtedly get those big messages plus many other little messages, which may have diluted the priming effect regarding the big issue. Thus, the cacophony of messages that comes to any highly attentive television news viewer or newspaper reader over a period of days may actually reduce the impact of coverage of any single issue.

Another possible explanation for the interest effect we observed is suggested by recent psychological studies of priming. Priming manipulations in the laboratory have the greatest impact when they occur without people paying much attention to them (Lombardi, Higgins, and Bargh 1987; Strack, Schwarz, Bless, Kubler, and Wanke 1993). When people attend closely to and are aware of the potential impact of context on their judgments, they correct for it. In our case, highly interested readers and viewers are likely to have noted the content of the news they received, and might therefore have adjusted the weights they attached to issues in order to correct for any news media impact. In contrast, less interested readers and viewers probably absorbed news media content without much awareness, so they were unlikely to make the correction. This would then have yielded larger priming effects among these individuals, just as we observed.

The hypotheses that knowledge structures might facilitate priming and that multiple priming manipulations might dilute any given priming effect are not especially radical ones for psychology. They can easily be accommodated within the reigning conceptual perspectives used to understand priming effects generally. But they are hypotheses that have not yet been carefully addressed in that literature to date. Perhaps the biggest payoff of this research will be as psychological political science, in terms of an understanding of which citizens are most influenced by the news media and why. But there is also a potential payoff as political psychology true to its name, in terms of the evolution of basic priming theory.

Attitude Importance and Policy Issues

The last example I will describe also began with the widely accepted notion that policy attitudes are relatively peripheral to American citizens' thinking about politics. In the view of political theorists, this idea challenged the viability of democratic governments because it called into question the motives and/or capabilities of democratic electorates (Dahl 1956; Pennock 1979). Yet stashed at the end of Phil Converse's (1964) monumental chapter on nonattitudes was a compelling hypothesis that, at its core, stood to rescue the apparent competence of democratic citizens. Rather than attending to the entire array of policy issues facing the nation, and forming crystallized and consequential attitudes on each one, asserted Converse, the ordinary citizen focuses on just the handful of issues that touch his or her life most directly. And in doing so, his or her attitudes on those issues become firmly anchored within cognitive structures and have significant consequences for political thought and action. In this sense, each citizen presumably falls into one or more "issue publics," groups of people passionately concerned about those particular issues.

As compelling as these ideas were conceptually, they had rarely been subjected to empirical scrutiny as of the early 1980s. No doubt, an important part of the challenge here was that Converse provided no clear guidelines on how to identify members of any given issue public. He alluded vaguely to having used open-ended survey questions to identify the issues about which survey respondents were most concerned. Yet Converse (1964) did not report his findings in detail, and later studies that used the same approach failed to produce evidence that issue public members (as gauged via open-ended questions) did indeed have more crystallized and consequential attitudes (e.g., Maggiotto and Piereson 1978; Natchez and Bupp 1968).

When I began to address these questions, I chose to rely on a device of convenience: closed-ended rating questions asking NES survey respondents how important various issues were to them personally. My first moves were to assess whether issue public members (as identified in this way) did indeed have more crystallized attitudes and whether their attitudes did in fact have more impact on cognition and action. All this turned out to be true: highly important ratings were associated with greater attitude stability, greater ideological constraint of attitudes across issues, and greater impact of attitudes on candidate preferences and voting (see Boninger, Krosnick, Berent, and Fabrigar 1995; Krosnick 1990).

These initial findings had payoffs both for political science and for psychology. From the political science perspective, this evidence demonstrated the utility and validity of the issue public notion, and it suggested that policy issues were having more impact on election outcomes than individual regression coefficients in full-sample analyses of survey data sets had heretofore suggested. Thus, American voters appeared to be more "responsible," to borrow Key's (1966) term, and "rational," to borrow Goldberg's (1969), than had appeared to be the case.

For psychology, my initial work contributed to the emerging literature on attitude strength. As Raden (1985) illustrated in his extensive review article, various attributes of attitudes had been shown to be related to their strength (as gauged by stability and consequentiality). These attributes include intensity of feeling, the amount of knowledge one had about the object, the certainty with which the attitude was held, and many more. My findings on attitude importance added to this list and in some instances expanded the correlates of strength dimensions that had thus far been documented. But the more valuable contributions to psychology have come in our subsequent work. In it, we have explored the mechanisms for the basic effects of importance we initially demonstrated.

For example, consider one of our initial findings: that people who consider an issue more important perceive larger differences between competing candidates in terms of their stands on the issue (Krosnick 1988). People who aren't very concerned about an issue tend to see competitors as taking relatively similar, moderate stands. In contrast, people who attach more importance typically see the candidates as more extreme on opposite sides and therefore see them as quite distinct.

In thinking initially about the possible mechanisms of this effect, I speculated that it might be due to increased perceptual accuracy among issue public members. And consistent with this idea, subsequent survey analyses revealed that these individuals were more likely to know on which side of an issue a candidate stood (Krosnick 1990). We therefore set out to explore the cognitive mechanisms of this apparent accuracy.

In particular, we suspected that two possible processes might be at work (see Berent and Krosnick 1993a, 1993b). The first is "selective exposure." In using this term, we do not mean selective exposure to attitude-supportive information, as the dissonance theory–inspired literature on the concept initially did (Festinger 1957). Rather, we mean that people may selectively expose themselves to information on issues they care deeply about, thus giving them the raw information base with which to build accurate perceptions. Second, we suspected that attitude importance might inspire "selective elaboration" of attitude-relevant information. That is, people who care deeply about an issue may be especially likely to think deeply about information relevant to that issue, thereby leaving a strong, integrated trace of that information in memory that should be easy to retrieve later.

To test these ideas, we began by conducting a survey study in which we telephoned a regional sample of adults before and after a nationally televised debate during the 1988 U.S. presidential campaign. In the post-election interviews, we administered free recall and recognition measures gauging respondents' memory for specific statements made by the candidates the night before. In addition, we measured the personal importance that respondents attached to the various issues addressed. As expected, higher importance was associated with better memory.

This result could have been due to selective elaboration in part, but it could also have been due solely to selective exposure, whereby viewers might completely stop paying attention to the debate when it turned to issues they did not care about. We therefore attempted to replicate the same finding in our laboratory using videotaped presentations of debate excerpts. Doing so allowed us to hold exposure levels constant and to see whether a memory effect remained that could be attributable to selective elaboration. Subjects viewed a thirty-minute videotape containing excerpts of various presidential debates and addressing a range of issues, and they returned to the laboratory one day later to complete free recall and recognition memory measures and to report the importance of the issues involved. As expected, higher importance was associated with better memory.

We then conducted three studies designed to document more definitively the mechanisms of the effect. In these studies, all of our laboratory subjects read one-sentence statements supposedly made by a set of political candidates on an array of policy issues. However, subgroups of the subjects differed from one another in terms of the conditions under which they were exposed to the initial candidate statements. One day later, all subjects returned to the laboratory to complete memory and importance measures.

Among subjects who initially read the statements at whatever pace they preferred, the expected relation between importance and memory accuracy appeared. But among subjects who were forced to read the statements very quickly and who therefore had no time to elaborate on the information, the relation disappeared. Furthermore, giving these latter subjects extra time to think about a set of statements (after they could no longer read them) reinstated the importance–memory relation. And finally, labeling the statements to indicate the issue each one addressed reinstated the importance–memory relation among rushed subjects, presumably because they could selectively expose themselves to only those statements on issues about which they cared deeply and thereby elaborate upon their implications within the limited time span allowed. In some supplementary studies, we have used more traditional laboratory paradigms for gauging selective exposure and have documented the expected relation between importance and this tendency.

Taken together, these recent findings do not have especially important implications for political science. From that discipline's perspective, simply knowing that higher importance is associated with relatively accurate candidate perceptions is enough to suggest that issue public members are equipped to be responsible and rational voters. Knowing precisely which cognitive mechanisms are responsible for this relation does not add a great deal of new understanding that would be of use in an analysis of political events.

But from the psychological viewpoint, our findings regarding mechanisms are indeed useful for the advancement of theory. We have shown for the first time how a dimension of attitude strength motivates information exposure and depth of processing in ways that shape memory for that information. In this sense, we have built a bridge between one dimension of strength (i.e., importance) and another (i.e., knowledge; see Wood, Rhodes, and Biek 1995), documenting how the former causes the latter. We have also helped to build the bridge between the literature on attitudes, in this case on attitude strength in particular, and the social cognition literature on memory.

In other work on attitude importance, we have investigated the relation of importance to various other psychological phenomena, and these studies yielded useful new insights for psychology as well. For example, in one study, we examined the "false consensus effect," whereby people tend to overestimate the prevalence of their own attitudes among others (Ross, Greene, and House 1977). The prevailing theoretical explanations of this effect presume that it occurs because people's attitudes shape their perceptions of others' attitudes (see, e.g., Marks and Miller 1987). If this is so, such effects would presumably be more powerful when attitudes are more personally important to individuals. Yet we found this not to be the case, thereby calling into question the prevailing views regarding the effect's mechanism (Fabrigar and Krosnick 1995) and lending support to some alternative possible explanations.

Another issue we have examined is the impact that small changes in question wording, format, or ordering have on people's reports of their attitudes. Many observers have taken for granted that these effects are concentrated primarily among people whose attitudes are weak and uncrystallized (Cantril 1944; Converse 1974; Gallup 1941:261). But in an investigation involving twenty-seven experiments conducted in the context of national surveys, we found this generally not to be the case (Krosnick and Schuman 1988). Again, this surprising result may push theory-building in the area of attitude measurement in new directions.

Our work on attitude importance began as psychological political science. The starting point was the evidence of apparently low stability of citizens' policy preferences and the apparently minimal impact of those preferences on their vote choices. In demonstrating the role of attitude importance in regulating these two processes, our contribution was initially to shed light on how contemporary American democracy operates. But in our more recent work, we have again shifted the focus to political psychology true to its name, with a primary interest in understanding how attitudes and information processing operate, regardless of implications for democratic theory.

This shift seemed natural when we made it, because our initial findings raised questions about the psychological mechanisms involved that prevailing theories could not readily answer. Now that we have generated plausible explanations, we are inclined to turn back to the agenda of psychological political science in doing research on attitude importance. That is, we are now planning studies that will attempt to demonstrate the political consequences of issue-public–driven decision making in elections.

It is useful to note that our work on attitude importance dovetails with our work on branching and labeling not only in terms of origins but in terms of implications as well. Like the branching/labeling work, our study of issue publics demonstrated that citizens' policy preferences have more impact on vote choices than previous studies had recognized. In this sense, incorporating measures of attitude importance into vote choice equations narrowed the gap between policy preferences and party identification in terms of predictive power, just as branching and labeling did. As more and more such steps are taken in future research, it is conceivable that the gap may disappear altogether. And that result would be a significant one indeed for our understanding of how democracies operate.

CONCLUSION

Perhaps making a distinction between psychological political science and political psychology will lead researchers to be a bit more self-conscious about whether their work at any given moment can be considered either or both. Although nearly all the research being published with the label "political psychology" appears to be primarily psychological political science, some of this work may also be of great use for basic psychological theory-building. If we all make efforts to identify those components or aspects of our work and portray them explicitly as such whenever possible, our research can eventually be seen as contributing both to political science and to psychology, and perhaps ultimately in even measure. Such a balancing would undoubtedly be highly desirable, because the support for our enterprise would then run wide and deep on both sides of the disciplinary fence.

Such a balancing would probably have a number of tangible effects, one of which is more cross-disciplinary publishing. At present, political psychologists within political science seem to publish in psychology journals only as a means of last resort to get their work in print. I have heard more than one story of a political scientist submitting an article to political science journals, only to have it rejected on the grounds that it is too psychological. Although there was plenty of psychology apparent in the work, the study seemed not to have made a useful and novel contribution to understanding politics. So the author's next inclination was to submit the article to a psychology journal on the assumption that if there is no contribution to political science, then perhaps the work contributes to psychology. Yet these papers are most often rejected by psychology journals as well, because the work was not initially designed to speak to the goals of psychology. To do so requires consciously and effortfully understanding the state of knowledge in that field and the directions in which future work could valuably move.

To do political psychology true to its name, and to contribute to both political science and psychology, are certainly not easy tasks. Trying to reframe an investigation after the fact to get it published somewhere is much more difficult than bearing in mind the goals of both disciplines from the start of a project or shifting one's goals as the data come in. Doing so, however, requires a mastery of both disciplines in ways that pose significant challenges.

One effective way to meet this challenge is for graduate students to take a good number of courses in the other discipline or to participate in unusual training opportunities such as the OSU Summer Institute in Political Psychology. Another, complementary approach is to form teams of political scientists and psychologists who work together and simultaneously shape and frame the work from the perspectives and value systems of both disciplines. The challenges to setting up cooperation and communication within such teams are no doubt significant, but the disciplinary payoffs are well worthwhile.

Whether an individual investigator strives to address both disciplines singlehandedly, or a multidisciplinary team works together to do so, it is important to recognize that the primary benefits of one's efforts cannot necessarily be mapped out in advance. Our work has moved through phases of contributing primarily to political science and primarily to psychology, largely in response to the findings of initial investigations.

Which direction is more fruitful at any given moment may not always be fully clear. And it will certainly not be clear long in advance. For this reason, interdisciplinary teams or individuals with joint departmental affiliations are probably best equipped to reap the biggest payoffs, because they will not shy away when the benefits of one's work begin to shift toward one discipline or the other.

With all this in mind, let's toast to a long and prosperous life for both political psychology and psychological political science. May the benefits of our enterprise serve the disciplinary goals of all!

References

Alt, James, and Alec Chrystal. 1983. *Political Economics*. Berkeley: University of California Press.

Anderson, John R. 1983. *The Architecture of Cognition*. Cambridge, MA: Harvard University Press.

Armstrong, J. Scott, William B. Denniston, and Matt M. Gordon. 1975. "The Use of the Decomposition Principle in Making Judgments." *Organizational Behavior and Human Performance* 14:257–63.

Bargh, John A., Shelly Chaiken, Rajen Govender, and Felicia Pratto. 1992. "The Generality of the Automatic Attitude Activation Effect." *Journal of Personality and Social Psychology* 62:893–912.

Bargh, John A., and Paula Pietromonaco. 1982. "Automatic Information Processing and Social Perception: The Influence of Trait Information Presented Outside of Conscious Awareness on Impression Formation." *Journal of Personality and Social Psychology* 43:437–49.

Berent, Matthew K., and Jon A. Krosnick. 1993a. "Attitude Importance and Memory for Attitude-Relevant Information." Unpublished manuscript. Columbus: Ohio State University.

———. 1993b. "Attitude Importance and Selective Exposure to Attitude-Relevant Information." Unpublished manuscript, Columbus: Ohio State University.

Boninger, David S., Jon A. Krosnick, Matthew K. Berent, and Leandre R. Fabrigar. 1995. "The Causes and Consequences of Attitude Importance." In Richard E. Petty and Jon A. Krosnick, eds., *Attitude Strength: Antecedents and Consequences*. Hillsdale, NJ: Erlbaum.

Campbell, Angus, Philip E. Converse, Warren E. Miller, and Donald Stokes. 1960. *The American Voter*. Chicago: University of Chicago Press.

Cantril, Hadley. 1944. *Gauging Public Opinion*. Princeton, NJ: Princeton University Press.

Collins, A. M., and Elizabeth F. Loftus. 1975. "A Spreading Activation Theory of Semantic Processing." *Psychological Review* 82:407–28.

Conover, Pamela J., and Stanley Feldman. 1986. "The Role of Inference in the Perception of Political Candidates." In Richard R. Lau and David O. Sears, eds., *Political Cognition: The Nineteenth Annual Carnegie Symposium on Cognition*. Hillsdale, NJ: Erlbaum.

Converse, Philip E. 1962. "Information Flow and the Stability of Partisan Attitudes." *Public Opinion Quarterly* 26:578–99.

1964. "The Nature of Belief Systems in Mass Publics." In David E. Apter, ed., *Ideology and Discontent*. New York: Free Press.

1974. "Comment: The Status of Non-Attitudes." *American Political Science Review* 68:650–60.

Dahl, Robert A. 1956. *A Preface to Democratic Theory*. Chicago: University of Chicago Press.

Easton, David. 1953. *The Political System*. New York: Knopf.

Einhorn, Hillel J. 1972. "Expert Measurement and Mechanical Combination." *Organizational Behavior and Human Performance* 7:86–106.

Fabrigar, Leandre R., and Jon A. Krosnick. 1995. "Attitude Importance and the False Consensus Effect." *Personality and Social Psychology Bulletin* 21:468–79.

Fazio, Russell. H., ed. 1990. "Illustrating the Value of Basic Research." Special issue of *Personality and Social Psychology Bulletin* 16:5–180.

Festinger, Leon. 1957. *A Theory of Cognitive Dissonance*. Evanston, IL: Row, Peterson.

Finn, R. H. 1972. "Effects of Some Variations in Rating Scale Characteristics on the Means and Reliabilities of Ratings." *Educational and Psychological Measurement* 32:255–65.

Gallup, George. 1941. "Question Wording in Public Opinion Polls." *Sociometry* 4:259–68.

Goldberg, A. S. 1969. "Social Determinism and Rationality as Bases of Party Identification." *American Political Science Review* 63:5–25.

Gollob, H. F. 1974. "The Subject-Verb-Object Approach to Social Cognition." *Psychological Review* 81:286–321.

Granberg, Donald, and E. E. Brent. 1974. "Dove–Hawk Placements in the 1968 Election: Application of Social Judgment and Balance Theory." *Journal of Personality and Social Psychology* 29:687–95.

Green, Donald P. 1988. "On the Dimensionality of Public Sentiment Toward Partisan and Ideological Groups." *American Journal of Political Science* 32:758–80.

Hastie, Reid, and Bernadette Park. 1986. "The Relationship between Memory and Judgment Depends on Whether the Task Is Memory-Based or On-Line." *Psychological Review* 93:258–68.

Heider, Fritz. 1958. *The Psychology of Interpersonal Relations*. New York: Wiley.

Higgins, E. Tory, and G. King. 1981. "Accessibility of Social Constructs: Information Processing Consequences of Individual and Contextual Variability." In Nancy Cantor and John Kihlstrom, eds., *Personality, Cognition, and Social Interaction*. Hillsdale, NJ: Erlbaum.

Iyengar, Shanto, Donald R. Kinder, Mark D. Peters, and Jon A. Krosnick. 1984. "The Evening News and Presidential Evaluations." *Journal of Personality and Social Psychology* 46:778–87.

Kahneman, Daniel, and Amos Tversky. 1973. "On the Psychology of Prediction." *Psychological Review* 80:237–51.

Kelley, Stanley. 1983. *Interpreting Elections*. Princeton, NJ: Princeton University Press.

Kernell, Samuel. 1978. "Explaining Presidential Popularity." *American Political Science Review* 72:506–22.

Key, Vladimir O. 1966. *The Responsible Electorate*. Cambridge, MA: Harvard University Press.

Kinder, Donald R. 1978. "Political Person Perception: The Asymmetrical Influence of Sentiment and Choice on Perceptions of Presidential Candidates." *Journal of Personality and Social Psychology* 36:859–71.

———. 1981. "Presidents, Prosperity, and Public Opinion." *Public Opinion Quarterly* 45:1–21.

Kinder, Donald R., and Thomas R. Palfrey. 1993. *Experimental Foundations of Political Science*. Ann Arbor: University of Michigan Press.

Krosnick, Jon A. 1988. "Americans' Perceptions of Presidential Candidates: A Test of the Projection Hypothesis." *Journal of Social Issues* 46: 159–82.

———. 1990. "Government Policy and Citizen Passion: A Study of Issue Publics in Contemporary America." *Political Behavior* 12:59–92.

Krosnick, Jon A., and Matthew K. Berent. 1993. "Comparisons of Party Identification and Policy Preferences: The Impact of Survey Question Format." *American Journal of Political Science* 37:941–64.

Krosnick, Jon A., and Laura A. Brannon. 1993. "The Impact of the Gulf War on the Ingredients of Presidential Evaluations: Multidimensional Effects of Political Involvement." *American Political Science Review* 87: 963–75.

Krosnick, Jon A., and Donald R. Kinder. 1990. "Altering the Foundations of Support for the President Through Priming." *American Political Science Review* 84:497–512.

Krosnick, Jon A., Fan Li, and Darrin R. Lehman. 1990. "Conversational Conventions, Order of Information Acquisition, and the Effect of Base Rates and Individuating Information on Social Judgment." *Journal of Personality and Social Psychology* 59:1140–52.

Krosnick, Jon A., and Michael A. Milburn. 1990. "The Psychological Determinants of Political Opinionation." *Social Cognition* 8:49–72.

Krosnick, Jon A., and Howard Schuman. 1988. "Attitude Intensity, Importance, and Certainty and Susceptibility to Response Effects." *Journal of Personality and Social Psychology* 54:940–52.

Kuklinski, James H., Robert C. Luskin, and John Bolland. 1991. "Where Is the Schema? Going Beyond the 'S' Word in Political Psychology." *American Political Science Review* 85:1341–56.

Lane, Robert E. 1963. "Political Science and Psychology." In S. Koch, ed., *Psychology: A Study of a Science*, Vol. 6. New York: McGraw-Hill.

Lingle, John H., and Thomas M. Ostrom. 1979. "Retrieval Selectivity in Memory-Based Impression Judgments." *Journal of Personality and Social Psychology* 37:180–94.

Lodge, Milton, Kathleen M. McGraw, and Patrick Stroh. 1989. "An Impression-Driven Model of Candidate Evaluation." *American Political Science Review* 83:399–419.

Lombardi, Wendy J., E. Tory Higgins, and John A. Bargh. 1987. "The Role of Consciousness in Priming Effects on Categorization: Assimilation versus Contrast as a Function of Awareness of the Priming Task." *Personality and Social Psychology Bulletin* 13:411–29.

Maggiotto, M. A., and J. E. Piereson. 1978. "Issue Publics and Voter Choice." *American Politics Quarterly* 6:407–29.

Marks, G., and Norman Miller. 1987. "Ten Years of Research on the False Consensus Effect: An Empirical and Theoretical Review." *Psychological Bulletin* 102:72–90.

McGuire, William J. 1968. "Personality and Susceptibility to Social Influence." In Edgar F. Borgatta and W. W. Lambert, eds., *Handbook of Personality Theory and Research*. Chicago: Rand McNally.

Milburn, Michael A. 1991. *Persuasion and Politics: The Social Psychology of Public Opinion*. Pacific Grove, CA: Brooks/Cole.

Miller, Joanne M., and Jon A. Krosnick. 1996. "News Media Impact on the Ingredients of Presidential Evaluations: A Program of Research on the Priming Hypothesis." In Diana C. Mutz and Paul M. Sniderman, eds., *Political Persuasion and Attitude Change*. Ann Arbor: University of Michigan Press.

Natchez, P. B., and I. C. Bupp. 1968. "Candidates, Issues, and Voters." *Public Policy* 4:409–37.

Neustadt, Richard E. 1960. *Presidential Power*. New York: Wiley.

Ottati, Victor, Martin Fishbein, and Susan E. Middlestadt. 1988. "Determinants of Voters' Beliefs About the Candidates' Stands on the Issues: The Role of Evaluative Bias Heuristics and the Candidates' Expressed Message." *Journal of Personality and Social Psychology* 55:517–29.

Pennock, J. Roland. 1979. *Democratic Political Theory*. Princeton, NJ: Princeton University Press.

Peters, David L., and Ernest J. McCormick. 1966. "Comparative Reliability of Numerically Anchored versus Job-Task Anchored Rating Scales." *Journal of Applied Psychology* 50:92–6.

Raden, David. 1985. "Strength-Related Attitude Dimensions." *Social Psychology Quarterly* 48:312–30.

Rahn, Wendy M., Jon A. Krosnick, and Marijke Breuning. 1994. "Rationalization and Derivation Processes in Survey Studies of Political Candidate Evaluation." *American Journal of Political Science* 38:582–600.

Ross, Lee, D. Greene, and P. House. 1977. "The False Consensus Effect: An Ego-Centric Bias in Social Perception and Attribution Processes." *Journal of Experimental Social Psychology* 13:279–301.

Ruble, Diane N., Philip R. Costanzo, and Mary Ellen Oliveri. 1992. *The Social Psychology of Mental Health*. New York: Guilford Press.

Snyder, Mark. 1993. "Basic Research and Practical Problems: The Promise of a 'Functional' Personality and Social Psychology." *Personality and Social Psychology Bulletin* 19:251–64.

Strack, Fritz, Norbert Schwarz, Herbert Bless, Almut Kubler, and Michaela Wanke. 1993. "Awareness of the Influence as a Determinant of Assimilation versus Contrast." *European Journal of Social Psychology* 23:53–62.

Webster's New World Dictionary, 3rd college ed. 1988. New York: Webster's New World.

Wood, Wendy, Nancy, Rhodes, and Michael Biek. 1995. "Working Knowledge and Attitude Strength: An Information-Processing Analysis." In Richard E. Petty and Jon A. Krosnick, eds., *Attitude Strength: Antecedents and Consequences*. Hillsdale, NJ: Erlbaum.

Wyer, Robert S., and J. Hartwick. 1980. "The Role of Information Retrieval and Conditional Inference Processes in Belief Formation and Change." In Leonard Berkowitz, ed., *Advances in Experimental Social Psychology*. Vol. 13. New York: Academic Press.

Zaller, John R. 1987. "Diffusion of Political Attitudes." *Journal of Personality and Social Psychology* 53:821–33.

1989. "Bringing Converse Back In: Information Flow in Political Campaigns." *Political Analysis* 1:181–234.

1993. *The Nature and Origins of Mass Opinion.* New York: Cambridge University Press.

Zimbardo, P. G. 1988. *Psychology and Life.* Glenview, IL: Scott, Foresman.

7

Political Psychology, Political Behavior, and Politics: Questions of Aggregation, Causal Distance, and Taste

ROBERT C. LUSKIN

The political beliefs, attitudes, and behaviors of ordinary citizens absorb a goodly share of the attention of modern political science. At a guess, they form the subject of as much as a quarter of the articles in the leading journals. Ours is a prosperous subdiscipline. Yet partly perhaps for that reason, partly because every subdiscipline occasions some ennui in other quarters, and partly for reasons we shall explore, it also has critics. Ignoring the egoistic ("it's boring") and the antiscientific (it deals in generalizations, worse yet in numbers), the most common complaint is that it is insufficiently political.

This is true even – especially? – when the objects of study are such familiar and psychologically macro variables as political sophistication, partisanship, and split-ticket voting – the domain of the field perhaps most commonly known as *political behavior*. It is also true when they are such less familiar and psychologically more micro variables as reliance on on-line versus memory-based processing, public responses to politicians' blame management strategies, and the use of likability heuristics to locate candidates on issues – the domain of current, cognitively influenced *political psychology*.

Needless to say, these fields overlap, as the oeuvres of this volume's contributors attest. As a matter of social rather than intellectual structure, political psychology is largely a subfield of political behavior: most political psychologists study mass politics. Perhaps intellectually it should be the other way around, with political behavior (and much of the rest of political science) regarded as applied psychology. But, for purposes of this chapter, I shall treat "political psychology," with some admitted injustice, as referring to the study of mass politics.

I am grateful to Jongho Lee for assistance, to George Marcus, Tali Mendelberg, Benjamin Page, and Daron Shaw for comments, and to Christopher Bratcher for both. Discussions with Christopher Achen and Laura Stoker have also been helpful.

Though fine, the distinction between political behavior and political psychology so construed is worth making because not all the skepticism of political psychology's utility comes from the far corners of the discipline. Indeed, my impression is that the most distant critics often take a more indulgent view of political psychology than of political behavior. At least it has the mystique of another and arguably more advanced discipline. No, not all of the skepticism comes from postmodernists, diehard institutionalists, or others of markedly different orientation or focus; some of it, at least toward certain strains of political psychology, comes from political behavior.

I am myself more than political behaviorite enough to share some of this skepticism. Yet I should like in these pages to argue the importance of the bulk of political psychology as well as, with somewhat fewer qualifications, the bulk of political behavior. In particular, I shall argue the importance of studying the dependent variables of these fields at their native individual level. As the reference to "taste" in the title suggests, the argument is relatively yielding – and thus, in theory, more difficult to resist.

I say "in theory" because persuasiveness is not the test of persuasion,[1] and much psychological research gives me reason to doubt my prospects of persuading confirmed critics. They are unlikely to be reading this chapter (Sears and Freedman 1967); if they read it, they will counterargue (Petty and Cacioppo 1986); etc., etc. The depreciation of political psychology and political behavior has roots in values, tastes, and *weltanschauungen*, not to mention professional and institutional interests. It is in some measure part of a rearguard struggle against quantification and, on the postmodern camp's part, against science. At minimum, however, it may be useful to us who do study mass politics to reflect on the value of the enterprise.

POLITICAL BEHAVIOR, POLITICAL PSYCHOLOGY, AND POLITICS

We are all at least somewhat parochial. Political scientists naturally care about politics, but how attached we should be to the criterion of political relevance depends on who "we" are. Political *psychologists* may not wish to cede the point that reliance on on-line versus memory-based processing and the rest are worth studying in their own right, regardless of their implications for the political systems in which they occur.

For argument's sake, however, let us assume from here on that we are all *political* psychologists, practicing what Krosnick (this volume) calls

---

[1] A play on Holmes's (1918) mot that "certitude is not the test of certainty."

"psychological political science." Then relevance for Politics, capital P – for the nature and interplay of elites and institutions, for the policies that result (who gets what), for the character of the democratic system – becomes vital. For this discipline, it is not enough to make the case, as Sniderman (1993) has, that Politics imbues the politics of ordinary citizens. The more pertinent questions are how far and in what ways the latter affects and conditions the former.

Although tracing the paths of such influence remains a challenge, the existence of some nontrivial influence is hard to deny, and I doubt that even those least enamored of political behavior and political psychology would deny it. At least in the aggregate, what ordinary citizens think, feel, and do about politics clearly makes some difference to elites, institutions, the policies they produce, and the political system. Even the most brutal regimes need sullen or terrified acquiescence for survival. Even under authoritarian government, the course of policy is channeled to some degree by popular sentiment, by what V. O. Key (1967) once called "opinion boundaries" (as witness for instance the gingerliness with which the Soviet Union under Gorbachev approached the freeing of prices, economically necessary though it was thought to be). In democracies, thanks to meaningful elections, the dependence on mass preferences is still greater. Despite both play and lag in the relationship, national policies tend to move in the direction of public preferences (Monroe 1979; Page and Shapiro 1983); at the state level, the most liberal electorates tend to get the most liberal policies (Erikson, McIver, and Wright 1987; Erikson, Wright, and McIver 1989).

The guiding or at least confining influences of aggregate policy opinions and vote choices are obvious. So is the importance of party identification, whose distribution has much to do with the means and variances of the parties' vote shares over repeated elections, and thus in turn with the mix of policies adopted, the frequency and fragility of coalition governments, and the danger of "flash parties" like the Poujadists of France and Wallaceites and Perotists of the United States. All this is well-trodden ground, in no need of being gone over here.

Let us tarry a little, however, over a couple of less obvious connections. Among the virtues commonly claimed for democracy is that the principle of majority rule maximizes aggregate "autonomy," meaning citizens' abilities to judge and pursue their own interests (Dahl 1989). The interests involved need not be wholly selfish: it is not just narrowly "adversarial democracy" (as in Schumpeter 1954; see Mansbridge 1980, 1990) to which the expression and distillation of interests is central.

In political behavior and political psychology, self-defined interests appear as *values*. Much has been written about the public's attachment to democratic values, especially those having to do with political tolerance (Gibson 1989, 1992; Stouffer 1955; Sullivan, Piereson, and Marcus 1982), and I don't doubt, feeble though the grip of these values on the majority of the public may be, that variation in the proportion of the public that holds them affects the tenor of political life. Much has also been written about the dependence of particular policy attitudes on particular values, especially on variations on the themes of freedom and equality (Feldman and Zaller 1992; McClosky and Zaller 1984; Rasinski 1987). Doubtless, too, the distributions of such basic values affect the flavor and outcomes of policy debate. It is no accident that the United States, with its peculiarly individualistic tilt (Dalton 1988; Smith 1987), has smaller government, lower taxes, and less encompassing social welfare programs than other democratic countries.

The point I want to stress, however, is the existence of individual and circumstantial variation in the accuracy with which people choose appropriate policy positions and cast appropriate ballots in light of their values. As regards voting, the variable I have in mind is close kin to Lau and Redlawsk's "normatively correct vote" (2001). If the free and fair contest of interests ranks high among democracy's raisons d'être, the variation in the degree to which people can identify the policies and vote choices most compatible with their values/interests has serious implications for democratic theory. The dependence of preferences on values could scarcely be more important.

This discussion of variability in the strength of the values–preferences nexus brings us to political *sophistication* (a.k.a. *expertise*, a.k.a. *cognitive complexity*) – roughly, the quantity and organization of a person's stored political cognition (Luskin 1987). Given the close correlations between quantity and organization and between quantity and accuracy, this is also roughly the same variable as *information*, in the sense of information already held, which omits organization, and as *knowledge*, which omits organization but requires accuracy. There are many reasons to think sophistication important (Delli Carpini and Keeter 1996; Luskin 1990, 2001), but perhaps its greatest importance lies in its conditioning of the relationship between values and policy and candidate preferences, which can be expected to be tighter among the more sophisticated. Given sophistication's correlations with such other characteristics as education, affluence, and economic conservatism, this conditioning of the values–preferences relationship has implications for the fairness of the contest among interests.

The same argument can be extended to the less examined but similarly leaky relationship between values and objective interests. Here the leakage is "false consciousness." Of course what constitutes "true consciousness" is contentious, which may be why this relationship has received less empirical attention. But take a person's objective interests for what we may, he or she should be more likely to have adopted political values conformable with them, the more he or she thinks and knows about politics.

These few examples by no means exhaust the strands linking mass politics with Politics. Tales of similar political consequence could be told of most of the other variables in the standard palette. Much of what we study in political psychology and political behavior has implications for matters of interest to institutionalists, policy specialists, comparativists, and political theorists.

How is it, then, that political psychology and political behavior elicit so many yawns and shrugs from so many of those of more institutional, historical, or philosophical bent? Antipathies toward quantification or science aside, I see three related reasons: *First*, impatience with the explanation of these fields' dependent variables at their native individual level. Their effects on politics are mainly in the aggregate, after all. *Second*, a preference for nonpsychological variables, which do frequently have the advantages of more agreed-upon conceptual boundaries and more precise measurement. This second reason is closely entwined with the first, since aggregate-level explanations tend, partly of necessity, to have a less psychological cast: psychological measures may simply be unavailable for sufficient numbers of the relevant aggregates; national surveys do not generally break down into adequate state, much less county, samples; survey time-series are short and confined to relatively few items; closely comparable surveys have not generally been done in more than a handful of countries at any given time; etc. Thus aggregate models tend from the psychological perspective to be reduced form, couched in sociodemographic, environmental, and other prior variables. *Third*, a disinclination to pursue the sequence of causal relations back beyond the aggregate opinions and participation that directly affect politics. One may recognize the need to include these as explanatory factors without feeling much curiosity about their antecedents in turn. The line, for any given discipline as for any given study, must be drawn somewhere. But let me return to this last point below.

POLITICS AND AGGREGATION

As the foregoing suggests, these issues of how Political political psychology and political behavior are and ought to be devolve in large part to differences over the levels of aggregation that are interesting, consequential, or illuminating from the standpoint of politics. At what levels do the interesting or important dependent variables reside? At what levels may they be most satisfyingly explained?

Several sorts of aggregation are involved, three more or less hierarchically related. *Psychological aggregation*, the most basic, refers to the intrapersonal dimension ranging upward from subatomic particles (to start with the absurdly micro) to neurons and neural networks to the "abstract neurons" of parallel distributed processing models (Rumelhart 1989; Rumelhart, McClelland, and the PDP Research Group 1986) to associative networks (e.g., Anderson 1983) to such more molar entities as beliefs, attitudes, values, and emotions. *Physical aggregation*, the only sort we are actually accustomed to thinking of as aggregation, refers to the extrapersonal dimension ascending from the individual to (unarticulated) groups of increasing inclusiveness. These first two dimensions meet at the skin. The more abstract third dimension, *relational aggregation*, translates further from people, whether individuals or groups, to such relational entities as institutions and events.[2]

Here we shall focus on physical and psychological aggregation, but two other sorts will also come up. *Temporal aggregation*, a matter of "tense" – present or past versus past perfect – refers to the dimension ranging upward from transient episodes to lifetime accumulations or residues. The dependent variables of experiments, more or less perforce, are temporally disaggregated, those well measured by ordinary surveys temporally aggregated. *Conceptual aggregation* is a matter of how broadly one's variables, at whatever level of physical, psychological, relational, or temporal aggregation, are drawn. Socioeconomic status, for example, is a more conceptually aggregate version of education, income, and occupation. Both temporal and conceptual aggregation are positively but only moderately correlated with the physical, psychological, and relational sorts.

A large part of the difference between practitioners and detractors of political psychology and political behavior lies in differing preferences as regards physical and relational aggregation. The dependent variables and explanatory models of political psychology and political behavior are fundamentally individual level. Changes or differences in aggregate party identification, political sophistication, or vote choice may be important but must stem from individual-level changes or differences and the heavily individual-level mechanisms that account for them. But politics, for the detractors, resides somewhere above the individual level. It is more physically and relationally aggregate, and they see a gap between

---

2 Psychological aggregation stands apart from the other two in aggregating within rather than across individuals, but it is probably relational aggregation that is the most distinctive, since physical and psychological aggregation involve only more or less tidy supersetting (more in the former, less in the latter), whereas relational aggregation involves relationships among lower order elements.

the characteristic concerns of political behavior and political psychology and politics.

In much the same way, the more intramural reservations about current political psychology, as distinct from political behavior, also boil down to questions of aggregation, only in this case of the psychological and temporal sorts. The skeptics' sense is that phenomena like on-line versus memory-based processing and the exact furniture of individuals' political schemas may be too psychologically and sometimes too temporally disaggregated – too distant from party identification, political sophistication, and the like and sometimes too fleeting to reveal much about political behavior, let alone, through the latter, about Politics.

PHYSICAL AGGREGATION AND INTERACTIONS

For reasons that will soon be evident, it is important to note that at the individual level many of the effects on these and other dependent variables of political psychology and political behavior are interactive (nonadditive). For too long, our treatment of interactions has tended to be all or nothing. The "all" is represented by the numbing practice, in analysis of variance, of estimating every possible interaction of every possible order – data wallowing at its worst. (Come to mention it, analysis of variance itself is fairly anesthetic; the regression model with dummy regressors is formally equivalent and more felicitously put.[3]) The "nothing," much more common, is represented by the linear (strictly speaking, linear and additive) models of missionary-style regression.

This may finally be changing, if the chapters in this and the accompetying volume are indicative. I am particularly pleased to see political sophistication, my own first and enduring love among variables, singled out in a number of chapters as a key conditioning factor. The sophisticated and unsophisticated can be expected to process political information very differently. We have already come across one example in sophistication's conditioning of the values–preferences relationship. Another is the interaction between sophistication and message type in persuasive communication: more closely reasoned appeals succeed better with the more sophisticated, more purely symbolic ones with the less sophisticated (Chaiken 1980; Newton, Masters, McHugo, and Sullivan 1987; Petty and Cacioppo 1984, 1986). In Zaller's (1992) fugue on Converse (1962) and McGuire (1968, 1969), the divisions of opinion in mass publics come to mimic those among elites more or less closely and more or less rapidly as a function of sophistication.

3 See King (1986).

Another conditioning factor is mood, as Marcus and MacKuen argue and show for anxiety (Marcus and MacKuen 1993, 2001). In Marcus and MacKuen's account, anxiety increases the role of "candidate enthusiasm" and decreases that of standing dispositions like partisanship in determining candidate preference. More generally, negative emotions prompt closer attention, more earnest processing, and greater learning than occur in their absence (Clore, Schwarz, and Conway 1994). Bliss, it seems, is ignorance.

Still other nonadditivities, putative or established, involving other conditioning variables, also abound. Masters (1989, 2001) argues that the emotional reactions elicited by leaders' facial displays are different for men and women. Kuklinski and Hurley (1994) show that blacks and whites differ radically in the extent to which they form different impressions of statements varyingly attributed to black or white speakers. Stoker (2001) shows that the degree to which regarding private behaviors like homosexuality or euthanasia as immoral feeds support for prohibiting them and depends on commitments to individual autonomy. And so on, and so on.[4]

The prevalence of interactions has an important bearing on the desirability of physical aggregation. Though fundamentally individual level, the dependent variables of political behavior and political psychology generally have effects that are felt only in the aggregate. As MacKuen, Erikson, and Stimson (1989) note of partisanship, for example, it is the polity- or constituency-wide distribution of partisanship that matters to the probability of electoral success, the likelihood of flash parties, and so forth. And for this reason, as well as to escape the noise of individual-level measurement, a number of studies have trained their sights on aggregate versions of these individual-level variables as they vary over time (MacKuen et al. 1989; Page and Shapiro 1992; Stimson 1991) or across political units (Erikson et al. 1987; Erikson et al. 1989).

This strategy has disadvantages, however. Tracing the implications of citizens' thoughts, feelings, and behaviors for politics requires aggregation at some point; the question is when. Where only aggregate measures are available (as is sometimes the case for vote choice or turnout), we must either use them or abandon the analysis. "If a thing is worth doing," G. K. Chesterton once said, "it is worth doing poorly." Something is better than nothing. But if individual-level data are available, it will generally be preferable to aggregate *after* modeling and estimation at the individual level.

The reason is not the classical "ecological fallacy" of using aggregate data to address individual-level relationships (Robinson 1950). In linear

---

4 More radically, Rivers (1988) argues for allowing different effects for each person.

models, as is now widely recognized, the supposed "ecological fallacy" is just model misspecification (see Erbring 1990; Hanushek, Jackson, and Kain 1974). If the individual-level model is

$$y_i = \beta_0 + \beta_1 x_i + u_i \tag{1}$$

the aggregate-level model is

$$\bar{y}_g = \beta_0 + \beta_1 \bar{x}_g + \bar{u}_g,$$

where $\bar{y}_g$, $\bar{x}_g$, and $\bar{u}_g$ are the sample means of the individual-level disturbance within the gth "group" (geographical unit, time point, or whatever). The individual- and aggregate-level models are the same, except that $\bar{u}_g$ must be heteroskedastic if u_i is homoskedastic, which merely complicates the estimation.

This commonplace needs qualification, however. One qualification is that it remains preferable to estimate at the individual level if individual-level data are available. On the surface, the aggregate-level results may present the more pleasing aspect. The R^2, in particular, will be higher – typically much higher – thanks to reduced noise (Cramer 1964). The coefficient estimates, however, will actually be *less* precise, owing to the loss of individual-level information (Greene 1993; Kmenta 1986).

A more crippling qualification is that the parallelism of individual- and aggregate-level models, and indeed the estimability of the latter, hinge on the linearity of the former (see Green 1964). Thus consider, in contrast to (1), the simple nonadditive (interactive) model in which x_1's effect on y depends linearly on the value of a second variable, x_2:

$$y_i = \beta_0 + \beta_1 x_{i1} x_{i2} + u_i. \tag{2}$$

This implies

$$\bar{y}_g = \beta_0 + \beta_1(\bar{x}_{g1}\bar{x}_{g2} + s_{12g}) + \bar{u}_g \tag{3}$$

$$= \beta_0 + \beta_1\bar{x}_{g1}\bar{x}_{g2} + \beta_1 s_{12g} + \bar{u}_g \tag{4}$$

$$\neq \beta_0 + \beta_1\bar{x}_{g1}\bar{x}_{g2} + \bar{u}_g, \tag{5}$$

where s_{12g} denotes the sample covariance of x_1 and x_2 within the gth group.[5] Now the aggregate-level equation differs from its individual-level

---

5 The proof is simple. Summing both sides of (2) and dividing by n yields

$$\bar{y}_g = \beta_0 + \beta_1(1/n)\sum x_{i1}x_{i2} + \bar{u}_g.$$

Since the "computational formula" for the covariance s_{12g} is

$$S_{12g} = (1/n)\sum x_{i1}x_{i2} - \bar{x}_{g1}\bar{x}_{g2},$$

substitution does the rest.

progenitor, and in a way that still involves individual-level information, in the form of s_{12g}.

As phrased in (4), this is a classic omitted variable problem (with the minor additional wrinkle that the coefficient of the omitted variable s_{12g} is known to be the same as that of the included variable $\overline{x}_{g1}\overline{x}_{g2}$), and as usual the omission spells bias and inconsistency. Denote the OLS estimator of β by $\hat{\beta}_1$. It is easy to show that the probability limit of $\hat{\beta}_1$ is

$$\text{plim } \hat{\beta}_1 = \beta_1 \left[1 + \frac{\text{COV}(\overline{x}_{g1}\overline{x}_{g2}, s_{12g})}{\text{VAR}(\overline{x}_{g1}\overline{x}_{g2})} \right] \neq \beta_1,$$

where VAR and COV denote sampling variance and covariance. For samples of increasing size, the sampling distribution of $\hat{\beta}_1$ collapses on a value that is not β_1.[6]

Note that these results do not apply to "contextual models," where one of the interacting variables in the individual-level equation (2) is measured only at the group level (so that, say, $x_{i2} = \overline{x}_{g2}$ for all i in g), since then the sample covariance $s_{12g} = 0$ for all g; $\text{COV}(\overline{x}_{g1}\overline{x}_{g2}, s_{12g})$ consequently $= 0$; and plim $\hat{\beta}_1$ in turn $= \beta_1$.

When the interacting variables x_1 and x_2 are both individual level, however, the only escape is if s_{12g}, though nonzero, is the same ($s_{12g} = s_{12}$) for all g. Then, from (3),

$$\overline{y}_g = (\beta_0 + \beta_1 s_{12}) + \beta_1 \overline{x}_{g1}\overline{x}_{g2} + \overline{u}_g,$$

which differs only in the intercept from (5). Then, too, $\text{COV}(\overline{x}_{g1}\overline{x}_{g2}, s_{12g}) = 0$, and plim $\hat{\beta}_1 = \beta_1$. In this case, the aggregate model has the effects essentially right. But there is no particular reason to expect such happy invariance.

These results have serious implications for the use of aggregate-level models to capture essentially individual-level processes. Nonadditivities of the sort depicted by (2) are both common and beyond the reach of purely aggregate data. With individual-level data, it makes sense to estimate the individual-level model (2). Without them, the usual aggregate model (5) is inappropriate, meaning that it cannot be estimated satisfactorily, while the appropriate aggregate model (4) is not wholly aggregate and thus cannot be estimated at all.

---

6 The GLS estimator $\tilde{\beta}_1$, more appropriate in view of the heteroskedasticity of $\overline{u}_g$, is also inconsistent:

$$\text{plim } \tilde{\beta}_1 = \beta_1 \left[1 + \frac{\text{COV}(w_g, s_{12g})}{\text{VAR}(w_g)} \right] \neq \beta_1$$

where w_g denotes $\overline{x}_{g1}\overline{x}_{g2}\sqrt{n_g}$, and n_g is the number of observations in the gth group.

PHYSICALLY AGGREGATE MEASUREMENT

So far we have been considering the perils of aggregation prior to estimation in *explanations* of individual-level dependent variables like those of political psychology and political behavior. Related pitfalls lie in aggregate *measurement*.

Measuring individual-level variables in intrinsically aggregate fashion (as opposed to aggregating individual-level measures) may seem obviously misguided, but there is in fact a well-established tradition, dating back at least to Converse (1964), of reckoning political cognition from the cross-respondent patterning of survey responses. Converse's device, much replicated, was a matrix of correlations among policy attitude items. Early refinements corrected for attenuation from random measurement error (Achen 1975; Erikson 1979), but more sophisticated efforts now focus on the coefficients of covariance structure models taking policy attitude items as indicators.[7]

Structurally, these models concern "true attitudes'" effects on other "true attitudes." Panel I of Figure 7.1 renders them in very bold strokes, in terms of just two true attitudes, although of course they typically involve more than two in the flesh. Their most characteristic feature, in the flesh, is hierarchy: they typically allow more general and abstract attitudes to affect narrower and more concrete ones but not vice versa, and forbid those at the same level of generality and abstraction from affecting each other (as in Hurwitz and Peffley 1987; Peffley and Hurwitz 1993; Rohrschneider 1993). The unidirectional relationship between Attitudes A and B, the former implicitly the more general and abstract, reflects this hierarchy.

Both correlation matrices and covariance structure models share two targets and associated axioms of measurement. One target is *cognitive structure*. The correlations or interattitude coefficients are taken as reflecting cognitive associations. In this role, covariance structure models may be seen as (absurdly crude) mappings of associative networks (as in Anderson 1983). The other target is *cognitive structuredness*, i.e., sophistication. Collectively, the magnitudes of the correlations or interattitude coefficients are taken as reflecting the level of cognitive organization or "constraint."

One immediately unappealing thing about all these devices is that despite requiring individual-level data, they afford only aggregate results. This is most obviously a problem for the measurement of cognitive structure. Take, for example, Peffley and Hurwitz's (1993) consideration

7 Correlations and covariance structure models by no means exhaust such aggregate-level approaches. For a more complete discussion, see Luskin (1987).

I.   The Usual

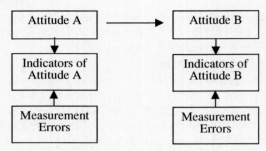

II.   More Realistic but Probably Unidentified

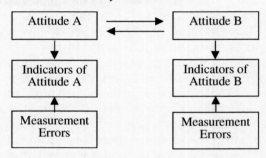

III.   Still More Realistic but Still Probably Unidentified

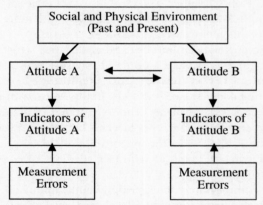

Figure 7.1. Covariance structure models of political attitude structure (in a thumbnail sketch).

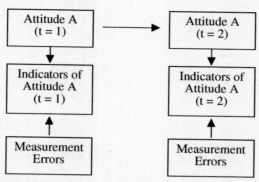

Figure 7.2. Covariance models of political attitude stability (also in a thumbnail sketch).

of whether the cognitive linkages between super- and subordinate foreign policy attitudes are mainly quasi-deductive (top-down) or quasi-inferential (bottom-up). The question is obviously too simple. Not everyone thinks in terms of the same broad postures; not everyone has attitudes on the same policies; not everyone reasons from given postures to the same policy attitudes; not everyone thinks top-down, as opposed to bottom-up, to the same extent.

It is also a problem for the measurement of cognitive structuredness. At best, the correlations or interattitude coefficients may say something about the political sophistication of the whole public or sizable groups within it. But they mask wide individual-level variation, a grave limitation in view of the preceding section. As either left- or righthand-side variable, sophistication is more likely to belong by rights in an equation like (2) than like (1). We have already seen that sophistication is a key conditioning variable – a frequent candidate for the role of x_2. There is also good reason to make the equation for sophistication as y non-additive (Luskin 1990).

Much the same applies to the slightly different covariance structure models aimed at gauging the substantiality or *crystallization* of particular attitudes (as in Achen 1983; Feldman 1988, 1990; Judd and Milburn 1980). These are depicted in similarly bold strokes in Figure 7.2, which simplifies most notably in showing only two waves. Here the stability coefficients relating the true attitudes to their later selves are taken as reflecting the extent to which the attitudes are more than "nonattitudes." But people have unequally crystallized and therefore unequally stable true attitudes and give unequally error-laden responses. And as Brady (1993) has shown, it is extremely difficult to infer anything about the proportion of guesses (nonattitudes) from the estimated stability and reliability coefficients in models of this sort.

The basic point here is common sense: why settle for aggregate measurement of individual-level cognition? Individual-level measures of cognitive structuredness and attitude stability are readily derived from the same or similar data (Luskin 1987). And though, as I shall argue, individual-level measures of cognitive structure are a more ambitious undertaking, of less certain cost effectiveness, the contours of individual cognition are too idiopathic to be mapped at anything but the individual level.

For argument's sake, however, let us take these measures on their own terms. Suppose, that is, that we should be satisfied with aggregate measurement, so long as it could be trusted. Now four further problems arise.

The first is that any measure of this sort must almost inevitably lose a whacking great chunk of the sample. With decent filters, a great many respondents are typically missing data – "don't know," "no opinion," or "not ascertained" – on one item or other. On the order of half the sample may fall away. Judd and Milburn (1980) lose two-thirds of theirs. The remainder, on which these measures are calculated, is of course vastly more sophisticated than the sample as a whole. As regards structuredness, therefore, these measures are biased up.[8]

In the nature of missing data, it is impossible to say what the correlations or estimated coefficients for the whole sample would be, but individual-level measures taking professions of ignorance at face value can illustrate the bias involved. To this end, I have constructed a binary variable from six policy items in the 1976 National Election Study (NES) survey. This variable distinguishes respondents who gave substantive responses to all six and thus would be included in the estimation of a covariance structure model based on these items from those who did not and thus would not.[9] Note that six is very few items: a real covariance structure model, involving more numerous items, would lose a higher proportion of the sample. Even so, nearly half the sample (46.2%) drops out.

I have chosen these questions to avoid overlap with the eleven I have previously used in constructing a knowledge-based measure of political

---

8 This on top of the effective sampling bias from designated interviewees who cannot be found or decline to be interviewed.

9 The six ask about school integration, cutting government spending "even if it means cutting back on programs like health and education," stricter handgun controls, the extent to which the United States should ignore "problems in other parts of the world," foreign aid, and rationing energy consumption versus charging higher prices for energy.

sophistication.[10] This measure (denoted D in Luskin 1987) counts the number of issues on which the respondent places the two major parties correctly, where for seven of the eleven a correct placement is one that has the Democrats to the left of the Republicans. For two issues, placements at the same scale point also count as correct; for the remaining two, any ordering does.[11]

The sample mean of this knowledge-based measure of sophistication is only 5.53, well *below* the mean of 6.14 for a population guessing randomly (from a bivariate uniform distribution) on every item.[12] The reason the sample mean falls short of the mean for random guessing is that many of those who do not know the parties' locations do not bother guessing. It would presumably be somewhat higher than 6.14 if everyone guessed. A correction for guessing, however, would then bring it right back down. This is a stunningly weak performance, no matter how you slice it. It is not much to know that the Democrats are to the left of the Republicans on major policy issues. Two items, moreover, are absolute "gimmes," requiring only that respondents place themselves and the parties, no matter where.

The point of this little analysis is the difference between those who give substantive responses to all of the other six policy questions and thus would be included in a covariance structure analysis based on them and those who did not and thus would not. The former have a mean of 6.12, the latter a mean of 4.88. The difference is statistically significant far beyond the .001 level. If the measure of sophistication is altered to require that the Democrats be placed strictly to the left of the Republicans on all eleven items (which now seems to me an improvement), the difference of means increases from roughly 1.25 to roughly 1.50.

10 These eleven ask about "(1) federal guarantees of jobs and a 'good standard of living'; (2) the balance to be struck between protecting the rights of the accused and preventing crime; (3) school busing to achieve integration; (4) federal efforts to 'improve the position of blacks and other minority groups'; (5) government-provided medical and hospital insurance; (6) the best response to urban unrest (forcible suppression versus amelioration of causes); (7) the penalties for marijuana smoking; (8) how graduated the federal income tax should be; (9) an equal role for women 'in running business, industry, and government'; (10) government power; and (11) military spending" (Luskin 1987:883).

11 See Luskin (1987) for details. Zaller (1990, 1992) has offered a partly similar measure, as under another rubric have Hamill, Lodge, and Blake (1985).

12 In view of what this measure accepts as correct orderings, the expected value for someone randomly guessing both parties' locations from a uniform distribution on all issues is $2(1) + 2(4/7) + 7(3/7) \cong 6.14$. I expand a bit on calculations of this sort below.

The second problem, in covariance structure models and correlations corrected for attenuation, is the removal of error. It is hardly surprising that "true attitudes," purged of error, are highly stable or that they are much more closely interrelated than their observed indicators. The question is how to regard the error that is being removed. If, as massive side evidence (reviewed by Converse and Markus 1979; Kinder 1983; Kinder and Sears 1985; Luskin 1987) suggests, it is chiefly a function of respondent ignorance (cf. Achen 1983; Feldman 1990), the most revealing parameters are not the stability or interattitude coefficients but the chronically huge measurement error variances (Converse 1980; Luskin 1987). For gauging structuredness, as opposed to structure, the coefficients of purely structural models, sans measurement equations, may actually be preferable.

The third problem, in covariance structure (and other structural) models, is identification. Hierarchical specifications are debatable at best. Surely people infer as well as deduce, reasoning bottom-up as well as top-down. Surely they reason laterally as well. A person's position on the budget deficit may affect his or her position on tax policies or vice versa; at a more abstract level, his or her attachment to individualism may affect his or her attachment to equality or vice versa. A truer picture than Figure 7.1's Panel I may therefore be its Panel II. But no model of this sort, dense with coefficients corresponding to bottom-up and lateral as well as top-down reasoning, is likely to be identified.

The final problem is the epistemic chasm separating the covariation of responses across respondents from anything that may or may not be going on in anyone's mind. Models akin to Figure 7.1's Panels I and II presume that the only source of the covariance between Attitudes A and B is the effects that either has on the other, which are cognitive or inside the head. But this is a crying underspecification. As a function of self-interest, social pressure, or both, people in given environments tend to hold given sets of opinions. Inner-city blacks may tend to oppose capital punishment and favor more liberal welfare policies; rural whites may hold the opposite pair of opinions. Put them together in the same population, and you've got covariance, even if no one in either group has ever reasoned his or her way – or internalized anyone else's reasoning – from one attitude to the other (Luskin 1987).

The reality, in other words, is sketched in Figure 7.1's Panel III. Without controls for environmental variables, the structural coefficients, to some sizable degree, represent the outside-the-head covariance from experiences and reference points that are shared within but vary between social locations. Bringing these variables into the model (as in Jackson 1983; Peffley and Hurwitz 1993) should help, but since all the additional variables are likely to affect all the attitudinal ones, identification will be as problematic as ever.

PSYCHOLOGICAL (AND TEMPORAL) AGGREGATION AND POLITICAL PSYCHOLOGY

One reason I have chosen to talk about values and sophistication is that they occupy the intersection of political behavior and political psychology, contributing to the case for the political relevance of both. More generally, the variables from political psychology that have a direct and obvious effect on politics are, like values and sophistication, relatively molar and shared with political behavior. But the domain of political psychology also includes the contents of cognitive structures commonly called "schemas," the process of political evaluation (whether on-line or memory-based), and other psychologically more micro phenomena.

Potentially, at least, it could descend several further rungs of psychological disaggregation. The great bulk of the past couple of decades' worth of developments in cognitive psychology have never really made it into political psychology. The initial spate of cognitively influenced political psychology scarcely ventured beyond "schema theory," and although more recent work has begun to fan out, large portions of cognitive psychology remain to be drawn on.

Things are beginning to change. "Schema theory" has been chuting rapidly and mercifully back to oblivion, its day in political psychology having ended by the early 1990s. Jim Kuklinski, John Bolland, and I (Kuklinski, Luskin, and Bolland 1991) criticized the studies parading "schema theory" on several grounds, but primarily because we thought the applications cosmetic and the theory redundant.[13] Trumpeted "measures of schemas" turned out to be measuring only their outsides: either the central tendency, on some specified dimension, of their cognitive contents (which might as easily be seen as beliefs, perceptions, or cognitive component of the corresponding attitude), the central tendency on some positive–negative dimension of their affective contents (which might as easily be seen as the affective component of the corresponding attitude), or their level of "development" (which might as easily be seen as "attitude structure" or "topic-specific expertise") (Kuklinski et al.

---

13 Lodge and McGraw (1991) cite Hastie (1986:21) to the effect that there is no single entity appropriately called "schema theory." Perhaps not, but there are a lot of people who think they are using it and have made much of doing so (including Conover and Feldman 1991 in the article immediately following theirs). I am inclined to agree with Humpty-Dumpty and Juliet about the importance of names; our criticisms stand regardless.

1991:1342). The measures themselves are often indistinguishable from preexisting attitudinal ones.[14] By and large, this is just standard public opinion and voting research with a makeover.

By way of unavowed confirmation, all the principals in this receding wave of "schema theory" have now long since moved on to other, more genuine and more rewarding uses of psychological theory. As regards the Lodge and McGraw (1991), Conover and Feldman (1991), and Miller (1991) defenses of their earlier efforts, therefore, my advice would be to mind what they have done, not what they have said.

One sort of measurement that would have been new and interesting is individual-level cognitive mappings of the sort sketched by Lodge and McGraw (1991). Alas, they have never actually been done. Lodge and McGraw's diagram is only hypothetical. One reason, no doubt, is that it would be prohibitively time-consuming to map more than a small corner of more than a handful of individuals' political cognitions in this way. Taber, Lodge, and Glathar (2001) thus sensibly propose tabling measurement in favor of simulation.

There is also still some considerable doubt about how much we as political psychologists should gain from detailed mappings of political cognitions. Again the question is one of psychological aggregation. Knowing the precise contents and structure of somebody's political cognitions may be about as useful for understanding what he or she thinks, feels, and does about politics "as knowing the chemical composition of the ink [would be] for reading a newspaper" (Kuklinski et al. 1991:1347). Though fascinating as psychology, this may be too remote from Politics to be interesting as political psychology.

Other questions pertain to temporal aggregation. The dependent variables of information-processing experiments – perceptions of and reactions to particular, slightly lagged stimuli – exist principally in the moment. If the moment in question resembles one in or just before getting to the voting booth or during or just before a survey interview, these variables may be critically important. For most purposes, however, it is the accumulation or residue of such momentary responses that seems likelier to affect the variables closer to politics, like attitudes and vote choice.

These same reservations attach with more certainty to much of the rest of cognitive psychology, the bulk of it psychologically if not always

---

14 To be fair, a few studies, notably by Lodge and his colleagues (e.g., Hamill et al. 1985; Lodge and Hamill 1986), have added some new and worthwhile instrumentation. Other new measures, however, have been either familiar or strange. Conover and Feldman's (1984) "schemas," from a Q factor analysis, include "Hobbesian–Freudian," "conservative integrationism," and "liberal sex roles-nonreligious."

temporally still more micro. I doubt that an understanding of neural functioning will be very helpful; I doubt that "connectionist" or parallel distributed processing models (Rumelhart 1989; Rumelhart et al. 1986), more aggregated but still not too much above the neural level, will help much either.

On the other hand, there remain veins of cognitive psychology that do not seem too micro yet have been little exploited. The Kahnemann–Tversky corpora on prospect theory and heuristics, coming to grips with how (and with what biases) people value and judge the probabilities of outcomes, leap to mind (Tversky and Kahnemann 1974, 1981). It is difficult to think of any other work so often and deservedly cited, yet – in political psychology, anyway – so little actually used. Other undermined veins lie in Tajfel's (1981), Turner's (Turner 1987), and others' work on social categories, and the recent work on emotions by Gray (1987), Frijda (1988), Ortony, Clore, and Collins (1988), and others (although Marcus has been making good use of Gray; see Marcus 1988; Marcus and MacKuen 1993).

Similarly limited use has been made of the full panoply of measurement devices in cognitive and cognitively influenced social psychology (see Bower and Clapper 1989; Srull 1984). A variety of response time measures are potentially revealing. To gauge stereotypes, for example, the experimenter can present subjects with a list of trait adjectives, having first made some social category like race salient by means of the preceding question, then ask them to say how desirable the adjectives are, distinguish them from interspersed nonsense words, or simply say them aloud. The shorter the response time, the stronger the association between adjective and stereotype. Dovidio's and Gaertner's work on racial attitudes provides examples from social verging on political psychology (Dovidio, Evans, and Tyler 1986; Gaertner and McLaughlin 1983; Perdue, Dovidio, Gutman, and Tyler 1990).

CONCEPTUAL AGGREGATION

I shall say little about conceptual aggregation, except to note that, as with the other sorts we have looked at, there are dangers in both too much and too little and that Zaller's measure of "political awareness" is in my opinion a prime example of too much. Zaller commingles sophistication, which is what he really seems to have in mind, with education, political interest, media use, and political participation. If these are all the same variable, we shall have a hard time using some of them to explain others. But a fairly high proportion of the twenty ordered pairs that can be formed from these five variables must correspond to nonzero effects. Does education affect sophistication? I don't think it does, much, but how can we tell if they are operationally inseparable? Surely interest affects sophistication, and vice versa. Surely interest and sophistication affect participation. These are standard hypotheses. In Zaller's own model, the operative elements of "political awareness" may differ from equation to equation. I suspect that message acceptance is a function of sophistication, but message reception a function of interest. We cannot tell without unpacking "awareness."

WHAT SHOULD BE EXOGENOUS? QUESTIONS OF CAUSAL DISTANCE – AND TASTE

As should by now be clear, the reason these various sorts of aggregation bear on the issue of political relevance is that most of them bear on the variables' causal distance from politics. There is always the question, in carving out some portion of what we must take to be an approximately block-recursive reality (Fisher 1961; Fisher and Ando 1962), of how far back to extend the analysis. At some point, the exogenous variables must be left exogenous. But where? The dependent variables of political behavior and political psychology, though arguably not Political, capital P, themselves, do affect Politics, at least in the aggregate, and directly enough to make them hard to ignore. The question, from the standpoint of *political* psychology, is whether they for their part are sufficiently interesting to be worth explaining in turn.

I am reminded of the cosmology lecture at whose end a lay member of the audience objects that the lecturer has got it all wrong. The entire universe, he says, is resting on the back of an enormous turtle. The lecturer, deciding to humor him, asks what the turtle is resting on. "Another turtle," he says. "And what," the lecturer persists, "is that turtle resting on?" "Another turtle." The lecturer starts to ask again but is cut off: "Save your breath, professor, it's turtles all the way down."

Where one draws the line is ultimately a matter of taste. "Explanation," it has been said, "is where the mind comes to rest." The variables of political behavior and political psychology are undeniably helpful for explaining politics. But it is impossible to refute – or establish – the claim that they are uninteresting and thus not worth explaining themselves. Essentially the same may be said of many of the more psychologically disaggregated variables distinctive to political psychology in relation to the more psychologically aggregated ones shared with political behavior. The former may help explain the latter, but at what level of psychological disaggregation should the task of explaining the former be ceded to the nonpolitical psychologists (or neurobiologists)?

One tolerant solution is to recognize that not everyone need draw the line in the same place. Phenomena of scant interest to particular researchers may nonetheless be important to the discipline as a whole. As the cultural anthropologist Robert Redfield once said in another connection (arguing against cultural relativism), we should want balanced libraries, not necessarily balanced books. One need not have much interest in explaining party identification, political sophistication, or reliance on on-line versus memory-based processing oneself to recognize the desirability of others' doing so.

TOWARD THE FUTURE

Reviewing the state of the subdiscipline some years ago, Kinder (1983) suggested refocusing from *how much* to *how* people think about politics – from the extent to the nature of political cognition. And a goodly volume of literature has, with varying degrees of success, answered his call. The early applications of schema theory, for example, can be viewed as a largely unrewarding effort on these lines.

In my view, however, a somewhat different refocusing – on explanation rather than merely finer description – will prove more useful. Whether considering the "how much" or the "how" of political cognition, we should be trying to explain it and to use it to explain other things. This prescription includes questions about the nature of whatever organized thinking occurs. But it also includes questions about its causes and consequences.

In the past perfect, this last variable is sophistication, whose importance by now should be clear. Let me therefore devote this penultimate section to indicating a few of the other topics I think particularly worth exploring. My selection is balanced toward the psychologically aggregated and correspondingly close to politics, reflecting my own sense of the turtle of diminishing returns. I shall make some suggestions but also raise questions.

Offhand versus Serious Processing

The most psychologically disaggregated topic concerns the distinction between *offhand* and *serious* information processing, which I offer as umbrella terms covering a number of more specific distinctions already extant. As Sears (2001) points out, processing has been divided on congeneric but nonidentical lines into *automatic* versus *controlled* (Shiffrin and Schneider 1977), *on-line* versus *memory-based* (Hastie and Park 1986), *category-based* versus *piecemeal* (Fiske and Pavelchak 1986), *peripheral* versus *central* (Petty and Cacippo 1986), and *heuristic* versus *systematic* (Chaiken 1980). As Petty and Cacioppo (1986) point out, it has also been divided, also on congeneric but nonidentical lines, into *nonsemantic* versus *semantic* (Craik and Lockhart 1972), *effortless* versus *effortful* (Tyler, Hertel, McCallum, and Ellis 1979), and *mindless* versus *mindful* (Langer, Blank, and Chanowitz 1978). Plainly one task before us is to smelt these distinctions down into whatever conceptually independent dimensions they contain.

Owing chiefly to Lodge, McGraw, and Stroh (1989), it is the on-line versus memory-based distinction that has most penetrated political psychology, with most attention centering on the question of which mode is more prevalent. Lodge, McGraw, and Stroh's results suggest that the great majority of processing is on-line, whereas Zaller's (1992) model of the survey response assumes memory-based processing. I suspect this debate will benefit from the kind of conceptual clarification I have just urged.

The more important questions, in any event, are who engages in which sort of processing under what conditions and what differences that makes to coding, retention, attitude change, and other cognitive and affective variables with implications for mass politics. The authors responsible for these distinctions (most notably Petty and Cacioppo 1986) have already provided some answers, partially sketched by Sears (2001), but much remains to be done.

Let me confine myself here to suggesting that both offhand and serious processing vary widely in both determinants and consequences, depending on sophistication. Is offhand processing the exercise of efficient routines by the highly sophisticated or of unreliable heuristics by the unsophisticated? Is serious processing a desperate ransacking of largely empty shelves or something akin to scholarly research? A few minutes' concentrated thought by the sophisticated and the unsophisticated are by no means the same thing. The same goes for a few seconds' cursory thought. One might in fact distinguish between high- and low-information processing of each kind, although a cleaner solution is to keep processing mode and sophistication as separate variables interacting in the determination of others.

The second half of this suggestion, similar in spirit to Petty and Cacioppo (1986), is that the choice of processing mode should also depend nonadditively on sophistication, in this case interacting with the difficulty of the material and the incentives to get the most from it. For the highly sophisticated, easy material should tend to be processed offhand, regardless of incentives; difficult material either offhand or seriously, depending on incentives. For the highly unsophisticated, weak incentives should tend to elicit offhand processing, regardless of difficulty; strong incentives either offhand or serious processing, depending on difficulty (cf. McGraw, Lodge, and Stroh 1990; Rahn, Aldrich, and Borgida 1994).

My one reservation about this topic concerns temporal aggregation. These processing variables, the processing outcomes they are presumed to affect, and many of their determinants are transient phenomena. How much do we need to explain such fleeting snips of processing? This is not a rhetorical question – there is a case to be made for temporally disaggregated variables – but it is worth noting that processing mode can be temporally aggregated into an individual differences variable. People have characteristic mixes of processing modes in the political domain, and the mix may be at least as consequential as the mode on any given occasion.

Cognitive Ability

The second topic is the effects of cognitive ability, which for all the recent attention to cognitive processing remains largely neglected. It continues to play wallflower to education, that Prom Queen of explanatory variables, and to a lesser degree to sophistication. Yet it is difficult to imagine that cognitive processing and its outcomes – behaviors, attitudes, accumulations of knowledge, and the rest – are not conditioned in some measure by the accuracy, speed, efficiency, and capabilities of the hard- and software involved. There is much evidence in psychology to suggest that they are (see Brody 1992; Gordon 1997; Gottfredson 1997).

One reason for this neglect is practical. Not many surveys contain relevant tests, the lone major exception being the General Social Survey (GSS) of the National Opinion Research Center of the University of Chicago, which includes the ten-item Gallup–Thorndike vocabulary test in many of its annual outings. Another reason, however, is ideological. Whether from modesty, insecurity, or excessive egalitarianism, many academics outside the relevant specialties in psychology will vehemently deny the existence and observability of individual differences in cognitive ability (except, of course, in hiring, graduate admissions, and everyday appraisals of others). Any reference to "intelligence," a closet synonym, draws particular hostility.

So it is with some pessimism that I urge the variable's importance nevertheless. I do not suggest that it is all-important, as in Herrnstein and Murray's (1994) distasteful hyperbole.[15] Very little in this world is determined wholly or even primarily by intelligence. Motivation and application matter – greatly. So do other abilities. So does knowledge. So do temperament and style. So, regrettably, do looks, wealth, and

15 For the record, although it is irrelevant to the questions I am raising here, the environmental differences between groups seem to me to be more than large enough to account completely for any group differences in measured intelligence.

connections. So do opportunities. But intelligence does *affect* many things, if only as one factor among several to many (Brody 1992; Gordon 1997; Gottfredson 1997).

It is important in this vein to distinguish intelligence from education and sophistication, with which it is substantially correlated (to the tune of roughly .4 with sophistication and roughly .6 with education). Both conceptually and empirically these are different variables. Sophistication is a matter of knowledge, education (as conventionally cast) a matter of schooling, intelligence a matter of ability.[16] My work with Joe Ten Barge suggests that the three affect somewhat different sets of political variables (Luskin and Ten Barge 1995).

Of particular interest is the contest between education and intelligence in the explanation of sophistication. Two current books have yet again stressed education's role (Delli Carpini and Keeter 1996; Nie, Junn, and Stehlik-Barry 1996). But Delli Carpini and Keeter do not control for intelligence, while Nie, Junn, and Stehlik-Barry, who do control for it, assign education the ultimate credit for its effect, based on a model in which education affects intelligence but not vice versa. Education's *direct* effects on political sophistication–like variables (there are several) in Nie et al.'s results are generally quite modest – and would presumably be reduced further, quite possibly erased, by controlling for political interest, of which Nie et al. take no account.[17]

My own work with a more elaborate model including interest as an endogenous variable alongside sophistication showed that when an admittedly make-do measure of intelligence was inserted in an equation for sophistication, education's effect disappeared (Luskin 1990). The obvious vulnerabilities of this measure, the interviewer's rating of the respondent's "apparent intelligence," made for reasonable doubts (Delli Carpini and Keeter 1996; Luskin 1990), but Ten Barge and I have more recently estimated a similar model using a more psychometric measure of intelligence and found the same thing. When intelligence enters the model, education's effect steps off a cliff. Political interest is more influential than either, but as between education and intelligence, it is the latter that has the direct effect (Luskin and Ten Barge 1995). We may leave aside for present purposes the thornier question of indirect effects, except to note that any model making intelligence endogenous but education exogenous (as in Nie et al. 1996) is patently misspecified.

16 Education is also an element of class, and of social location, giving it main effects on directional variables like vote choice that sophistication and intelligence lack.
17 Smith (1989) also has relevant results, which he interprets as showing education with little effect, but actually showing it with a good deal. In addition to whistling past obvious simultaneities, however, he too fails to control for intelligence.

My suggestion from all this is that education is overrated and over-used, and intelligence underrated and underused. Across the broad range of politico-psychological dependent variables, both are doubtless impor-tant, but we have been enshrining the one while ignoring the other. I should similarly suggest that it is misleading to substitute education for intelligence or sophistication (as, for example, in Sniderman, Brody, and Tetlock 1991) and undesirable to bundle these and other variables into conglomerate measures of "political awareness," "political involve-ment," or somesuch (as for example in Zaller 1992).

Emotion

The third topic is emotion. Even in the day of "cognitive imperialism" (Tomkins 1981), now fading, it was hard to argue that emotions are not at least as important as cognition. Zajonc's (1980) contentions that emotion arises from a physiologically different system than cognition and precurses all but the most rudimentary cognition look increasingly if qualifiedly right. Some emotions involve more processing than others, but they all seem to involve the limbic system, especially the amygdala and anterior cingulate (Damasio 1994; Ledoux 1989, 1992). Probably Zajonc's contention that emotion dominates cognition in most evalua-tive contexts is also about right.

The role of emotion in political evaluations and decision making, however, remains largely unexplored. What emotions matter to mass politics, and how? In marking off the distinctive roles of anxiety and enthusiasm, Marcus and MacKuen (1993, 2001) have made a significant advance. Yet fundamental questions remain. The circumplex model would be more compelling if we could see more plainly how the full spec-trum of commonly recognized emotions – joy, contentment, gratitude, fear, regret, sorrow, and the rest – could be interpreted as combinations of these two (and perhaps some cognitive) dimensions.

Another question concerns temporal aggregation. Is the tense in which these and other emotions enter political information processing and deci-sion making present or past perfect? Is it the emotional response at the moment of choice in the voting booth or some residue of cumulative emotion over the course of the campaign that matters? (Are they the same?) The answers will make a great difference to the variables we look at and for.

Television

The most psychologically aggregate and directly political topic is the influence of the electronic media, particularly television, in politics. With the average American spending more time watching television than doing anything else except working and sleeping, there can be few influences more pervasive.[18] It is a fair suspicion, moreover, that television is heavily implicated in a number of disturbing trends. Partisanship is down and candidate personae up as influences on vote choice. Turnout is down, disenchantment with politics and government up. And by no means just in the United States. Other Western democracies seem to be riding the same curve, only some distance behind (Dalton 1996; Lijphart 1997).

What is television's role in this? It may partly be the increasingly cynical portrayal of politics in television news. Doubtless this bias has been with us since before Marconi, but it has become more acute in the television age (Patterson 1993). It may partly be the vividness, accessibility, and (thus) audience penetration of the medium. It is plausible, for one thing, that we have come to know candidates in a more familiar way (Hart 1994), about which there is an adage. We are just now beginning to see how television news, political ads, and other shows affect our perceptions of politicians, understandings of issues, issue positions, and votes (Ansolabehere and Iyengar 1995; Iyengar 1991; Iyengar and Kinder 1987; Newton et al. 1987; Neuman, Just, and Crigler 1992). Here, too, much remains to be done.

CONCLUSION

How do we know anything is worth studying? Why should we study *politics*, never mind political psychology or political behavior? The answer must be framed in terms of politics' effects – on societal qualities like justice, on the pleasures and frustrations of quotidian life. In short, we must claim that politics has consequences, and for things we value.

Both consequences and values are always disputable, of course, but if politics is worth studying, then so are political behavior and political psychology, to the extent they affect it. The characteristic disaggregation of these fields' dependent variables – physical in both, psychological and temporal in the latter – leaves them open to charges of insufficient political relevance, but in neither case are such charges justified. At least in the aggregate, the variables of political behavior are manifestly relevant. So, ipso facto, are many of the more psychologically

---

18 A methodological implication is the desirability of presenting information in audiovisual form. For example, the information boards of Lau and Redlawsk (2001), while ingenious, ignore all the visual and paralinguistic cues that are so important in televised news stories – and that come through whether or not they are what the story is about.

macro variables of political psychology, heavily overlapping those of political behavior.

It is true that the interface with Politics, capital P, is at the aggregate level, and it is a position as defensible – and indefensible – as any to pale our models there, taking the aggregate distributions of political thoughts, feelings, and behaviors as explanations but not explananda. But one's curiosity may well be unsatisfied by such relatively proximate explanation. For us who study political psychology and political behavior, it is important to examine the variables that affect the public's political thoughts, feelings, and behaviors – and thus, at a greater remove, the process and outcomes of Politics in turn.

It will not do, however, to explain – or measure – these phenomena strictly at the aggregate level. The phenomena themselves are fundamentally individual level, with heavily if not preponderantly individual-level roots, many of which combine nonadditively, as numerous contributions to Kuklinski (2001) attest. Under these circumstances, as I have argued, aggregate-level measures and models are caricaturish at best. Aggregate *implications* remain important, of course, but we shall want to derive them from individual-level measures and models.

When it comes to political psychology, as distinct from political behavior, the questions concern psychological and temporal rather than physical aggregation. Many of the variables of political psychology are more psychologically and temporally disaggregated and thus admittedly more distant from Politics than those of political behavior. But how troubling this is depends on one's disciplinary vantage point. Some political scientists may find much political psychology too distant from politics. And so it may be, for them. But not necessarily for everyone. *De gustibus*, in the end, *non est disputandum*.

There are limits, to be sure. Methodologically, in particular, not everything goes. Semiotic fantasias on "political culture," aswirl in metaphors and metonymies so clever no communicator could ever have intended them, nor any ordinary citizen ever have perceived them, are plainly useless.[19] Gauging the distributions, sources, and effects of values, beliefs, attitudes, and behaviors requires systematic observation, in the form of surveys, experiments, and the like; general if conditional hypotheses (conditionality being what interactions are about); and empirical (usually statistical) tests. In the realm of the empirical, *il n'y a pas de hors-science*.[20]

---

19 I am thinking of specific cases but shall content myself with suggesting genres and approaches like "cultural studies" and "postmodernism" as the places to look for examples.

20 A less admiring play on Derrida's (1967:227) claim that *"il n'y a pas de hors-texte."*

Substantive boundaries are harder to draw. At some level of temporal or psychological disaggregation, there may be consensus that the variables are too causally distant from politics to be of great interest. But there remains a wide range of variables we should be willing to consider worthwhile for somebody ultimately interested in explaining politics to examine. My own view, and what I have been arguing here, is that the majority of the variables of political psychology and a still greater majority of those of political behavior fall within this range.

References

Achen, Christopher H. 1975. "Mass Political Attitudes and the Survey Response." *American Political Science Review* 69:1218–31.

——— 1983. "Toward Theories of Data: The State of Political Methodology." In Ada W. Finifter, ed., *Political Science: The State of the Discipline*. Washington, DC: American Political Science Association.

Anderson, John R. 1983. *The Architecture of Cognition*. Cambridge, MA: Harvard University Press.

Ansolabehere, Stephen, and Shanto Iyengar. 1995. *Going Negative: How Political Advertisements Shrink and Polarize the Electorate*. New York: Free Press.

Bower, Gordon H., and John P. Clapper. 1989. "Experimental Methods in Cognitive Science." In Michael I. Posner, ed., *Foundations of Cognitive Science*. Cambridge, MA: MIT Press.

Brady, Henry E. 1993. "Guessing, Stability, Reliability in Attitude Items: Why Wiley-Wiley Models Do Not Tell You Enough." Paper presented at the annual meeting of the Midwestern Political Science Association, Chicago.

Brody, Nathan. 1992. *Intelligence*. San Diego, CA: Academic Press.

Chaiken, Shelly. 1980. "Heuristic versus Systematic Information Processing and the Use of Source versus Cue Messages in Persuasion." *Journal of Personality and Social Psychology* 39:752–66.

Clore, Gerald L., Norbert Schwarz, and Michael Conway. 1994. "Affective Causes and Consequences of Social Information Processing." In Robert S. Wyer, Jr. and Thomas K. Srull, eds., *Handbook of Social Cognition*, 2nd ed. Hillsdale, NJ: Erlbaum.

Conover, Pamela Johnston, and Stanley Feldman. 1984. "How People Organize the Political World: A Schematic Model." *American Journal of Political Science* 28:95–126.

——— 1991. "Where Is the Schema? Critique." *American Political Science Review* 85:1364–9.

Converse, Philip E. 1962. "Information Flow and the Stability of Partisan Attitude." *Public Opinion Quarterly* 26:578–99.

——— 1964. "The Nature of Belief Systems in Mass Publics." In David E. Apter, ed., *Ideology and Discontent*. New York: Free Press.

——— 1980. "Comment: Rejoinder to Judd and Milburn." *American Sociological Review* 45:644–6.

Converse, Philip E., and Gregory B. Markus. 1979. "Plus ça change . . . : The New CPS Election Study Panel." *American Political Science Review* 73:32–49.

Craik, Fergus I. M., and Robert S. Lockhart. 1972. "Levels of Processing: A Framework for Memory Research." *Journal of Verbal Learning and Verbal Behavior* 11:671–6.

Cramer, J. S. 1964. "Efficient Grouping, Regression and Correlation in Engel Curve Analysis." *Journal of the American Statistical Association* 59: 233–50.

Dahl, Robert A. 1989. *Democracy and Its Critics*. New Haven, CT: Yale University Press.

Dalton, Russell J. 1988. *Citizen Politics in Western Democracies: Public Opinion and Political Parties in the United States, Great Britain, West Germany, and France*. Chatham, NJ: Chatham House.

1996. *Citizen Politics in Western Democracies: Public Opinion and Political Parties in Advanced Western Democracies*. Chatham, NJ: Chatham House.

Damasio, Antonio R. 1994. *Descartes' Error: Emotion, Reason, and the Human Brain*. New York: G. P. Putnam's Sons.

Delli Carpini, Michael X., and Scott Keeter. 1996. *What Americans Know About Politics and Why It Matters*. New Haven, CT: Yale University Press.

Derrida, Jacques. 1967. *De la Gramatologie*. Paris: Editions de Minuit.

Dovidio, J. F., N. Evans, and R. B. Tyler. 1986. "Racial Stereotypes: The Contents of Their Cognitive Representation." *Journal of Experimental Social Psychology* 22:22–37.

Erbring, Lutz. 1990. "Individuals Writ Large: An Epilogue on the 'Ecological Fallacy.'" *Political Analysis* 1:235–69.

Erikson, Robert S. 1979. "The SRC Panel Data and Mass Political Attitudes." *British Journal of Political Science* 9:89–114.

Erikson, Robert S., John P. McIver, and Gerald C. Wright, Jr. 1987. "State Political Culture and Public Opinion." *American Political Science Review* 81:797–813.

Erikson, Robert S., Gerald C. Wright, Jr., and John P. McIver. 1989. "Political Parties, Public Opinion, and State Policy in the United States." *American Political Science Review* 83:729–50.

Feldman, Stanley. 1988. "Structure and Consistency in Public Opinion: The Role of Core Beliefs and Values." *American Journal of Political Science* 32:416–40.

1990. "Measuring Issue Preferences: The Problem of Response Instability." *Political Analysis* 1:25–60.

Feldman, Stanley, and John Zaller. 1992. "The Political Culture of Ambivalence: Ideological Responses to the Welfare State." *American Journal of Political Science* 36:268–307.

Fisher, Franklin M. 1961. "On the Cost of Approximate Specification in Simultaneous Equation Estimation." *Econometrica* 29:139–70.

Fisher, Franklin M., and Albert Ando. 1962. "Two Theorems on Ceteris Paribus in the Analysis of Dynamic Systems." *American Political Science Review* 56:108–13.

Fiske, Susan T., and Mark A. Pavelchak. 1986. "Category-Based versus Piecemeal Affective Responses: Developments in Schema-Triggered Affect." In Richard M. Sorrentino and E. Tory Higgins, eds., *The Handbook of Motivation and Cognition*. New York: Guilford Press.

Frijda, Nico J. 1988. "The Laws of Emotion." *American Psychologist* 43: 349–58.

Gaertner, S. L., and J. D. McLaughlin. 1983. "Changing Not Fading: Racial Stereotypes Revealed by a Non-reactive, Reaction Time Measure." *Social Psychology Quarterly* 46:23–30.

Gibson, James L. 1989. "The Structure of Attitudinal Tolerance in the United States." *British Journal of Political Science* 19:562–71.

1992. "Alternative Measures of Political Tolerance: Must Tolerance Be Least Liked?" *American Journal of Political Science* 36:560–77.

Gordon, Robert A. 1997. "Everyday Life as an Intelligence Test: Effects of Intelligence and Intelligence Context." *Intelligence* 24:203–320.

Gottfredson, Linda S. 1997. "Why g Matters: The Complexity of Everyday Life." *Intelligence* 24:79–132.

Gray, Jeffrey A. 1987. *The Psychology of Fear and Stress*, 2nd ed. Cambridge: Cambridge University Press.

Green, H. A. John. 1964. *Aggregation in Economic Analysis: An Introductory Survey*. Princeton, NJ: Princeton University Press.

Greene, William H. 1993. *Econometric Analysis*, 2nd ed. New York: Macmillan.

Hamill, Ruth, Milton Lodge, and Frederick Blake. 1985. "The Breadth, Depth, and Utility of Class, Partisan, and Ideological Schemata." *American Journal of Political Science* 29:850–70.

Hanushek, Eric A., John E. Jackson, and J. F. Kain. 1974. "Model Specification, Use of Aggregate Data, and the Ecological Correlation Fallacy." *Political Methodology* 1:87–106.

Hart, Roderick P. 1994. *Seducing America: How Television Charms the Modern Voter*. New York: Oxford University Press.

Hastie, Reid. 1986. "A Primer of Information-Processing Theory for the Political Scientist." In Richard R. Lau and David O. Sears, eds., *Political Cognition*. Hillsdale, NJ: Erlbaum.

Hastie, Reid, and Bernadette Park. 1986. "The Relationship between Memory and Judgment Depends on Whether the Task Is Memory-Based or On-Line." *Psychological Review* 93:258–63.

Hauser, Robert M., J. T. Sheridan, and J. R. Warren. 1999. "Socio-Economic Achievements of Siblings in the Life Cycle: New Findings from the Wisconsin Longitudinal Study." *Research on Aging* 21:338–78.

Herrnstein, Richard J., and Charles Murray. 1994. *The Bell Curve: Intelligence and Class Structure in American Life*. New York: Free Press.

Holmes, Oliver Wendell, Jr. 1918. "Natural Law." *Harvard Law Review* 32:40–4.

Hurwitz, Jon, and Mark Peffley. 1987. "How Are Foreign Policy Attitudes Structured?: A Hierachical Model." *American Political Science Review* 81:1099–120.

Iyengar, Shanto. 1991. *Is Anyone Responsible? How Television Frames Political Issues*. Chicago: University of Chicago Press.

Iyengar, Shanto, and Donald R. Kinder. 1987. *News That Matters*. Chicago: University of Chicago Press.

Jackson, John E. 1983. "The Systematic Beliefs of the Mass Public: Estimating Polling Preferences with Survey Data." *Journal of Politics* 45:840–65.

Judd, Charles M., and Michael A. Milburn. 1980. "The Structure of Attitude Systems in the Public: Comparisons of a Structural Equation Model." *American Sociological Review* 45:627–43.

Key, V. O., Jr. 1967. *Public Opinion and American Democracy.* New York: Alfred A. Knopf.

Kinder, Donald R. 1983. "Diversity and Complexity in American Public Opinion." In Ada W. Finifter, ed., *Political Science: The State of the Discipline.* Washington, D. C.: American Political Science Association.

Kinder, Donald R., and David O. Sears. 1985. "Public Opinion and Political Action." In Gardner Lindzey and Elliot Aronson, eds., *Handbook of Social Psychology*, Vol. 2. New York: Random House.

King, Gary. 1986. "How Not to Lie with Statistics: Avoiding Common Mistakes in Quantitative Political Science." *American Journal of Political Science* 30:666–87.

Kmenta, Jan. 1986. *Elements of Econometrics*, 2nd ed. New York: Macmillan.

Kuklinski, James H., ed. 2001. *Citizens and Politics: Perspectives from Political Psychology.* New York: Cambridge University Press.

Kuklinski, James H., and Norman L. Hurley. 1994. "On Hearing and Interpreting Political Messages: A Cautionary Tale of Citizen Cue-Taking." *Journal of Politics* 56:729–51.

Kuklinski, James H., Robert C. Luskin, and John Bolland. 1991. "Where Is the Schema? Going Beyond the 'S' Word in Political Psychology." *American Political Science Review* 85:1341–56.

Langer, E. J., A. Blank, and B. Chanowitz. 1978. "The Mindlessness of Ostensibly Thoughtful Action: The Role of 'Placebic' Information in Interpersonal Interaction." *Journal of Personality and Social Psychology* 36:635–42.

Lau, Richard R., and David P. Redlawsk. 2001. "Decision Making during a Political Campaign." In James H. Kuklinski, ed., *Citizens and Politics: Perspectives from Political Psychology.* New York: Cambridge University Press.

Ledoux, Joseph. 1989. "Cognitive–Emotional Interactions in the Brain." *Emotion and Cognition* 3:267–89.

1992. "Emotion and the Amygdala." In J. P. Aggleton, ed., *The Amygdala: Neurobiological Aspects of Emotion, Memory, and Mental Dysfunction.* New York: Wiley.

Lijphart, Arend. 1997. "Unequal Participation: Democracy's Unresolved Dilemma." *American Political Science Review* 91:1–15.

Lodge, Milton, and Ruth Hamill. 1986. "A Partisan Schema for Political Information Processing." *American Political Science Review* 80:505–19.

Lodge, Milton, and Kathleen McGraw. 1991. "Where Is the Schema? Critique." *American Political Science Review* 85:1357–64.

Lodge, Milton, Kathleen M. McGraw, and Patrick Stroh. 1989. "An Impression-Driven Model of Candidate Evaluation." *American Political Science Review* 83:399–420.

Luskin, Robert C. 1987. "Measuring Political Sophistication." *American Journal of Political Science* 31:856–99.

1990. "Explaining Political Sophistication." *Political Behavior* 12:331–61.

2001. "The Heavenly Public: What Would the Ideal Democratic Citizenry Be Like?" In George Rabinowitz and Michael B. MacKuen, eds., *Electoral Democracy.* Ann Arbor: University of Michigan Press.

Luskin, Robert C., and Joseph C. Ten Barge. 1995. "Education, Intelligence, and Political Sophistication." Paper presented at the annual meeting of the Midwest Political Science Association, Chicago, April 6–8, 1995.

MacKuen, Michael B., Robert S. Erikson, and James A. Stimson. 1989. "Macropartisanship." *American Political Science Review* 83:1125–43.

Mansbridge, Jane J. 1980. *Beyond Adversary Democracy*. New York: Basic Books.

——— ed. 1990. *Beyond Self Interest*. Chicago: University of Chicago Press.

Marcus, George E. 1988. "The Structure of Emotional Response: 1984 Presidential Candidates." *American Political Science Review* 82:735–61.

Marcus, George E., and Michael B. MacKuen. 1993. "Anxiety, Enthusiasm, and the Vote: The Emotional Underpinnings of Learning and Involvement During Presidential Campaigns." *American Political Science Review* 87:672–85.

——— 2001. "Emotions and Politics: The Dynamic Functions of Emotionality." In James H. Kuklinski, ed., *Citizens and Politics: Perspectives from Political Psychology*. New York: Cambridge University Press.

Masters, Roger D. 1989. "Gender and Political Cognition." *Politics and the Life Sciences* 8:3–39.

——— 2001. "Cognitive Neuroscience, Emotion, and Leadership." In James H. Kuklinski, ed., *Citizens and Politics: Perspectives from Political Psychology*. New York: Cambridge University Press.

McCloskey, Herbert, and John Zaller. 1984. *The American Ethos: Public Attitudes toward Capitalism and Democracy*. Cambridge, MA: Harvard University Press.

McGraw, Kathleen M., Milton Lodge, and Patrick Stroh. 1990. "On-Line Processing in Candidate Evaluation: The Effects of Issue Order, Issue Importance, and Sophistication." *Political Behavior* 12:41–58.

McGuire, William J. 1968. "Personality and Susceptibility to Social Influence." In E. F. Borgatta and W. W. Lambert, eds., *Handbook of Personality Theory and Research*. Chicago: Rand McNally.

——— 1969. "The Nature of Attitudes and Attitude Change." In G. Lindzey and E. Aronson. Reading, eds., *Handbook of Social Psychology*, 2nd ed. MA: Addison-Wesley.

Miller, Arthur H. 1991. "Where Is the Schema? Critique." *American Political Science Review* 85:1369–76.

Monroe, Alan D. 1979. "Consistency Between Public Preferences and National Policy Decisions." *American Politics Quarterly* 7:3–19.

Neuman, W. Russell, Marion R. Just, and Ann N. Crigler. 1992. *Common Knowledge: News and the Construction of Political Meaning*. Chicago: University of Chicago Press.

Newton, James S., Roger D. Masters, Gregory. J. McHugo, and Dennis G. Sullivan. 1987. "Making Up Our Minds: Effects of Network Coverage on Viewer Impressions of Leaders." *Polity* 20:226–46.

Nie, Norman H., Jane Junn, and Kenneth Stehlik-Barry. 1996. *Education and Democratic Citizenship in America*. Chicago: University of Chicago Press.

Ortony, Andrew, Gerald L. Clore, and Allan Collins. 1988. *The Cognitive Structure of Emotions*. Cambridge: Cambridge University Press.

Page, Benjamin I., and Robert Y. Shapiro. 1983. "Effects of Public Opinion on Policy." *American Political Science Review* 77:175–90.

——— 1992. *The Rational Public: Fifty Years of Trends in Americans' Policy Preferences*. Chicago: University of Chicago Press.

Patterson, Thomas E. 1993. *Out of Order*. New York: Alfred A. Knopf.

Peffley, Mark, and Jon Hurwitz. 1993. "Models of Attitude Constraint in Foreign Affairs." *Political Behavior* 15:61–90.

Perdue, Charles W., John F. Dovidio, Michael B. Gutman, and Richard B. Tyler. 1990. "Us and Them: Social Categorization and the Process of Intergroup Bias." *Journal of Personality and Social Psychology* 59:475–86.

Petty, Richard E., and John T. Cacioppo. 1984. "The Effects of Involvement on Responses to Argument Quantity and Quality: Central and Peripheral Routes to Persuasion." *Journal of Personality and Social Psychology* 46:69–81.

1986. *Communication and Persuasion: Central and Peripheral Routes to Attitude Change.* New York: Springer-Verlag.

Rahn, Wendy M., John H. Aldrich, and Eugene Borgida. 1994. "Individual and Contextual Variations in Political Candidate Appraisal." *American Political Science Review* 88:193–9.

Rasinski, Kenneth A. 1987. "What's Fair Is Fair – Or Is It? Value Differences Underlying Public Views about Social Justice." *Journal of Personality and Social Psychology* 53:201–11.

Rivers, Douglas. 1988. "Heterogeneity in Models of Electoral Choice." *American Journal of Political Science* 32:737–57.

Robinson, W. S. 1950. "Ecological Correlations and the Behavior of Individuals." *American Sociological Review* 15:351–7.

Rohrschneider, Robert. 1993. "Environmental Belief Systems in Western Europe: A Hierarchical Model of Constraint." *Comparative Political Studies* 26:3–29.

Rumelhart, David E. 1989. "The Architecture of Mind: A Connectionist Approach." In Michael I. Posner, ed., *Foundations of Cognitive Science.* Cambridge, MA: MIT Press.

Rumelhart, David E., James L. McClelland, and the PDP Research Group. 1986. *Parallel Distributed Processing: Explorations in the Microstructure of Cognition.* Cambridge, MA: MIT Press.

Schumpeter, Joseph A. 1954. *Capitalism, Socialism and Democracy*, 3rd ed. New York: Harper Torchbooks.

Sears, David O. 2001. "The Role of Affect in Symbolic Politics." In James H. Kuklinski, ed., *Citizens and Politics: Perspectives from Political Psychology.* New York: Cambridge University Press.

Sears, David O., and J. L. Freedman. 1967. "Selective Exposure to Information: A Critical Review." *Public Opinion Quarterly* 31:194–213.

Shiffrin, R. M., and W. Schneider. 1997. "Controlled and Automatic Human Information-Processing: Perceptual Learing, Automatic Attending, and a General Theory." *Psychological Review* 84:127–90.

Smith, Eric R. A. N. 1989. *The Unchanging American Voter.* Berkeley: University of California Press.

Smith, Tom W. 1987. "The Welfare State in Cross-National Perspective." *Public Opinion Quarterly* 51:404–21.

Sniderman, Paul M. 1993. "The New Look in Public Opinion Research." In Ada W. Finifter, ed., *Political Science: The State of the Discipline II.* Washington, DC: American Political Science Association.

Sniderman, Paul M., Richard A. Brody, and Philip E. Tetlock. 1991. *Reasoning and Choice: Explorations in Political Psychology.* New York: Cambridge University Press.

Srull, Thomas K. 1984. "Methodological Techniques for the Study of Person Memory and Social Cognition." In Robert S. Wyer and Thomas K. Srull, eds., *Handbook of Social Cognition*, Vol. 2. Hillsdale, NJ: Erlbaum.

Stimson, James. 1991. *Public Opinion in America: Moods, Cycles, and Swings.* Boulder, CO: Westview Press.

Stoker, Laura. 2001. "Political Value Judgments." In James H. Kuklinski, ed., *Citizens and Politics: Perspectives from Political Psychology.* New York: Cambridge University Press.

Stouffer, Samuel. 1955. *Communism, Conformity, and Civil Liberties.* New York: Doubleday.

Sullivan, John L., James Piereson, and George E. Marcus. 1982. *Political Tolerance and American Democracy.* Chicago: University of Chicago Press.

Taber, Charles F., Jill Glathar, and Milton Lodge. 2001. "The Motivational Construction of Political Judgments." In James H. Kuklinski, ed., *Citizens and Politics: Perspectives from Political Psychology.* New York: Cambridge University Press.

Tajfel, Henri. 1981. *Human Groups and Social Categories.* Cambridge: Cambridge University Press.

Tomkins, Sylvan S. 1981. "The Quest for Primary Motives: Biography and Autobiography of an Idea." *Journal of Personality and Social Psychology* 41:306–29.

Turner, John C. 1987. *Rediscovering the Social Group: A Self-Categorization Theory.* New York: Basil Blackwell.

Tversky, Amos, and Daniel Kahneman. 1974. "Judgment under Uncertainty: Heuristics and Biases." *Science* 185:1124–31.

1981. "The Framing of Decisions and the Psychology of Choice." *Science* 211:453–8.

Tyler, S. W., P. T. Hertel, M. McCallum, and H. C. Ellis. 1979. "Cognitive Effort and Memory." *Journal of Experimental Psychology* 5:607–17.

Zajonc, Robert B. 1980. "Feeling and Thinking: Preferences Need No Inferences." *American Psychologist* 35:151–75.

Zaller, John R. 1990. "Political Awareness, Opinion Leadership, and the Mass Survey Response." *Social Cognition* 8:125–53.

1992. *The Nature and Origins of Mass Opinion.* New York: Cambridge University Press.

Part IV   Political Psychology and
Aggregate Opinion

8

The Micro Foundations of Mood

JAMES A. STIMSON

Public opinion matters in a democracy because it is presumed to influence government. The level at which that influence is realized is the macro level, the polity. Thus work that aspires to connect public opinion to the myriad political activities beyond the public is aggregate. Theories that connect aggregate opinion to politics are macro theories.

My own work (Stimson 1991, 1998) and Erikson, MacKuen, and Stimson (2001) push public opinion to macro theoretic connections, a scholarly trend that can also be seen in works by Page and Shapiro (1992) and Mayer (1992). My own work on domestic policy mood (along with most of Page and Shapiro's efforts) is macro in another sense as well. It begins with fully aggregated data. It attempts universal coverage of the American survey research record of measured policy preferences, an attempt much too ambitious to permit analysis of individual-level data – even though all survey data are collected from individuals and a large proportion of the studies are available as individual-level data. The task of analyzing all those micro data is too daunting. Analyses therefore build on survey marginals, the national percentages choosing one or another survey response option.

Beginning with survey marginals is a wonderfully efficient noise reduction mechanism. The marginals retain the information one wants about movements of opinion between studies and over time but lose the vastly larger variance associated with between-individual differences. The price one pays is twofold. First, one loses the ability to address questions at other levels of aggregation. Do preference trends vary by race, or region,

---

This chapter is based upon a paper written earlier. Since that time, some revised sections of the paper, particularly the analysis of aggregated effects, have been incorporated in Chapter 6 of Erikson, MacKuen, and Stimson (2001). The remainder of the chapter is partially revised to incorporate data that became available after the original paper was written.

or gender? These sorts of questions cannot be addressed because the needed distinctions are already lost in the marginals data from which analysis begins. Second, and more important, the method deprives us of the opportunity to witness the aggregation process that underlies everything. We wish to know what macro movements mean, and for that it is important to know who – what kinds of citizens – is doing the changing when aggregate change is recorded.

It is this second limitation that motivates this chapter. Having observed aggregate variation that is descriptively intriguing and consequential for elections (Erikson et al. in press; Stimson 1991, 1998) and of direct influence on public policy (Erikson et al. in press), it now becomes important to find out more about what drives these aggregate preferences.

The strategy for finding out more about aggregation is to abandon, for the moment, the fully aggregated data and attempt a similar analysis that begins with individuals. A convenient means to do so is to focus on the General Social Survey (GSS) series. The GSS presents many of the same indicators of policy preferences year after year in a tightly controlled survey design that maximizes opportunities for longitudinal analysis. This, to be sure, is not the full survey record from which the aggregate policy mood measure is developed (Stimson 1991). It spans 1973–96 in this analysis, a little more than half of the full period of analysis. And it provides a very limited set of indicators continuously present for the full period.

With the policy mood series in hand, we have the advantage of knowing what an aggregation of GSS (or any other) series ought to look like if its items are representative of the universe of policy preferences. Thus we need not ask about the face validity of the GSS indicators – and if we did, we wouldn't like the answers. We can instead go ahead and construct a series that aggregates the items and ask if it does or does not track the policy mood concept. That is how we shall proceed.

The tasks ahead are to review the macro mood concept and measure, to develop an analogue from the GSS individual data, to validate the latter against the former, and then, having done so, to inquire into the micro foundations of mood. We turn first to the concept and measure of mood, dealing with it as first presented, at the macro level.

THE CONCEPT AND MEASURE OF MOOD

Imagine a mass public that has views about the role of government and that generalizes those views toward most of the activities that government engages in. Such favorable or unfavorable views, along with the supporting emotional orientation, would be expected to rise and fall over time, as government intervention is alternately viewed as the solution to public problems or as a problem in itself. This rising and falling, seen as a passive response of whole publics, is "domestic policy mood" (Stimson 1991, 1998).

Policy mood is global, rather than particular, in two senses. The first of these is that it conceives not of movements back and forth from left to right, or from right to left, by small numbers of citizens, but rather of whole distributions of opinion that move gently back and forth over time and circumstance. Liberals, moderates, and conservatives all stay in place in relative terms, while at the margin the whole becomes more eager for government solutions or more antagonistic to them.

Second, mood is conceived as global in the sense that it applies generally to all government domestic activities. In this conception, citizens need not distinguish between environment, public health, education, or the myriad other activities in which government plays a role. They can be for more or less government in general.

The global policy perspective may be seen as a common factor model. We conceive a common set of attitudes, attitudes toward government itself, to cause some of the variation observed in each specific policy controversy. The events and debates specific to a given domain then are allowed to explain the balance of attitudes in that area. How much of the variation in each policy area is common and how much is specific to the domain then become empirical questions, subject to estimation of a rough and ready sort.

This conception demands little of the public. It is the public opinion of the "cognitive miser." The individual citizen need only (1) have a general orientation toward government and (2) change it modestly over the years in response to events, conditions, symbols, and rhetoric. He or she need not be informed of any of the specifics of policy debates, needs to know no facts or arguments. The "constraint" (Converse 1964) that makes mood global requires only a consistent attitude toward government, the common element in all public policy debates and in survey questions about opinion. That requires no intellectual investment and minimal cognitive ability.

Opinion that is global across policies has, in principle, testable empirical implications. It leads us to expect that separately derived series of attitudes toward various policy specifics should move in tandem over time. Such analyses are performed in Stimson (1991, 1998) and will be briefly reprised here. The assumption that movements in opinion represent movements of whole distributions of citizen views over time, on the other hand, is necessarily an assumption for macro analyses. Moving from primitive assumption to testable assertion is the principal burden of this chapter. We digress to review the evidence about a connection between policy views over time. We ask, "Are opinion tracks parallel?"

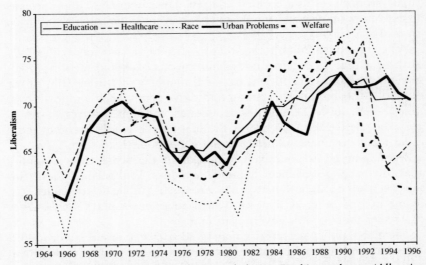

Figure 8.1. Five issue tracks from the extended New Deal issue cluster. (All series are smoothed with a three-year moving average.) Source: Modified from Stimson (1999).

Is Opinion Parallel?

Expectations about the longitudinal track of public opinion series are clearly a function of our beliefs about the structure of opinion. If we believe that Americans view most policies as separate domains calling for attitudes suited to the facts of the case, then we would expect policy attitudes to be independent of one another over time. We could, for example, witness consensus on the need for greater government involvement in one area – say health care – and at the same time large-scale support for drawbacks in another – education, the environment, racial equality, and so forth. Much commentary about American politics is consistent with such an expectation. If, on the other hand, we believe that attitudes are global, toward government activity in general, then we expect to see relatively parallel tracks of opinion in the various policy domains.

The data are voluminous, and our opportunity to deal with them here is quite limited, so we present a highly summarized snapshot of parallelism in Figure 8.1.[1] The figure contains independently estimated issue

---

1 The estimates are central tendencies of all available survey marginals for policy preferences questions asked in an identical format over time. The estimation technology (see Stimson 1991, 1999) has a logic akin to that of principal components analysis, and thus the estimates may be thought of as something like factor scores.

tracks for the domains of education, welfare, racial equality, health, and urban problems, a reasonably complete canvas of the extended New Deal issue domain. Each of the series is smoothed with a three-year moving average, a process that dampens sampling fluctuation (particularly in the early years, when the estimation is based on relatively thin data) and highlights long-term movement.

With some pretty limited exceptions, the message of Figure 8.1 is that policy preferences move in parallel. One can see little movements here and there that suggest reaction to policy specifics. But what is mainly seen is common movement, back and forth, as Americans have altered between relatively favorable and relatively unfavorable views of government activity. Indeed, the parallelism is so substantial that a policy maker could use knowledge of the tracks of opinion in any one area to estimate opinion drift accurately in another. This suggests that attending to global public opinion shifts is both effective and economical as a means to factor knowledge of public opinion into public policy decisions. This particular evidence cannot tell us that policy makers *do* attend to public mood; it does say that they *could*.

Figure 8.1 suggests that we might encapsulate most of what we know about these five policy domains (and others) within a single concept and a single measure. That measure is estimated from all domestic policy survey marginals, without regard to specifics, and displayed in Figure 8.2. It has some of the appearance of the descriptive lore of political eras, and tends to validate some common assertions as the liberal character of the 1960s or the reverse in the 1980s. It deviates a bit from the lore in appearing to build to its peaks of liberalism and conservatism before those movements were generally recognized to be underway. This suggests a sustained but subtle buildup of demands for government action (in the late 1950s) or inaction (in the late 1970s), eventually recognized and acted upon in the eras that become known as distinctive. This is consistent, we shall see, with a similar lag between changes in policy preference (mood) and changes in self-identified ideology.

All of this is a restatement. We turn now to the novel task of this chapter, exploring the micro-level phenomena captured in macro mood. We begin the task by developing an individual-level measure of the phenomenon.

A MICRO VIEW OF MOOD

For the larger task of measuring the movement of policy preferences over time, one would not wish to be restricted to particular policies, particular survey houses, or particular questions. And thus our strategy has been to use all existing series of policy preference data. But for the task at

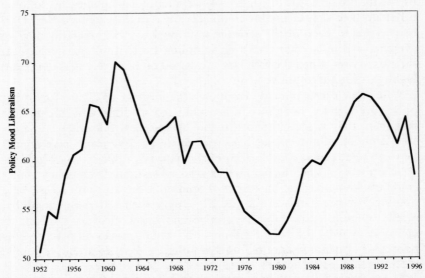

Figure 8.2. Domestic policy mood, estimated from all survey organization series of domestic policy preferences: 1956–96.

hand, examining the views of the individuals who are the ultimate data source, we need the design control of a single set of studies posing exactly the same questions over time. That isn't possible for the full span of our interest, but for the period beginning in 1973 – with only occasional lapses – the GSS does provide the leverage needed. Their national cross sections answer many of the same policy preference questions year after year, giving us an opportunity to dip below the marginals and study individual behavior.

Before we can know that we are dealing with the same concept at both the macro and micro levels, we need to develop an alternative measure from the GSS materials and then to demonstrate that it taps the same concept, domestic policy mood, as do the more diverse materials with which we started. We begin with measurement development.

Step 1: A Measure from Micro Data

The GSS presents an impressively rich collection of measured policy preferences. But most of the measures span only subsets of the twenty-four-year GSS series. And strict continuity of questions is necessary for developing a valid over-time measure with individual data. Within the GSS, the only series that are lengthy enough to span a worthwhile period are the spending priorities questions. These begin with a common lead-in:

We are faced with many problems in this country, none of which can be solved easily or inexpensively. I'm going to name some of these problems, and for each one I'd like you to tell me whether you think we're spending too much money on it, too little money, or about the right amount. Are we spending too much, too little, or about the right amount on?

and then probe particular spending priorities:

1. *. . . solving the problems of the big cities?*
2. *. . . improving and protecting the nation's health?*
3. *. . . welfare?*
4. *. . . improving the conditions of blacks?*
5. *. . . improving and protecting the environment?*
6. *. . . improving the nation's education system?*
7. *. . . the military, arms, and defense?*

These data are available for all the same years, 1973–96, except for four years (1979, 1981, 1992, 1995) when there was no study. Although they cover a limited range of controversies, these series are very well behaved. And we shall soon see that this limited range of materials tracks well with the full range of domestic policy captured in the policy mood concept. Because the same measures are available for all years, the established technology of principal components analysis is a straightforward means to extract the common component, if any, that underlies them. Such an analysis, based now on individual data, produces an obvious single-factor solution with strong positive loadings for all domestic spending preferences and the expected negative loading for national defense. A factor score can be extracted from the micro data. Once rescaled (mean, 50; standard deviation, 10) to approximate the aggregate policy mood measure, it serves as the micro-level analogue to the policy mood concept. Its virtue for these analyses is that it takes on a value for each (nonmissing) GSS respondent.

Step 2: Validation

The measure (see Figure 8.3) shows the same general pattern, for this limited eighteen-year period, as seen before – a growth of conservatism climaxing in 1980, followed by steady movement toward liberal preferences after 1980, peaking around 1990. Although now an individual-level measure, with no respondent appearing in more than one study, the aggregation of the individual values takes on much the same appearance as the aggregate time series with which we began. Such a side-by-side comparison is presented in Figure 8.4, where we see aggregate policy

Figure 8.3. Domestic policy mood estimated from GSS spending priorities questions: 1973–96. Source: GSS.

mood, based upon marginals from the universe of survey organizations, arrayed against the GSS factor score data aggregated by year. In Figure 8.4, we see substantial longitudinal similarity between the macro mood measure (derived from marginals) and the factor score here derived from GSS micro data. Correlating at about .95, the separately derived series are clearly tapping the same concept for the period for which the GSS measure is available. Thus we shall proceed to call the GSS measure the "policy mood" and use it in individual-level analyses to stand in for the macro level concept.

WHO MOVES MOOD?: THREE STORIES ABOUT AGGREGATION

When we observe macro behaviors, such as systematic movements in policy preferences, and wish to ascribe them to individual-level behaviors, there are three sorts of common stories we would tell. Each connects what we know about individuals to what we observe in the aggregate, but they make different assumptions about the process and yield remarkably different conclusions about the meanings to be ascribed to public opinion shifts. We take them up here.

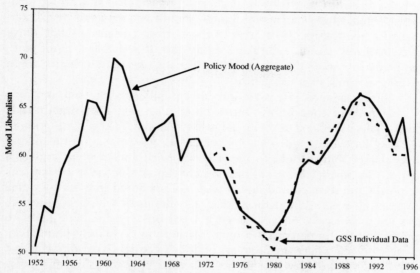

Figure 8.4. Domestic policy mood, all survey organizations 1956–96, and GSS, 1973–96.

The simplest of the stories we'll call the "baseline model." It holds that the macro behavior is the same as the individual behavior. A macro opinion shift of x points thus arises from an electorate in which each citizen moves x points. For more realism, we allow individuals to vary in their opinion movements, some more, some less, and assert that the macro movement arises from a distribution of individual movements, randomly distributed around a central tendency that is identical to the macro opinion change. This inference, when it is in fact wrong, is the classical ecological fallacy (Robinson 1950).

A plausible alternative to the baseline model postulates that mass electorates are mainly inert, not moving at all. In this story, macro-level movements arise from an opinion elite, a refined segment of the electorate that is atypically informed about and interested in public affairs. The opinion elite story has macro variation arising from a mass component varying randomly around a true mean of zero and a small elite segment with highly patterned movement. The usual mathematics of aggregation gain tell us that in such a scenario the macro signal would faithfully mirror the elite movement, entirely ignoring the large, more typical, mass opinion shifts, whose randomness yields a zero expectation. Given the standard view that opinion elites evince committed political behavior that is both stable and predictable – in a word, ideo-logical – macro movements in opinion should be seen as of trivial con-sequence to politics. In a world where most citizens do not move (systematically) at all, and where those who do move have prior com-mitments to one or the other side in politics, aggregate changes might connote nothing of consequence.

A third standard interpretation, one popular in the old standard Michigan voter conceptions, turns the opinion elite conception upside down. This peripheral voter model is like the opinion elite conception in rejecting large-scale individual movement as an explanation for macro-level change, but it looks to the least informed and involved segments as the "dynamic element" of opinion change. In this view, it is citizens atypically uninformed and uninvolved, not anchored in place by stable motivation, who account for change. If millions of teenagers, after all, can know precisely when to switch from one style of blue jeans to another, policy preference too might be little more than fashion. If so, those who don't care much about politics, who lack commitment to a motivated point of view, should be most susceptible to fashionable polit-ical views. This peripheral voter explanation also tends to discount the importance of macro-level movements. It holds that most persons do not change at all; it disparages those who do. Fashion and fad are real enough and can have important short-term impacts, but those who follow fashion in politics will predictably move on to other views.

The three stories are ideal types. We do not expect any of them to be fully accurate. Politics, more likely, will be some mixture of all. It becomes important to determine the recipe for the mix. In addressing the question, we have a crucial design advantage. Because we ask "Who moves mood?" we have the observed macro movement itself as a stan-dard against which to judge individuals. As a consequence, we don't suffer the usually debilitating inability to observe change and judge whether its character is systematic or random.

Estimating the Incidence of Nonattitudes

The question to be investigated is, who moves when mood moves? Which of the ideal types seems best to comport with the data? To gain some leverage, we observe changes of preference by citizens over time in categories of their personal attributes that ought to be associated with "elite," "peripheral," or "mass" standing. The GSS offers few attractive choices for this stratification, so we shall have to content ourselves with what's there. One of these is the old standard, years of formal education.

We know how macro mood moves over time. What we now wish to know is what sorts of citizens, by the criterion of education, contribute

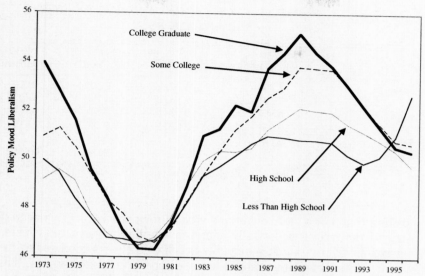

Figure 8.5. GSS policy mood for four education groups. Source: GSS.

most to the observed movement. Is it the best educated who most resemble the macro result, support for an opinion elite model? Is it the least, support for a peripheral voter model? Or is movement relatively uniform?

We begin by coding education into standard categories: "less than high school," "high school graduate," "some college," and "college graduate (or more)." It is then easy enough to observe opinion movements in these subaggregates, which we do in Figure 8.5.

What we can see from the figure is that the better educated are a little more responsive. They move in the same pattern as the nation, but do so more dramatically. The pattern of movement shows monotonic declines in responsiveness as we move from college graduates, to college attenders, to noncollege groups.

The data in Figure 8.5 are flatly inconsistent with the peripheral voter conception of opinion change. Insofar as we can locate possible peripherals among the least educated, the pattern observed is the opposite of that expected. This group shows the least, not the greatest, apparent responsiveness. It makes the smallest contribution to the macro movement.

Employing variance as an indicator of systematic movement, a clear pattern emerges: the better educated move more (and, from Figure 8.5, move more systematically) over time. Variance is monotonically related

Stimson

Table 8.1. *Regressions of Within-Education Group Policy Mood on Macro Policy Mood*

	Less Than High School	High School Graduates	Some College	College Graduates
Intercept	11.88	3.22	4.51	9.74
	(7.63)	(4.13)	(4.86)	(6.97)
Slope	0.80	0.95	0.92	0.84
	(0.13)	(0.07)	(0.08)	(0.12)
R^2	0.64	0.89	0.85	0.70
Group variance	19.82	23.73	30.08	49.99

For all groups, $N = 20$.

to education. For a more quantified view of the phenomenon, we regress each of the series on the fully aggregated policy mood series.[2] These regressions tell us, one at a time, how each of the parts is related to the whole – which contribute more, less, or nothing to the aggregate. The unambiguous message of Table 8.1 is that all education groups move largely in parallel, and all contribute substantially to macro variation. Slopes range from .80 to .95, R^2 from a low of .64 to a high of .89.

The question then reduces to the mixture of the remaining alternatives: baseline and opinion elite. The baseline model clearly predicts movements that are relatively uniform and of equal magnitude across the categories of this criterion. If the opinion elite model holds, we would expect most movement to originate among the best educated, with inertia elsewhere the norm.

To gain further leverage on the question, let us presume that the data are generated by a "black and white" (Converse 1964) sort of model, where each of the groups is an aggregate of some respondents who respond strongly and regularly to changes in political context and some who do not respond at all – because their survey responses express no meaningful attitudes.

We then ask: What proportion of each group is of each type? An opinion elite conception would predict that most of the systematic response arises from the better educated. If only an elite is in tune with national political cues, then the observed responses should be a (gray) aggregation of small numbers responding very strongly and large

2 Each of the series is first transformed to match the mean and variance of the fully aggregated series. In this way, the unstandardized slope coefficients capture the series' impact without the distortion of differences in variance.

numbers who are unresponsive. A strong version of the opinion elite conception – where the size of the elite is very small – leads us to expect elite influence only among the best educated, where it would be numerically small. As one moves down the ladder of educational attainment, the elite proportion should virtually vanish. The baseline conception, on the other hand, leads us to expect a substantially meaningful response from all educational strata.

We use the observed responses to calibrate the proportions of systematic opinion changers (labeled "meaningful") versus those whose opinions are not meaningful and who therefore cannot experience meaningful change (labeled "random"). We employ as a measure of group responsiveness the range of opinion change, from 1980 to 1990, low and high points, respectively. This simple yardstick captures much of the systematic movement in opinion for the period of analysis.

Since those who respond randomly produce no systematic change in the aggregate, we assume that the range of opinion change is proportional to the number of meaningful responders. Without further assumptions, then, we can easily characterize the relative proportions of meaningful and random response by education. To estimate absolute proportions, one further assumption is required. We assume further that the highest education category, college graduates and beyond, consists of 90% meaningful responders and 10%, who, despite their relatively elite educational backgrounds, still have so little interest and involvement in politics that they lack meaningful policy preferences. Obviously arbitrary, that assumption still is more realistic than its alternative, the assumption that all of the well educated are meaningful responders.

Now we can proceed to estimate the incidence of attitudes and nonattitudes with just a little algebra. We observe a net range of 9.96 points among the best educated. We presume that the observed range is an aggregation of the $p = 90\%$, whose response is unknown (denoted x_s for systematic) and the $q = 10\%$, whose response is zero by assumption (denoted x_r for random). Thus:

$$\sum_{i=1}^{p+q} \frac{x_i}{(p+q)} = \sum_{j=1}^{p} \frac{x_{js}}{p} + \sum_{k=1}^{q} \frac{x_{kr}}{q} \quad \text{with} \quad E(x_{.r}) = 0.0$$

Nature presents us with the left side of the equation, with the two types already mixed. We wish to know $E(x_{.s})$, the undiluted response of the systematic responders only. That can be derived simply by dividing the overall estimate by p, our assumed .90 proportion of systematic types. The result, about 11.06, is now an estimate of the true, but unobserved, systematic response. With that in hand, we can now solve the

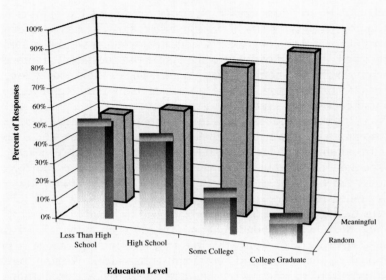

Figure 8.6. Estimated incidence of meaningful and random response for four education groups. Source: GSS.

equations for each of the education groups for p and q, the proportions of meaningful and random responders, respectively.

The estimated proportions for each group are graphed in Figure 8.6. The breakdowns are 90–10% (by assumption) for the college graduates, 80–20% for those with some college, and about 52–48% for the two noncollege groups. The absolute numbers are only as good as our assumption about the college graduates. But it is important to notice the relative pattern, which is of gentle, gradual decline in the number of systematic responses as one moves from highest to lowest educational group. With traces of support for an opinion elite conception, these data are mainly supportive of more uniform opinion response by all sectors of the electorate. For further leverage on this issue, we try a different criterion, vocabulary usage.

Vocabulary Usage.[3] The GSS administers, on an intermittent basis, a variation on the Gallup–Thorndike Verbal Intelligence Test. This is a passive recognition scheme in which respondents are presented, one at a time, with ten vocabulary items. The items are introduced as things not generally known, and respondents are urged to "guess" at the correct

3 I am grateful to David Sears for suggesting this criterion.

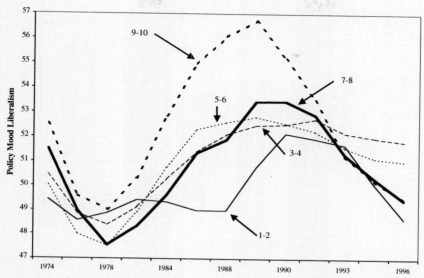

Figure 8.7. Policy mood by vocabulary knowledge test. Scores are numbers of correct answers. Source: GSS.

meaning of the word from a list of five synonyms.[4] The scale is then simply the number correct, recoded here to five categories.

An unusual sort of criterion, this test of verbal skills ought to be associated with unusually high or low standing in the electorate. To examine whether it is, we repeat the procedure followed with the education criterion. We first look at what sorts of verbal skills are associated with systematic responses of policy preference in Figure 8.7.

Figure 8.7 shows a pattern notably similar to what we have already seen with education. All verbal levels seem to move pretty much in tandem and to match closely the aggregated series. Those with the very lowest verbal skills are most different from the others. This evidence, again, is flatly inconsistent with the peripheral voter conception of opinion change. If the periphery can be equated with minimal verbal skills, then the result is just the opposite; the low-skill respondents disrupt the general pattern, they do not produce it. The question again

4 The National Opinion Research Center does not divulge the items used in order that it may administer the same items over time without fear that respondents might have been sensitized to the words from publicity of a previous study. The GSS codebook for the variable, "WORDSUM," gives as an example "beast," with an answer set that includes "animal" and four obviously wrong alternatives.

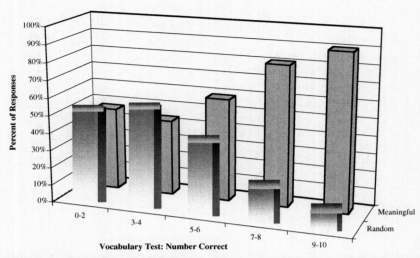

Figure 8.8. Estimated meaningful and random response for five vocabulary skills groups. Source: GSS.

comes down to choosing as between opinion elite and baseline conceptions of change. With four of five groups behaving almost identically, the preliminary nod must go to the naive baseline conception.

We break the five vocabulary groups into systematic responders and nonattitudes responders in Figure 8.8. We have again assumed that the highest group, those scoring 9 or 10 out of 10, are 90% systematic types and 10% nonattitudes types. That produces an estimate of true response of about 10.67, a little lower than the education-based estimate. The pattern of Figure 8.8 is similar to what we saw before, showing relatively gradual declines in systematic response as one moves from highest to lowest verbal skills, but with the lowest-scoring two groups slightly out of expected ordering. Verbal skill clearly matters for systematic opinion holding and systematic opinion change, but with half or more of the electorate looking systematic, there is no basis for an opinion elite model. The naive conception is again triumphant. Impressive aggregate change in opinion is produced, that is, by large-scale and relatively uniform change at the individual level.

What then is the micro foundation of policy mood? What is going on among individuals that gives rise to the systematic aggregate change? The dominant evidence is consistent with a story of individual responses that look much like the aggregate response. Domestic policy mood moves from left to right or right to left because millions of ordinary citizens are themselves moving. There are clear indications of opinion leadership among the best educated, to be sure, but it is far from dominant. The whole is consistent with a global view of opinion that holds that observed aggregate shifts result from marginal shifts in the whole distribution of attitudes. And we may also assert the negative. The systematic patterns in the aggregate do not arise from systematic movements by only a relative handful of citizens.

EXPLAINING POLICY MOOD

Public policy mood in its original development is a wholly longitudinal concept. It is the over-time movement of central tendencies of public policy preferences. In this analysis we can go beyond central tendencies, for the GSS data permit analysis across individuals as well as over time.[5] We can take up the old question, "What sorts of people hold what sorts of preferences?" along with "How do preferences move over time?" That allows us additionally to examine whether compositional effects, that is, changes in the proportions of various kinds of people over time, can explain all or part of the longitudinal movement.

From fifty years of voting behavior research we derive expectations about cross-sectional explanations of preferences. Within the limits of parsimony and the measures available in the GSS, we examine seven such variables. Party identification, the Michigan measure scored 0 (strong Democrat) to 6 (strong Republican), should be negatively related to mood (itself scored in the liberal direction). The relative conservatism of the South should be captured by a region dummy variable, scored 1 for "South" and "Border" regions, 0 otherwise. For education (scored as years) we have weaker priors. In bivariate analyses its association with income and social class often connects it with conservatism. In a multivariate context, where income and race are controlled, we expect positive association with liberalism. Income, measured in standard categories, is regularly expected to be associated with conservatism. For race, we create two dummy variables for the categories black and other, both of which are expected to be more liberal than the white reference group. And last, women are now (at least) regularly more liberal than men, modeled here with a female dummy variable.

To capture the longitudinal variation in policy mood, we create dummy variables for all of the years in which the measure is available except the last, 1996. To model the variation in mood, both cross-sectional and longitudinal, we estimate a pooled regression (ordinary

---

5 This design does not, however, permit the fine-grained analysis of movements over time, as in Durr (1993). That requires more, and more closely spaced, time points than the GSS permits.

least squares) of the dependent mood variable for the cumulated GSS respondents. We expect the cross-sectional variables to operate as they normally do and the time dummy variables jointly to pick up the same over-time variation as in the aggregate mood measure. For the dummy variable portion of the model, the intercept term will stand for the reference category, white male in 1996.

The estimates are presented in Table 8.2. There we see the cross-sectional priors faithfully mirrored. Republican identification, residence in the South, and high income have negative coefficients, predicting relative conservatism. Black and other racial identities and female gender produce greater relative liberalism. Education, the one we were not quite sure about, is positively associated with liberal policy preferences. A cross-sectional only model (not shown) produces a fit (adjusted R^2) on these noisy individual-level data of .143. To assess whether changes over time matter as well, the set of time dummies is added to the model. The longitudinal information produces an improvement in fit to .181, the difference highly significant ($F = 40.04, p < .00001$) with this large sample.

To assess the import of changes over time, we need to go a step further. We can imagine a scenario in which adding a set of time dummies improves fit but without really explaining the phenomenon at hand. One such possibility is a relatively random set of year-to-year differences that are significant without being the postulated phenomenon. Thus we need to demand that these estimated coefficients be orderly approximations of the postulated movements in mood (which are independent of these GSS data). To determine whether in fact they are, we transform the coefficients by setting 1996 equal to the intercept term and then computing the level for every other year as the intercept plus dummy variable coefficient for that year.

The regression dummy variable coefficients are graphed in Figure 8.9 along with the GSS version of the policy mood concept seen before. It is unimportant that the regression estimates are uniformly more conservative. That is a function of the chosen reference categories (white and male) as well as the values of the other variables. What we do care about is whether the regression estimates track the same over-time pattern. Clearly, they do. The parallelism between the two sets of estimates is striking. The regression estimates look identical to the original (factor analytic) variable, with only the minor distinction of being a bit smoother.[6]

---

6 The greater relative smoothness appears to be a somewhat greater resistance to sampling fluctuation. Since the cross-sectional explanations are controlled in the estimation process, sampling-induced fluctuations in composition have little impact. Fluctuations in the numbers of blacks, for example, both a small

If some portion of the over-time movement of mood were a compositional effect – if it were produced, that is, not by attitude change but by changes in the types of people populating survey samples – then we would expect the regression estimated mood to be an attenuated version of the original. After a control for composition, it should capture only true attitude change. There is no such attenuation. Hence composition effects can be set aside as a possible explanation for over-time attitude shifts.

MOOD AND SELF-IDENTIFICATION

Policy mood represents the longitudinal track of left–right ideology in the American electorate. But it is not the only such representation. Ideological self-identification in the usual language of liberalism and conservatism is a more direct alternative. We simply ask people whether they think of themselves as "liberal" or "conservative" and go from there. Here we examine whether the two approaches measure similar or different ideologies, taking up the issue first at the macro level and then at the micro level.

Macro Connections

To examine the longitudinal movement of self-identified ideology, we exploit the same technology used in developing the policy mood indicator. Using the universe of survey administrations of variations on the question – 557 administrations of twenty-two separate series – we solve for a single time series representing the central tendency of whatever it is that these questions tap. Some cautions are in order before we look at the result. Many survey respondents are clearly unfamiliar with the concepts "liberal" and "conservative," as we have long known (Converse 1964). That is evidenced in the incidence of nonresponse of about a third or more. And we ought to worry, given this evidence, that many of the two-thirds who do attempt a response are trying a little too hard to be cooperative. If ideological terms are an empty vessel for many, it is likely that the void will be filled irregularly. Thus we know that self-claimed liberals and conservatives bring different, but not opposite, connotations to the two terms (Conover and Feldman 1981).

proportion of the electorate and highly distinctive in their views, could produce considerable fluctuations in uncontrolled estimates, which would not appear in the regression estimates, where the contribution of blacks to the overall estimate is explicitly controlled.

Table 8.2. *A Regression of Mood on Cross-Sectional Explanatory Variables and Time Dummy Variables*

Variable	Without Year Dummies	With Year Dummies
Party Identification	−1.03	−1.09
	(0.04)	(0.04)
Region: South and Border	−1.50	−1.61
	(0.21)	(0.20)
Education, years	0.53	0.51
	(0.03)	(0.03)
Income Category	−0.08	−0.19
	(0.03)	(0.03)
Race: Other	3.15	2.11
	(0.55)	(0.54)
Race: Black	7.41	6.90
	(0.24)	(0.24)
Gender: Female	1.45	1.40
	(0.15)	(0.14)
Intercept	45.10	47.24
	(0.37)	(0.51)
1973[a]		0.08
		(0.41)
1974		0.16
		(0.42)
1975		−0.85
		(0.42)
1976		−2.36
		(0.41)
1977		−3.62
		(0.41)
1978		−3.22
		(0.41)
1980		−4.23
		(0.41)
1982		−1.52
		(0.39)
1983		−0.36
		(0.40)
1984		0.68
		(0.57)
1985		0.62
		(0.49)
1986		0.65
		(0.49)
1987		1.13
		(0.53)

Table 8.2. (*contin.*)

Variable	Without Year Dummies	With Year Dummies
1988		2.27
		(0.50)
1989		2.68
		(0.49)
1990		3.73
		(0.51)
1991		2.02
		(0.49)
1993		1.47
		(0.48)
1994		0.14
		(0.40)
N	15,746	15,746
Adjusted R^2	.1426	.1812

[a] A test of the exclusion of the year dummy variables produces an F of 40.04 with an associated p value $<.00001$.

Source: GSS, 1973–93 cumulative.

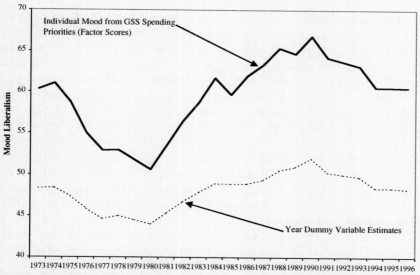

Figure 8.9. Policy mood estimated by factor score and by coefficients from a pooled regression model. Source: GSS.

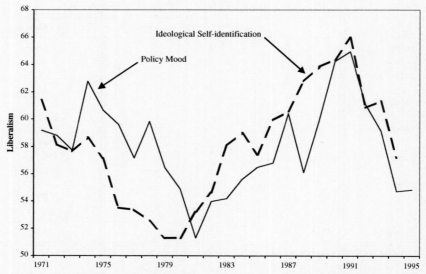

Figure 8.10. Policy mood and liberal–conservative self-identification: 1956–96.

Less documented, but even more troublesome for longitudinal analysis, it seems quite likely that connotations of "liberal" and "conservative" shift with time and political context. As different sets of issues, domestic and foreign, come and go in the national spotlight, the positions that survey respondents think define liberal and conservative ideologies are likely to shift as well. Given a very limited grasp of the central ideological concepts, we would expect many to be highly susceptible to priming effects and, in particular, to defining ideology in terms of the relatively narrow debates of recent weeks more than with enduring and fundamental differences. This is troublesome because the priming is uniform, and therefore this source of error in self-identification will be systematic with respect to time, not random. Aggregation, the usual elixir for random error, will strengthen and compound errors that are uniform or systematic.

We examine the association between the two series, policy mood and self-identified liberalism–conservatism, in Figure 8.10. The story suggested by the figure is that mood and self-identification are loosely connected. The form of that connection is that self-perceptions, in the aggregate, follow changes in policy preferences by a year or two. Over the sweep of almost four decades the two show similar, but far from identical, cycles. A micro story consistent with these aggregates is that citizens change their preferences in response to the state of the economy and in response to previous public policy (Erikson et al. 2001) and then are slow to shift their self-perception to match those new preferences but eventually do so. An error correction scenario is a good fit. Preferences (mood) set an appropriate target level of self-identification. A person with mainly conservative preferences, for example, should think of him- or herself as somewhere near the conservative end of the spectrum. When perception is off target, over time and with experience the person will come to realize that this is so and adjust the self-identification to match the preferences. Given that ideological terms are a near-empty abstraction for most citizens and that political involvement is intermittent at most, we expect the loose abstraction to adjust more readily to the more concrete preferences rather than the reverse. Given that it is an "identification," a part of the self-image, we expect the adjustment to be slow.

For aggregates the time sequence is a testable issue. Whether changes in preference lead to changes in identification or the reverse (or neither) can be determined by a Granger test. The result of numerous such tests is decisive in ruling out the prospect that self-identified ideology causes policy mood. The tests are indecisive in making the case for mood causing self-identified ideology. Over a large number of such tests with slightly differing series and different numbers of lags, about half the time the tests produced evidence of significant (i.e., .05) Granger causality. In the other half they did not. Thus, whether or not such causality exists is best left an open question.[7]

Micro Connections

We can think about the connection of policy preferences to self-identification at either level of analysis.[8] But as is so often the case, when we turn to the individual level for analysis, things get murky. It is simple enough to ask, "Do those who have, say, liberal policy preferences also think of themselves as liberals?" Answering the question is not so simple. The preference measure is correlated with the identification measure ($r = .27$). But that suggests a glass much less than half full. The great bulk of the explanation for why people think of themselves in ideological terms must come from elsewhere than their policy preferences,

7 The Granger test demands significant explanatory ability of the presumed independent variable when the dependent variable is already well explained by its previous values. This is much more than mere correlation. By that lesser standard the two series are definitely associated.

8 We cannot, however, examine hypotheses about preference and identification change with the GSS micro data, for we observe individuals only at a single time.

Table 8.3. *Micro Connections: Self-Identification and Policy Mood*

	Bivariate	With Year Dummies
Policy mood	−0.0387	−0.0408
	(0.0010)	(0.0010)
18 annual dummies		(not shown)[a]
Intercept	6.0040	6.2701
	(0.0529)	(0.0562)
Adjusted R^2	0.0839	0.0928
N	15,053	15,053

[a] For test of a set of 18 annual dummies, $F(18, 15,033) = 9.22$, $p = .0001$.

this analysis must say. Acting from the suspicion that much of what the identification scale measures is simply error, we shall not attempt an explanation here.

Two sorts of analyses promise to help reveal the micro-level links between preference and identification. The first of these addresses the possible spuriousness of the observed connection. In the second, we ask whether the individual-level confusion is lessened by looking at whole categories of self-identification.

We have observed that preferences and identification might or might not move together over time and that they are loosely associated for individuals examined cross-sectionally. In a last statistical step, we use the individual data to examine the robustness of the aggregate association. Aggregate time series might move together causally or spuriously. In the latter case, the association might result from common or parallel movement in time that should be attributed to some third factor tracing a similar path. One means to examine this spuriousness thesis is to model both the cross-sectional and time-serial variation in a pool of dated individual data and ask whether the cross-sectional association for individuals is robust against a challenge from modeling the time-serial variation. We do this by including dummy variables for each GSS study (i.e., year) in a regression of self-identification on policy preferences. If the time-serial connection is wholly or partly spuriously associated with a third factor moving over time, then the individual evidence of association should be attenuated when this blind control for time-serial variation is introduced.

The regressions of Table 8.3 address the issue. The first column is simply a bivariate regression of identification – the 7-point scale – on policy preference (mood). The estimated coefficient is very small and negative, as it should be because (1) the variables have opposite polarities and (2) the variance of the preference measure is much greater than the identification measure. This first regression serves chiefly as a baseline for comparison to the second. There we introduce eighteen annual dummy variables for the nineteen study series and ask whether any part of the cross-sectional association disappears when we control for the common movement over time of the two series. The answer clearly is that none does. The association becomes slightly stronger in the face of controls for time than it was without them.

These two concepts, policy preference and self-identification, are both heralded as measures of "ideology." It is disquieting that their correspondence, both in the aggregate and for individuals, is so limited. But it is not news. Since Free and Cantril (1967) observed that the chasm between them was "so marked as to be almost schizoid," we have known, if not understood, not to expect a close connection. Part of the mismatch is simply that the self-identification measure is unreliable, and therefore its associations with all other variables are strongly attenuated.

To get a feeling for how much attenuation might result from simple unreliability, we break down the preference measure into the categories of self-identification, "extremely Liberal" to "extremely Conservative." If the limited association between preference and identification indicates limited association of the underlying concepts, then we should expect those limits to persist under aggregation. If, on the other hand, unreliability accounts for the slight connection, then the random errors it represents should be self-canceling, leaving strong evidence of an association for aggregates. The visual evidence may be seen in Figure 8.11, where a range of views for each ideological group is presented. The presentation is of one standard deviation above and below the mean mood measure for each group.

Figure 8.11 continues the evidence of contrariness in the mood–identification relationship. One can see monotonic association between identification and mood. The mean levels of mood march steadily downward on the graph as one moves from "extremely liberal" to "extremely conservative." This is the expected evidence of association. But the range of views tells another story. When we look at plus or minus one standard deviation (i.e., the middle 68% of all responses for each group), we see both that the ranges are quite large and that they invariably span both sides of the zero neutral point. Thus every group includes numerous members who claim to be one thing by self-description and advocate the opposite by policy preference choices. That would be expected in the middle of the identification scale. That the relative handful of Americans who are willing to characterize their views as "extreme" includes many who are inconsistent is unexpected. Note also a more subtle pattern: the

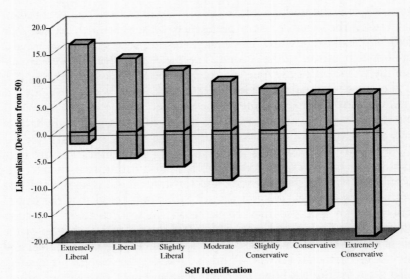

Figure 8.11. Domestic policy mood by self-identified liberalism–conservatism. Bars represent one standard deviation above and below the mean for each group.

discrepancy between preferences (mood) and self-identification is greater for those who claim to be conservatives than for those who claim to be liberals. Those who claim to be liberals by and large are liberals. But relatively many Americans who claim to be conservatives are *not* conservative in their preferences for more or less government. Perhaps a third of all those who style their political views as "conservative" have preferences that lie well on the liberal side of the median voter.[9]

All this does not suggest that self-identification is meaningless. It is behaviorally important that a citizen chooses to call him- or herself "conservative," for example. *It is the inference that this description has anything to do with the issues that usually divides liberals from conservatives in the national elite political dialogue that is dangerous.*

9 A detailed analysis of the domestic spending items that are a prominent part of the GSS Mood measure in Erikson et al. (2001) pinpoints the discrepancy. Many self-styled conservatives advocate more or less across-the-board expansion of government spending in the domestic arena, obviously bringing some connotation to the word "conservative" that does not include the main-line debate between liberals and conservatives about the size and scope of the federal government. Indeed, the modal response to controversial domestic spending issues by self-described liberals, moderates, *and* conservatives is "spend more."

Ever since such measures were introduced, we have been observing self-description and inferring preferences. Because there is huge slippage between description and preference – and particularly because of the asymmetry in this slippage – we ought forever to refrain from drawing this inference. Americans are symbolically conservative; on balance, they prefer conservative self-descriptions to liberal ones. But they are also operationally liberal; given the choice between more government and less, they prefer on balance more. If we choose *either* characterization and think we understand the American electorate, we will be wrong.

CONCLUSIONS

This chapter is about how domestic policy preference, a species of ideology, moves in time and across people. That preference varies between individuals is what gives it interest. That it moves in patterns over time we knew. This chapter, then, is about explaining the one in terms of the other. What we have seen that matters is that the small movements of whole electorates over time may be best understood as arising from small systematic shifts of the whole distribution of opinions over time. Left remains left, right is right, and center is still center. But what left, right, and center mean in concrete policy preferences shift as aggregate opinion shifts.

There would seem to be a simple psychological message in these shifts. We explain individual views as some mix of cognition, affect, and identification. When whole populations move over time, we must look to cognition to account for change. For if change involves some consensual response to the perceived political and policy world, accounting for the consensual aspect requires shared cognitions. The natural view of systematic change is to posit it as a response to experience, and that entails changing cognitions. That suggests that we look to real politics and real policy to explain changing attitudes.

To look at the same phenomenon across time and across people is to come to terms with how different these modes of explanation are. The over-time pattern that motivates this research is really very small. But small movements that are wholly systematic take on great importance. The difference between people, the cross-sectional variance, is really very large. Because that is so, nothing as small as the systematic over-time variation is ever likely to arise from cross-sectional analyses. One doesn't pursue small sources of variance at the expense of large ones. But aggregate-level research must be wholly uninformed about how aggregates move. Jamming both together has proven worthwhile.

References

Conover, Pamela Johnston, and Stanley Feldman. 1981. "The Origins and Meaning of Liberal/Conservative Self-Identifications." *American Journal of Political Science* 25:617–45.

Converse, Philip E. 1964. "The Nature of Belief Systems in Mass Publics." In David E. Apter, ed., *Ideology and Discontent.* New York: Free Press.

Durr, Robert H. 1993. "What Moves Policy Sentiment?" *American Political Science Review* 87:158–70.

Erikson, Robert S., Michael B. MacKuen, and James A. Stimson. 2001. *The Macro Polity.* New York: Cambridge University Press.

Free, Lloyd A., and Albert Hadley Cantril. 1967. *The Political Beliefs of Americans.* New Brunswick, NJ: Rutgers University Press.

Mayer, William G. 1992. *The Changing American Mind: How and Why American Public Opinion Changed Between 1960 and 1988.* Ann Arbor: University of Michigan Press.

Page, Benjamin I., and Robert Y. Shapiro. 1992. *The Rational Public: Fifty Years of Trends in Americans' Policy Preferences.* Chicago: University of Chicago Press.

Robinson, W. S. 1950. "Ecological Correlations and the Behavior of Individuals." *American Sociological Review* 15:351–7.

Stimson, James A. 1991. *Public Opinion in America: Moods, Cycles, and Swings.* Boulder, CO: Westview Press.

1998. *Public Opinion in America: Moods, Cycles, and Swings,* 2nd ed. Boulder, CO: Westview Press.

9

From Denial to Extenuation (and Finally Beyond): Political Sophistication and Citizen Performance

ROBERT C. LUSKIN

For a long time now, an extremely large chunk of political psychology has revolved around political *sophistication*, meaning roughly the extent and organization of an individual's stored political cognition, and more or less equivalent variables. Two other terms having some currency, *expertise* and *cognitive complexity*, are synonymous (the former entirely, the latter in its most usual sense). *Constraint*, a term whose popularity is mercifully fading, has frequently been used to mean the correlations or other statistical patterning of attitudes across individuals but was originally intended and is still sometimes used to mean sophistication's organizational side. *Ideology*, in certain of its numerous meanings, is also related, an ideology being what someone who is highly sophisticated has. Perhaps the most currently popular term is *information*, which in its relevant sense is just the complement of constraint in its original sense – the quantity of stored cognition, organization aside. *Knowledge*, also popular, is the same, except for the additional connotation of accuracy.

In practice, even these last subtle distinctions melt away. A few poor scraps of information do not need or receive much cataloging, while great vast heaps of it cannot be retained without it. It is somewhat easier to find people who have lots of well-organized but frequently incorrect information, a case well illustrated, a few years ago, by the followers of Lyndon Larouche. But this combination too is rare. By and large, the people who have lots of information are also those whose information

I worked on this chapter while Chercheur Associé at the Centre d'Etude de la Vie Politique Française of the Fondation Nationale des Sciences Politiques, Paris, supported by a Faculty Research Assignment from the University Research Institute of the University of Texas. I am grateful to Jongho Lee for assistance, to George Marcus, Tali Mendelberg, Benjamin Page, and Daron Shaw for comments, and to Christopher Bratcher for both.

is better organized and more largely correct, making information, knowledge, and sophistication highly collinear. From here on I shall treat these terms too as synonymous.[1]

DENIAL

The essay that did more than anything else to put this cognitive variable stage center was Converse's (1964) "The Nature of Belief Systems in Mass Publics." The most prominent of the questions Converse posed, and answered darkly – the degree to which ordinary citizens are in the main sophisticated or unsophisticated – has occasioned reams of revisionist and counter-revisionist research. At long last, and despite some flickering dissent (for example, in Dalton and Wattenberg 1993), there now seems to be near-consensus that by anything approaching elite standards most citizens think and know jaw-droppingly little about politics.

This evolution has been partly methodological, toward better measurement. Practice is hardly uniform, even now, but there has been a gradual shifting away from the physically aggregate devices critiqued in my other contribution to this volume, which for reasons given there tend to give a grossly exaggerated view of the structuredness of the underlying cognition. The only other evidence of purportedly high (or even moderate) or increasing sophistication has been of three sorts. One batch of literature used shoddy knockoffs of *The American Voter*'s famed "levels of conceptualization" (Nie, Verba, and Petrocik 1976). Long since discredited (Luskin 1987; Smith 1989), these measures initially showed a dramatic increase in mean sophistication, then (as their authors fell silent) an equally dramatic decrease.[2] As Luskin (1987:888) remarks, "people do not build or forget complex [political belief systems] so quickly."[3]

The second sort of evidence, this supposedly indicating considerable if not necessarily increasing sophistication, comes from intensive, probing interviews of the sort pioneered by Robert Lane (1962, 1969,

1 For more on such definitional matters, see Luskin (1987).
2 Mistakenly, in my view, Smith (1989) argues that the original levels of conceptualization, too, were fatally flawed. I present evidence that a somewhat redrawn and streamlined version performs very well, if not quite as well as the factual measures I plump for in the end (Luskin 1987 and this volume).
3 Interestingly, Nie's latest book spends a good deal of its length trying to explain why political sophistication has *not* increased, despite massive increases in education and what he and his coauthors see as education's sizable individual-level effect on sophistication (Nie, Junn, and Stehlik-Barry 1996).

1973) and more recently undertaken by Jennifer Hochschild (1981). As a means of gauging sophistication, this approach mainly misses the point, valuable though it may be for generating – never testing – hypotheses about the nature of such cognition as exists. I expand on the nature of this misdirectedness, what I call "forgetting the denominator," below.

But the approach is also unreliable and biased in roughly statistical senses, and the latter in ways destined to produce an impression of greater sophistication than exists. One problem is sorting out what affects what, even within the sample. With dozens of variables romping around a book based on fifteen observations (as in Lane 1962), degrees of freedom run heavily in the red. Another problem is knowing what to make of the sample. The interviewees are not a probability sample, and even if they were, the slender *n* would bar confident generalization. Yet another problem is knowing what to make of measurement that goes beyond obtrusive to intrusive. This is where part of the bias comes in, as the probing style of the unstructured interviews almost certainly creates opinion as much as measures it. And a final problem is knowing how far to trust the analyst's constructions. This too is a source of bias, as the interpretive style of analysis, coupled with the necessity of saying *something*, in the interest of publication, invites the attribution of reasoning and motives well beyond anything actually in the psyches of the interviewees.[4]

The third sort of evidence, this supposedly indicative of increasing sophistication, lies in the spread of formal education, acclaimed by Inglehart and followers as "cognitive mobilization," on the mistaken assumption that increases in formal education bring comparable increases in political knowledge (Dalton 1984; Inglehart 1977, 1990).[5] In fact, education is only lightly related to sophistication (Luskin 1990; Luskin and Ten Barge 1995), as should hardly surprise anyone who has observed the enormous range of ability and knowledge (about no matter what) among students all getting university degrees, indeed all from the same university.[6]

By contrast, the methodological turn that has gradually been settling this question has been toward more direct measurement, of what people actually know and more often don't know about politics. Measures of this sort paint a very dark picture indeed. The gap between the most and least informed is almost unimaginably vast, "orders of magnitudes of

---

4 See Feldman and Zaller (1992) for a similar critique.
5 Dalton's most recent treatment (1996) is more complex, making an independent but highly circumstantial case that political information, not just education, has increased.
6 Cf. Delli Carpini and Keeter (1996); Nie et al. (1996); and Luskin (this volume).

orders of magnitudes" (Converse 1990:373). The mass public contains lay members resembling political commentators. For that matter, it contains political commentators. But it also contains a great many more people who know next to nothing about politics. A certain small percentage of the American public, at any given time, do not know who the president is. Roughly a quarter do not know who the vice president is. The average American's ability to place the Democratic and Republican parties and "liberals" and "conservatives" correctly on issue dimensions and the two parties on a liberal–conservative dimension scarcely exceeds and indeed sometimes falls short of what could be achieved by blind guessing. The verdict is stunningly, depressingly clear: most people know very little about politics, and the distribution behind that statement has changed little if at all over the survey era (Bennett 1989, 1993, 1995; Delli Carpini and Keeter 1996; Kinder and Sears 1985; Luskin 1987; Price 1999).

EXTENUATION

Yet the controversy over how sophisticated most people are has not really died so much as transformed itself. The Panglossian line has merely shifted from denial to extenuation. People are said to practice low-information rationality, implicitly claimed to be not too much inferior to the high-information kind (Popkin 1992). Their beliefs may lack the overarching structure of "ideology" but are nonetheless lent coherence by more psychologically disaggregated entities like schemas and values (Conover and Feldman 1984; Feldman 1988; Hamill, Lodge, and Blake 1985). They engage in "on-line" as distinct from "memory-based" processing, updating their attitudes in response to new information without needing to retain the information past the moment of updating (Lodge, Steenbergen, and Brau 1995). They can still navigate the political landscape by noting the locations of the leaders of parties or groups they like or dislike (Brady and Sniderman 1985; Popkin 1992; Sniderman, Brody, and Tetlock 1991). They may vote heavily on the basis of the candidates' personal characteristics but are doing so as a means of generating reasonable predictions about performance in office (Miller, Wattenberg, and Malanchu 1986; Rahn, Aldrich, Borgida, and Sullivan 1990). Or their opinions may be awash in nonattitudinal noise at the individual level but are nonetheless stable and sensible in the aggregate (Page and Shapiro 1992).

As this recounting suggests, both *physical* and *psychological aggregation* (distinguished in Luskin, this volume) are part of this story. Physical aggregation, with its canceling out of purely random individual-level error, makes beliefs and attitudes look more interconnected, stabler, and more responsive to relevant cues than they are.[7] Less inherently, psychological aggregation or disaggregation may also obscure ignorance, depending on what is being aggregated or disaggregated, how far, and to what end.

One claim based on physically aggregate evidence, for example, is that citizens generally find their way to policy positions and vote choices consistent with their positions on liberal–conservative or left–right scales. Dalton and Wattenberg (1993) call these latter "super issues." And so they would be, in a population of George Wills and Morton Kondrackes. In the real world, however, they are super issues for some, amorphous quasi-issues for others, and essentially uncognized by yet others. Even at the aggregate level, the evidence is not entirely flattering. Inglehart's (1984) correlations between left–right self-location and positions on a baker's dozen of policy issues average only a trifle over .2.

More direct, because individual-level, and thus considerably less flattering evidence lies in the definitions people are able to give when asked to say what these "ideological" distinctions entail. Conover and Feldman (1981:641) conclude that "the meaning of ideological labels is largely based on symbols rather than issues." Klingemann (1979:230), by a definition he himself calls "very generous indeed," finds an average of only 40% of five national publics able to provide a reasonably well-developed, policy-relevant definition of "left" or "right" (see also Butler and Stokes 1969; Converse 1964; Levitin and Miller 1979; Sani 1974). Among other things, this count evidently includes "ideological" but circular definitions – say, of "the right" as "conservative."

In this light, the correlations between liberal–conservative or left–right self-location and policy positions and vote choice are still less impressive. For many German voters, for instance, right may be a near-synonym for the CDU, and left a near-synonym for the SPD. In other cases, both self-location and vote choice may be driven by some real but meager policy content, which may or may not bear any strong resemblance to the rest of the voter's policy preferences, much less his or her values or interests.

But what of voters' ability to locate the parties and ideological groups in roughly the right regions of policy issue scales? Sniderman et al. (1991) show that the mean locations ascribed to liberals and conservatives on the National Election Studies' (NES's) standard 7-point scales concerning government-guaranteed jobs and the rights of the accused are sensibly to the left and right of the midpoint, respectively. In their view, this poses a "conundrum." How do voters manage to get such locations right despite ignorance and inattention? Their answer is what they term the

---

7 Especially with measurement error sheared off, as in covariance structure models.

"likability heuristic" (Brady and Sniderman 1985). The trick, simply put, is to infer that groups you don't like take positions you don't agree with.

Somewhat different but equally undemanding cueing devices can be found in Lupia's (1992) "costly entry" and "endorsement" models of referendum voting.[8] Let me treat these first, then return to the likability heuristic and its parent conundrum. In the costly entry model, voters get information about the cost of getting the proposition on the ballot and thus its distance from the status quo; in the endorsement model, they receive perfectly reliable information, say from some trusted person or group, about which side of the status quo the proposition is on. In each case, Lupia shows that under stated assumptions some voters will always choose correctly, in terms of their own preferences, between the proposition and the status quo, while the remainder can at least use the information to reduce the probability of choosing incorrectly.

Keep in mind, however, that these results rest on an assumption of universally apprehended, perfectly reliable information, whose implications, in the case of costly entry, are universally grasped. In the real world, where by no means everyone receives, accurately construes, or considers the implications of even these simple pieces of information, only some modest portions of the electorate can come close to obeying either of these models. The remainder come closer to obeying Lupia's "control case" model, in which voters have some probabilistic prior notions about the proposition's location in the model's unidimensional policy space but no further cues. Indeed, many voters doubtless come still closer to a purer null model lacking even these prior probabilities.

So while these models shed light on some of the ways in which voters may put even crude information to use, they do not necessarily imply that very many voters successfully do so. In Lupia's experimental results, roughly a quarter of the costly entry subjects and a third of the control case subjects vote incorrectly. (He does not test the endorsement model.) The purer null model best describing some nontrivial portion of the electorate could be expected to produce a still higher proportion of incorrect votes, on the order, depending on further assumptions, of 50%. Thus even with some voters behaving as in the costly entry or endorsement model, the electorate as a whole makes errors aplenty.

Much the same is true of Brady and Sniderman's likability heuristic. No doubt some people use it. No doubt some thereby succeed in placing parties and ideological groups correctly when they otherwise might not. But "some people" is not everybody. Those not using the likability

8 More precisely, Lupia's models are of "direct legislation," including but not confined to referenda.

heuristic may get these locations quite wrong. So, for that matter, may many of those using the heuristic.

But then what explains Sniderman, Brody, and Tetlock's conundrum? How do so many people get the issue locations of liberals and conservatives and Democrats and Republicans approximately right? The answer is, they don't. There is no conundrum. It only appears that most people are getting these locations approximately right, thanks to the physical aggregation in the mean locations. Let us review the evidence, using the same 1976 NES data as Sniderman, Brody, and Tetlock and focusing on the placements of liberals and conservatives.

The mean locations mislead in three ways, laid out in Table 9.1. First, they obscure the substantial proportion of respondents who place a given ideological group incorrectly (see Converse and Pierce 1986:ch. 4). Granted, what counts as correct placement can be a nice question, especially as regards the midpoint. Placements at the midpoint may be treated leniently, as correct, or strictly, as incorrect. The evidence favors the strict definition: in every case, the mean sophistication (as measured in Luskin, this volume) of those placing liberals or conservatives at the midpoint is about the same as the mean sophistication of those making more unambiguously incorrect placements (to the wrong side of the midpoint) but far lower than the mean sophistication of those making more unambiguously correct ones (to the right side of it).[9] The relevant comparisons appear in Table 9.2. Still, Table 9.1 reports results for both definitions. The complements of the first two columns show that even with the midpoint counted as correct, some 20–30% get these placements wrong and that with the midpoint counted as incorrect, some 40–50% get them wrong.

Second, the percentages who do get these placements right still need correction for guessing. The appropriate correction depends on what counts as correct and what one assumes about guessing. The simplest assumption is that guesses are distributed uniformly, so that the probability of guessing right by chance is $3/7$ under the strict definition and $4/7$ under the lenient one.[10] For every four people answering incorrectly under the strict definition, there should be another three guessing

---

9 Even though, as the next paragraph notes, those making correct placements are not an especially pure group. They include a great many respondents getting the correct side by chance.

10 One likely departure from uniformity, consistent with the results just mentioned, is that guessers may well tend to congregate at the midpoint (a mean-squared-error-minimizing choice for guessers operating in complete ignorance). If so, the corrections imposed here will be somewhat too strong under the strict definition, where the probability of guessing right will be somewhat less than $3/7$, and somewhat too weak under the lenient one, where the probability of guessing right will be somewhat more than $4/7$.

Table 9.1. *Placements of Liberals and Conservatives in Government-Guaranteed Jobs and Rights of the Accused*

	Percentage of Placements				Percentage of Sample		
	Correct (LD)	Correct (SD)	Knowingly Correct (LD)	Knowingly Correct (SD)	Don't Know	Knowingly Correct (LD)	Knowingly Correct (SD)
Liberals on Government-Guaranteed Jobs	76.87%	58.33%	32.63%	27.08%	41.48%	19.20%	15.85%
Conservatives on Same	79.19%	61.16%	51.44%	32.03%	39.86%	30.94%	19.26%
Liberals on Rights of Accused	82.80%	64.79%	59.87%	38.38%	40.36%	35.71%	22.89%
Conservatives on Same	71.59%	51.79%	33.71%	15.63%	39.36%	20.44%	9.48%

Note: LD and SD denote lenient and strict definitions of correctness, as explained in the text. The don't knows include those who could not place themselves on these issues and thus were not asked to place liberals or conservatives plus those who placed themselves but could not place liberals or conservatives. The Knowingly Correct columns incorporate corrections for guessing, as also explained in the text.

Source: 1976 NES.

288

Table 9.2. *Mean Sophistication by Placement Type*[a]

| Response Type | Ideological Group/Issue | | | |
	Liberals, Govt.-Guaranteed Jobs	Conservatives, Govt.-Guaranteed Jobs	Liberals, Rights of Accused	Liberals, Rights of Accused
No Placement (Don't Know)	1.51	1.43	1.65	1.63
Midpoint	2.96	2.90	3.28	3.40
Unambiguously Incorrect	3.18	3.03	3.43	2.83
Unambiguously Correct	5.47	5.42	4.65	5.76

[a] Entries are means of the revised 0–11 sophistication scale described in the text.
Source: 1976 NES.

correctly by chance, while for every three people answering incorrectly under the lenient definition, there should be another four guessing correctly by chance. Thus the percentage who should really get credit for placing liberals correctly on the rights of the accused is more like 59.9% $(= 82.8 - (4/3)(100 - 82.8))\%$ than 82.8% by the lenient counting and more like 38.4% $(= 64.8 - (3/4)(100 - 64.8))\%$ than 64.8% by the strict one. These corrected percentages, in Table 9.1's third and fourth columns, range downward from the 59.9% just cited to 32.6% under the lenient definition and from the 38.4% just cited to 15.6% under the strict definition.[11]

Third, the accuracy of the means is inflated by the missing data bias already discussed. Like Sniderman, Brody, and Tetlock's means, the first four columns of Table 9.1 are calculated only on those respondents who do place liberals and conservatives on these issues. But, as the fifth column shows, roughly 40% of the sample do not even try. Thus the truest picture of the public's (in)ability to place liberals and conservatives correctly lies somewhere between the final two columns of Table 9.1, which multiply the corrected percentages placing the ideological groups correctly (in the third and fourth columns) by the percentage placing them at all (the complement of the fifth column). These are the percentages of the whole sample who can be presumed to have know-

11 The corrected percentages can also be regarded as proportional reductions in error from a baseline of random guessing from a uniform distribution.

ingly placed liberals and conservatives correctly on these issues. With correctness leniently defined, these percentages range from roughly 19% to 36%; with correctness strictly defined, they range from 9% to 23%.

I have been following Sniderman, Brody, and Tetlock in proceeding item by item, but a much better way of using these sorts of items is to total the number of them on which the respondent both ventures a placement and gets it right. But this is very close to the measure of political sophistication I have adopted in Luskin (1987; this volume), on which the mean performance is actually inferior to random guessing.

Other illusions are a function of psychological aggregation. The prevalence of "performance-relevant" criteria like competence and integrity in evaluating candidates may give the impression of electoral sagacity (Abelson, Kinder, and Peters 1982; Kinder, Peters, Abelson, and Fiske 1980; Miller et al. 1986; Rahn et al. 1990). But it is important to ask just what the perceptions of candidates on these dimensions are made of. Very frequently, as the Rosenberg (Rosenberg, Bohan, McCafferty, and Harris 1986; Rosenberg and McCafferty 1987) and Masters and Sullivan studies (1989, 1993; Sullivan and Masters 1988) suggest, they are based on attire, countenance, physical and vocal mannerisms, and other such flimsy and unreliable cues. Not surprisingly, they are frequently inaccurate. The historical record is replete with egregious misperceptions. Many voters thought that Carter had competence, that Nixon had integrity, and that Reagan had both. (Many still do.)

Yet other illusions are fostered by, though not intrinsic to, psychological *dis*aggregation. The trap here is not actually psychological disaggregation per se but the loss of perspective that readily accompanies it. Too microscopic a focus makes gossamer cognition, barely visible in everyday conversation, look impressive. True, even the thoroughly unideological have numerous political cognitions and affects, schemas and values. True, even they succeed in making some sense of politics thereby. But this is not particularly redemptive. "Some sense," empirically, is quite often little enough, and errors remain common, in even such basic tasks as placing the Democratic and Republican parties and liberals and conservatives on issue dimensions, as we have seen.

Essentially the same danger lies in heavily idiographic approaches – even in unfulfilled idiographic aspirations, to judge from some "schema theory" (Conover and Feldman 1984, 1991) – whatever the level of psychological aggregation. It is easy in the detailed charting of what political cognition *is* present to lose sight of the vastly greater quantity that *is not*. Lane's (1962, 1969, 1973) differences with Converse (1964, 1975), *pace* MacKuen (this volume), are a case in point. Both Lane and Converse were dealing with beliefs, attitudes, values, and so forth – with psychological entities at approximately the same level of aggregation.

Method aside, the differences were not of aggregation but of perspective. While admitting that his Eastportians' political beliefs were highly "morselized," Lane (1962) emphasized the cognition that *was* present – celebrating the numerator while forgetting the denominator.

This loss of perspective reminds me of the indignant Scotsman who wrote back to Dr. Johnson that there was *so* a tree in the highlands – he knew of one not ten miles from where he stood.[12] Of course nearly everyone has some meaningful political cognitions. Of course these almost always have some organization to them. Of course nearly everyone, in consequence, makes some sense of politics. But the overwhelming evidence remains that the sense is generally limited and often erroneous.

Still more important, the degree of limitation and error varies widely. Indeed, the main trouble with these extenuations, apart from their disregard of what are in fact serious constraints on democratic processes, is that they paper over individual differences. Not everyone is woefully unsophisticated about politics. Some few are highly sophisticated, with many more in between. And this variation matters.

It is not just, as Sniderman et al. (1991), who actually stress individual differences in cognitive processing, must be read as contending, that the unsophisticated cope with political information and choices differently but more or less equally well. Quite a number of studies show or imply the contrary: that the more sophisticated generally see policy and vote options more clearly and make more sensible choices, on what most of us would regard as more sensible (policy-relevant) grounds. In fact, the correlations in Luskin (1987:885) show that the more sophisticated, as reckoned by other measures (based on their use and understanding of abstractions like "liberal" and "conservative"), do far better at placing the political parties correctly than do the less sophisticated, the same sort of task at which Sniderman et al. (1991) suggest nearly everybody contrives to do pretty well, regardless of sophistication.

To some extent, as this last suggests, these extenuationist claims shade back into the same old implausible contention that most people are actually quite sophisticated. Even some of the evidence has a familiar ring. The items Sniderman et al. (1991) use to show that people get the parties' locations about right despite being unsophisticated are very much the kind I have used to measure sophistication itself (Luskin 1987).[13] Again the only real difference, apart from whether the objects being placed are

---

12 Lifted from Hess and Hess (1989:40) and probably too droll to be true. I cannot find the incident in Boswell.

13 Zaller (1992) puts similar items to similar use, but throws a good many other disparate ingredients into his measure as well. See Luskin (this volume).

ideological groups or parties, is of physical aggregation. By focusing on the means, Sniderman et al. (1991) paint a flattering picture; counting the number of issues on which individual respondents get the parties' locations right shows how unimpressively most people actually fare at this.

Of course, this last argument still comports with a final extenuation. Aggregate clarity may coexist with individual-level confusion, but since it is aggregate opinion that politicians read in the polls and aggregate vote choices that decide elections, perhaps it is only the aggregate clarity that matters (Page and Shapiro 1992). At the individual level, people may make more sensible choices with more (and better) information, but would improved information alter the *aggregate* distribution of opinions or votes?

Pretty clearly it would. The largely forgotten coda of Converse's (1964) seminal essay suggests some of the aggregate consequences. That the more privileged tend both to be more sophisticated and to favor the right gives parties of the right more dependable mass bases – more participatory and less likely to be swayed from their interests – than parties of the left.

More generally, it needs only some plausible assumptions about the correlations between sophistication and other righthand-side variables to get from sophistication's individual-level conditioning of policy preferences and votes to the conclusion that the aggregate distributions of policy preferences and votes would be noticeably different if everybody approached the average congressman's or political commentator's level of sophistication. To the extent that the more sophisticated both pursue their interests or values more successfully and have different interests or values than the less sophisticated, the distribution of policy preferences should be altered by increased sophistication; so, to the extent that they both pursue their interests, values, or policy preferences more successfully and have different interests, values, or policy preferences, should the distribution of votes.

Empirical confirmation is beginning to come in. In Lupia's (1992) experiments, the subjects in the control case condition, where the only force promoting the "complete information majority preferred alternative" is sheer aggregation, produce majorities for the right alternative only slightly more than half the time. Aggregation by itself achieves little. More directly to the point, Delli Carpini and Keeter (1996), Bartels (1996), Althaus (1998), and Luskin and Globetti (1997) estimate full-information distributions of policy preferences (in Delli Carpini and Keeter's case) and votes (in Bartels's and Luskin and Globetti's).

The basic idea is as follows. First estimate the parameters of

$$E(y_i|x_i, S_i) = g(\gamma_0 + \gamma_1' x_i + \gamma_2' x_i S_i), \tag{1}$$

where y_i is either a policy preference measured numerically or binary vote choice scored $\{0,1\}$, x_i a $K \times 1$ vector of either sociodemographic or attitudinal regressors, S_i a scalar measure of political information, γ_1' and γ_2' $1 \times K$ parmeter vectors, γ_0 a scalar constant, g a function (in these analyses, identity, logit, or probit), and $E(y_i|x_i, S_i)$ the expected value of y_i conditional on x_i and S_i, equal to the probability that $y_i = 1$ in the case of vote choice. Then estimate "full-" (actually "fuller-") information attitudes or vote choices by combining the estimated γs with the actual x's and maximum S.

The results? Delli Carpini and Keeter (1996) find modest but consistent differences in full-information versus actual mean policy attitudes. Althaus (1998) finds that more than half of his forty-five dichotomous policy items show differences of more than 5 percentage points between the full-information and actual percentages endorsing a given side, that more than a quarter show full-information versus actual differences of more than 10 percentage points, and that a fifth show a clear reversal of majority opinion.[14] Bartels (1996) estimates that full information would have shifted the popular votes in recent presidential elections by up to 5.6 percentage points. Luskin and Globetti (1997) estimate that full information would have shifted the popular vote in the 1988 presidential election by between 1.6 and 3.9 percentage points. These are *net* changes. In both Bartels's and Luskin and Globetti's analyses, the *gross* changes – the proportions of individuals changing votes in either direction – run roughly twice as large. Aggregation does help, but the net changes remain large. The "magic of aggregation" (Converse 1990) is half-illusion.

Since 1.6%, 3.9%, or even 5.6% may not sound like much, it is worth noting explicitly that these are important changes. One fanciful way of establishing their importance would be to ask major-party candidates, many of whose victories or losses would have been reversed by changes of this magnitude. (The thought experiment should suffice.) From this, no doubt the most important perspective, these numbers are large because they would alter outcomes.

From another perspective, they are large because they are sizable fractions of what they could realistically be. Even with the typically modest information most people actually have, many must already be at their full

---

14 Several other items come very close to reversed majorities, and would presumably exhibit them with a still better measure of information, whose maximum value would represent still fuller information, if we assume at least local monotonicity. See below.

information positions (even while many are not). In two-candidate elections, roughly 50% must be voting "correctly" strictly by chance, lacking any information. The actual percentage must be substantially higher. How low a percentage remains available for change may be gauged as follows. Take the actual vote distribution for what it is, for example, 52.4% for Bush and 47.6% for Dukakis in the 1988 presidential election (as reported by the NES respondents). Set the correlation between actual and full-information vote at some plausible minimum, say .4, and the imbalance among full-information switches at some plausible maximum, say 5 : 1 (five times as many Bush voters switching to Dukakis as Dukakis voters switching to Bush).[15] These specifications are enough to solve for gross and net change, which are in this example 32.5% and 21.7%, respectively. The parameters may be jiggled somewhat, but it is difficult to find plausible settings under which these soft ceilings could be much higher.

That much is a matter of methodologically informed interpretation, taking the estimated changes as given. But from a more purely methodological perspective these are probably underestimates to begin with. For one thing, they contrast "full" with actual, not "zero" information, thus missing roughly half of information's full potential. For another thing, "full" information is measured by survey items that would all be regarded as "gimmes" by anyone reading this chapter. To avoid degenerate distributions, with nearly everyone sitting at zero, the selection of information items for any mass survey involves a great deal of "item sampling bias" toward very easy items.[16] Thus a maximum score does not necessarily indicate anything remotely close to "truly full information, even at the level of Kinsley or Will, let alone God" (Luskin and Globetti 1997). A maximum closer to truly full information might be expected to produce still larger changes. (Or then again might not – I say "probably" advisedly. Read on.)

A couple of studies seeming to suggest much smaller information effects do not really do so. One is the well-known article by Lupia (1994), encored in Lupia and McCubbins (1998). Lupia claims that simply knowing which of California's five side-by-side 1987 auto insurance referenda was supported by which interest group enabled otherwise

---

15 There is no way of estimating the correlation, but the estimates of the imbalance flow from Bartels's and Luskin and Globetti's estimates of gross and net changes. In Bartels's case, the ratio averages 1.99 : 1, never exceeding 2.85 : 1. In Luskin and Globetti's, it is somewhere between 3.17 : 1 and 4.52 : 1, depending on which of their estimates is used. In all, it seems clear that 5 : 1 is a very high value.

16 The term is from Luskin et al. (2002), who discuss the implications for measuring information gains.

ill-informed voters to behave as if fully informed. But Lupia's results are both (1) very likely wrong, the product of several highly questionable specification and measurement decisions and (2) overinterpreted. I hope to establish (1) elsewhere – there is no space here – but it should for present purposes suffice to establish (2).

Three tributary observations are involved. First, the distinction between "simple cues" and other information is largely false. Who favors what proposition *is* information, not a substitute for information. It is particularly important information, particularly relevant to voting decisions in referenda, just as the parties' locations in policy or ideological space is to voting decisions in representative elections (Fishkin and Luskin 1996; Luskin and Ten Barge 1995). I have built a measure of political information entirely of just such party-location items (Luskin 1987), and Zaller (1991) has made heavy use of them in his measures. It is information, moreover, that is highly correlated with other information (see Delli Carpini and Keeter 1996; Luskin 1987). Someone who knows a lot about a referendum generally is unlikely not to know where the major players stand on the question, and those who know at least the latter are likely to know a great deal more about the former than those who do not. In this light, Lupia's results are just another confirmation that information matters, especially information of a sort others have already identified as particularly important.

Second, Lupia's student-selected, nonprobability sample of Los Angelinos seems to be perceptibly closer than the whole voting electorate to their full-information votes, just as you'd expect of a sampling design involving some degree of interviewer selection.[17] To see this, take the percent-

17 To be fair, Lupia tries to minimize the unrepresentativeness of his sample by choosing sites (polling stations) that varied in "the cost of auto insurance, the average number of accidents, and the cost of insurance claims" and by asking his student interviewers to approach every fifth person exiting the polling station. But even the every-fifth-person method, even if faithfully implemented, is not truly random, and the selection of sites is far from it. As anyone who has worked with survey houses and with volunteer student interviewers knows, moreover, even the "professionals" need eagle-eyed surveillance, and the students will get lots of things wrong (no doubt including the every-fifth-person method). The interviewing was also confined to a four-hour period, also (apparently) a nonrandom selection. Lupia mentions not gearing the interviewers' incentives to the number of interviews completed, but this probably cuts both ways: students finding that they do not need to meet any quota to earn their extra credit may not be motivated to approach quite every fifth exiting voter. Perhaps, on average, they try only every twelfth, or seventeenth. (Lupia reports no response rate.) But once they abandon strict adherence to the every-fifth-voter rule, they wind up making unconstrained selection, and the usual biases toward sociodemographic characteristics associated with information come in.

ages voting "yes" among the well-informed sample members who also know the relevant cues (in the first column of his Table 4) as distributions of more fully informed votes. Then consider whether the percentages voting "yes" in his sample or in the Los Angeles election statistics (in the last and next-to-last columns of his Table C-1) are closer to the corresponding more fully informed votes. On four of the five proposals, Lupia's sample is closer, by an average of roughly 3.5%, across all five. This apparent sampling bias leaves less room for information effects.

Third, and most important, the percentages possessed of interest group cues are still not impressively large. According to Lupia's Table B-1, each proposition was favored by exactly one of the three active interest groups (trial lawyers, the insurance industry, and consumers, in the person of Ralph Nader). Generously calculated, the percentages identifying the correct backer run from only 23.0% to 55.5%, averaging only 38.8%[18] – and that's without correction for guessing.[19] Thus a major hole in Lupia's argument from these data is essentially the same as the major hole in his argument from his formal model (Lupia 1992): simple cues may arguably make voters more likely to reach the "right" vote, but not that many people typically know the cues.

The other apparently discordant piece of evidence comes from Lau and Redlawsk (1997), who find that in the five presidential elections from 1972 through 1988 the percentage of NES respondents voting just as they would with full information or, in Lau and Redlawsk's terms, casting "normatively correct votes," ranged from 67.8% to 79.0%, averaging 75.2%.

Two points must be made about these figures, however, one interpretational and one methodological. The interpretational point is that these figures are once again much less impressive than they seem at first blush. They must either be considered as proportional increases in the agreement between actual and full-information votes over the 50% achievable by blind guessing or, equivalently, be corrected for guessing.[20] The

18 These are the percentages of the 339 respondents saying that the right interest group supported the given proposal. They are generous in the sense that respondents who mistakenly identify more than one interest group as having supported a given proposal (as the structure of this series of questions permits them to do) are still counted as correct.

19 And among what seems from the previous paragraph to be a much better than averagely informed sample. Behind the 3.5% difference in votes is almost certainly a much larger difference in information, operationalized as the percentage of information items answered correctly, given the large percentages voting "correctly" by chance and the partially self-canceling nature of information's aggregate effects.

20 See footnote 11.

corrected figures – the percentages knowingly casting normatively correct votes – range only from 45.6% to 58.0%, averaging only 52.5%.

The methodological point is that even these corrected figures may well be too high. Lau and Redlawsk's normatively correct votes are based on psychological variables like the respondent's policy preferences and party identification rather than sociodemographic ones. This matters, as Lau and Redlawsk note, not quite concernedly enough, because actual policy preferences and party identification have already strayed from their full-information counterparts (as Althaus 1998 and Delli Carpini and Keeter 1996 plainly show). Much of the disconnect between interests (or even values) and votes is being swept out of sight. Normatively correct votes based on sociodemographic variables would very likely differ still more often from actual ones.

So the burden of these cross-sectional analyses is that information does matter, that the distributions of policy preferences and votes would often enough be palpably different under full information. But a degree of "internal validity" is missing. The basic strategy, perforce, is to compare otherwise similar individuals having different levels of sophistication. Nobody's sophistication actually increases. What would happen if given individuals actually knew more? The question can be addressed experimentally, by getting a probability sample to learn more about politics and then observing the effects on policy preferences and vote intentions.

The largest-scale effort in this direction is Deliberative Polling (Fishkin 1991, 1995; Luskin, Fishkin, and Jowell 2002). A probability sample is interviewed, sent carefully balanced briefing materials; brought for a weekend to one place to discuss the issues in small groups and put questions to panels of policy experts, policy makers, and politicians; and then given the same questionnaire as at the beginning. There have now been eighteen Deliberative Polls: five national ones in Britain, two national ones in Australia, one national one apiece in the United States and Denmark, and nine regional ones in the United States.[21]

The samples, issues, and numerous other details have varied, but the results have generally shown both sizable information gains and frequent and sizable changes of attitude, even in the net (Fishkin and Luskin 1999; Luskin and Fishkin 1998; Luskin et al. 2002; Luskin, Fishkin, and Plane 1999). In the 1997 Deliberative Poll on the British general election of that year, for example, the Liberal Democrats gained nearly twenty points, at the roughly equal expense of Labour and the Tories, far outpolled the Tories, and very nearly outpolled Labour (Luskin, Fishkin,

---

21 By the time this chapter appears, there will have been at least one more national Deliberative Poll, in Canada.

Jowell, and Park 1999). In the 1999 Deliberative Poll on the Australian constitutional referendum to make the nation a republic, cutting its vestigial ties with the British crown, the percentage voting "yes" increased by seventeen points (Luskin, Fishkin, McAllister, Higley, and Ryan 2000). Other, broadly similar devices – the Choice Questionnaire in the Netherlands (Neijens 1987; Neijens, de Ridder, and Saris 1992) and the Planning Cell in Germany (Dienel 1978, 1989; Renn, Stegelman, Albrecht, Kotte, and Peters 1984) – have produced broadly similar results. Better informed publics have noticeably different policy and voting preferences.

BEYOND

Sad to say, this debate has still not taken us terribly far, dwelling as it has on something in the nature of an "existence proof." *Whether* information matters is an important question, but while I cannot yet say, reportorially, that we are all agreed on the answer, the trend is clear, as I believe are the merits. One sign of how strongly the evidence argues the affirmative is the striking *volte face* recently executed by Popkin, whose book *The Reasoning Voter* (1992) has been a pillar of extenuationism but whose more recent convention papers have contended that information matters – a lot.[22] Soon it will be time to move on to the next questions, of *how* information matters – how much, to what, with what sign, and under what conditions.

The seeds of a literature are already present. One emerging question concerns aggregate sign. Would the distributions of policy and candidate preferences move left or right if everyone were "fully" informed (operationally, if everyone had the maximum score on whatever index is being used to measure information)? Full information might most straightforwardly be thought to benefit the left, given the correlations between information and efficiency in the pursuit of one's interests, between social location and information, and between social location and interests, conventionally construed. If everybody had full information, the people whose information would be hoisted furthest would be disproportionately from the less favored strata of society, whose interests, by conventional definition, should incline them to the left.

This was what Converse (1964) anticipated, and what Delli Carpini and Keeter (1996) find in their models of policy preferences. In every

---

22 Like Nie's cite in footnote 3, this sort of winning-over by the evidence stands in admirable refutation of the cynical and antiscientific view of political science as simply the continuation of politics by other means (although for those holding this view it may be).

issue domain they examine – redistributive and safety-net programs, abortion rights, affirmative action, and gay rights – the full-information distribution of opinion is more liberal than the actual one. But this is *not* what Bartels (1996) finds in his model of presidential vote choice. The model is the same, saving only the dependent variable, the measure of information, and the functional form, which is logistic. The sociodemographic regressors are virtually identical. The method of confecting the full-information distribution, in this case of votes, is the same. Yet the results are quite different. The biggest full-information impacts Bartels finds, for the 1980 and 1988 elections, benefit the Republicans. Delli Carpini and Keeter also examine presidential vote choice, working with a model more or less identical to Bartels's (again bar the measurement of information), but, oddly, do not in this case report the impact of universal full information, leaving the suspicion that their results for this vote choice model resemble Bartels's rather than their results for policy attitudes. Apparently, full information makes the distributions of policy preferences unfailingly more liberal yet the distribution of vote choices sometimes more Republican.

The plot thickens with Suzanne Globetti's and my analysis taking vote choice as a function of more proximate, psychological variables – candidate images, policy proximities, partisanship, and simple retrospections – plus information (Luskin and Globetti 1997). Using the same NES data as Bartels, we find that universal full information would have advantaged Dukakis, not Bush, in 1988. We use a different – superior – measure of information, but that does not appear to be responsible for this difference in sign. So apparently it is only for vote choice predicted from social location that full information sometimes tilts preferences starboard. Policy preferences predicted from social location become more liberal, vote choices from political attitudes more Democratic.

But even this more limited generalization is too simple. Althaus (1998) finds that opinions move to the left on some of his array of forty-five policy issues but to the right on others. His fully informed public is generally more inclined to endorse higher taxes in the interest of either reducing the deficit or increasing government services but more opposed to big government, generally more inclined to endorse the policies favored by minority, gay, and women's organizations but more opposed to affirmative action.

The results from Deliberative Polling have been similarly mixed. Some of the changes in policy preference have been to the right, others to the left, yet others in directions not easily labeled as either left or right (Fishkin 1995; Luskin et al. 2002). The one Deliberative Poll so far to focus on vote preference in a representative election (as opposed to a referendum) – just prior to the British general elections of May 1, 1997 –

produced striking shifts away from both the Conservative and Labour parties and toward the Social Democrats (whose share of the vote intentions zoomed from 11% to 33%).

This variety of results nudges us toward deep questions. Some of the variance may be methodological. Perhaps survey-based simulations miss some of the possibilities for change in conservative directions that quasi-experiments reveal. Or perhaps, on the other hand, the results showing more informed electorates voting more Republican rest on inadequately specified models. Most obviously, the social locations defined by individual sociodemographic variables in the roles of the x's in (1) may not be configural enough. Conceivably, if (1) contained products of the x's with one another as well as of the x's with S, the results might run more consistently as expected.

The more interesting and important possibilities, however, are more substantive. Perhaps the generally implicit but common assumptions about how information matters (reflected in both of my contributions to this volume) have been too facile. Perhaps

the conventional notions of what policies people in given social locations should prefer . . . [are not always] shared by the best informed people in those locations. Perhaps the conventional notions are wrong – perhaps, indeed, by definition, if we equate appropriateness with the positions held by the best informed people in given locations. Or perhaps sophistication's conditioning of the relationship between social location and policy preference is nonlinear, with the moderately well-informed most likely to endorse the conventionally appropriate positions, and the most and least informed less likely to do so, from random choice and independent thought, respectively. . . .

[This question comes down to] what is really in most people's best interest, disagreements over which are the warp and woof of political debate, and it is possible to construct eminently plausible arguments, for example of the rising-tide-lifts-all-boats variety, that policies whose most immediate and transparent effects favor the well-off may actually serve the less well-off better than redistributive alternatives. (Luskin and Globetti 1997:25, 30)

In short, increased sophistication may sometimes haul the distribution of policy preferences or votes to the right. It may depend on the issue or the election. Empirically, that seems so far to be true, at least for policy preferences, although the possibility that this variation in sign is wholly artifactual, a function of varying specifications and methods, cannot yet be dismissed. The other possibility is of nonmonotonicity, perhaps for all issues and elections. If the conservatives are right, increasing sophistication should first move the public leftward but then, at levels high enough to make long-term and indirect effects visible, rightward again.[23]

---

23 For more on the question of sign, see Luskin (2001).

These questions of sign – of when, if ever, increased sophistication does or should move the distribution of opinion right instead of left – are among the most important on the horizon, but others also loom. Who becomes more or less sophisticated? There is a controversy brewing over the role of education in promoting political sophistication (compare Delli Carpini and Keeter 1996 or Nie, Junn, and Stehlik-Barry 1996 with Luskin 1990 or Luskin and Ten Barge 1995 and see Luskin, this volume). What are the sources of such cross-national variation as exists? Getting up truly comparable measures is difficult, but see Gordon and Segura (1997) for an interesting attempt. What are sophistication's other consequences – for political participation, political tolerance, political extremism, etc.? Delli Carpini and Keeter (1996) and Luskin and Ten Barge (1995) have recently examined several such effects, as, in more single-shot fashion, have a number of studies scattered across the years. But the real work is just beginning.

References

Abelson, Robert P., Donald R. Kinder, and Mark D. Peters. 1982. "Affective and Semantic Components in Political Person Perception." *Journal of Personality and Social Psychology* 42:619–30.

Althaus, Scott. 1998. "Information Effects in Collective Preferences." *American Political Science Review* 92:545–58.

Bartels, Larry M. 1996. "Uninformed Voters: Information Effects in Presidential Elections." *American Journal of Political Science* 40:194–230.

Bennett, Stephen Earl. 1989. "Trends in Americans Political Information, 1967–1987." *American Politics Quarterly* 17:422–35.

1993. "Out of Sight, Out of Mind: Americans' Knowledge of Party Control of the House of Representatives, 1960–1984." *Political Research Quarterly* 46:67–81.

1995. "Americans' Knowledge of Ideology, 1980–1992." *American Politics Quarterly* 23:259–79.

Brady, Henry E., and Paul M. Sniderman. 1985. "Attitude Attribution: A Group Basis for Political Reasoning." *American Political Science Review* 79:1061–78.

Butler, David, and Donald E. Stokes. 1969. *Political Change in Great Britain: Forces Shaping Electoral Choice.* New York: St. Martin's Press.

Conover, Pamela Johnston, and Stanley Feldman. 1981. "The Origins and Meaning of Liberal/Conservative Self-Identifications." *American Journal of Political Science* 25:617–45.

1984. "How People Organize the Political World: A Schematic Model." *American Journal of Political Science* 28:95–126.

1991. "Where Is the Schema? Critique." *American Political Science Review* 85:1364–9.

Converse, Philip E. 1964. "The Nature of Belief Systems in Mass Publics." In David E. Apter, ed., *Ideology and Discontent.* New York: Free Press.

1975. "Public Opinion and Voting Behavior." In Fred I. Greenstein and Nelson W. Polsby, eds., *The Handbook of Political Science*. Reading, MA: Addison-Wesley.

1990. "Popular Representation and the Distribution of Information." In John A. Ferejohn and James H. Kuklinski, eds., *Information and Democratic Processes*. Urbana, IL: University of Illinois Press.

Converse, Philip E., and Roy Pierce. 1986. *Political Representation in France*. Cambridge, MA: Harvard University Press.

Dalton, Russell J. 1984. "Cognitive Mobilization and Partisan Dealignment in Advanced Industrial Democracies." *Journal of Politics* 46:264–84.

1996. *Citizen Politics: Public Opinion and Political Parties in Advanced Western Democracies*. Chatham, NJ: Chatham House.

Dalton, Russell J., and Martin P. Wattenburg. 1993. "The Not So Simple Act of Voting." In Ada W. Finifter, ed., *Political Science: The State of the Discipline II*. Washington, DC: American Political Science Association.

Delli Carpini, Michael X., and Scott Keeter. 1996. *What Americans Know About Politics and Why It Matters*. New Haven, CT: Yale University Press.

Dienel, Peter C. 1978. *Die Planungszelle: Ein Alterntive zur Establishment-Demokratie*. Der Bürger plant seine Umwelt. Oplkaden: Westdeutscher Verlag.

1989. "Contributing to Social Decision Methodology: Citizen Reports on Technological Problems." In C. Vlek and G. Cvetkovich, eds., *Social Decision Making for Technological Problems*. Dordrecht: Kluwer Academic.

Feldman, Stanley. 1988. "Structure and Consistency in Public Opinion: The Role of Core Beliefs and Values." *American Journal of Political Science* 32:416–40.

Feldman, Stanley, and John Zaller. 1992. "The Political Culture of Ambivalence: Ideological Responses to the Welfare State." *American Journal of Political Science* 36:268–307.

Fishkin, James S. 1991. *Democracy and Deliberation: New Directions for Democratic Reform*. New Haven, CT: Yale University Press.

1995. *The Voice of the People: Public Opinion and Democracy*. New Haven, CT: Yale University Press.

Fishkin, James S., and Robert C. Luskin. 1996. "The Deliberative Poll: A Reply to Our Critics," *Public Perspective*, 7:45–9.

1999. "Bringing Deliberation to the Democratic Dialogue: The NIC and Beyond." In Maxwell McCombs, ed., *A Poll with a Human Face: The National Issues Convention Experiment in Political Communication*. Mahwah, NJ: Erlbaum.

Gordon, Stacy B., and Gary M. Segura. 1997. "Cross-National Variation in the Political Sophistication of Individuals: Capability or Choice." *Journal of Politics* 59:126–47.

Hamill, Ruth, Milton Lodge, and Frederick Blake. 1985. "The Breadth, Depth, and Utility of Class, Partisan, and Ideological Schemata." *American Journal of Political Science* 29:850–70.

Hess, John L., and Karen Hess. 1989. *The Taste of America*. Columbia: University of South Carolina Press.

Hochschild, Jennifer. 1981. *What's Fair? American Beliefs about Distributive Justice*. Cambridge, MA: Harvard University Press.

Inglehart, Ronald. 1977. *The Silent Revolution*. Princeton, NJ: Princeton University Press.

1984. "Changing Cleavage Alignments in Western Democracies." In R. Dalton, S. Flanagan, and P. Beck, eds., *Electoral Change in Advanced Industrial Democracies*. Princeton, NJ: Princeton University Press.

1990. *Culture Shift*. Princeton, NJ: Princeton University Press.

Kinder, Donald R., Mark D. Peters, Robert P. Abelson, and Susan T. Fiske. 1980. "Presidential Prototypes." *Political Behavior* 2:315–37.

Kinder, Donald R., and David O. Sears. 1985. "Public Opinion and Political Action." In Gardner Lindzey and Elliot Aronson, eds., *Handbook of Social Psychology*, Vol. 2. New York: Random House.

Klingeman, Hans-Dieter. 1979. "Measuring Ideological Conceptualization." In Samuel Barnes and Max Kasse, eds., *Political Action*. Beverly Hills, CA: Sage.

Lane, Robert E. 1962. *Political Ideology*. New York: Free Press.

1969. *Political Thinking and Consciousness: The Private Life of the Political Mind*. Chicago: Markham.

1973. "Patterns of Political Belief." In Jeanne Knutson, ed., *Handbook of Political Psychology*. San Francisco: Jossey-Bass.

Lau, Richard R., and David P. Redlawsk. 1997. "Voting Correctly." *American Political Science Review* 91:585–98.

Levitin, Theresa E., and Warren E. Miller. 1979. "Ideological Interpretations of Presidential Elections." *American Political Science Review* 73:751–71.

Lodge, Milton, Marco Steenbergen, and Shawn Brau. 1995. "The Responsive Voter: Campaign Information and the Dynamics of Campaign Information." *American Political Science Review* 89:327–43.

Lupia, Arthur. 1992. "Busy Voters, Agenda Control, and the Power of Information." *American Political Science Review* 86:390–403.

1994. "Shortcuts versus Encyclopedias: Information and Voting Behavior in California Insurance Reform Elections." *The American Political Science Review* 88(1):63–76.

Lupia, Arthur, and Matthew D. McCubbins. 1998. *The Democratic Dilemma: Can Citizens Learn What They Need to Know?* New York: Cambridge University Press.

Luskin, Robert C. 1987. "Measuring Political Sophistication." *American Journal of Political Science* 31:856–99.

1990. "Explaining Political Sophistication." *Political Behavior* 12:331–61.

2002. "The Heavenly Public: What Would the Ideal Democratic Citizenry Be Like?" In George Rabinowitz and Michael B. MacKuen, eds., *Electoral Democracy*. Ann Arbor: University of Michigan Press.

Luskin, Robert C., and James S. Fishkin. 1998. "Deliberative Polling, Public Opinion, and Democracy: The Case of the National Issues Convention." Presented at the American Association for Public Opinion Research Annual Meeting, Saint Louis, MO, May 14–17.

Luskin, Robert C., James S. Fishkin, and Roger Jowell. In press. "Considered Opinions: Deliberative Polling in the U.K." *British Journal of Political Science*.

Luskin, Robert C., James S. Fishkin, Roger Jowell, and Alison Park. 1999. "Learning and Voting in Britain: Insights from the Deliberative Poll." Paper presented at the annual meeting of the American Political Science Association, Atlanta, September 2–5.

Luskin, Robert C., James S. Fishkin, Ian McAllister, John Higley, and Pamela Ryan. 2000. "Information Effects in Referendum Voting: Evidence from the

Australian Deliberative Poll." Paper presented at the annual meeting of the American Political Science Association, Washington, DC, August 31–September 3.

Luskin, Robert C., James S. Fishkin, and Dennis L. Plane. 1999. "Deliberative Polling and Policy Outcomes: Electric Utility Issues in Texas." Paper presented at the annual meeting of the Association for Public Policy Analysis and Management, Washington, DC, November 4–6.

Luskin, Robert C., and Suzanne Globetti. 1997. "Candidate versus Policy Considerations in the Voting Decision: The Role of Political Sophistication." Manuscript, Department of Government, University of Texas at Austin.

Luskin, Robert C., and Joseph C. Ten Barge. 1995. "Education, Intelligence, and Political Sophistication." Paper presented at the annual meeting of the Midwest Political Science Association, Chicago, April 6–8, 1995.

Masters, Roger D., and Dennis G. Sullivan. 1989. "Non-Verbal Displays and Political Leadership in France and the United States." *Political Behavior* 11:123–56.

1993. "Nonverbal Behavior and Leadership: Emotion and Cognition in Political Attitudes." In Shanto Iyengar and William McGuire, eds., *Explorations in Political Psychology*. Durham, NC: Duke University Press.

Miller, Arthur H., Martin P. Wattenberg, and Oksana Malanchuk. 1986. "Schematic Assessments of Presidential Candidates." *American Political Science Review* 80:521–40.

Neijens, Peter. 1987. *The Choice Questionnaire: Design and Evaluation of an Instrument for Collecting Informed Opinions of a Population*. Amsterdam: Free University Press.

Neijens, Peter, Jan de Ridder, and Willem Saris. 1992. "An Instrument for Collecting Informed Opinions." *Quantity and Quality* 26:245–58.

Nie, Norman H., Jane Junn, and Kenneth Stehlik-Barry. 1996. *Education and Democratic Citizenship in America*. Chicago: University of Chicago Press.

Nie, Norman, Sidney Verba, and John Petrocik. 1976. *The Changing American Voter*. Cambridge, MA: Harvard University Press.

Page, Benjamin I., and Robert Y. Shapiro. 1992. *The Rational Public: Fifty Years of Trends in Americans' Policy Preferences*. Chicago: University of Chicago Press.

Popkin, Samuel L. 1992. *The Reasoning Voter*. Chicage: University of Chicago Press.

Price, Vincent. 1999. "Political Information." In John P. Robinson, Phillip R. Shaver, and Lawrence S. Wrightsman, eds., *Measures of Political Attitudes*. San Diego, CA: Academic Press.

Rahn, Wendy M., John H. Aldrich, Eugene Borgida, and John L. Sullivan. 1990. "A Social-Cognitive Model of Candidate Appraisal." In John A. Ferejohn and James H. Kuklinski, eds., *Information and Democratic Processes*. Urbana: University of Illinois Press.

Renn, O., H. U. Stegelmann, G. Albrecht, U. Kotte, and H. P. Peters. 1984. "An Empirical Investigation of Citizens' Preferences among Four Energy Alternatives." *Technological Forecasting and Social Change* 26:11–46.

Rosenberg, Shawn W., Lisa Bohan, Patrick McCaffery, and Kevin Harris. 1986. "The Image and the Vote: The Effect of Candidate Presentation on Voter Preference." *American Journal of Political Science* 30:108–207.

Rosenberg, Shawn W., and Patrick McCafferty. 1987. "The Image and the Vote: Manipulating Voters' Preferences." *Public Opinion Quarterly* 51:31–47.

Sani, Giacomo. 1974. "A Test of the Least-Distance Model of Voting Choice: Italy." *Comparative Political Studies* 7:193–208.

Smith, Eric R. A. N. 1989. *The Unchanging American Voter*. Berkeley: University of California Press.

Sniderman, Paul M., Richard A. Brody, and Philip E. Tetlock. 1991. *Reasoning and Choice: Explorations in Political Psychology*. New York: Cambridge University Press.

Sullivan, Dennis G., and Roger D. Masters. 1988. "Happy Warriors: Leaders' Facial Displays, Viewers' Emotions, and Political Support." *American Journal of Political Science* 32:345–68.

Zaller, John R. 1992. *The Nature and Origins of Mass Opinion*. New York: Cambridge University Press.

Political Psychology and the Micro–Macro Gap in Politics

MICHAEL MacKUEN

Political science thrives in the space that connects the individual and the collectivity. From its roots in ancient Greece, the discipline has always aimed to help individuals live artfully together in a community. It is in this sense that the discipline necessarily concerns the links between individuals' personal lives and the operation of the broader polity. It is not that we might choose to, but instead we must, bridge the micro–macro gap.

In this chapter, I argue that political psychology has already contributed much to the understanding of how individual and polity join together. And yet, much work remains to be done.[1] In particular, when we want to employ political psychology to bridge the micro–macro gap, we need to think explicitly about the *mechanisms* that link the individual to the broader polity. But more than that – the nature of the microworld depends on the macroworld for its very meaning. By this I do not mean only that individuals interact with and try to make sense of a social environment, though this is true. Instead, I want to suggest that what is *political* about people lies rooted in their shared collective life rather than in their personal lives.

A story might illustrate the point. In the 1960s both Robert Lane and Philip Converse were asked to participate in an American Political Science Association panel on the character of the public's political beliefs. Fireworks were expected. Unfortunately (for the spectators), the principals had met the evening before and came to understand their differences.

---

1 Clearly, much more good work exists than I can summarize in this chapter. And, to be sure, political psychology has already made a greater contribution than might seem apparent here. Yet, I believe that the discipline has even more to offer as it begins explicitly to address the nature of the collectivity or, rather, the individual's construction of the collectivity.

Contemporary observers then saw a stark contrast between Lane's and Converse's positions. Lane (1962) argued from intensive interviews that people hold highly complex and dynamic political views. Converse (1964), analyzing mass surveys, found that individuals' political views were unconnected across issues and over time and inferred "nonattitudes." If the question is whether individuals understood anything about the political world, the disagreement could not be stronger.

Yet, the fundamental questions were different. Lane's evidence and conclusions were intentionally micro-centered. That is, he showed that individual citizens' political views were highly developed and embedded in their personal psychologies. Many of Lane's discussants revealed unusual lines of "reasoning" and saw the broader political system from largely personal perspectives.

Converse's inferences, on the other hand and thus ambiguously, were of both a micro and a macro nature. He understood that the highly idiosyncratic views Lane heard were hardly connected to the politics of government. For politicians to deal with their constituents, they needed a systematic organization of political views. Merely understanding each person's psyche to be wholesomely unique does little good. Politicians, like other observers of the social scene, must necessarily abstract from the hodgepodge of complex psyches to a crisper view of reality. First, they need to know how the public might react to specific policy questions as they appear in government: citizen angst means less than a preference for lower taxes. Second, they employ such terms as "liberal" and "conservative" to describe *sets* of political beliefs and preferences – so that they may project public preferences concerning future matters not yet crystallized. In short, politicians expect that citizens hold meaningful preferences concerning policies on which politicians must decide. Converse's results showed that people's political views are not well described by such disarmingly naive abstractions.

Key to this story is an understanding that politics is about the way people live together. Government, not cognition, is the discipline's touchstone. Knowing how public opinion translates into the institutions of government requires not only knowing about individuals' beliefs and values but also, crucially, knowing how government officials make sense of their constituents' beliefs and values. Less clear here, but more important in the long run, we also need to know how people's beliefs and values depend on politicians' actions and how those actions are informed by politicians' understanding of the systematic relationship between people's beliefs and values and politicians' actions. We need to understand the systemic relationship between micro and macro behavior.

Thus, while the larger macroentity is composed of its parts, its *political essence* is by no means equivalent to a simple projection of the microparticles. My overall line of argument here is that, when it aims to push political science, political psychology needs to show how individual psyches connect to the broader political system and how this connection enriches our overall understanding of politics.

To be sure, much of our work has been built into conventional political science. Practically all freshman textbooks include discussions of "political behavior" that reflect four decades of political psychology. Yet, many aspects of that psychology, while entirely satisfactory as an individual-centered science, need elaboration or recasting before they are relevant for a macropolitical science. This may be especially true of much recent work. Of course, this need for theoretical linkages is a natural result of our science being a "division of labor" enterprise: it is up to the macrotheorists to catch up with the microlevel work.

SOME THEORETICAL CONSIDERATIONS

Before considering the nature of political psychology, let us turn to matters rather more abstract. When we want to know about bridging the micro–macro gap, we need to think about what sorts of factors constitute that gap. And then we need to think about the peculiar strengths and weaknesses inherent in a psychological explanation of politics.

Dimensions of the Micro–Macro Gap

The distinction between what constitutes a micro or a macro phenomenon is a matter of scale. Micro clearly reflects something smaller than macro. It is the nature of that scale that matters. For political science, the scales typically represent dimensions of time and population.

When an experimental psychologist decides to study a subject's choice mechanisms, that scientist has made an arbitrary choice of analytic units. Here the time frame is one of a few minutes, and the population unit is the human individual. Clearly, matters can be moved both up and down the scale. On the one hand, the analyst may wish to examine subsets of time and population – say, the momentary reactions of neural networks to different sorts of visual input. On the other hand, the analyst may be interested in how different societies react to historical change in the means of material production.

Obviously, these differences may be said to be matters of aggregation. After all, historical societal change must be made up of (many!) nanoseconds and neural networks. This truism misses the point. The analytic strategies that abstract to the proper units of analysis necessarily must be simple enough, and general enough, to allow some bridging of the micro–macro gap. The methods of aggregation will prove crucial, and causal theories will clearly reflect different levels of abstraction. For example, social historians may be pardoned for ignoring neural networks and, similarly, neural physiologists cannot expect to say much about social theory. We shall want to be conscious of the danger of mindlessly applying microlevel theory to macrolevel phenomena (and, less plausibly, the reverse).

I wish to consider this point for the application of an individual-centered political psychology to national politics.[2] To maintain familiar ground, I shall concentrate on the politics that link people's political preferences with governmental outcomes in the United States. I do so for two reasons. First, the connection between citizens and government is an illustration of the broader issue of micro–macro modeling. And second, I believe that the link between people's lives and government policies to be of compelling political theoretical interest in its own right.

A Caricature of Micro and Macro Modeling

For a moment, I should like to suggest two "pure types" of models for studying politics – the first clearly micro- and the second macro-oriented. These two types represent simplifications that ignore the subtleties in real work.

On the one hand, consider a purely micropolitical science. Here, researchers would focus entirely on how individuals understand and experience political life. We would study how people develop their partisan views or how legislators cast their votes. The emphasis would lie on extrapolations from subsets of psychological theory – say, dynamic psychology or decision theory. As a subject, such a political science would have enormous intrinsic merit. When we are interested in the quality of human life, we surely want to know how people deal with the political side of that life. So it matters if the poor feel alienated from their society or if politicians choose policies consistent with their personal philosophies.

On the other hand, a macropolitical science would deal in abstract aggregates. It would ask about the relationships between the public and

2 I want to distinguish the smaller-canvas stuff here from the grander matter of political culture. Clearly, culture matters enormously. The question of authority, for example, is entirely different in Germany and the United States. The notion of economic equality seems to be perceived differently in different industrial nations. And, of course, the world looks very different from Rwanda. I do not wish to minimize the crucial importance of political culture, as it is clear that definitions of politics vary enormously as a function of peculiarities of history and literature. Instead, in this chapter, I want to concentrate on more mundane matters – those that may be more mechanical in nature.

government or, at a lower scale perhaps, between interest groups and Congress. Such a political science surely employs a political psychology, albeit an elementary one. It characterizes each aggregate or institution with motives and behavior that reflect a sort of typical voter or lobbyist or legislator – writ large. Thus, for example, it makes some sense to say that when Congress disappoints the public, Congress will change its policy course.

Yet, we typically want more from our theoretical apparatus. The essentially micro science misses the collective nature of politics, while the essentially macro science limits itself to schoolbook simplifications. A richer and more subtle intellect wants to combine the micro and macro elements into a conceptual framework that yields more. To proceed, it will be necessary to see how understanding the mental processes of voters or politicians enlarges our understanding of aggregates and institutions. The simpleminded psychology works well enough for college textbooks and television journalism. And, to be fair, most political scientists will remain skeptical about how much real payoff comes from studying psyches rather than social systems.

Reductionism, Emergent Properties, and Macro Politics

Think of the micro–macro gap in the following way. Start by understanding that the macroconcept may make good sense because it is useful. That is, while we know full well that the macroentity is made up of microelements, it is more useful to use the macroentity as a unit of analysis. We must abstract away from a complex reality and may find it helpful to do so by using lumps of people as a form of shorthand. Thus, it makes sense to talk about the United States and France engaging in a trade war rather than about all the complex interactions among American or French vintners, farmers, politicians, public officials, and ordinary citizens. Or it may be useful to talk about the Democrats or small businessmen as an entity without worrying about the complexity below. This is the first cut at micro–macro conceptualization.

Then think more seriously about the linkages. While the macro is comprised of the micro, it need not be a transparently simple additive summation. That is, it may be more or less than the sum of its parts. In conceptual terms, we take a reductionist stance starting with individuals (rather than neural nets) as the unit of analysis and see how individuals interact so as to produce a collective outcome. Of course, when people do interact, they are aware of others' actions and are thus subject to a collective influence: we expect something other than simple aggregation as the outcome. Here the micro–macro link focuses on the *mechanisms* that translate individual behavior into collective behavior, that is, on the mechanisms that do the aggregation (or disaggregation).

But the macro is of more interest than as a cumulation of the micro. It also plays a crucial part in determining the ways in which the micro units see themselves and directly shapes their behavior. That is, the macro acts on the micro units, which, in turn, generate the macro. More prosaically, collective outcomes affect individual beliefs, values, and decisions – which in turn produce the collective outcomes. This possibility is genuinely interesting.

It is potentially powerful because to the extent to which the micro and macro are self-referenced in their production functions, they will produce something that is a great deal more than the sum of its parts. In current language, the interactions between micro and macro yield "emergent properties" that are not obvious from an understanding of the micro units alone.

Thus, the argument comes full circle. The macro may be useful as a mere abstraction from the complex micro reality. As such, it is a convenient though perhaps imperfect representation of the world. However, when we come to understand that the macro drives itself through the micro units, we begin to see that macroanalysis demands a different sort of conceptual apparatus. Even if it were possible to understand the summation of the micro parts, we would need to do more. The macroanalysis now means something in and of itself.

Political Psychology as a Reductionist Strategy

When we explain macrophenomena with political psychology, we necessarily look at reductionist solutions. That is, because political psychology is primarily rooted in how individuals think, we produce explanations by showing that when we combine individuals we produce surprising or powerful macroresults. Two strategies suggest themselves. First, we may consider how ordinary people interact to produce surprising results for the macropolity. And, second, we may want to look closely at how political actors, those operating on the macrostage, produce surprising macro behavior that, in turn, affects ordinary people.

Political psychologists have long been engaged in the first sort of activity. We already know a lot about how ordinary people, and some extraordinary people, think about politics and react to events on the larger stage. What I want to suggest in this chapter is that the real payoff will lie in moving toward a political psychology that is explicitly embedded in a dynamic social system. When we study individuals, we want to study individuals as they translate their external world into a response that affects other people as well as professional political actors. And when we think about professionals, we want to think about how their thoughts and actions peculiarly influence each other and the broader polity – "peculiarly" in the sense that the results produce something other than a simple summation.

To be sure, most of political science deals with macrophenomena on their own terms, in their own logic, and short-circuits the reductionist pathway. That is, political scientists most often talk about Congress as an institution rather than about how the psychological makeup of individual members affects the collective entity. A political psychologist takes a different path and needs to show that doing so produces additional explanatory leverage.

THE STANDARD MODEL

Before arguing for more explicit concern about the connection between micro- and macroanalysis, we need to establish a baseline. The argument for political psychology will carry force only if it improves upon an elementary baseline model. In fact, such an elementary model is far from a straw man.

The obvious candidate is additive aggregation. That is to say, the macropolity reflects the sum of individual-level politics. Current discussion suggests that the mere aggregation of individuals produces a politics that makes much more sense than theory alone would suggest.

The basic idea is straightforward. It recognizes that individual citizens' views are ill informed, poorly integrated, and unstable. It posits that each individual has a "central tendency" attitude toward political objects and understands that the momentary expression of that attitude may reflect any number of (essentially random) deflections from the central tendency. For example, responses to surveys will reflect not only the "true" attitude but also "noise" elements due to the momentary events of the day, imprecise or peculiar questionnaire design, or other idiosyncratic factors. Further, the simple theory notes that the linear summation of such responses – across individuals or over time – will produce a cleaner measure of the true attitudes simply because the random noise will cancel out. Finally, aside from any correspondence with reality, this view has an additional appeal because it posits an "average" citizen who makes judgments about public policy. The aggregate or macro public opinion looks and sounds like a metaphorical person, and thus charms many.

In practice, this baseline model aims to represent a "public preference" not merely as a metaphor but also as an "adequate approximation" of politics. Most often, it reflects a public opinion poll about preferences and draws inferences about the direction of public sentiment. (More careful analysts speak of changes in the direction of public sentiment.) For example, from the mid-1970s through the early 1980s, public opinion polls showed that support for defense spending first rose and then fell. The inference was that the public changed its collective mind about the matter, presumably in accord with changes in actual conditions and political argument (Fan 1988).

When stated in this form, we understand the standard model to be a linear model – linear in the sense that individuals independently form the aggregate by adding up their experiences. This is, of course, a convenient simplification. Here I should like to add three complications that have the ability to change our fundamental view of how the micro and macro are connected: (1) the aggregation process affects the composition of the collectivity and how individuals interact with one another to produce something different from a simple sum of the parts; (2) the quality of the macropolitical life directly affects how individuals view the political world; and (3) the micro and macro worlds interact in a feedback system that makes the micro–macro connection implicitly nonlinear, if not chaotic, in its character.

I want to stress that the standard model makes much sense. While theoretically inadequate, it may serve as a useful social construct. To abandon this fiction, we need to find serious deleterious consequences of using the simplification – and suggest alternative views that make more sense.

THE IMPORTANCE OF AGGREGATION

It is common for politicians and political observers to speak casually of the public as though it were a single actor. It is not.

Importantly, we now fully appreciate how implausible is the very notion of a "public preference" concerning outcomes. Except under extraordinary circumstances, there exists no public preference about a set of alternatives (Arrow 1963; Riker 1982; and a host of others). This familiar theoretical result, sometimes regarded as a parlor trick, carries profound implications for the study of politics. For our purposes, political outcomes reflect not only (or even mainly) individual preferences but also the institutional mechanisms that translate those individual preferences into a collective choice (for example, Riker 1980). Thus, any attempt to speak of macropolitical action as a function of micropolitical preferences will need to consider the "institutional" translation mechanisms.

This much is well known. Most of political science studies those institutions and the actors within. Such topics as interest groups, parties, legislatures, bureaucracies, courts, and the mass media dominate typical departmental curricula. We fully understand that any references to a public preference represent a metaphor rather than a scientific construct. The real question is not whether institutional mechanisms are theoretically necessary components of the micro–macro connection; they are.

Instead, we ask how (or whether) political psychology can better inform our understanding of macropolitical outcomes. Most political science finds little of interest in political psychology. The question for us is whether this judgment is correct.

Compositional Factors

It is clear that the mass public includes different sorts of people. Any community will include individuals from different cultural political traditions who have distinctive political views. Importantly, some are more (or less) wealthy, educated, attentive to politics, likely to participate in politics, and so on. Does this matter?

Relative Weight. It is now a commonplace that the political public is different from the overall public. While this is surely true for the "electorate" of active voters as opposed to the citizenry of voters and nonvoters, it is more strongly true for other forms of political manifestations. The key is, of course, participation. The poor and poorly educated are less likely to vote – and much less likely to campaign or to contribute to candidates – and very much less likely to roam the halls of Washington to press home their points.

Given the flavor of the participant public, we can expect that politicians will naturally pay attention to those who pay attention. That is, politicians may ignore interests that have no active supporters because, other things being equal, politicians care about political power and unsupported interests are powerless. This argument is so widely appreciated that it hardly needs stating.

Being widespread, though, is not the same as being true. Clearly, the fundamental economic interests of the participant – as opposed to those of the nonparticipant – public will be slightly different. The homeless can hardly be expected to take full advantage of a specially reduced capital gains tax. However, our best evidence on the matter suggests that voters and nonvoters have similar preferences about policy – at least as posed in survey questionnaires. So, ignoring the interaction between micropreferences and macrobehavior that I shall emphasize later, it appears that using voting results as a simplification for public preferences works well enough. In any case, this is easily seen as a matter for political psychologists.

Composition Itself May Change. The composition of the "active" public is not set in stone. From time to time we may expect that different sorts of people will become more and less active. At the very least people may choose to get into politics when they see their interests and lives threatened. Thus, we observe increases in attention and turnout during the darkest days of 1932's Depression political campaign to the point where it may be argued that the fundamental shifts of the 1930s may have been due as much to the mobilization of nonvoting immigrant workers as to the policy questions of the day (Anderson 1986). Or, more recently, we observe an increase in the turnout rate of fundamentalist Christians during the 1994 election and another increase among African-Americans in 1998 – with the result that the "electorate" changed its preferences concerning political outcomes.

One might note that all of these shifts occurred at the margin. However, given the likelihood that political outcomes will often be balanced around the 50–50 point, we can expect that even slight changes in the composition of the electorate will have consequences for the winners and losers of election campaigns.

Marginal Behavior versus Typical Behavior

From the days of Robinson's (1950) warning, social scientists have been wary of the "ecological fallacy." We now well understand that aggregate behavior is not always a simple sum of individual behaviors. In fact, confusing the two will sometimes produce inferences that are just dead wrong. In the classic case, for example, southern counties with the largest percentage of blacks were the most likely to go for the segregationist candidates Strom Thurmond and George Wallace – because those counties were the ones in which black voters were most likely to be disenfranchised and white voters most likely to vote on segregationist lines.

More often, of course, the "individual" model will closely approximate macrobehavior. The distinctions will be subtle rather than sledgehammer – with the result that the investigator might be less inclined to see the distinctions.

Of course, given the differentiation in the mass public, simple representational models of the "average citizen" may not project into macrobehavior. If subsets of the public produce macrochange, then that change may reflect mechanisms different from those that typify the model citizen. This is particularly important for dynamic behavior.

Political Sophistication and Election Outcomes. An early, and widely propagated, version of the micro–macro distinction reflected the link between the distribution of political sophistication in the mass public and the way that elections were determined. Early evidence suggested that the most sophisticated people were also those most likely to have adopted strong partisan predispositions and least likely to shift their vote in any election. The marginal voters, those who actually determine macro-outcomes, were those least able to understand public affairs and most likely to base their vote on trivial concerns. Logically, then, the fact that many voters were reasonably knowledgeable did not matter because the voters deciding the outcomes were quite ignorant. And, naturally, the implication was that political decisions based on the macroelection result reflected an intelligence considerably less keen than that of the typical voter. (It turns out that this characterization carries less weight than it once did. For a surprising contradiction, see Zaller 1998. However, see the discussion below.)

Attentiveness and Macromovements. A few studies (for example, Converse 1962; MacKuen 1984; Weatherford 1983; Zaller 1992) have found that attentiveness to elite political debates conditions people's susceptibility to change.[3] This is characteristic of relatively low-level flows of information (say, year-to-year fluctuations in policy debate as opposed to presidential election campaigns). Thus, when the mass public changes its apparent preferences, it is typically the more attentive members who do the changing.[4]

In some regards, the more attentive merely do the work for their neighbors. When the essential political interests of the attentive and the inattentive are similarly distributed, the macroresult resembles that that might obtain if everyone were equally involved. This, it is claimed, typifies both the voting and nonvoting populations (for example, Wolfinger and Rosenstone 1980). Whether the same result holds for the chronically attentive and inattentive remains to be seen.

Dividing the whole into the attentive and the inattentive may produce distinctive dynamics. For example, month-to-month modest changes in opinion may be entirely limited to the attentive subset. If this is the case, then large-scale shifts will not necessarily result from the same factors that produce the smaller shifts.

3 Though, of course, for high-visibility presidential races the reverse holds. See Dreyer (1972) and Zukin (1977). For more subtlety, see Zaller (1990).
4 Note that Page and Shapiro (1992) report essentially no differences in opinion change when the public is broken down into subclassifications – one of which was education. Zaller (1992) is very careful to stress that awareness (rather than education or reported media usage) is a useful measure of how closely people are connected to the elite political debate. On the measurement point, he makes perfect sense. The theoretical–empirical matter is yet to be settled.

When highly sensitive citizens provide the juice for short-term movements, the source for change may lie in the elite political discussion that they routinely monitor. However, large-scale shifts necessitate messages (and communication mechanisms) that penetrate into the lower, less attentive strata of the public. Perhaps here we might expect the need for (1) *emotional engagement* – a redefinition of how issues get framed, or (2) *reality changes* – that are reflected in the day-to-day lives of apolitical citizens, or (3) *interpersonal communications* – that begin to get revved up only when real-world situations require close consideration by ordinary people (note the diffusion models of Rogers 1962 and others).

We need to work on understanding the difference between superficial and profound public opinion change. The political psychology of attitude change may thus incorporate subtleties the importance of which depends on the character of change that is of interest.

Partisanship and Presidential Approval. In our study of macrolevel partisanship and presidential approval (MacKuen, Erikson, and Stimson 1989), we expected to see that fluctuations in this level of partisanship would affect current and subsequent presidential approval. After all, in cross-sectional microanalysis, we always observe Republicans favoring Republican presidents and Democrats favoring Democrats. Adding to or subtracting Republicans (or Democrats) from the aggregate would seem likely to produce higher or lower approval ratings for Republican (or Democratic) presidents.

This microlevel expectation is disappointed. Shocks to the level of macropartisanship affect not at all the public's judgment of the incumbent president. A little thought suggests that merely extrapolating from an individual to the collectivity might be a mistake.

Consider the fact that the microlevel relationship between partisanship and presidential approval is probably due to colored perceptions of presidential performance. That is, Democrats are likely to dwell on good news about Democratic presidents while dismissing bad news as unimportant, irrelevant, or mean-spirited attacks from the press. These sorts of mechanisms are likely to be most powerful for an emotionally charged partisanship – one based on a sort of "yellow dog" loyalty. Yet, such partisans are those least likely to shift their orientation in accord with the year-to-year political-economic forces that move macropartisanship. Instead, the macromovement comes from Fiorina Key–type[5] people for whom partisanship is merely a "standing voting decision." And, of course, these are the individuals who are *least* likely to color their

5 As in Fiorina (1981) and Key (1966).

emotional perceptions of the political world in general and the president in particular.

Nonindependence of Individuals

A long-standing interest of political psychology (or social psychology) has been the way in which people interact. Visions of a "mass society" populated by automatons have been unfulfilled. Instead, we now understand that people live in social groupings that affect their political lives. The political social psychology of human interaction suggests real consequences both for how people form their opinions and for how they transmit those views to the broader polity.

The Importance of Social and Political Contexts. In the most straightforward way, people interact and influence each other. A fairly long research tradition, if not yet fully developed, has shown that people's political behavior depends in part on their social context. Earlier work by Berelson, Lazarsfeld, and McPhee (1954), Miller (1956), and Butler and Stokes (1969), as well as that of MacKuen and Brown (1987), Krassa (1990), and Gibson (1992), gave indications of such phenomena: people's preferences, and changes in their preferences, depend on the preferences of their social milieu.

More recently, Huckfeldt and Sprague, in a sustained collaboration, have begun to explore the subtleties of social influence processes. It is now clear that mutual influence depends both on the views of partners and on the character of the broader social setting (1987, 1988, 1990, 1991). Further, local institutions such as the political party (1992) and the church (Huckfeldt, Plutzer, and Sprague 1993) appear to play a crucial role in carrying social signals in indirect, and thus hidden, ways.

This work, yet to attract enough attention, serves to remind us that people's political behavior depends critically on the context in which it is formed. The macroenvironment, the collections of microenvironments, exerts influence on individuals both through simple reductionist interactions and through local institutions that structure those interactions.

While we now appreciate the structural form of social relations, its importance for macroprocesses has yet to be fully appreciated. At the very least, these social effects produce *nonlinear* relationships between opinion and outcome – both over space and over time. That is to say that, in response to external stimuli, collective political behavior should exhibit the sorts of irregularities common in nonlinear models rather than the scatterplot linearities with which social scientists are familiar and comfortable. We are just now beginning to appreciate the theoretical implications of nonlinearity.

THE SPIRAL OF SILENCE, POLITICAL DELIBERATION, AND THE APPEARANCE OF CONSENSUS

Most individuals, to some extent, prefer positive rather than negative feedback from their conversational partners. Noelle-Neuman (1984) describes this as a "fear of social isolation." If people perceive their social environment to be sufficiently friendly, they will talk about politics; if they see it as sufficiently unfriendly, they will talk about other matters. Because minorities are unwilling to speak out, they spiral toward silence (Noelle-Neuman 1984).

The result is an artificial hegemony (MacKuen 1990). Within any grouping, only one view or the other will dominate – opponents will encounter instant and decisive negative reactions. Social collectivities appear (but in reality are not) unified on matters. Further, they reflect little deliberation because "opponents" rarely raise their voices.

Given this appearance of consensus, then, democratic politics appears to work well. Politicians have no trouble satisfying the desire for unanimity, and the classic public choice problems obligingly vanish from sight. This appearance is misleading. Of course, the key mechanism is the fact that many private opinions never become public opinion. That is, public judgments that are expressed forcefully are clearly different from a mere summation of individual judgments. Important for our theoretical point, the social mechanisms that govern the translation of private considerations into public opinion are crucial. We need to understand the mechanisms as much as the individual psychology.

This matter is interesting for politics because so much of politics finds its roots in geographical or social collectivities. Politicians represent regions, lobbyists represent social interests, and so on. When such social factors are important, political deliberation becomes fragmented into pockets of false consensus – with clear-cut implications for democratic governance. In the contemporary American South, it is hard for liberal ideas to get a serious hearing; in the African-American community it is equally hard for conservative views to be considered. The marketplace of ideas, so vital for democracy, resembles less the vast free trade zones of North America or the European Union and more the isolated local monopolies of the nineteenth century.

THE IMPORTANCE OF MACROPHENOMENA FOR MICROBEHAVIOR

While it is clear that the aggregation of individuals into a collectivity is far from a simple matter, it should also be obvious that phenomena at the macro level affect the views, decisions, and behavior of individuals at the micro level. This connection, one that begins to close the feedback loop between micro and macro, is pregnant with theoretical import.

Users' Choice

Start with the idea that people use the concept of a macroentity if it proves useful. Macrophenomena are, of course, constructs rather than objective facts. That is, such entities as "society" or the "electorate" or "politicians" are conceptual overlays (familiar ones, to be sure) on a complicated mix of human life. Note that the simplification – that the macro can be identified as particular aggregates of individuals – works if it serves its users. Most people need some simplification because it does them little good to say that "things are complex." Think of three needs that the simplification serves. First, people have *instrumental* needs. Politicians need to think about the public or their constituency in terms simple enough to have meaning. Of course, successful politicians will also understand complexity and nuance. Nevertheless, the shorthand works pretty well most of the time. Second, a social collectivity allows people to *identify themselves* in a broader scheme of things. They belong to something. People may consider themselves Americans or Republicans or college professors or liberals. And, finally, they deal with the macroworld to *express themselves* in a broader sense. They are able to project anger, pleasure, disappointment, and hope onto the world stage.[6]

This macrocollectivity is more important than it seems. Of course, collective decisions depend on the institutions that transform individual preferences into public outcomes. But the macrocollectivity is, in itself, an important feature of those transforming mechanisms. The obvious example is the fact that elected politicians must correctly understand the collective preferences (and subsequent behavior) of their electoral constituencies. They make mistakes at the risk of losing their jobs.

When people use the collectivity, they use it as a sort of mirror that shows the relationship between themselves and everyone else. The mirror, of course, has utility to the extent to which people achieve either their instrumental, identificatory, or expressive goals using that fiction (or people would invent other fictions). Importantly, Mutz (1998) suggests that this mirror allows people to carry on a proto-conversation with

---

6 This view has become common over the years. For different perspectives in early work, see Lasswell (1930) and Katz (1960).

the social other (in the same sense as George Herbert Meade) to create a sense of their political selves.

Whether this macromirror reflects the collectivity directly is not in question. It cannot. We know that no method of aggregation can produce a correct reflection of the many. (Though people who do survey research, with its atomistic probability samples, may be forgiven for simply assuming that their methodology picks up something inherently real.) Instead, we want to know both (1) how people create this mirror of reality and (2) how the constructed mirror warps people's perceptions and, ultimately, their behavior.

This matter is interesting both for political elites and for ordinary citizens. For example, most politicians and observers communicate with each other, and in many ways cooperate, in constructing the fictional representation of the collectivity. Journalists share in their production of a widely visible "social reality." Politicians have strong incentives to develop an appreciation for that social reality and, perhaps, may profit from sharing their perceptions with one another.[7] Saying that many people share the same construction does not mean that the construction is any more real than another construction – except to the extent to which a widely shared construction may have more weighty consequences than idiosyncratic constructions. And that is a matter for investigation, not implicit assumption. In the end, we shall want to know more about how the political community's perceptual mechanisms serve its interests and affect political outcomes.

When we think of the macropolity as an instrumental construct, it is easiest to see how it works for politicians. But it may work equally powerfully for ordinary people. We have known for some time that people use cues in their social environment to determine the nature of the world. Given the inherently ambiguous nature of social information, they find a "social reality test" especially appropriate for making judgments about distant events. Now this has been especially important

---

7 Note that politicians deal with a more predictable world when they and their opponents share an understanding about the outside world. When politicians rely on idiosyncratic views (or must anticipate that opponents do so), uncertainty rises immensely. Of course, uncertainty may be desirable for politicians who seek to win only the next election. Yet, politicians must endeavor to manage political careers extending over decades. Successfully managing a career means successfully managing uncertainty. It thus may be possible that politicians, even opposing politicians, will by evolutionary mechanisms develop processes that produce widely shared images of the collectivity because deviants will find their careers foreshortened (and thus disappear from the population of politicians).

from the late twentieth century on because people's views of what
is worth thinking about seem most clearly pointed toward national
and international affairs.[8] And it is just those distant affairs, distant in
space, time, and personal control, about which people have, and can
have, practically no personal knowledge. They must rely on social
cues to make sense of what is happening. And those social cues must be
rooted in the macropolitical system. For example, when people make
judgments about the state of economic affairs, they may consider the
nature of their own personal environment (that is, the economic state
of their family, friends, and workplace). In addition, they may want to
consider news about the local or national (or international) economy.
Alternatively, when people must evaluate the safety of modern times,
they may consider their own personal experience with crime or they may
consider the flow of news about crime in the larger society. It seems that
different sorts of people use different sorts of information to make such
social judgments.

Anticipated Reactions

The simple model may appear to work when in fact the observed relationship between changes in public sentiment and politics represents a
(genuine) spurious link. Consider "third person effects" (see Davison
1983). These occur when political actors presume that their actions will
be closely watched by another audience, which will act unless it is
satisfied. (Politicians look into the mirror and see their image reversed.
They act to please that image.)

Such a phenomenon fits a commonsense understanding of ordinary
politics. Elite actors engage in a policy debate. Mass publics then pick
up that debate and react in accord with their predispositions – conservatives and liberals choosing sides predictably. Politicians then react to
the elite debate in anticipation that their constituents will act on their
"mimicked" beliefs. After a while, it may not matter at all what the mass
public actually does. The anticipated reaction will be enough.

Of course, from time to time, elites will be caught out when they discover that the public misunderstands the elite debate or the public stops
paying attention. Numerous are the instances of politicians who claimed,
and were believed, to represent the voice of an enormous faction – only
to find their presumed followers disconnected.

8 For a useful argument about the roots of this phenomenon, see Wiebe (1973), who
  suggests that the national press, for its own reasons, focuses on national and international stories. People thus are exposed to this frame for news and attend to its
  character.

Individuals Writ Large

When the linear aggregation approximation works, political psychology still has things to say that suggest that the "rational reaction" model may be enhanced.

Schemas, Stereotypes, and Opinion Formation. People clearly use models of the world to understand how it works. These mental constructs may take various forms, and over the years we have developed different ways to describe them. However, the basic point remains that when people encounter information about policies or politicians, they associate the information with internal representations. What is of interest here is the extent to which those representations are built up from the ground or are plucked from similar, though more familiar, phenomena.

These matters affect the dynamics of the macropolity. Clearly, to the extent to which people rely on old stereotypes to process information, the macrosystem will have difficulty adjusting to new events and conditions. The question is, how quickly can people and politicians reshape their understandings of the political world?

The Collective Meaning of Individual Life. In an odd way, the collectivity seems to help individuals make up their minds about their own lives. It appears that media coverage of political problems (which are, by convention, treated as national or community problems) heightens people's awareness of those problems in their own lives. For example, people who are unemployed begin to see unemployment as a serious problem when they are told by the press that their job loss is a systemic problem rather than a personal one (see Erbring, Goldenberg, and Miller 1980; Mutz 1994). In this sense, the individual life takes on special meaning from the collective experience.[9] Important for politics, people's lives are transformed by the character of political discussion – a political discussion that is rooted in the strategies and tactics of politicians maneuvering on the macropolitical battlefield. And those understandings of personal lives can further fuel the political drives of politicians who seek popular support.

---

9 There is nothing mystical about this. People are entirely reasonable in revising how they see their own lives in the context of the broader experience. People who are laid off during hard times should surely see their future differently than those laid off during booms. At a minimum, the prospects for obtaining a new job should be much less favorable. More telling, a broader societywide depression emphasizes to people that their own fortunes are linked to palpable outside social circumstances in a way that is not nearly so obvious for the boom-time layoff.

Agenda Setting, Framing, and Priming. We now well understand that people must decide among different reference criteria (or considerations) when they think their way through difficult political questions. We also understand that their choice among those "frames" depends in some ways on the mass media (Iyengar 1991; Iyengar and Kinder 1987; and the mass communication agenda-setting literature). These understandings go partway toward explaining opinion shift and opinion stability in the general public. They also inform our understanding of the fundamental character of political judgment that must energize a democracy.

Understanding more clearly how individuals choose among competing considerations will move us forward. Rudimentary factors such as salience and centrality clearly make sense. Yet, we have far to go before we can appreciate the nature of this problem. And we should pursue the matter because it will inform our fundamental judgments about the character of macropolitics as well as microdecisions.

THE POLITICS OF THE MICRO–MACRO CONNECTION

While we understand that microbehavior is sensitive to macrophenomena, we need to explore the ways that political actors understand this phenomenon and try to take advantage of it. When this happens, it produces a feedback system that connects microdecisions to macrophenomena, which then affect microbehavior.

Composition and Differential Feedback

Composition factors have implications beyond the well-appreciated linear bias. To be sure, when the active polity represents disproportionately a particular class of political interests, we expect politicians to weight that class's interests disproportionately in their calculations. But when we consider the interaction between micro and macro, this sort of composition has even richer dynamic implications.

Take, for example, the character of political communications. While the voting public is only modestly more upscale than the population as a whole, other relevant subgroups are decidedly more filtered in their nature. Writers of letters to the editor, radio talk show callers, political contributors, Kiwanis Club members, and party activists are of a different stripe. While distinct from each other, each group represents a keenly attentive potential clientele for politicians and journalists. And it is the politicians and journalists who are of primary interest because these are the "firms" who must sell their "products" – their ideas – to a particular market made up of attentive and activist citizens. The producers of public debate thus shape their discourse to appeal to their market, and so we have a political dialogue that reflects the active strata of the general public.

What makes this observation powerful is the realization that the active strata thus define the terms of political debate and, indirectly, the political views of the less keenly attentive. Thus, observing a similarity in views between the overall population and the voting public misses the point. The poor and alienated, when they dip into daily political discussion, must deal with an intellectual framework congenial to the activist elite strata. The desperate two-job-a-day marginal income earner gets to think about the implications of capital gains tax reduction for the flow of international capital! In a sense, the poor must choose between options that are already stacked toward elites – or they drop out. The positive feedback system here pushes the deliberation of ordinary governance away from the language and lives of ordinary people and toward the language and lives of the politically active.

While this particular observation makes sense and may be worth closer investigation, the more general phenomenon surely does. When systems exist with feedback, the dynamics will often produce interesting results, ones not always evident from a linear-type analysis.

Conditional Model of Voter Psychology

While the mechanisms of politics may change over time, equally, they may prove (partly) endogenous. It is surely the case that the public's political involvement (rather than any given individual's involvement) varies over time. This may have dramatic implications for how the representation system works.

A powerful example lies in Nie, Verba, and Petrocik's (1976) evidence on over-time variation in the cross-sectional correlation between citizen preferences (on class distributional issues) and the vote. For both the well informed and the ill informed, the correlation was highest during the unrest of the Depression years and the tumult of the 1960s. More notably, the difference in those correlations was smallest during these periods of "hot politics." That is to say, the inattentives began to cast a policy vote only during periods of macropolitical excitement.

The clear inference is that class voting depends on external stimuli to motivate the ill informed to pay attention and vote "properly." (During the quiescent 1950s and 1970s, they voted almost without regard to class issues.) Thus, political psychology turns out to be decisive for the method of aggregation. These external stimuli – here, the unrest of the Depression years and the tumult of the 1960s – activated the consciousness of the chronically less attentive – here, the less educated – so that their voting choices better matched their political attitudes.

Of course, the question remains, how? Was it the unrest, and hence anxiety, that characterized these eras (Marcus, Neuman, and MacKuen 2000)? Was it a matter of politics reflecting societal divisions? (Note that Depression-era politics was on everyone's lips, as were the cultural issues of the 1960s.) In any case, politics entered the active consciousness of a larger portion of the electorate. This mass mobilization – in which typically complacent members of the public suddenly become critically concerned and engaged – deserves more attention.

The Meaning of Elections

Let us revisit the matter of the electorate's being comprised of people with varying levels of political sophistication. Now throw in our understanding about politicians' strategies for political communication and the new generation of (political science–trained) political consultants. Such consultants understand (say, from the "levels of conceptualization" argument) that the citizens who are most susceptible to persuasion are those who think of politics in terms of "the nature of the times" or "the candidate's personality." Accordingly, they craft political communications suitable for the target audience – emphasizing the simplest versions of blame and scandal. After a time, such messages come to define the stakes of political campaigns, so that even more sophisticated participants begin to see barroom brawls as the essence of democratic deliberation.

At the end of the day, these subtle differences in feedback may lead to cynicism about the character of democratic rule. Note the divergence between the terms of ordinary political discussion – as defined by an activist's mindset – and the language of election campaigns – as defined by the casual voter. The observer might well be excused for taking election campaigns as cynical attempts to manipulate a foolish public. Rather than seeing a "feast of democracy," the contemporary observer of today's political chefs sees nothing more than pastries and wine.

Hyperdemocracy

Alternatively, the macropolitical world may generate modest changes in the microenvironment but completely misunderstand the linkages. The feedback between system and individual may produce a collective irrationality – a hyperrepresentation.

A good example is the Len Bias case in 1986. Shortly after the National Basketball Association draft, Len Bias – a star University of Maryland basketball player and first-round pick of the Boston Celtics – died of a cocaine overdose. The Washington press gave the case enormous coverage as an example of how drugs were destroying lives. Shortly thereafter,

Washington politicians descended on talk shows to make speeches about the terrible drug problem. When they went home for recess, they discovered that their home contacts (the politically attentive) were now concerned about the drug problem. Accordingly, they returned to Washington to make more demagogic speeches, found the public even more interested, and passed a lot of dramatic legislation.[10] "Drug kingpin" became part of our collective language. Only later did the public discussion notice that the drug problem in America had actually been declining.

A Common Political Language and a Common Political Landscape

Reconsider the "ideology" argument made by Converse in 1964. He was interested in the liberal–conservative dimension because that was the shorthand used by journalists and politicians to think about the political world. The surprise, of course, was that so few people used such abstractions or, for that matter, could explain what those terms meant.

The labels "liberal" and "conservative" continue to be meaningful for the attentive stratum in American politics. Politicians and people use these terms to signal one another about the bundle of policies, the public philosophies, that they favor. They remain the lingua franca of political life – despite the fact that the terms carry less and less intrinsic meaning. Note that:

1. People and politicians need stereotypes. The actual political world is too complicated to understand in its fullness, so everyone needs simplifications in order to make easy sense of it. This is particularly true for the media masters: they need such simple representations so that they can produce widely accepted symbolic arguments.

2. For many politicians, knowing the politics of the district is crucial. However, more important than knowing is the sense of knowing. Having *something* on which to base a judgment is a prerequisite to having confidence in one's decisions. (Surely the simplification is incomplete, yet it may serve the purpose. If the signal is correlated, even weakly, with the genuine article, then the signal will carry information and the user will do better attending to the signal than not.)

---

10 Given the contemporary budget constraints, they had to cut programs to get the proper symbolic increase in police spending. My favorite was the cut in school lunch programs because it was more important to keep students drug free then well fed.

3. The signal identifies friends and foes. This is especially important for politicians who are making their own way in a crowded political minefield. Especially in intraparty conflict, they need to find some way to attract potential supporters in an efficient manner. Individuals need friends and foes to make sense of the world as well (Sniderman, Tetlock, and Brody 1991).
4. Ideological signaling helps identify oneself in the broader political world. (This is helpful for both the politician and the person.)

Thus, the symbolic ideology of liberal–conservative serves politicians, journalists, and ordinary citizens. As long as everyone agrees on what these terms mean, the fiction works well enough.

However, we understand that these representations are highly fractionated images. Importantly, liberals and conservatives have different understandings about the meanings of the terms (Conover and Feldman 1981). Essentially, they bring different "considerations" (Zaller 1992) to this definition. These considerations reflect dominant American values, with a different emphasis on which values are taken as first. (Order and fairness are both well regarded, but the relative ranks differ for conservatives and liberals.)

This distinction reflects the sorts of deep ambivalence that characterize many other forms of politically interesting questions (see Hochschild 1981; Zaller 1992). These questions are of political interest precisely *because* they tap deeply felt ambiguities. Thus, politicians who seek *wedge* issues, those issues that divide the public, for their own professional advantage will, in the pursuit of their own interests, constantly chip away at any consensual definitions of the meaning of politics.

This fractionation of ideology is particularly interesting from a macropolitical viewpoint. We understand, from theoretical work, that the pressing problems of "majority cycling" – in which politicians continuously outmaneuver each other in a policy space – arise when the structure of the policy space is at least two-dimensional. Of course, in theory all policy spaces are multidimensional. However, in practical politics, single-issue dimensions can come to dominate political life. (In national politics such cases are termed "alignments," such as when the debate about government's role in the economy in the 1930s produced the New Deal alignment.) When governments can control the political agenda around a single dimension, policy outcomes prove more or less stable and reflect public desires. Otherwise, no straightforward result occurs. Alignment becomes dealignment or realignment.

Equally important, when a common single dimension dominates both popular understanding and elite signaling, the fuller polity will "speak a common language." They will share a common fiction. When matters fractionate, it will be difficult to communicate properly. Moreover, people who find that their views project poorly into the elite language will find it difficult to identify with, or even understand, the nature of national politics.[11] Disengagement, if not raw disgust, is sure to follow.

POLITICS AS PUBLIC PSYCHOLOGY

The main argument here is that the way people think and act in politics depends enormously on the way that others think and act. Politics, and the psychology of politics, are fundamentally social in character. This has implications both for the way we conceive political psychology and for the part that political psychology plays in real-world political life.

On the Science and Politics of Measurement

The fundamental meaning of a "public" depends on the mechanisms used to tap it. When the nation holds elections to make decisions, the electoral mechanism elicits a certain sort of response. Some types of people show up, while others do not. Some people think about the future, others about the past. For some, what matters is a tentative standing decision, while for others, the decision must be made from the evidence at hand. The nature of the collective entity is thus defined by the context in which the entity reveals itself. Yet, the same public might be probed by an atomistic telephone poll. Or the character of the public might be examined by means of depth interviews to uncover the individual person's thought processes. The character of the public will thus change, including some people and excluding others, motivating some and not others, and so on. The instruments used to measure or to identify the public will have much to say about what one sees.

For research purposes, it may make sense to use mechanisms that resemble natural mechanisms. But there are different natural mechanisms in the public. One model is that of the election – in which individuals are asked to make simple summary judgments about candidates or referendum-type questions. However, this mimicking of official mechanisms may miss the point. Equally interesting are poll results. Many observers consider polls genuine manifestations of the public's desires; thus the polls are an important feature of day-to-day political life. Here the researcher needs to construct probes that mimic poll questions – with all their transparent simplicity. And further, one might want to mimic the

---

11 Of course, when people cannot share in a common language with political elites, many will make up their own. Rich understandings about political psychology might emanate from closer scrutiny of the radio call-in shows.

sort of day-to-day political conversation that rumbles through the public. Here a focus group might be the instrument of choice.

The point here is that there exists no real public out there, eagerly awaiting discovery. Instead, there exist natural processes that may be emulated as defining the character of the public. Yet, it is not obvious that the natural mechanisms are uniquely to be preferred. The probing depth interviews of Lane (1962) and Hochschild (1981) revealed much about the character of the public in ways that hardly resemble anything in ordinary life. The choice of mechanism will help define the outcome, and no particular mechanism captures the true world. The investigator's scientific construct must be the primary consideration. My argument is that we need to think hard about what is politically interesting. Clearly, when one wants to see the public as politicians do, the mock election or the public opinion poll makes the most sense.

The Nature of Political Thought

At a more fundamental level, the essence of private microviews depends on the operation of the macropolitical system. We know that people's opinions depend on the context in which they are elicited. Zaller and Feldman (1992) show that people's attitudes toward standing issues in the public debate depend crucially on the considerations that they bring to bear – and that those considerations vary over time. The underlying processes that generate particular considerations may be either deterministic but unknown or they may be fundamentally probabilistic (in a quantum sense). In either case, we may suspect strongly that those psychological systems will depend in part on the external environment. In the narrowest sense of that external environment, the survey questionnaire, we have good experimental evidence that the context will sometimes shape survey responses. More important, we have both experimental and field evidence that people's assessments of the U.S. president or presidential candidates are affected by the way the judgments are framed by the media-public debate. The considerations are "primed" by outside forces to make some judgments more likely than others (Iyengar 1991; Iyengar and Kinder 1987; Krosnick and Kinder 1990; Nelson, Clawson, and Oxley 1997).

In one sense, this representation implies that people make up opinions as they go along. Most political scientists would reject that view as being too harsh. It is not. When people are asked to give judgments on matters that they have not previously considered, they must manufacture, not merely recall, a response. To be sure, for many people issues such as abortion or welfare or crime will have formed the subject of previous conversations. They will have *rehearsed* their opinions in the sense that they will have previously verbalized opinions in a social setting – a setting that will give external validation to the voiced view – and thus will have previously manufactured an opinion. However, even these people will have to fit their previously rehearsed opinions into the questionnaire frame or policy debate as it is articulated in the particular instance. For most people most of the time, the political situation will force them to create an opinion on the spot – inviting them to recall what they can from their own previous rehearsals and make sense of the particulars of the questionnaire or the nature of the public debate. Thus, they take some nascent ideas and see what they can do to fit those views into the current context – as though they were solving a little puzzle. We now understand why people's views are sometimes so sensitive to context – the context shapes how elementary considerations are formulated into an opinion.

What I want to say is this: people's political psychologies are fundamentally social. Their beliefs and values are embedded in a social system that produces, reinforces, and changes them. This is clearly true at the large-scale level. Political culture largely defines what is interesting and what is not, what is plausible and what is not. And political socialization teaches children, and later adults, what sorts of beliefs and values are to be considered at all.

But my point is sharper, and perhaps more radical, than the political culture argument. Day-to-day political views are also rooted in the macropolitical context. Imagine encountering a young man who was raised by wolves; now imagine asking his views on abortion, welfare reform, and foreign aid. Or imagine yourself transported to the 1890s to be asked about monetizing silver, civil service reform, and American imperialism. These attitudes only make sense in the political context of the time and only to those who have "followed" the reading of the text. Equally important, that "text," the framing of the debate by setting some considerations to the fore and relegating others to the background, is a product of the larger political environment. It is an outcome of self-conscious political actors pursuing strategies structured by the rules of the game that places "public attitudes" at the core of political power. And those political actors set the debate in terms that will elicit from the public the sorts of responses that the political actors deem helpful in their own pursuit of political policy and political power.

Systemic Elicitation of Public Opinion

Think about two ways in which the political system might tap public opinion. First, political actors struggle over the ways that opinion is elicited. Trivially, public opinion pollsters may choose questions, or question orderings, that produce predictable results. More interesting, politicians work hard to shape the terms of public debate and the character of particular election campaigns – so that their side has the best chance of winning. Thus, most often when we learn the public's opinion, we learn about how they respond to the particular questions put to them. When we want to know about politics, we must know not only the answers but also the questions that fit the answers.

Second, and perhaps more profound, the normal forms of democracy have built-in characteristic ways of eliciting opinion. Consider two extremes. In the first, imagine a small town setting where people need to decide about rebuilding a bridge over the local stream. When elections, or public decisions, are about the individuals' *scene* – that is, decisions are about people, places, and things that reside in the individuals' life spaces – then we expect the opinion elicited to be highly conscious and reflect some potential feedback. Poor decisions about the bridge will lead to a real, observable, collapse. In contrast, think about people deciding national affairs such as a balanced budget or foreign aid. It is hard to imagine anyone knowing, really knowing, success and failure. When public decisions are about matters far removed from people's personal scenes, we expect that the opinions elicited will contain strong doses of unchecked fantasy. That is to say, the opinion that national politics elicits is so weakly linked to any real-world evidence that it is largely a matter of imagination. And because the beliefs and values simply do not carry consequences for individuals, those individuals may produce thoughts that are entirely nonsense. That people don't know much about the national budget process or about foreign aid is no surprise. That these views are taken seriously is.

We want to know more about how people and political elites see the basic relationship between the shaping of political debate and the nature of the public response. We want to know how they think about these matters, how they strategize for political power, and how they evaluate political debate and the public response altogether. Anecdotal evidence suggests that some people do indeed think seriously about the implications of these connections. Yet, it appears that most do not, and further, most do not care.

THE MICRO–MACRO DISTINCTION RECONSIDERED

Understanding just how the micro and macro are interconnected will move us forward a great deal. This is true for two main reasons. First, as I've argued all along, the very meaning of politics stems from how people handle the micro–macro gap. We make our most telling contributions to political science when we develop our understanding about how the micro and macro worlds interact to produce something important for human lives. And second, the interaction between the micro and macro has profound implications for how we begin to rethink the nature of democratic governance. When the world is essentially linear (or atomistic), we can talk loosely about an aggregate public. However, when things get more complicated in terms of the generation of the macro, the reflection of the macro in the micro, and finally the conscious interaction between the two, we can readily anticipate theoretical relationships that are at least nonlinear and possibly chaotic in character. The connection between the individual and society may be fundamentally beyond practical understanding.

Political Meaning Rooted in the Micro–Macro System

When we care about politics and psychology, we care about how the way people think affects the way they live together. Usually this means we care about how people's thought processes affect, and are affected by, the battle over the right ordering of society, over the distribution of value, or over the terms of social cooperation.

In our original example, the matter of mass belief systems, we care about how individuals conceive politics because their conceptions affect the ways that politicians are likely to act. And, of course, those politicians' actions will, in turn, affect the ways that people view political life. Similarly, we want to know more about how people choose considerations and then formulate political preferences – and how political actors go about the business of shaping the ways that people derive their preferences. Or we want to know more about how the character of political conflict and consensus spills over to people's psyches to either stimulate or suppress political participation. In all these cases, we want to understand how ordinary people, political activists, and professional politicians deal with the broader macropolitical world as they go about their daily business.

My main argument here is that we are interested in political psychology as a fundamental way to study politics, not as a mere exercise ground for studying thoughts. And political psychology will be most powerful when it explicitly sites consciousness in the strategic operation of the political system.

A Nonlinear World

One primary implication of this discussion is that *in theory* we expect nonlinearities in the link between the individual and the polity. Or, alternatively, we understand that the richness implicit in the micro–macro connection will come into play as the empirical world becomes apparently nonlinear.

To be sure, for much of our political psychology, things look pretty well approximated by linear models. That is, when we model collective outcomes, they look pretty much as we would expect were the collectivity a loose atomistic aggregation of individual decision makers. When this pattern dominates, then the micro–macro mechanisms may be largely peripheral. (That is to say, they may operate but their import may be hidden.)

On the other hand, we understand that much of politics is full of surprises – dramatic collective actions that cannot easily be explained or (better) predicted by simply adding up individual actions. When the country went into its hyperdemocratic frenzy over the Len Bias cocaine story, no one could have predicted the actions from a linear model built around the nature of the public problem. It took intense positive feedback in the micro–macro link to produce such a dramatic consequence from such an ordinary disturbance. When the American electorate voted the Democrats out of Congress in 1994, the composition of the electorate changed – traditional Democrats became discouraged and sat the election out, while religious fundamentalists turned out in large numbers. In both cases, public opinion changed in the sense that the public manifestation changed. And, of course, this is the point.

Nonlinear politics requires a substantial revision of our commonsense view of democracy. Understanding that individuals' preferences do not imply collective choices revolutionized our appreciation of the very nature of democratic politics. Now, when we understand that micro- and macropolities are fundamentally interconnected, we understand that nonlinearities, even chaos, will result. Consider the implication. When we normally think about the dynamics between exogenous forces and political outcomes, we think in linear terms. That is, we expect that the exogenous forces will affect politics in a potentially predictable way. However, when the exogenous forces must feed through a highly coupled system, one in which small disturbances can produce major results, then the link between cause and effect practically disappears. That is, we cannot expect a standard pattern to connect economic change or foreign crisis or a political event with the ensuing political outcome. I don't mean to say that things are complicated and thus difficult to predict – though, of course, that is true. Instead, I mean that our ability to predict the political future is *fundamentally* flawed by the nonlinear connections about which we have spoken. This is a matter of mathematics, not intellectual capacity. When we see a political event, we cannot say whether it will be important or not.

Now, knowing that nonlinear politics is very different from the standard "linear aggregation" politics is helpful. However, it may not be crucial. At some levels of scale, say year-to-year changes, it may well be that the simpler linear understanding makes empirical sense. When the public wants more or less it gets more or less. The quick riffs that comprise the daily drama of the nightly newscasts may be totally unimportant for the politics of human lives. And catastrophic changes of the sort that characterized the Progressive Conservative demise in Canada and the fall of communism in Eastern Europe may be so rare as to be unpredictable in any case. So the theoretical argument and the examples set forth in this chapter may not be compelling. Yet, it seems to me that the argument is sufficiently strong on its face that we want to know more about when nonlinearities are likely to rise up and drive outcomes.

What we are looking for is some sort of life in the aggregate that is distinctive from a transparent aggregation of individuals. We are looking for emergent properties in macrobehavior. That is, we are looking for evidence that politics conducted at the macro level has its own character. There is nothing mystical here – the macro is in fact made up of aggregated microexperience – but what is interesting is the possibility that the rules of aggregation so combine the microinputs as to produce a systemic response that takes on a very different character.

In the most stark terms, we want to know if we must study the means of aggregation to get leverage on the macro-outcomes. The "straw man" opponent is a reductionist psychologist who claims that once you understand how the human mind works, the rest is trivial – just as a biologist might encounter a physicist who claims that once you understand particle physics, the rest is chemistry. In the physical sciences, it is clear that macrosystems do take on emergent properties – and that it is those emergent properties that constitute the nature of different scientific disciplines. Here we wonder if the emergent properties of a macropolitical system are sufficiently rich to demand a different scientific discipline for their study.

Having said all this, it is not yet clear that a simple macroconceptualization, rooted in the standard linear model, must be abandoned. Page and Shapiro (1992) show clearly that the public reacts to specific issues in ways that make perfect sense. So it is entirely reasonable to expect governments to reflect those sensible judgments.

Further, it appears that the macropolity reflects large-scale changes that also make sense. Stimson's (1991) analysis reveals that when people change their views on specific issues, they also change their views on others. This commonality should truly surprise political psychologists.

Finding that the public shifted from conservative to liberal to conservative to liberal over the past forty years suggests something systematic at the macro level that is not captured in microlevel analyses. This macrolevel change has macrolevel consequences. The movement in mood affects both presidential and congressional elections – in a way that is independent of the simultaneous changes in partisanship and national economic performance. Finally, these large-scale shifts also resonate in the policies that Washington has produced (Stimson, MacKuen, and Erikson 1995), and those policies reflect back on public opinion (Erikson, MacKuen and Stimson 2001).

Without getting bogged down in details, this entirely macrolevel analysis greatly expands our view of democratic governance. There may be more to the noble myth than has heretofore been realized.

References

Andersen, Kristi. 1986. *The Creation of a Democratic Majority.* Chicago: University of Chicago Press.

Arrow, Kenneth. 1963. *Social Choice and Individual Values,* 2nd ed. New York: Wiley.

Berelson, Bernard R., Paul F. Lazarsfeld, and William N. McPhee. 1954. *Voting: A Study of Opinion Formation in a Presidential Campaign.* Chicago: University of Chicago Press.

Butler, David, and Donald Stokes. 1969. *Political Change in Britain.* New York: St. Martin's Press.

Conover, Pamela Johnston, and Stanley Feldman. 1981. "The Origins and Meaning of Liberal–Conservative Self-Identifications." *American Journal of Political Science* 25:617–45.

Converse, Philip E. 1962. "Information Flow and the Stability of Partisan Attitudes." *Public Opinion Quarterly* 26:578–99.

    1964. "The Nature of Belief Systems in Mass Publics." In David Apter, ed., *Ideology and Discontent.* New York: Free Press.

Davison, W. Phillips. 1983. "The Third-Person Effect in Communications." *Public Opinion Quarterly* 47:1–15.

Dreyer, Edward. 1972. "Media Use and Electoral Choices: Some Political Consequences of Information Exposure." *Public Opinion Quarterly* 354: 544–53.

Erbring, Lutz, Edie Goldenberg, and Arthur H. Miller. 1980. "Front Page News and Real World Cues: A New Look at Agenda-Setting by the Media." *American Journal of Political Science* 24:16–49.

Erikson, Robert S., Michael B. MacKuen, and James A. Stimson. in press. *The Macro Polity.* Cambridge: Cambridge University Press.

Fan, David P. 1988. *Predictions of Public Opinion from the Mass Media: Computer Content Analysis and Mathematical Modeling.* New York: Greenwood Press.

Fiorina, Morris P. 1981. *Retrospective Voting in American National Elections.* New Haven, CT: Yale University Press.

Hochschild, Jennifer L. 1981. *What's Fair? American Beliefs About Distributive Justice.* Cambridge, MA: Harvard University Press.

Huckfeldt, Robert, Eric Plutzer, and John Sprague. 1993. "Alternative Contexts of Political Behavior: Churches, Neighborhoods, and Individuals." *Journal of Politics* 55:365–81.

Huckfeldt, Robert, and John Sprague. 1987. "Networks in Context: The Social Flow of Political Information." *American Political Science Review* 81: 1197–1216.

1988. "Choice, Social Structure, and Political Information: The Informational Coercion of Minorities." *American Journal of Political Science* 32:467–82.

1990. "Social Order and Political Chaos: The Structural Setting of Political Information." In John A. Ferejohn and James Kuklinski, eds., *Information and Democratic Processes.* Champaign-Urbana: University of Illinois Press.

1991. "Discussant Effects on Vote Choice: Intimacy, Structure, and Interdependence." *Journal of Politics* 53:122–58.

1992. "Political Parties and Electoral Mobilization: Political Structure, Social Structure, and the Party Canvass." *American Political Science Review* 86:70–86.

Iyengar, Shanto. 1991. *Is Anyone Responsible? How Television Frames Political Issues.* Chicago: University of Chicago Press.

Iyengar, Shanto, and Donald R. Kinder. 1987. *News that Matters: Television and American Opinion.* Chicago: University of Chicago Press.

Katz, Daniel. 1960. "The Functional Approach to the Study of Attitudes." *Public Opinion Quarterly* 24:163–204.

Key, V. O. 1966. *The Responsible Electorate.* Cambridge, MA: Harvard University Press.

Krassa, Michael A. 1990. "Political Information, Social Environments, and Deviants." *Political Behavior* 12:315–30.

Krosnick, Jon A., and Donald R. Kinder. 1990. "Altering the Foundations of Support for the President through Priming." *American Political Science Review* 84:497–512.

Lane, Robert E. 1962. *Political Ideology.* New York: Free Press.

Lasswell, Harold D. (1930) 1977. *Psychopathology and Politics.* Chicago: University of Chicago Press.

MacKuen, Michael B. 1984. "Exposure to Information, Belief Integration, and Individual Responsiveness to Agenda Change." *American Political Science Review* 78:372–91.

1990. "Speaking of Politics: Individual Conversational Choice, Public Opinion and the Prospects for Deliberative Democracy." In John A. Ferejohn and James Kuklinski, eds., *Information and Democratic Processes.* Champaign-Urbana: University of Illinois Press.

MacKuen, Michael B., and Courtney Brown. 1987. "Political Context and Attitude Change." *American Political Science Review* 81:471–90.

MacKuen, Michael B., Robert S. Erikson, and James A. Stimson. 1989. "Macropartisanship." *American Political Science Review* 83:1125–42.

Marcus, George E., W. Russell Neuman, and Michael MacKuen. 2000. *Affective Intelligence and Political Judgment.* Chicago: University of Chicago Press.

Miller, Warren E. 1956. "One-Party Politics and the Voter." *American Political Science Review* 50:707–25.

Mutz, Diana C. 1994. "Contextualizing Personal Experience: The Role of Mass Media." *Journal of Politics* 56:689–714.

1998. *Impersonal Influence: How Perceptions of Mass Collectives Affect Political Attitudes.* Cambridge: Cambridge University Press.

Nelson, Thomas E., Rosalee A. Clawson, and Zoe M. Oxley. 1997. "Media Framing of a Civil Liberties Conflict and Its Effect on Tolerance." *American Political Science Review* 91(3):567–83.

Nie, Norman H., Sidney Verba, and John R. Petrocik. 1976. *The Changing American Voter.* Cambridge, MA: Harvard University Press.

Noelle-Neumann, Elisabeth. 1984. *The Spiral of Silence: Public Opinion – Our Social Skin.* Chicago: University of Chicago Press.

Page, Benjamin I., and Robert Y. Shapiro. 1992. *The Rational Public: Fifty Years of Trends in Americans' Policy Preferences.* Chicago: University of Chicago Press.

Riker, William H. 1980. "Implications from the Disequilibrium of Majority Rule for the Study of Institutions." *American Political Science Review* 74:432–46.

1982. *Liberalism Against Populism: A Confrontation Between the Theory of Democracy and the Theory of Social Choice.* San Francisco: Freeman.

Robinson, W. S. 1950. "Ecological Correlation and the Behavior of Individuals." *American Sociological Review* 15:351–7.

Rogers, Everett. 1962. *Diffusion of Innovations.* New York: Free Press.

Sniderman, Paul M., Richard A. Brody, and Philip E. Tetlock. 1991. *Reasoning and Choice: Explorations in Political Psychology.* New York: Cambridge University Press.

Stimson, James A. 1991. *Public Opinion in America: Moods, Cycles, and Swings.* Boulder, CO: Westview Press.

Stimson, James A., Michael B. MacKuen, and Robert S. Erikson. 1995. "Dynamic Representation." *American Political Science Review* 89:543–65.

Weatherford, M. Stephen. 1983. "Economic Voting and the 'Symbolic Politics' Argument: A Reinterpretation and Synthesis." *American Political Science Review* 77:158–74.

Wiebe, G. D. 1973. "Mass Media and Man's Relationship to His Environment." *Journalism Quarterly* 50:426–32, 446.

Wolfinger, Raymond E., and Stephen J. Rosenstone. 1980. *Who Votes?* New Haven, CT: Yale University Press.

Zaller, John R. 1990. "Bringing Converse Back In: Modeling Information Flow in Political Campaigns." In James A. Stimson, ed., *Political Analysis: 1989,* Vol. 1. Ann Arbor: University of Michigan Press.

1992. *The Nature and Origins of Mass Opinion.* Cambridge: Cambridge University Press.

1998. "Know-Nothing Voters in U.S. Presidential Elections, 1948–1996." Paper presented at the annual meeting of the American Political Science Association, Boston, September 2–6.

Zaller, John R., and Stanley Feldman. 1992. "A Simple Theory of the Survey Response: Answering Questions versus Revealing Preferences." *American Journal of Political Science* 36:579–616.

Zukin, Cliff. 1977. "A Reconsideration of the Effects of Information on Partisan Stability." *Public Opinion Quarterly* 41:244–54.

Index

Abelson, Robert, 25
aggregate policy mood measure, 259
aggregate policy opinions, 219
aggregate-level models, 226
aggregates
  autonomy of, 219
  clarity of, 292
  of individuals, 320
  motion of, 279
  political response to, 165
  time series, 276
aggregation. *See also* physical
    aggregation
  additive, 312
  after modeling and estimation,
    224
  atomistic, 334
  conceptual, 222, 235–6
  importance of, 313–14
  of individual, 259
  levels of, 253–4
  linear, 323
  mechanisms of, 310–11
  methods of, 308–9
  in political behavior, 221
  in political psychology, 221, 236
  political relevance and, 236
  prior to estimation, 227
  relational, 222
  temporal, 222
  transparent, 335
Agrees, 68
  Knows correspondence with, 69
AK High
  classification as, 73

Opposes, 76
Supports, 76
AK Low
  classification as, 73
AK Medium
  classification as, 73
  Opposes, 77
  Supports, 76
Almond, Gabriel
  on behavior, 98
  on cross-national culture, 97
Altermeyer, Bob
  on authoritarianism, 33–4
Althaus, Scott, 293
  on opinion movement, 299
American Journal of Political Science,
    155, 166
American Political Science
    Association, 306
  political psychology section of, 158
American Political Science Review,
    155, 166, 193
American Voter
  attitude models constructed by, 36
Anderson, J. A.
  four-wave longitudinal study of,
    141
Anderson, Walter, 25
anthropology
  global culture sought through, 97
anticipated reaction, 322
Appleby, Joyce
  on human thought, 105
Aristotle, 57
  on citizenship, 91

Index

asymmetry hypothesis, 126
attitude change theory
  elite decision making pertinence of, 37
Attitude Question
  analysis of, 67–8
  with cue, 64–5
  with no cue, 64
  speaker's cue and, 69
attitude statements
  of candidates, 124–5
attitude theory
  political psychology and, 25
  of social psychology, 37
attribution theory, 177
  elite decision making pertinence of, 37
authoritarianism, 33–4
automatic activation processes, 196
Avery, R. K.
  four-wave longitudinal study of, 141

babbling equilibrium, 83
balance theory, 117
  projection theory and, 118
Bandura, Albert
  behavior theory of, 34
Barber, James David, 24
  on presidents, 175
  psychobiography and, 29
Bargh, John A.
  on autonomic activation processes, 196
Bartels, Larry M., 116, 127, 155–6, 293
  gross and netchanges predicted by, 294n15
  on media effects, 39
  model of presidential vote choice, 299
behaviorism, 28
Berelson, Bernard
  quantitative research of, 128
Berent, M. K., 12
Berkman, M. B., 125
Beyond Self Interest (Mansbridge), 159
Bianco, William
  rational choice model of, 27

Bolland, John
  schema theory criticized by, 233–4
Brabrooke, David, 104
Brady, Henry
  liability heuristic of, 168–9, 172, 174, 286–7
Brennen, Geoffrey
  on rational choice, 159
Brody, Richard
  on president approval ratings, 163
Bruner, J. S., 117

Cacioppo, John
  on cognition, 85
  ELM of, 58
candidate evaluation, 190–1
  accuracy of, 145
  cognitive consistency linked to, 191
  longitudinal data used to predict, 142
  model of, 174
  performance relevant criteria for, 290
  through memory-based processing, 191
  variance in, 139n6
Carmines, Edward
  on America's racial attitudes, 164
causal hypothesis testing, 144
Chaiken, Shelly
  on autonomic activation processes, 196
  on persuasion, 59
children
  emnification origins in, 30
  political thinking in, 33
Chong, Dennis
  collective action model by, 160
  rational choice model of, 27
citizen preferences. See also
  preferences
  and voting, 325
citizenship, 89
  civic activity in, 94
  elements of, 91–2
  focus groups' dialogues on, 100
  in Great Britain, 90
  ideal form of, 110
  "identity" and, 93
  individualism and, 99

340

Index

Hochschild, Jennifer
  interviewing method of, 283
Holmberg, Soren
  on perspective effects, 123n3
  rational democratic coefficient of,
    129–30
  on voting behavior, 176–7
Hovland, Carl, 57
human development, 25, 32–40
  needs, 31–2
Hurley, Norman L.
  on racial difference, 224

importance-memory relation, 208
individual preferences. *See also*
  preferences
  transformed into public outcome,
    320
individual-level cognition, 285
  aggregate measurement of, 230
individual-level relationships
  "ecological fallacy" and, 224–5
information processing
  dual-process models of, 39
Inglehart, Ronald, 32
  on cross-national culture, 97
institutions
  citizenship attitudes taught in, 106
  learning in, 105–6
  macrolevel causal explanations of,
    106
integrative complexity
  political elites studied in, 178–9
interdisciplinary research, 41
Interest Question, 65–6
  analysis of, 67–8
  responses to, 68t
  variables derived from, 77
interpersonal communications, 317
Iyengar, Shanto
  gulf war study by, 203–5
  on media effects, 39
  news media priming studies of,
    202

Janis, Irving L., 25, 57
  on conformity, 36
  on groupthink, 178
Johnson, Lyndon, 125
Jones, Bryan
  rational choice model of, 27

Jones, C. C.
  nonrecursive structural equation
    model of, 128
*Journal of Personality and Social
  Psychology*, 155, 193, 203
Judd, Charles
  on political candidate judgments,
    176
  on political expertise, 175–6
judgment formation
  memory's role in, 38
  sociotropic, 38

Kahneman, Daniel, 194–5
Keen, Sam
  on emnification, 30–1
Keeter, Scott, 293
  model of presidential vote choice,
    299
Kelley, Harold, 57
Kinder, Donald R.
  gulf war study by, 203–5
  on media effects, 39
  news media priming studies of, 202
  on sociotropic politics, 189–90
King, M.
  voter-candidate similarity predicted
    by, 132–3
Klapper, Joseph
  on persuasiveness, 58
Kleugel, James R.
  on inequality, 177
Knowledge Question, 65–6
  analysis of, 67–8
  responses to, 68t
  variables derived from, 77
Knows, 68
  Agrees correspondence with, 69
Knutson, Jeanne, 25
  humanistic psychology applied by,
    31–2
Krosnick, Jon A., 8–9, 11–13
  candidate perception accuracy of,
    145–6
  candidate perception analyzed by,
    142–3
  gulf war study by, 203–5
  news media priming studies of, 202
Kuklinski, James H., 169
  on racial difference, 224
  schema theory criticized by, 233–4

344

Index

Books in the series